Culture&Politics
China

Culture&Politics China

An Anatomy of Tiananmen Square

Peter Li, Marjorie H. Li and Steven Mark, editors

Transaction Publishers

New Brunswick (U.S.A.) and London (U.K.)

Second paperback printing 2009

Copyright @ 1991 by Transaction Publishers, New Brunswick, New Jersey.

This book is printed on acid-free paper that meets the American National Standard for Permanence of Paper for Printed Library Materials.

Library of Congress Catalog Number: 90-42374
ISBN: 978-0-88738-353-3 (cloth); 978-1-4128-0734-0 (paper)
Printed in the United States of America

Library of Congress Cataloging-in-Publication Data
Culture and politics in China : the anatomy of Tiananmen Square / edited by
Peter Li, Steven Mark, and Marjorie H. Li.
p. cm.
Includes bibliographical references and index.
ISBN 0-88738-353-X
1. China—History—Tiananmen Square Incident, 1989. 2. China—
Politics and government—1976. 3. Students—China—Political activity.
I. Li, Peter, 1935- II. Mark, Steven. III. Li, Marjorie H.

DS779.32.C84   1990   90-42374
951.05'8—dc20   CIP

The characters that appear on the cover of this volume are sung, "conflict," and its resolution, *jie*, or "deliverance." They were selected in accordance with the methods of the *I Ching*. the Book of Changes, and were written by New York calligrapher and painter C.C. Wang.

Cover photograph of the "Goddess of Democracy" by Victoria Chapman, graduat student in sociology at Princeton University.

Fang Lizhi's remarks on "Patriotism and Global Citizenship" reprinted with permission of Orville Schell.

Excerpts from Su Shaozhi' s "The Crisis of Marxism in China" reprinted with permission from *The World & I* and the author.

This Book Is Dedicated to Future Generations of
the Chinese People

Contents

Preface

The key to understanding China and things Chinese is patience. The Chinese people seem to have an inexhaustible reservoir of it, which has been both their bane and their strength. Patience keeps them optimistic and opportunistic, eager and able to take advantage of whatever situation arises. It is also fundamental to their fatalism, which too often keeps them from creating these situations for themselves.

So it is patience that the editors recommend to readers of this volume. The *I Ching*, China's ancient Book of Changes, advises that an appropriate attitude for readers to take would be *kun* (receptiveness). "The Receptive must be activated and led by the Creative, then it is productive of good," says the Chinese classic.

Patience will allow this book to reveal itself at its own pace. The story of Tiananmen Square is not easy to understand, even for Chinese people, and this is not only because it causes us such distress. Translating the words in documents and speeches is one thing, but it is another to try to translate a culture, with its values, its way of thinking, its peculiar mindset. This volume, in large measure, attempts to do just this.

To this end, we have adopted an unusual approach. After a brief introduction and recap of events at Tiananmen Square, we devote the first section of the book, chapters 1 through 5, to statements from some of the major players involved in the demonstrations. The intention is to allow the parties to speak for themselves as individuals and as a group.

We introduce each passage with a commentary designed to illuminate aspects that may not be apparent from the surface of the words. These introductions also provide some context relating them to the demonstrations as a whole. However, we have eschewed a strict chronological approach because we believe that the demonstrations should not merely be viewed as a series of events.

For the most part, the statements have been grouped according to the roles their subjects played in the drama of the demonstrations. The first chapter, of course, is devoted to the students, the main protagonists in the demonstrations. The second chapter introduces the hardline leaders, specifically Li Peng and Deng Xiaoping (as represented in the 26 April editorial in the *People's Daily*). More importantly, it shows the interaction between Li Peng and the students. The third chapter gives a fuller accounting of the hardliners' attitudes and their way of thinking. This may be a difficult chapter to read, not because the words seem so venomous but because they seem so cold.

The fourth chapter is devoted to the intellectuals, who represent the tradition of social responsibility and self-searching analysis that the students were trying to emulate. The fifth chapter outlines aspects of the reformist faction in the government and the voice with which it spoke.

The second section of this volume comprises a brief interlude followed by seven essays. These chapters discuss different aspects of the student movement, from its underpinnings as a cultural, political, and psychological phenomenon to its place in the world historical year of 1989. Some of these essays will talk directly about events on Tiananmen Square; others will refer to them only indirectly, focusing instead on the milieu out of which they came.

Because of the diverse nature of these chapters, some will be easier to understand than others. We have provided a special glossary of Chinese terms for chapter 8 (Conformity and Defiance on Tiananmen Square: a Social Psychological Perspective). There is also a glossary at the end of the volume explaining the most important historical and geographical references.

What may come as a surprise to the reader is the absence of a comprehensive and neutral account of the events on Tiananmen Square on the night of 3-4 June. Such reports inevitably deal with questions about how many people were run over by tanks, or how many soldiers were beaten to death by angry mobs, but add nothing to the broader discussion of why the demonstrations developed, why the government reacted the way it did, how the two sides interacted, and what forces influenced one or both sides. The fact that blood was shed may make these questions that much more important, but it does not provide any answers. We do present student leader Chai Ling's eyewitness account and Beijing Mayor Chen Xitong's report, knowing full well that each has its blind spots.

In fact, the essays that deal directly with the student movement refer almost exclusively to events that happened well before the invasion. It is these events and tendencies that led to that 3-4 June uprising, and the invasion merely represented their implosion. In addition, this book addresses the future of the student movement and the democracy movement in China only in broad terms.

We hope that by speaking with many voices this volume can introduce readers to some of the diverse forces and motivations that drew China into the drama of the student demonstrations. As China searches for a place in the modern world, these forces and motivations, like the patience of generation upon generation of Chinese, will continue to hold it back and push it forward; at the same time, they will erode away as slowly as the gray stones on Tiananmen Square.

Acknowledgments

This book is the product of the despair, frustration, and bewilderment that followed the tragic conclusion of the Chinese student movement in 1989. The bloody suppression of the mostly peaceful, nonviolent demonstrators caused Chinese the world over to undergo a soul-searching re-evaluation of Chinese culture and civilization in light of the harsh political reality of the present day.

This volume may therefore be looked upon as a sustained effort to examine the relationship between culture and politics in China and the effect that cultural values impose on political behavior. Marjorie recruited a variety of experts to give their views: political scientist Peter Nan-Shong Lee of the Chinese University of Hong Kong; Ph.D. candidate King Tsao, an eyewitness to the events on the Beijing University campus during the demonstration period; and social psychologist Chung-fang Yang of the University of Hong Kong. They all provide unique perspectives on the incident at Tiananmen Square.

In November 1989, a symposium on "The Challenge of Democracy" was held at Rutgers University. Two of the three speakers at the symposium were the eminent Chinese historian Ying-shih Yu of Princeton University and renowned sociologist and political scientist Irving Horowitz of Rutgers University. Their insightful comments analyze the Chinese condition within the context of Chinese and world history.

Finally, journalist Steven Mark, who had been in China a few months prior to the outbreak of the student demonstrations, was asked to join as in-house editor to fine-tune the manuscripts and documents, and make other contributions.

After months of contemplation, discussion, and plain hard thinking,

xiii

the result, we hope, is an intriguing and appropriate opening volume to a series of books on Asian studies that is being planned by Transaction Publishers.

There are many people whose assistance in this project was invaluable. The support and encouragement we received from Transaction Publishers were indispensable–any would-be author who encounters the combination of Irving Louis Horowitz's boisterous tail-whipping and Mary E. Curtis's precise interrogation will experience the pleasure of dealing with people who genuinely care about their product.

Thanks also to the Chinese Democratic Fund, which along with fifteen other Chinese-American organizations sponsored the above-mentioned symposium; and to Mary Hartman, dean of Douglass College, whose invitation to Peter to speak at a forum on Global Conflict and Resolution gave us added incentive and encouragement.

Professor Ching I Tu, head of the Chinese department at Rutgers University, came through by appointing an extra teaching assistant for Peter so that he could devote more time and energy to the book.

Jennifer Li donated her spring vacation from Douglass College to help type reports and documents. Later, Jenny and classmate Dawn McPhee also gave up a Saturday night—a not insignificant sacrifice for college students—to help read and copyedit the entire volume.

We also must thank the dozens of Chinese students and scholars who discussed current conditions in China with us and provided us with insights not only into the Chinese way of life but the Chinese way of thinking.

Finally, our families and friends deserve our appreciation, particularly Mrs. Hsu Shufen, who held the household together while we worked, and Caroline Li, whose unbridled energy at the tender age of nine reminded us always to believe in the future.

PETER LI
STEVEN MARK
MARJORIE H. LI

Introduction

It is a curious phenomenon in China that the government, in order to prove its position, usually winds up undermining it. It denounces dissident intellectuals and groups, meanwhile giving full play to their ideas in government publications. It admits its mistakes, thereby displaying its own incompetence.

Similarly, it expects the people simply to accept its word when it says the 1989 demonstrations were the work of "a small group of people with ulterior motives." These assertions fly in the face of the government's own statistics about the demonstrations, which appeared in a recent book, *Fifty-Six Earthshaking Days* (Jingxin dongpo wushiliu tian), published in Beijing.[1] Statistics do not normally make for interesting reading, but the numbers here are enough to give one pause. According to the book, there were demonstrations in every one of the twenty-nine provinces of China, in eighty-four cities, and involving more than six hundred institutions of higher learning. More than 2,800,000 students took part in the demonstrations. This figure undoubtedly includes multiple countings of students since, as the book points out, only 2,030,000 students are enrolled in all the colleges and universities in China. Nonetheless, the figure represents either a remarkable percentage of student participation, a very strong commitment on the part of some students who demonstrated day after day, or both.

The numbers for Beijing seem even more remarkable. The book reveals that in Beijing alone, from 15 to 19 May, more than seven hundred organizations of various sorts took part in the demonstrations. Among them were sixty adult schools and institutions of higher learning; sixty middle and technical schools; 120 occupational, high,

1

middle, and grammar schools; more than one hundred news agencies, party organizations, and national institutes; more than forty organizations from the Ministry of Culture alone; some twenty Beijing city municipal organizations; nine political party organizations; more than 160 factories, businesses, stores, and hotels; and thirteen hospitals. Students from over eighty different colleges and universities outside of Beijing converged on the capital to join their classmates on the front lines of protest.

Thus one can see how widespread the protests and demonstrations were, and can draw certain conclusions as to the extent of the discontent throughout the country. The government really had a crisis on its hands—one is tempted to even say it faced a near rebellion.

So there is a question that needs to be asked: How can such a widespread and large-scale grass-roots movement crumble overnight? We must ask the hard question: Why did the movement fail?

The easy answer, of course, is that the guns and tanks were enough to vanquish the movement, send it underground, and drive it overseas, but there is a more fundamental proposition to this: The student movement of 1989 is another manifestation of China's unsuccessful attempt at modernization since its opening to the West during the past ten years. Professor Tang Tsou has characterized the situation in China in this way: "Political life in China is now governed by a new 'paradigm' which is the product of the century-old confrontation between China and the West. In this paradigm, traditional and modern elements, the old and the new, foreign examples and Chinese reality, Western knowledge and Chinese mentality, are sometimes merely juxtaposed, sometimes combined in unstable mixtures, and sometimes fully integrated."[2]

The confrontation at Tiananmen Square can be seen as a conflict between the old and the new, between the young and the old, between the Chinese and the West, between the adherents of Deng's Four Cardinal Principles and the practitioners of bourgeois liberalism, between the authoritarian values of the old order and the individualism of the young. They were combined in not only an unstable mixture but a highly volatile mixture. The lofty ideals of a democratic society were not acceptable to the authoritarian, totalitarian values of the Leninist-Stalinist party-state. Ultimately when push came to shove, the authoritarian regime called in the troops and tanks.

Modernization, of course, is a curious term in that its measure can never be really calculated. The standard of living, the political process, technological and scientific advances, and the cultural achievements of a society can all be considered aspects of how modern a state is. China also has to contend with modernization of thought, since its traditional values invariably influence the people's ability to change one or more of the above.

In the Chinese context, modernization might well be seen partially in terms of trying to strike a balance between two concepts: turmoil and harmony (harmony in Deng's terminology is unity and stability). Chinese culture, more so than most, disdains the former and seeks the latter, but the extent to which the society can find a definition in which the two can accommodate each other will dictate its capacity to accept change.

The Student Demonstrations

These concepts figured heavily in the demonstrations on Tiananmen Square. The students had at their disposal a wide arsenal for demonstrations but, in order to appear in harmony with society, they decided that above all theirs would be a nonviolent, peaceful demonstration. They would not even encourage the ordinary Beijing citizens to join them, fearing that they could be infiltrated and their movement disrupted. The tactics they adopted—marches, demonstrations, sit-ins, petitions, boycotting classes, dialogues, and, most drastic of all, a hunger strike—all reflected this intention. In their experience, this would not be considered a "turmoil."

Nonetheless, some aspects of the demonstrations do not suggest a completely harmonious situation. On every one of the fifty-six days of the movement, there were marches and demonstrations of some sort. At some of the high points, such as on 27 April, 17 May, and 23 May, there were more than 1 million demonstrators on the Square, although not all of them were students. Class boycotts began on 24 April at thirty-five different colleges and universities in Beijing.

Petitions were presented at various stages in the student movement. They were presented to the Standing Committee of the Politburo on 17 April and to the Beijing Municipal Party Committee on 19 April. However, the third and the best known presentation was on 22 April.

On this occasion, after the formal memorial service for Hu Yaobang was over, the students, who were holding a peaceful sit-in on the east side of the Great Hall of the People, sent three student representatives to present a petition to Li Peng. After standing for half an hour with no one coming to receive the petition, two of the students knelt down, holding the petition above their heads in a gesture of supplication. After an hour and a half of kneeling, still no one from the government came forward to receive the petition.

But there was an interesting act of defiance in this drama. One student refused to kneel because he considered it a contradiction in terms to kneel down (a feudal gesture) to request democratic reforms. The young man who refused to kneel was none other than Wu'er Kaixi, a Beijing Normal University student who would become the most charismatic figure of the student movement. Here we have an interesting mixture of traditional and modern methods of protest. Both the students who kneeled and Wu'er were sincere, but there was a difference as to the appropriate tactics.

Another petition was handed to the government on 2 May. It was almost an ultimatum, demanding a reply by noon on 3 May. Finally, another one was delivered to the National People's Congress, the State Council, and the Party Central Committee on 6 May. So, while the demonstrations remained peaceful, degenerating into violence only when authorities resorted to force, the students obviously had become more confrontational and more overbearing.

As a way of spreading their message, the students also employed a large repertoire of slogans, symbols, and gestures. They would chant them, write them on banners, and carry them in the demonstrations, which at various times spread because of local and foreign news media coverage. These slogans often targeted specific party leaders, an extraordinary occurrence in China. They were clearly insulting to the leadership, which probably gave the leaders even less incentive to listen to the students, no matter how festive the atmosphere on Tiananmen Square was.

A powerful symbol for the students was the Goddess of Democracy, which was erected on the Square the night of 29 May. Given the fact that it was Western in style, modeled after the Statue of Liberty, it certainly irked the authorities even more.

Another form of discourse demanded by the students was to have "equal" dialogues. A number of them were held in an effort to resolve some of the issues, but none was conclusive. The first was held on 29 April between some forty student representatives and three government representatives; another was held on 14 May.

The final and the highest level meeting was on 18 May. More than ten students representing the hunger strikers met with Premier Li Peng and a number of other officials. Again, both sides were adamant in their demands. The atmosphere was one of confrontation, belligerence, and mutual suspicion. There was no possibility of negotiation or dialogue. The conditions were probably made worse because the event was being broadcast live on television—no side wanted to appear weak by giving in to the other side. The final meeting ended with no resolution of any of the differences. The government refused to back down on its editorial of 26 April and the students refused to end their hunger strike.

Although the meeting was highly charged, Li Peng began in a patronizing tone by discussing his own children, the youngest of whom was older than the student demonstrators. Thus, he wanted to set himself up as a parent figure to the students. Li was rudely cut short by Wu'er Kaixi, who interrupted him. However, Wu'er Kaixi later did an about face by referring to Premier Li Peng as "teacher" Li because he considered the premier to be old enough to be his teacher. And throughout the discourse he always addressed Li Peng using *nin* (the polite form of you) rather than *ni*. Here again the tradition of respect for elders was juxtaposed with the defiant attitude of the students.

On 13 May, after a series of deadlocks and in light of the coming summit meeting with Gorbachev, the students proceeded with their most drastic and yet nonviolent means of protest: the hunger strike. As it turned out, this was the most effective of the methods that the students adopted. It aroused the sympathy of the whole nation and the whole world; even the government was forced to make conciliatory moves behind the scenes.

Without a shot being fired, the students had succeeded in making the government appear as if it were killing them. True to their word, the student movement had remained peaceful. There were even reports that crime had decreased and that the people of Beijing were friendlier than ever toward one another.

The Government's Response

However, from the moment the students stepped out on the Square, the government was angered and concerned that the movement might spread beyond the confines of the student groups. The government ignored the festivities on the Square and moved to quell the movement. Puzzled as to how to avoid even greater disruption, the government did not take strong measures at first. However, once the decision was made, it took blunt, definitive steps. The first was on 26 April, after a week of demonstrations, when it decided to condemn the student demonstrations as "turmoil." This legitimized an effort to marshal party forces against the demonstrations. But the government totally miscalculated its effect among the people at large. The editorial not only provoked the students but angered the common people as well and spurred the demonstrations on. The editorial became a self-fulfilling prophecy. If there was no turmoil before, now there was.

The second decisive act on the part of the government was on 19 May when the decision was made to implement martial law in parts of Beijing. This decision again angered the students and citizens of Beijing greatly. Once more the people and the students took to the streets, and they even successfully, if only temporarily, blocked the entry of the troops into Beijing. But this triumph was short-lived. After the declaration of martial law it was just a matter of time before the troops and tanks would enter the city and bring an end to the student movement, although there were still times when violence could have been prevented.

That leaves the interim period from 27 April to 18 May, which was the most troublesome period to the party because of a power struggle that was going on within the leadership. If there was any "turmoil" going on, it was here. The demonstrations prompted a showdown between the hardline faction and the reform faction, which had been building in the late 1980s as China's problems in the reform era grew. It is ironic that Deng Xiaoping, the man most responsible for the opening of China during the reform era, had to side with the hardline faction and repudiate his reformer protégé Zhao Ziyang. In the same way, he had repudiated his other famous protégé, Hu Yaobang, in 1987.

The struggle between Deng and Zhao is made more difficult because of the mentor-protégé relationship between the two men. Zhao opposed Deng's stand on calling the student demonstrations turmoil, but he faced a dilemma in that he, being the protégé, was not in a position to directly defy his mentor. Therefore, on several occasions Zhao showed his disagreement with Deng by making public statements to the effect that the students were in the right, that they were merely displaying their patriotic fervor in the demonstrations. On 13 and 16 May, Zhao, at the meeting of the Standing Committee of the Politburo, proposed that the 26 April editorial be repudiated, but on both occasions his proposals were rejected by the committee. Zhao also tried his best to convince the students to stop their hunger strike, to go back to their classes, and to stop the demonstrations. But the momentum of the student movement had reached such a point that there was no turning back. Zhao knew that his days were numbered. Finally, rather than being present when the order to impose martial law in Beijing was issued, Zhao chose to be absent, indicating unmistakably his loss of power. Thus Zhao also became a tragic figure in this drama of power struggle within the party. If he had succeeded in turning back the students, he might have been able to maintain his position as party general secretary and prevent the final bloodshed.

In the end, of course, Deng Xiaoping and the hardliners had their way in putting down the "turmoil," transforming it in their minds into a "counter-revolutionary rebellion." Zhao was ousted, and the students were driven from the Square. The party elders were unified, and the juniors scared into submission.

To the party's way of thinking, this amounted to peace and harmony. At the time of this printing, dissension and unhappiness in the party and society at large are said to be widespread, but not expressed in public. A campaign urging Beijing citizens to "take a walk" on Tiananmen Square on 1 April 1990 as a "display of solidarity" was forestalled. The party, so focused on the "ulterior motives" of "a small number of people" during the demonstrations, is now happy to look at the surface of the masses of society and believe, or try to believe, that all is well.

But perhaps one does not need to end on such a pessimistic note. The difference between turmoil and harmony was blurred during the demonstrations, and the focus on this difference may actually force people to think about what this means in terms of modernization. The statements of the hardliners during and after the demonstrations should now give a reasonable definition as to what constitutes turmoil and what does not. The students proved to be quick learners in the art of protest; they may now take some lessons from 1989 and apply them to the future.

The government, for its part, may be less inclined to use the term so quickly and so harshly in the future. Despite all of its declarations that the student movement was a turmoil, one has to believe that a substantial number of people agree with Zhao Ziyang, who thought the 26 April editorial was a mistake. If the government can avoid pinning such condemnations on demonstrators, then it may get to the substance of what they are saying rather than getting caught up in an argument over semantics. Deng Xiaoping said in 1986, "It is no simple thing to introduce reform and modernize our country." Although said only in passing, Deng had hit on the crux of the problem confronting China. In a way, Deng Xiaoping had sown the seeds of his own destruction in the late 1970s with his policy of reform that came to fruition ten years later. He was in favor of learning from the West and of opening China to the West economically; he was also in favor of studying the Western social sciences. His policy of "seeking truth from facts" led him to promote the study of social science subjects such as economics, management, political science, law, sociology, and world politics. These studies, however, questioned the viability of the socialist system, and the product of these studies was the rise of discontent and growing expectations which resulted in the 1989 student movement.

Changes in any society can be seen in a variety of ways. The Tiananmen incident, in terms of a sudden, short-term revolutionary change, showed that the prodemocracy movement was a failure. But, seen in terms of long evolutionary changes in history such as the growth of knowledge and technology, urbanization, and democratic ideals, the Tiananmen incident is a step in the building of a foundation that will lead to a democratic future for China. It will not come tomorrow, it may not come in five or ten years. But we must have that faith, that leap of faith that will carry us into the future.

Notes

1   The book and the figures quoted are in *Tansuo* (The Quest) 73 (January 1990): 4. A book of a similar nature, but covering the whole nation is

Xuechao, dongluan, baoluan (Student Movements, Turmoil, and Violence) (Chengdu: Sichuan People's Press, 1989).

2   Tang Tsou, *Cultural Revolution and Post-Mao Reforms* (Chicago: University of Chicago Press, 1986), p. xxxiv.

Part I

Voices from the Square

1

The Voices of Youth

A Battle of Love and Hate
Chai Ling (Commander-in-chief of the Tiananmen Square Command Center)

[*The powerful combination of emotion and idealism that inspired the 1989 student movement is evoked in this report of the movement's final hours. In this moving account given just days after the 3-4 June attack, student leader Chai Ling, a twenty-three-year-old psychology major at Beijing University, vividly portrays not only the students' actions but their thoughts as the onslaught unfolded before them. What is particularly revealing is her description of the transformation of the students' attitude that occurred as it became more and more apparent that the soldiers and tanks were bearing down on Tiananmen Square. Rather than thinking of saving their lives, the students briefly adopted a confrontational attitude, then assumed a sacrificial posture, aware that martyrdom would carry special significance with the people. It was only when the situation became truly hopeless that they decided to flee; for many of them, this decision apparently came too late.*

While appearing on the verge of breakdown at times, Chai only rarely directs an outburst against specific members of the Communist leadership and is cautious about estimating the number of casualties. She does not view the struggle so much as an ideological or political conflict but rather as "a battle of love and hate." This characterization provides some insight into why the students, despite their rage, decided that their only true weapon could be peaceful resistance.]

The Troops Invade

Today is 8 June 1989. The time is 4:00 P.M. I am Chai Ling, commander-in-chief of the garrison that was guarding Tiananmen Square. I am still alive. With regard to all that happened at Tiananmen Square from 2 to 4 June, I think that I am the most qualified to comment upon it. I have a responsibility to report the truth to the world, to every compatriot, and to every citizen of China.

On the night of 2 June, at around 10:00 P.M., our very first indication of what was to come occurred when a police vehicle struck four innocent bystanders, instantly killing three of them. Immediately thereafter came another ominous sign when a group of soldiers arrived. [But] they deliberately surrendered, leaving behind truckload upon truckload of guns, military uniforms, and other equipment, abandoning them to the citizens, who had blockaded the military vehicles, and our fellow students. As far as these events are concerned, the students were very cautious. We immediately gathered these weapons together, and gave them to public security officials [police]. We have a receipt to prove it.

Our third sign came that afternoon. On 3 June, at 2:00 or 3:00 P.M. at Liubukou and Xinhuamen, many of the troops went into action, beating up the students and the citizens of Beijing. At this point, some of the students stood up on vehicles and used megaphones to call out to them: "The People's Army loves the people; the People's Army doesn't fight the people!" One student had just made this appeal when a soldier climbed up, kicked him in the stomach, and said "Your mother! That's who loves you!" then clubbed him on the head. The student fell to the ground.

From that point on…. Let me take a moment and tell you about our position. I was the commander-in-chief. At the time, there was a broadcast station on the Square. This station was called the Hunger Strikers' Broadcasting Station. I stood fast by that post and directed the movement of the students from there. Of course, other students were also at our command post, like Li Lu and Feng Congde. We were constantly receiving emergency bulletins from everywhere about students and city residents being beaten and killed.

From about 8 or 9 until 10 that night, the situation worsened. News of people being killed were reported to us at least ten times. At 7:00 or 8:00 P.M., our command center held a press conference. We told all that we knew to the foreign and Chinese journalists. However, there were very few foreign reporters because, it was rumored, the hotels where they were staying were under surveillance by the military and their rooms were being searched. There were only one or two foreign reporters at the Square that day.

Our command post issued a declaration to which we all pledged: to fight against Li Peng's illegitimate government. At precisely 9:00 P.M., all of us at Tiananmen Square stood up, raised our right hands, and took an oath:

For the advancement of democracy in our country, for the development and prosperity of our country, to protect the nation against a small group of conspirators, to prevent 1 billion citizens from a reign of terror, I pledge my young life to the defense of Tiananmen Square and the republic. I may lose my head, my blood may flow, but the People's Square shall not be lost. We are willing to fight to the very end of our young lives, until the very last person.

At 10:00 P.M. sharp, the Democracy University was founded at the Square. Deputy commander Zhang Boli was installed as president. The establishment of a Democracy University received warmhearted support from all quarters [on the Square]. At this time, the command post was receiving emergency reports from various sources. The situation was very tense. At the northern section of the Square, our founding of the Democracy University was receiving thunderous applause. The University was established near the statue of the Goddess of Democracy. However, on the eastern and western sides of Changan Boulevard, blood was flowing like a river. The butchers, the soldiers of the Twenty-seventh Army, pointed tanks, submachine guns, and bayonets—the effect of the tear gas already had worn off— at those people who dared to yell out even one slogan. Those who dared to throw one brick were chased down by machine gun-bearing troops. All the bodies on Changan Boulevard were bloodstained on the chest [where they were shot]. Our fellow students came running toward headquarters, their hands, their bodies, their arms soaked with blood—the last drop of their comrades' blood. Furious and outraged, they embraced their dead classmates and nursed the wounded.

The Students' Stand: Peace

After 10:00 P.M., the command center pleaded with everyone for restraint. Why? Because when our patriotic democratic student movement had begun in April and continued in May as a general democratic movement, our principle, our purpose, was to petition peacefully. The spirit of our struggle had been peaceful. Many students, workers, and residents of Beijing came to our command post and said, "Since things are like this, we should use weapons too." The male students were also infuriated and wanted to use weapons. The students of our command post told everyone, "We believe in petitioning peacefully. The supreme sacrifice of a peaceful demonstration is self-sacrifice." Slowly, one by one, we came out of our tents, hand in hand, side by side, singing the "Internationale." Holding hands, we circled the

Monument north, east, west, and south and, our calmness overcoming our fears, sat down quietly to greet the butchers' knives.

Because we knew that we had entered into a battle between love and hate rather than between military forces, because we all knew that if we used peace and harmony as our highest principle in this democratic patriotic struggle, the final result would be ...

[There was a break in the narrative here. Chai Ling was on the verge of sobs. The "final result," of course, was a reference to death that she was not able to say.]

If our fellow students were to take up sticks, bottles, and other things, weapons that are not really weapons, to go against those with submachine guns and those irrational madmen driving tanks, that would be the greatest tragedy of our whole democratic movement. The students just sat there quietly, waiting to be sacrificed.

At this time, some megaphones rigged up inside the command post shed and some speakers in several nearby sheds were playing the song "Descendants of the Dragon." The students were singing in harmony with the music, their eyes streaming with tears. They hugged each other, joining hands because each one knew that these were the last few moments of their lives. It was time to sacrifice themselves for democracy.

There was a young student called Wang Li. He was only fifteen and he wrote his final testament. I do not recall exactly what he wrote, I only remember that he said something like this: "Sometimes it is very strange, but it's a pity there is no time." He said that sometimes, when he saw a little insect crawling and he wanted to stomp on it, that little insect would immediately cease to move [as if waiting to be killed]. He was only fifteen years old and he was already contemplating the meaning of death.

[Chai Ling could not hold herself back any longer and cried. Then, with difficulty, she continued.]

Our republic! Don't forget! Don't forget! These are the children of your struggle!

At about one hour past midnight, the command center had to abandon the broadcast station at the pedestal of the Monument and retreat [up the steps] to the Monument to command the Square. I was commander-in-chief. I and the others in command walked along the four sides of the Monument to check on the condition of the students and to mobilize them for one final stand. The students were just sitting there silently. They said, "We will just sit here peacefully; we in the first row are the most determined. Our classmates said to sit quietly. We don't care that those in the first row will be killed, we will sit quietly. We won't move, and we never will kill anyone."

I made a short speech to everyone. I said:

> There is an ancient story. Everybody knows it already. There was an ant colony of about 1.1 billion ants. One day the hill was afire. The ants had to get past the fire if they were going to save the colony. So they clung together to make a ball and rolled through the fire. A few ants burned to death, but a vast number survived. Fellow students on the Square, we already stand on the outermost layer of the people. We know in our hearts that only through sacrifice can we have an effect on the survival of the republic.

Then the students sang the "Internationale," again and again, our hands clasped tighter and tighter. By this time, four comrades, Hou Dejian, Liu Xiaopo, Zhou Tuo, and another, couldn't continue. They said "Children, you should not sacrifice yourselves any more." But each student was very determined, so the four went to negotiate with the military leader, the one supposedly in charge of the troops. They told him, "We will withdraw from the Square, but we hope you will ensure the students' safety. We will leave in peace."

The Final Assault

At this time, the command center polled the students for their opinion on abandoning the Square. They agreed to withdraw, so we decided to leave. But just at that moment, those butchers failed to keep their promise. Just as the students were leaving, helmeted soldiers, lugging machine guns, attacked the Monument. They didn't wait for the command center to tell everybody of the decision to leave. The speakers that we had set up around the memorial were [suddenly] pockmarked like honeycombs [by their machine gun fire]. This was the people's Monument! A monument to the heroes of the people! They actually opened fire on the Monument.

Most of the other students came down. We could only cry as we left, but the citizens said not to. We told them we would be back, because this was the people's square, but ... but afterwards we knew. There were some students who still had some hope for this government and this army. They thought the army would simply drag everybody away. They were too exhausted to move and stayed in the tents.... The tanks came and crushed them into ground meat. Some people say there were two hundred students or more.... There are some people who said more than four thousand people died on the Square.

[The recording had to be stopped at this point because Chai Ling was sobbing so violently.]

The exact figure I still don't know but, on the edge of the Square, members of the Workers' Autonomous Association fought fiercely but all died. There were at least twenty or thirty of them.

I have heard that, as the students were planning to leave the Square, the tanks and troop carriers coated the sheds and the students' corpses with gasoline and burned them all up. Afterwards, they used water and flushed the Square clean of all evidence. Our democratic movement's statue, the Goddess of Democracy, was crushed to pieces by the tanks.

Walking arm in arm, we circled Chairman Mao's Mausoleum. As we retreated from the Square to the south and west, we saw on the south side of the mausoleum a crowd of more than ten thousand helmeted soldiers sitting there. The students yelled "Dogs" and "Fascists." As we retreated to the west, we saw row upon row of soldiers running toward Tiananmen Square to regroup. The citizens and students, baring their teeth in anger, cursed them: "Fascists," "Dogs," "Animals." The soldiers ignored us, running quickly toward our Square.

In our withdrawal, as we passed through Liubukou, all the members of the command post were in the front row. It was here on 3 June at noon that the first of the bloody battles had taken place. There was rubble everywhere. Even the trash cans were burnt and dented.

From Liubukou we walked to Changan Boulevard. The streets were awash with blood, flowing toward.... All that could be seen were burnt-out trucks and rubble strewn along the ground. Evidence of the just-finished battle could be seen, but there was not one corpse.

Afterwards, we learned that the front rows of this band of fascists had used machine guns and, after they killed the people, the rear guard carried the bodies to buses and pedicabs. Some people hadn't even died, hadn't taken their last breath, but were carted away and suffocated to death.

This band of fascists took their sins and buried them in broad daylight, without a shadow, without a trace. With only our spirits left, we wanted to return to the Square again for another rally. At this time some soldiers came to dissuade us, saying "Children, don't you know that they have machine guns inside? Don't sacrifice yourselves again." We had no choice but to return through Xidan, back to the western district [where the universities are]. Along the way we saw a mother crying loudly, her child dead. On the roads we saw four bodies that were of the citizens of Beijing. They had been beaten to death, and their bodies were exposed on the street.

We turned north, back toward our university. Every citizen's eyes were filled with tears. Some said, "I bought government bonds. Was it for them to purchase bullets to slaughter innocent people? To massacre innocent children?"

We were inundated with news from everywhere, some that students had witnessed themselves, some told to them by citizens. This band of executioners was just killing, attacking citizens on both sides of Changan Boulevard, and shooting rockets. Children, elderly people, all lost their lives in the assault. What crime had they committed? They hadn't even chanted a slogan!

A friend told me he had been passing through Changan Boulevard at 2:00 A.M., trying to stop the tanks, when he saw a little girl waving her right hand, standing in front of the tanks. The tank ran right over her, turning her into ground meat. A student had his hand around a student when a bullet whizzed by and struck his friend down. And he said "I have just escaped death!"

On our way back, we saw a mother looking for her child. She said that her child was named so and so. "Yesterday he was alive, is he still alive?"

Wives looked for their husbands; teachers looked for their students. A banner was hanging from the government building saying "Support the correct decision of the Party Central Committee." Our classmates furiously tore it down and burned it. The radio blared out, saying the military had entered Beijing to quell a band of hooligans and to maintain law and order.

I think I am the most qualified person to say that these students were not hooligans. Every conscientious Chinese, put your hand on your heart and think: Young children, hand in hand, shoulder to shoulder, sitting quietly below the Monument, meeting the butchers' knives with only our hopes—were they hooligans? If they were, could they sit there so calmly? What level have the fascists sunk to, to lie with a straight face and feel no guilt? Lying before the world. If it could be said that those machine gun-toting soldiers who killed the innocent were beasts and animals, then what of those people on the television screen, those in front of the cameras—what kind of people were they?

As we retreated from the Square hand in hand, walking along Changan Boulevard, a tank came spreading tear gas. It rolled over students, over their legs, their heads—many would never again be whole. Who are the hooligans? Those students in front kept going at the original pace, just as before. If they wore face masks, it was because their throats already were being choked by the tear gas. These students who already had sacrificed so much, what can bring them back to life? They are forever lost, forever on Changan Boulevard!

Our fellow students formed a column and walked north to the Beida campus, where many students from other campuses had come. For each student, Beida had set up a bed. But we were very, very troubled. We were still alive, but there were many more left on the Square, left on Changan Boulevard, who would never ever come back!

[The recording had to be stopped again at this point because Chai Ling was sobbing violently.]

Some were very, very young. They will never come back!

With the departure of the students from Tiananmen Square to Beida, the student movement that had begun on 13 May with hunger strikes and ended with a peaceful sitdown was forced to a conclusion.

Afterwards, we heard a report that said on 3 June, at 10:00 P.M., Premier Li Peng have given three commands: First, the military should open fire; second, the military should move at top speed on 4 June to recover the Square at all costs; and, third, the leaders and organizers are to be shot on sight, no questions asked.

Comrades, this is our mad, conscienceless illegitimate government. A massacre is going on in Beijing. A massacre that will spread slowly through the whole country is just underway.

But comrades, the darker it becomes, the sooner dawn will come. When a group of fascists can lose their minds and crack down then a genuine people's democratic republic is born. The crucial moment of the life and death of our nation is at hand.

Comrades, every citizen with a conscience, every Chinese, wake up. The final victory belongs to the people. The false Central Committee of the party under the leadership of Yang Shangkun, Li Peng, Wang Zhen, and Bo Yibo is not far from its doomsday. Down with fascism! Down with the militarists! The people must win! Long live the republic!

Petition to Li Peng Following the Funeral Service for Hu Yaobang

Students of Beijing University, Planning Committee of the Beijing University.

[For eight weeks prior to 4 June, the students demonstrated peacefully on Tiananmen Square. While the slogans and placards calling for democracy gained the attention of the news media, the students' official demands were presented in petitions to the government.

This is one of the earliest petitions, drafted on 21 April, but it generated the most controversy. On 22 April, four student representatives tried to present it to the government; three of them, in a traditional show of submission, kneeled for one hour on the steps of the Great Hall of the People, where officials were attending services for former Communist Party General Secretary Hu Yaobang. No one came to receive it, and this was taken as the height of government insensitivity.

Most of the demands are self-explanatory, but some background is appropriate: item number one refers to Hu, a popular figure among students and intellectuals who had been ousted from the leadership for refusing to crack down on student demonstrations in 1986-87; item number two refers to an incident on 20 April in which police beat up several students; and, item number six refers to the party's repeated attempts to stifle Western influence, which it calls "bourgeois liberalism."]

1. To reevaluate Comrade Hu Yaobang's accomplishments and shortcomings; to affirm his democratic, liberal, generous and friendly attitude;
2. To strictly punish those who beat the students and people, and demand those who did the beatings to apologize to the ones who suffered;
3. To issue as soon as possible the regulations regarding the news media, to guarantee freedom of the press, and to allow the people to publish newspapers;
4. To request that the nation's leaders make a detailed disclosure to the people about their property and income; to investigate official profiteering;

5. To request that the nation's leaders investigate the merits of the educational policy; report to the people after a careful inspection; request a large-scale increase in educational funds; and raise the salary of intellectuals.
6. To reevaluate the "antibourgeois liberalization" movement and to review the verdict of those who were unjustly treated during that period;
7. To urge that the patriotic democratic movement be given open, just, and timely coverage by the press.

A Tide of Democracy
Wang Dan

[Wang Dan was one of the original leaders of the student movement and an organizer of the so-called "democracy salons" on the Beijing University campus in the late 1980s. As a history major at Beijing University, the twenty-four-year-old Wang views China's problems from a long-range perspective, seeing democratic reform as a way to solve China's long struggle to modernize itself rather than as an end in itself.

Wang shows enthusiasm for democratic reform along Western lines, quoting Patrick Henry. But, in calling for a "tide of democracy" to be launched "from the bottom up," he exhibits the pervasive influence of the Maoist rhetoric and mentality on Chinese youth. And, despite the student movement's success so far (this statement was issued in mid-May), Wang realizes that the establishment of a democratic system in China is only a long-term goal.]

Since the Opium War of 1839, China has been forcibly invaded, its economy impoverished, and its society plunged into chaos. These and other problems have inflicted deep wounds on a formerly healthy nation.

In the forty years since the Communist party came to power, there have been some achievements in planning. But these have come at a heavy cost: a disastrous decline in the status of intellectuals, lagging economic development that falls behind day by day, and a deterioration in public order. Most important, the people have been deprived of democracy, freedom, and human rights.

Every Chinese, especially the new generation of intellectuals here on the mainland, wishes to see a prosperous and thriving country. However, we realize that without initiating political reform it is impossible to spur China along the road to modernization. Reform of the political structure will naturally affect the fundamental interest of the ruling party. Given the Communist party's vested interests, it is hard for it to change. In fact, it has not done so at all.

In this situation, we can't help but feel it necessary to launch a democracy movement from the bottom up, to enlighten the masses, resulting in a great tide of democracy that the government, based on the people, cannot resist.

This plan has been under discussion among liberal-minded people and has gradually ripened over the past few years. As it happens, 1989 is the seventieth anniversary of the May Fourth Movement and the bicentenary of the French Revolution. People's yearnings for democracy, science, human rights, freedom, reason, and equality, which lack a fundamental basis in China, have once again been aroused. The new enlightenment movement that has sprung up on the mainland reflects the attempt of intellectuals to carry forward a democratic campaign that will inspire the people. This attempt has already been so effective that many people are thinking the same question: How can we bring about democracy in China?

Democratic movements on the mainland have often been unleashed by incidental events. The death of Hu Yaobang ignited like a burning fuse the enthusiasm and courage of young intellectuals. This is how the patriotic democratic movement that has attracted world attention began, erupting last month at universities throughout the country.

We make no attempt to conceal the aim of the current student movement, which is to exert pressure on the government to promote the progress of democracy in China. Nor do we wish to hide the fact that our political views differ on some points from those of the government and the party.

We openly declare what we are advocating: full freedom of speech, of association, and of the press; building Westernized political mechanisms; and doing away with obsolete political ideology. I think the current student movement has at least one function: In the future we can declare, "Yes, we support dissidents."

As an organizer of—and active participant in—this student movement, I feel I can already say I have a clear conscience, for this movement has made the party realize the actual opinion of the people and has made the people, for the first time in forty years, aware of their own power.

I think that with this achievement we can say that the student movement has made a great contribution to the progress of China's democracy movement.

I have great respect for those colleagues abroad who campaign and cry out for democratization in China. On behalf of the students of the mainland, I would like to express our thanks to them for their support. At the same time, I would like to encourage every warrior fighting for the final victory of democracy all over the globe. I hope that you will support the democracy movement on the mainland with even greater enthusiasm. We assure you that we will fight to the very end for the realization of democracy in China.

"Give me liberty or give me death!"

The Hunger Strikers' Statement
The Beijing University Hunger Strikers' Group

[On 13 May, after the government had taken what were considered to be only minimal steps to address the students' demands, three thousand students began a hunger strike. This action was especially drastic in that they refused to take even liquids, inducing a life-threatening condition within days. The hunger strike quickly attracted worldwide attention and sympathy and put an extraordinary amount of pressure on the government.

The emotional impact of the statement below was quite strong on the Chinese people. With a childlike innocence, the students express their regret over their action and declare their readiness to die for their cause. In appealing to citizens and parents, and in asking "If we do not act, who will?" the statement also represents the students' attempt to gain broader public support.]

On this bright, sunny day in May, we are going on a hunger strike. In this the most beautiful period of our youth, we have no choice but to sever ourselves from all of life's goodness and beauty and leave them behind. We do this unwillingly and with great regret.

But our country has reached a point where inflation is soaring; official profiteering is running out of control; authority and power are looming high above the people; the bureaucracy is corrupt; large numbers of well-intentioned scholars and students are drifting overseas; and society is becoming more and more chaotic. At this crucial moment of life and death in our national history, dear countrymen, all those who have a conscience, please listen to our plea!

The country is our country.
The people are our people.
The government is our government.
If we do not call out, who will?
If we do not act, who will?

Even though our young shoulders are not yet hardened to the task, even though the weight of death seems too much for us, we are going to do it. We cannot do otherwise. History demands it of us.

Our sincerest expressions of patriotism, our most profound acts of humanity, are being misrepresented as "hooliganism," as "pursuing ulterior motives," as "being manipulated by a small clique."

We would like to ask all unbiased Chinese, all workers, farmers, soldiers, citizens, intellectuals, celebrities, government officials, policemen, and all those who are trying to concoct charges against us, put your hand on your heart and ask your conscience, "What crime have we committed?" Have we caused unrest? We are boycotting our classes, we have demonstrated, we are on a hunger strike, we have dedicated our lives to our cause, but to what ultimate purpose? Our feelings have been toyed with again and again. We will endure a near-fatal hunger strike in the search for truth, yet we are the victims of savage beatings by the military police. Our student representatives have begged for democracy on their knees but have been ignored. Requests for an equal dialogue have been postponed again and again. The student leaders have placed themselves in great danger.

What are we to do? Democracy is the most noble condition of human existence. Freedom is the inalienable right of all people. But for these we must exchange our young lives. Is this something that the Chinese people can be proud of? A hunger strike is an act of last resort, and right now there is no alternative.

We will use the spirit of death to struggle for life. But we are still children, just children! Mothers in China, please look upon your sons and daughters in earnest! As hunger mercilessly destroys their youth, as death draws near, how can you remain unmoved and unsympathetic?

We do not want to die. We would like to live full, happy lives because we are at the most wonderful age of life; we do not want to die, we want to study and learn. The fatherland is still so poor. It may seem that we are abandoning the fatherland. But death is certainly not what we are seeking—if the death of one or a few can improve the lives of many, if it will make the fatherland thrive and prosper, then we do not have the right to be cowards and continue to live.

When we are near starvation, fathers and mothers, don't grieve. When we bid farewell to our lives, aunts and uncles, please don't let your hearts ache. We have only one wish, and that is to allow us to make a better life. We have only one demand, and that is that you remember that it is not death that we seek! Democracy is not the business of but a few people; it certainly is not a task that can be accomplished in only one generation.

Death is awaiting a far-reaching and eternal echo. A man about to die speaks virtuous words; a horse about to die brays sorrowfully.

Farewell, comrades, take care! Both the dead and the living are equally sincere.

Farewell, loved ones, take care. We cannot bear to leave you, but we must say farewell.

Farewell, fathers and mothers! Please forgive us. Your children cannot be both filial to you and loyal to their country.

Farewell, our countrymen. Please allow us to reluctantly express our loyalty this way. We are using our lives to write our oath. It must clear the skies over the republic!

The People's Decree
29 May 1989
The Beijing Workers' Autonomous Union

[Workers, along with most other groups in society, showed support for the students early in the demonstrations but did not join them until mid-May. Their support was considered of major significance because communist China, while predominantly an agrarian society, has tried to mold itself into a workers' state.

Although somewhat abstruse in its presentation, the workers' statement amounts to a catalogue of questions and complaints that the Chinese people had about their society by the late 1980s. It is a harsh condemnation of the Communist leaders for their failure to develop the country and their refusal to listen to the people. The statement uses particularly strong language, adopting a sarcastic tone and invoking the thoughts of Mao Zedong and the words of Zhou Enlai to criticize the leaders.

The statement adopts a broad perspective in evaluating China vis à vis other nations. It expresses a great desire for democracy, but it does not examine exactly how democracy would function or what form it would take in China. It also refuses to reject socialism.]

For many years, this great nation of 1.1 billion people has been ruled by a small clique of bureaucrats. They have held up the banner of socialism but practiced authoritarian rule, carried out a policy of keeping the people ignorant, and persecuted intellectuals. They are so high and lofty that they disregard the law of the land and party discipline. To safeguard their own rule, they have dragged in conspiring factions and flagrantly practiced cronyism and favoritism in their appointments.

One person in particular, like a present-day "Empress Dowager Ci Xi" listening in on affairs of state from behind the curtain, has divided the people and played them off against each other. He knows only how to play bridge and poker [Deng Xiaoping was known to be an avid bridge player], but does not concern himself with the people's suffering, the ever-growing debt, the increasing burden of taxes, soaring inflation, or the fact that all these factors have led this nation of a billion people to be last among the nations of the world. Furthermore, he has restricted freedom of speech, publicizing only that our gross national product and gross national income surpass those of other nations. But if one knows what the population of these other countries is, then the per capita income of our country's people comes out to be one-tenth or one-twentieth of that in other countries.

[Taking these into consideration,] can our country still be considered a "great nation"? We are no different from other people, but why are our people so poor, so backward? Is it because we are incapable? If we say our population is large, then how about Japan, which also has a population density equal to ours. Why are they better off than us? If we say that the United States has had a longer time to develop, then how about South Korea and Taiwan? Why are they better off than us?

In recent years, the bureaucracy has become more and more corrupt, but the leaders cannot stop it. What is the reason? The talk these days is that Li Peng tells us that his three children do not participate in official profiteering. However, when you are the premier, it is not enough just to say that your children are not taking part in official profiteering; you must eradicate and forbid all profiteering activities. Moreover, up to this point you still don't know who the biggest profiteers and the most corrupt bureaucrats. If you cannot find out who these people are, what right do you have to sit there and gobble down your rice? If you are going to be this incompetent, why are you prime minister?

China is a vast land rich in natural resources; the people's energy is abundant. But you have made a mess [of the country]. You say you had no experience with socialism and are trying to lead 1 billion people across the river by feeling for the stepping stones. So many people have been searching for those stones for the past ten years, but where are they now? Inevitably, there were many people who couldn't find the stones. Wouldn't they drown as a result? Is it not the case that the officials are playing with the people's lives, like children playing games? Reform has been in effect for ten years, with no direction or goal. Ultimately, where will our 1 billion people be? Can any of the officials give us an accurate and clear answer? It was said that it didn't matter whether the cat was white or black—that as long as it caught mice, then it was a good cat. But if there is only one mouse to catch, then wouldn't the two cats be fighting over the same mouse? Disorder has been created; it produces more conflict, and the divisiveness becomes deeper and deeper. This must lead to the "official cat's" eating more and getting fatter, while the "people's cat" gets poorer and poorer. Is this the right way to govern a country?

Prime Minister Zhou Enlai once said, "Whoever wins the students wins the future." Chairman Mao once said, "He who suppresses student movements is certain to come to a bad end. If you do not defeat all the reactionary elements, they will not fall by themselves; where the broom does not reach, the dust will not run away by itself. If one wants to succeed in the struggle, there must be sacrifice. Power comes from the barrel of a gun."

If we desire democracy, we must make sacrifices. If we do not strike at those in power, they will not fall by themselves. They surely will not bestow the rights and benefits of democracy on us, so we must go out and struggle and fight for democracy. Without genuine democracy, official profiteering and corruption cannot be eradicated.

If we want to realize a true democracy, we must abolish the institution of life-time tenure in office. Otherwise, under a one-man dictatorship, the people will dare to be angry but dare not speak out. In that case, what sense is there in talking about democracy? If there is no democracy, there can be no human rights. If there are no human rights, then it is slavery. Let us who do not want to be slaves stand up right now, chest out, back straight. Don't say that we don't have anything; we want to be masters of the world. Only by quickly fanning the flames of the patriotic democratic movement will we capture the opportunity to succeed.

The fact is that, at the present moment, the primary concern of the democratic movement is political power. Only by knocking down the authoritarian leaders and eliminating the obstacles to democracy can the prodemocratic movement move forward. Otherwise, our democratic movement inevitably will meet with the dictators' "settling accounts" with us. Therefore, the patriotic democracy movement calls to us!

Take the following verses as our "school fight song": Workers, students, and businessmen unite! Head toward the forefront of the patriotic movement! Listen! The cry of democracy is calling! Look! The flag of democracy is waving. Workers, students, and merchants altogether, we rush through the storm in waves to greet the bright and shining light. Workers, students, shopkeepers, and all the people, rush toward the forefront of this patriotic movement.

Comrades, our opposition to some of the leaders of the party does not mean that we oppose all the leaders of the party. Our opposition to some of the leaders of the government does not mean that we oppose all of socialism. The reactionary apostles of dictatorship have labeled us arbitrarily [as counter-revolutionary] and beaten us at will. Isn't this because democracy has not been established? Do you mean to say that we are going to let this kind of phenomena keep recurring? The people will not permit this! All the people must unite and save the nation. In order to save the nation, we must quickly banish the dictator Deng Xiaoping from the annals of history. Let the whole of China begin to establish the prerequisites of democracy and freedom.

How Naive We Were
Wu'er Kaixi

[Wu' er Kaixi, 21, was an education major at Beijing Normal University when he rose to prominence as one of the most outspoken and aggressive of the student leaders. He was one of the few student leaders to escape China after 4 June.
As the most charismatic and controversial figure in the student movement, the Communist party singled him out for attack and conducted a massive propaganda campaign to discredit him. In this statement, given shortly after his escape, Wu' er attempts to answer some of those charges. He also launches his own rhetorical attack on the government, describes the scene at Tiananmen Square, pleads for support, and gives his views on the basic principles of democracy. The statement is therefore representative of the thinking of the students: quick, well-intended, but quixotic.]

To all my compatriots who love freedom and democracy, to all Chinese everywhere, I am Wu'er Kaixi of Beijing Normal University, one of the organizers of the Beijing student movement and the Beijing University Students' Autonomous Union. I am also one of the twenty-one most-wanted "hooligans" that the false (or counterfeit) government wants arrested. I want to say this to everyone, especially since everyone on this earth, on this world, already knows what has happened in Beijing, on Tiananmen Square. I think also many of our friends already know.

Let me say simply that 4 June is the darkest day of the republic. Our China is ill. Led by Li Peng and Yang Shangkun, and directed behind the scenes by Deng Xiaoping, the reactionary warlords, the reactionary government, the fascist army, early in the morning of 4 June on Tiananmen Square in Beijing, thoroughly revealed their treacherous fascist countenance when they opened fire on thousands of students who were demonstrating peacefully. I cannot say at this time exactly how many people were killed. But I can tell you that the number killed on Tiananmen Square that night must be at least a thousand. As to the total number [killed or wounded] during the bloody suppression, I would estimate it without any exaggeration at about ten thousand. This is a conservative estimate.

We all know that, several days after the massacre, one could often hear the crack of rifle fire. Many people in the streets were killed. On 4 June, I was at Tiananmen Square. During the massacre I saw with my own eyes many of my schoolmates and compatriots being shot and beaten with clubs by beasts that had lost their conscience and humanity. I saw this clearly with my own eyes. They were shot in the head and in the stomach. Blood was flowing. We were peacefully making our demands when the massacre occurred—we were peaceful.

In the ambulance there were three people, I was one of them. [According to one account, Wu'er Kaixi was talking to the students on the evening of 3 June by the Monument for the People's Heroes, when he collapsed and was taken away by ambulance to the hospital.] One was a student who already had died. Another was a soldier who was hit by another soldier while he was on the Square. He was sent to the hospital and later was executed.

We were hoping for peace, but how naive we were. We did not expect [this kind of] fascist violence. We never thought that they would be this base and beastly.

Many of my schoolmates were crushed by tanks—flattened on Tiananmen Square. Their bodies were shoveled away by bulldozers. Our investigating team from Beijing Normal University saw with their own eyes the troops putting the bodies in plastic bags, throwing them into a pile and burning them.

A student from Qinghua University told me one of his classmates together with two others were holding hands trying to stop a tank. They were shot, and then the tank ran them over.

I think the Beijing Autonomous Student Union, which the government proclaims to be illegal, is absolutely legal. We are totally righteous; it [the government] is illegal. This government can no longer represent the people. A government that opens fire on its people obviously is illegitimate. The real counter-revolutionaries and hooligans are Li Peng, Deng Xiaoping, Yang Shangkun, and those reactionary warlords and fascists. These human-faced, animal-hearted leopards and wolves, they seized governmental power, military power, but actually they are the people's public enemy. They will face the judgment of history.

What happened to many of my schoolmates and friends is still not clear. This bunch of fascists is still ruthlessly hunting them down, killing them. They want to kill us off in one sweep. Didn't Li Peng say that he did not want to see us rise up again? They are shameless, base. They are also hypocrites. Many of my friends perhaps saw the video they took of me with a hidden camera [it was shown on national television] and said that I was "wining and dining," whereas in fact I was merely having a meal at the Beijing Hotel with my friends from Hong Kong. If they consider this to be "wining and dining," then I want to ask them, the fascists, what about their national banquets, welcome parties, and various other kinds of feasting that they hold? They are using the people's blood and sweat to fatten themselves. If they consider me to be "wining and dining" then what about their "wining and dining"? This government has become so hypocritical that even when a student goes to have a meal, they will stealthily videotape it, play it on national television, and tell the people that this person is a counter-revolutionary. I believe this government is not going to last very long, because they are the enemy of the people.

The people feel that they have been wronged, they feel temporarily disadvantaged, but definitely there is no reason to feel defeated. The history of the past few days tells us that our movement is an antigovernment movement. At the shortest, half a year, seven or eight months; at the longest, three years, not more, the government will totally collapse. Then the people will be in charge of their own political future.

I know many friends are concerned about us, concerned about me. It has been about half a month from the time of the massacre. I am safe. It has been difficult; I barely escaped with my life, but I am still alive. Compared to many of my schoolmates who are left forever on the Changan Boulevard and the Square, [I am very lucky]. To the many brave spirits crying in anguish, may your soul rest in peace.

To those of us who are alive, our lives no longer belong to us. The lives of our fellow students are now part of us. Our compatriots gave up their lives for our freedom and democracy, for our beautiful ancestral land, for the prosperity of our land. Their lives are interwoven with ours.

We must continue standing straight, chest out, and struggle to the end. Li Peng's government has cheated the people; his victory is only temporary. The likes of Deng Xiaoping, Li Peng, and Yang Shangkun are merely little pebbles trying to stop the forward movement of the wheel. It is ludicrous, it's pitiable, perhaps they will be successful for the moment. They have cheated the army. Fortunately, history is written by the people, and made by the people.

Now we can say that we have achieved a great victory. Every Chinese who loves China, every compatriot who loves freedom and democracy, every one of us is shouldering the heavy responsibility of history. We must be responsible for our democracy, for the struggle for science, for our martyrs. We must bear the burden for those fighters who personally took part in the democratic movement this time, for ourselves, and more so for the thousands upon thousands of overseas Chinese and their descendants [who helped us]. Therefore, our burden is very heavy. Therefore, we must raise our head, stand straight, and struggle to the end. We must continue to stand tall; otherwise we will not be able to take the ponderous first step, otherwise China will not progress!

We must pull China, this sinking ship, from the shallow waters of the reef, pull it from danger. Only then can we reach the bright shining sea. Now more and more people have joined our ranks. Therefore, this great ship will be able to leave the dangerous shoals and sail toward the shining ocean. The martyrs who have sacrificed their lives will never be forgotten. Long live the republic! Long live democracy! Long live truth! Long live freedom!

My compatriots, my comrades, patriotic fighters of the democratic movement, I am Wu'er Kaixi. I want to say that the massacre is over. Our country is temporarily at a low point. But I believe that our movement will inevitably succeed. What we seek will inevitably be achieved. We must bring about a greater and greater democratic movement; completely overthrow the reactionary warlord Li Peng, Yang Shangkun, and the behind-the-scenes supporter Deng Xiaoping. On this foundation, we want to build a democratic consciousness in every Chinese.

What is democracy? Now that the people's minds are awakened, an excellent opportunity has arisen. We want to make this foundation even better. What is democracy? Democracy is when the people are in control of the political power, and not political power controlling the people. [Democracy is when] the people can choose their own political and economic life according to their wishes. Democracy is taking these glorious democratic ideas and instilling them in the minds of every citizen of the republic. We did not do this very well in the past;

our education has been poor. The educational level of our children is very low, the educational level of our citizens is also very low. Our responsibility is to raise this level.

Another point: our student movement really wanted to promote democracy in order to make China strong and prosperous. We really did not want to create disorder; nobody wanted disorder. We only wanted to destroy reactionary authority as soon as possible. Besides destroying reactionary authority and reactionary warlords, and all their activities, I want to say that it was actually not our objective to remove Li Peng. To get rid of him was not important; it was important, however, that we decided to use the slogan "Down with Li Peng." Our primary objective was not just to get rid of him, but to establish a system of balance of political power, to establish a democratic mechanism. I believe all of us, including patriotic overseas Chinese, have the responsibility and duty to cooperate with the people in bringing about this system of balance of political power, to give the people a voice. This is our great distant goal.

In the short run, we want to have freedom of information, to instill a democratic consciousness; in the long run, we want to establish a system of balance of power. This is our goal!

2

Confrontation

Resolutely Oppose Turmoil

This Is Not a Dialogue

Resolutely Oppose Turmoil
People's Daily, 26 April Editorial

*[Published after just one week of relatively peaceful student
demonstrations, this editorial was the key to the entire course of
events on Tiananmen Square. It was bannered across the front page of
the nation's largest newspaper and therefore had the personal
approval of Deng Xiaoping, the nation's paramount leader. Deng
himself was largely responsible for its harsh tone, declaring in a 25
April speech to local party leaders that the student movement was a
"turmoil aimed at negating the leadership of the Communist party and
the socialist system."*

*The editorial reflects Deng's hardline policy in dealing with critics
of the party, and student movements in particular. It tries to intimidate
them into submission, threatening the demonstrators with severe
political consequences. It also attempts to sow division within the
movement by making students wary of "a small number of people,"
who it alleges "are taking advantage" of them.*

*Although government officials in the following weeks called the
students patriotic and well-intended, their steadfast refusal to formally
retract this editorial angered and agitated the students. The students,
believing that Chinese tradition granted intellectuals and students the
right of dissent, were acutely aware of the significance of being called
"turmoil"; the term had been applied to the 1986-87 student
movement that had been suppressed (albeit nonviolently) and that had
led to the dismissal of their favorite leader, Hu Yaobang. That incident
established a precedent for the government in its treatment of future
student demonstrations.*

*The editorial's use of the same term essentially invoked this
precedent and amounted to a criminal sentence hanging over the
students. They therefore demanded a retraction as a "reversal of
verdict"—a traditional concept in Chinese culture that would allow
them to keep their good standing in society.*

*The government, meanwhile, had created a no-win situation for
itself with the editorial. Regardless of how the students saw their
movement, the editorial had condemned them and cast them as an
"enemy." In confronting this danger, real or perceived, the
government could not afford to be accommodating lest it be perceived
as weak. Moreover, Deng Xiaoping's personal policy was at stake;*

*retraction would repudiate him and cause him to lose face. And yet,
the longer the government stayed with the editorial, the more defiant
the students became.]*

During the memorial services for Hu Yaobang, a vast number of
party members, workers, farmers, intellectuals, cadres, PLA soldiers,
and students found their own way of expressing their sense of loss.
Moreover, they indicated the desire to turn sadness into strength, to
realize the Four Modernizations, and to contribute their strength to
invigorate the nation.

During the services, there were also some unusual events. A small
minority of people, taking advantage of the opportunity, circulated
rumors and singled out several party and national leaders for attack.
They misled the crowd into attacking the Zhongnanhai Compound
inside Xinhuamen, where the Party Central Committee and the State
Council are housed. It got to the point where there were even people
yelling reactionary slogans like "Down with the Communist party." In
Xian and Changsha, there were several serious incidents in which
hooligans were involved in assaults, vandalism, theft, and arson.

In consideration of the great sadness of the crowds, the party and
the government adopted a tolerant and restrained attitude toward such
inappropriate words and actions by the young students when their
feelings were aroused. On 22 April, prior to the beginning of the
funeral services for Hu Yaobang, with regard to the students who had
arrived earlier on Tiananmen Square, the government did not follow
its usual practice and clear them away. Instead, it asked them to take
part in the funeral services in an orderly fashion. Due to the
cooperative efforts of everybody, a dignified, solemn atmosphere
prevailed during the funeral proceedings.

But after the service, a small minority of people with ulterior
motives continued to take advantage of the students' sympathies for
Comrade Hu Yaobang. They circulated every kind of rumor,
confusing the people's minds, and used wall posters to slander, revile,
and attack the party and national leaders. They openly defied the
Constitution, encouraging opposition to the Communist party
leadership and socialism. In some of the institutions of higher
learning, they established illegal organizations, grabbing power from
the student associations. Some even commandeered the student
broadcasting station. At other institutions, they encouraged students to

boycott classes and teachers to stop teaching; they even forcefully stopped students from going to class. They pirated the good name of the workers' associations and circulated reactionary handbills. Moreover, they banded together and traveled from place to place, plotting to create even greater trouble.

These facts prove that this small minority was not supporting the activities for Comrade Hu, that it was not promoting the improvement of socialism and democracy in China, and that it was not airing its grievances. It was raising the banners of democracy to destroy democracy and rule by law. Its purpose was to distract the people's attention, to throw the whole nation into disorder, and to destroy the stability and unity of the political situation. This is a planned conspiracy. It is a turmoil designed to negate socialism. This is a serious political struggle that has been placed before the entire party, the nation, and every citizen.

If the government is lenient, passes over this turmoil lightly, and lets them do as they say, then in the future an even more chaotic situation will occur. The wishes of the whole nation, including the students' hopes for openness and reform, for the eradication of mismanagement, for development, for control of inflation, for raising the standard of living, for opposing corruption, for developing a democratic system, all could disappear into the shadows. Even the great rewards of ten years of reform could be lost or put in very grave danger. The whole nation could be shaken up and the republic's ambitious wishes difficult to fulfill. A China full of hope and promise could become a hopeless China ridden with strife and unrest.

The party and the entire nation must fully recognize the seriousness of this struggle. We must unify, take a clear-cut stand against the turmoil, and be determined to protect the Constitution and preserve socialist ideology and the socialist system. We must not allow the establishment of any kind of lawless system but take determined, forceful action to stop the activities of any organization that makes a pretext of speaking for the rights of students. Against those harboring ideas of perpetuating false accusations from afar, the party and the people will depend on the law to insistently pursue those responsible for crimes. Illegal demonstrators must be outlawed; they must be forbidden from going to factories, to farms, and to schools to promote conspiracy. The nation must depend on the law to restrain thugs, vandals, thieves, and arsonists and to protect the students' legitimate right to learn and study. A vast number of students genuinely hope to eliminate corruption and to advance democracy. This is also the party's and the government's demand. This demand for the eradication of mismanagement, for the rapid advance of reforms, and for the building of socialism, democracy, and law can only be realized under the leadership of the party.

All party comrades, all people of the nation must clearly recognize that if this turmoil is not forcefully stopped, the nation's future will have no peace. This struggle could bring an end to the open reforms and the successful development of the Four Modernizations; it could bring to an end the advance of the whole nation. Committees on every level of the Chinese Communist Party, party members, Youth League members, all the democratic parties, all patriotic, democratic persons, and all citizens who want to make a clear distinction between right and wrong, arise and actively struggle to forcefully put down this turmoil!

This Is Not a Dialogue
Li Peng at a Meeting with the Students.

[On 18 May, after a month of student demands for a dialogue with government leaders, Premier Li Peng and other government officials met with student representatives in an effort to end the five-day-old hunger strike. The event was televised live throughout the nation, putting the untelegenic Li, already a target of severe criticism, at a distinct disadvantage in comparison to the attractive and spontaneous youths.

With the 26 April editorial in the People's Daily still in effect, Li was not expected to stray from the party line, but he further weakened his case with his demeanor toward the students. Although his opening remarks may appear to be kindly and paternalistic, they were viewed as an attempt to put himself in the superior position—the traditional role of the parent—which irritated the students. Wu'er Kaixi immediately counterattacked, saying "you did not invite us here, we invited you," and the tables were turned.

Based on that exchange alone, the students were considered the winners of this confrontation. But they make some interesting revelations about their movement here. The students basically admit that they have lost control of their movement, that the majority can be manipulated by a tiny minority, even by one person. This indicates that the demand for unanimity of opinion is still prevalent within the student movement, despite its belief in democracy and the democratic process, i.e., tolerance of differing opinions and the minority following majority rule. As it turns out, the student representatives do not even have the power to make the fasting students leave the Square.

The course of the discussion dramatizes the personal animosity between the students and the hardliners more than it does the ideological conflict. There is virtually no give-and-take. The students deliver what amounts to an ultimatum, demanding the retraction of the 26 April editorial and public dialogues. The officials appear open to the issue of dialogue but then begin proposing measures to get the hunger strikers off the Square, ignoring the issue of the editorial entirely. The students, perhaps out of frustration, forgetfulness, or merely excitement from having scored some debating points, never return to it. Li Peng fuels the tension with an abrupt lecture, saying "Beijing has fallen into a state of anarchy."

In the end, the students recognize that their victory is symbolic and, upon taking their leave, will not even recognize that the meeting constitutes a "dialogue." Neither side has given in, nothing has been left on the table for future negotiation, and the threat of future conflict seems inevitable. Although it appears that he was ready to do so in any case, Li Peng declared martial law the day after this encounter.]

LI PENG: I am glad to meet you. Today we only want to talk about one subject: how we can bring an end to the students' hunger strike. The party and the government are very concerned about this matter, deeply disturbed, and worried about the health of the students. I want to solve this problem first; the rest can all be easily discussed. We do not have any other motives, just concern. You are all young; the eldest among you are not more than 22 or 23 years old. My youngest child is older than you. I have three children, none are involved in official profiteering, and all are older than you. You are all like my own children, related by flesh and blood.

WU'ER KAIXI: Premier Li, if we go on like this, it seems that we will not have enough time. We should begin discussing substantial questions as soon as possible.

Now I would like to say what we came here to talk about. A moment ago you said that we will only talk about one question. The fact is you did not invite us here. It was all of us at the Square who invited you to come to talk with us. [Therefore,] it should be up to us to decide what the topic of discussion should be. Fortunately, our points of view are in agreement.

Now, many students have already passed out from fasting. You probably know about it. I think the main point is how to solve the problem.

Yesterday, we heard and read Comrade Zhao Ziyang's written talk. Why is it that the students still have not returned [to school]? I believe that the reply was not satisfactory, very unsatisfactory. The conditions that we stipulated and the present situation on the Square you already know.

WANG DAN: Let me briefly review the situation on the Square. There are about two thousand people who have fainted on the Square. In order for them to leave the Square and stop the hunger strike, you must completely resolve the issues that we have raised. In our meeting with Minister Yan Mingfu last time, we also talked about this problem. The government must listen to the will of the people and resolve the problem as quickly as possible. Therefore, my suggestion is very clear: In order to have the students leave the Square, the only way is to promise to fulfill the two conditions that we raised.

WU'ER KAIXI: You are of such an elderly age, I could call you Teacher Li [Li laoshi]. Teacher Li, there is no need to persuade us [the student representatives]; we also want the students to leave the Square as soon as possible. The situation on the Square is such that the minority does not obey the majority; rather, the 99.9 percent obeys the 0.1 percent. If there is one student who does not leave the Square, all the rest of the hundreds of thousands will not leave either.

WANG DAN: Yesterday, after Comrade Yan Mingfu came to speak to us, we took an opinion poll of more than one hundred students to see if they would agree to leave the Square. The result of the survey was that 99.9% of the students indicated that they do not want to leave.

Let me make our demands clear again: First of all, you must positively affirm that the student movement is a patriotic democratic movement, that it is not a social turmoil as stated in the editorial of 26 April. Second, we must have a dialogue as soon as possible and it should be broadcast live. If these two conditions are met, we can return to our work of persuading the students to leave the Square as soon as possible. Otherwise, it will be very difficult to do our work.

WU'ER KAIXI: As to these two demands, I would like to make clear that our demands must be fulfilled as soon as possible. First, the student movement must be positively affirmed and the editorial of 26 April that the movement is a turmoil must be retracted. Up to now, no one has said that the movement is not a turmoil.

Another point is that the nature of the movement should be defined. Then we could think of several ways of carrying this out. The first is to have either Comrade Zhao Ziyang or Li Peng—it would be best to have Comrade Zhao Ziyang—speak to the students directly at the Square. The second is to issue another editorial rejecting the 26 April editorial, apologizing to the people of the country, and admitting the great significance of the student movement. Only under these conditions can we do our utmost to convince the students to change their hunger strike to a sit-in. Then we can proceed to solve the other problems. We will do our best to persuade them, but still we cannot guarantee that we will be successful. However, if these two points cannot be carried out, then what happens hereafter will be difficult to say.

As for the dialogue, it must be done immediately and must be open, equal, direct, sincere, and with genuine representatives of the masses of the students. The State Council has also said there should be a dialogue. Well then, why is it that we cannot suggest it? Open means that it should be broadcast live on television. This is being truly open. And there should be both Chinese and foreign correspondents present. As for equality, the dialogue should take place between those leaders who have decision-making powers and student representatives who have influence and are elected by the students themselves. This is the true meaning of direct and equal. During the dialogue there should not be answers such as "There is no way that I could answer that question." If there are questions we raise that the government has not discussed yet, then [the government] should call a meeting immediately to discuss them. This is really solving the problem.

WANG DAN: We have come as representatives of the students on the Square who are on the hunger strike. It is for the sake of their lives that we have come. Therefore, we hope each of you leaders here will clearly indicate his attitude toward our two demands. Being the initiators and organizers of the movement, we are concerned about the safety of the students. I think each of you also feels the same way. Based on our common objective, we fervently hope that you will give us a reply as soon as possible.

XIONG YAN (student at Beijing University): It does not matter whether the government or some other agency recognizes the greatness of this patriotic democratic movement. History will recognize it. Then why do we want the government to recognize it? This is because the people have a wish. We want to see if the government is really our own government. That is our real question.

Second, we are all fighters for communism; we have a conscience, a sense of humanity. In order to solve the problem at hand, we should not be concerned with face-saving devices. As long as the people's government admits its mistakes, the people will support it.

Third, if we have disagreements with Premier Li Peng, it is not a personal grudge against you. It is because you are the premier of the country.

WANG XUEZHEN (party secretary of Beijing University): I believe that the great majority of the students are patriotic and hope to promote economic and political reform. The great majority of the students are not part of the turmoil. As to this point, I hope that the government will affirm ...

WANG ZHIXIN (student at Political Science and Law University): Slogans about democracy and science have been bandied about for seventy years, but we still have not achieved them. Now we have raised them again. I would like to ask our government another question: On 22 April, we presented a petition to you, but you did not come out [to receive it]. On 13 May, we began our hunger strike. It has been six days now. According to international practice, a government should respond when a hunger strike has lasted seven days. Even a country like South Africa complies.

Still another question: The demonstrators now include kindergarten teachers and all sorts of other people. I don't know what the government's attitude is.

WANG CHAOHUA (postgraduate student at the Academy of Social Sciences): I believe that the students are self-consciously staging a democratic movement according to the rights stipulated by the Constitution. This is one point I wish to affirm. If it were merely patriotic fervor, then anything could happen, otherwise there would be no way of explaining the cool, rational, restrained, and orderly way [in which the demonstrations are proceeding].

LI PENG: Let me raise a point, I hope that when someone is speaking there will be no interruptions. After that person has finished, there will be plenty of time for comments.

SHAO JIANG (student at Beijing University): The student movement probably has already become a nationwide people's movement. If this is the case, then, whereas the students are relatively peaceful and reasonable, we cannot guarantee that a nationwide people's movement will be orderly and rational. I would like you to address this matter.

[The Government Officials have their say.]

LI TIEYING (Politburo member and minister of the State Education Commission): With regard to the matter of the Education Commission's setting up more opportunities for dialogue and for listening to the opinions of teachers and students, we should regularize them; they should be on various levels, and in various formats, so that people will have the opportunity to speak out. We have not done enough. That the student movement this time has grown to its present size is something we did not wish to see. Because it has actually already become a large-scale event, national in scope, the problem has become political and has created great reaction in the society, and the situation is still evolving.

As for my views of the student movement, the large majority of the students are patriotic. They made many criticisms, suggestions, and presented their points of view. But many things are not determined by our subjective views and wishes. The final judgment will be made by history.

The events ... may develop into something different from what you students had originally conceived. Everyone is opposed to turmoil. If there is no stability in China, then everything will be lost.

YAN MINGFU (a member of the Secretariat of the Party Central Committee): In the past few days, I have been in contact with the students many times. Now what I am most concerned about is to save those children who are on hunger strike on the Square, those who are very weak and whose lives are in danger.... I believe the problems will ultimately be resolved, but right now we must send the students who are in critical condition to the hospital. I think we can come to an agreement on this point. Let us separate the two issues.

The developments as they appear now, as I have discussed already with Wu'er Kaixi and Wang Dan on 13 May, have already transcended the well-intentioned wishes of the students. The situation now is already beyond your control.

On 16 May, I went to the Square to exchange views with you. At the time, I made three proposals: (1) we wish that you would leave the Square immediately and convince your fasting fellow students to go quickly to the hospital to get medical attention; (2) as a representative of the government with the authority invested in me, I declare that there will be no harm or punishment brought to bear on the students, i.e. the so-called problem of "retribution"; and, (3) if the students do not believe me, then, before the meeting of the People's Congress, I will offer myself as hostage and will return with you to your university.

I heard that, after I left, Wang Dan and some of the other students discussed my proposals. Some of the students agreed with my views, but the majority did not. [Even] under these circumstances, leaders of the government tried several times to go to the Square to talk with the students. But because we did not know the proper procedures, we were not able to get in. This you probably know already.

Now all the indications are that the student-initiated organizational measures are losing their effectiveness. The ability to influence the course of developments is becoming less and less. But the people involved are increasing [in number], and it is more difficult to get them to listen to you. How events will develop causes us deep concern. Now the only sector you have influence over is the fasting students. Decide now to have them leave the Square.

From the point of view of the Party Central Committee and the State Council, we sincerely wish and have the desire to resolve the issues that you the students have raised. Now the key issue is the lives of the children. This is the question of the greatest concern. It must be viewed seriously. We must be responsible for the lives of the children.

CHEN XITONG (the mayor of Beijing): When I came to this meeting, there was a lot of traffic, so I was late. As the mayor of Beijing, I would like to say a few words. Comrades, you have all seen the developments of the past few days. Workers, farmers, intellectuals, and cadres from various departments are all concerned about the events that are taking place. What is our predicament at this point? Many of the citizens, workers, and farmers of Beijing called the city government and Municipal Party Committee requesting that we convey this message. [The government] should follow democratic and legal procedures. The problems should be resolved in accordance with democratic and legal procedures as suggested by Zhao Ziyang.

The second point is that the city's transportation system has come to a standstill. Production has been [adversely] influenced. [Some] factory workers have come out to support the movement, but a greater number hope that the situation will not continue. If our entire transportation system is paralyzed, then supplies will not be forthcoming, and it will greatly affect our people and the country. This point you all understand.

Another matter that is of great concern to us is the students' hunger strike. Medical workers and doctors of the Red Cross all are very concerned about the health of the students. They just requested that they be granted the greatest convenience so that all those students who are in poor health can be sent to the hospital as quickly as possible. They asked that we not play games with the lives of the children—the lives of the students—that we not use their lives to bargain for other things. This point I think you all understand. We must insure the physical health of the students. What good is it to ruin your health or to sacrifice your life? As the mayor of Beijing, I would like to make these two points and hope that the students will cooperate so that the Red Cross may carry out its humanitarian duty and insure the safety of the lives of the striking students. Our municipal government is determined to take necessary measures to protect the students from rain and cold. We have already made ample preparations.

LI XIMING (secretary of the Beijing Municipal Party Committee and member of the Politburo): I do not have much to say. The most important thing is not to let the life of even one child on the hunger strike be threatened.

LI PENG (premier of China): Now let me express some of my views. Since you all wish to talk about substantial questions, I will first bring up one matter. I suggest that the national and Beijing Red Cross societies send all the students on hunger strike safely to the hospital. I hope that all the other students on the Square will support and cooperate with them. This is my first concrete suggestion. At the same time, I will order the medical workers in all the hospitals in Beijing, whether they belong to municipal or central government departments, to care for the hunger strikers and to assure the absolute safety of their lives. Whatever disagreements or agreements we may have, the most important thing is to save them. In this the government is duty bound. Every student on the Square should also cooperate for the sake of caring for their fellow students. I have issued directives that all hospitals must try their best to prepare beds and necessary medical equipment for treating the students.

The second question is that neither the government nor the Party Central Committee have ever said that the students are creating turmoil. We have never said this. We have been affirming the students' patriotic enthusiasm, and many of the things that you have done are right. Many of the questions you have raised are just the ones that the government hopes to deal with. Frankly speaking, you have actually helped the government to a certain degree in its efforts toward solving these problems. There are some problems that we have long been trying to solve but could not solve in time because of many obstacles. The students have very perceptively pointed out these problems and have helped the government and the party overcome them. I think this is positive.

But the development of the situation does not follow your best intentions, desires, and patriotic enthusiasm. These are objective conditions that no one can control. This is to say, in fact, great disorder has already appeared in Beijing and it is spreading across the whole country. I can tell you that yesterday our lifeline, the railroad, was obstructed for three hours at Wuhan and the transport of goods was interrupted.

Now, in quite a few cities, some students, and others who are not students but society's idle members, are using the banner of the students to make their way to Beijing. In the last few days, Beijing has fallen into a state of anarchy. I have no intention of putting the blame on Wu'er Kaixi or Wang Dan, but these are the objective facts.... As the government of the Republic of China, we have a responsibility to the people. We cannot ignore the situation. We must protect the life and property of the people and the students, and guarantee the safety of the students. We must protect the factories and the socialist society.... Turmoil China has experienced many times. People naturally do not want turmoil, but ultimately it occurs.

The third point is that, even though many government functionaries, city residents, workers, and even some personnel from the State Council have taken to the streets to show their support for the hunger strikers, I hope that you will not misunderstand their intention. They are showing you their concern, hoping that you will not harm your life and health. But among them there are also many people whose actions I do not approve. If they come with food and ask the students to take food and drink, or want to care for their health or to persuade them to leave the Square as soon as possible and to discuss the problems with the government later, these are all correct. But there are many people who are encouraging you to continue your hunger strike. I am not saying what their motivations are, but I disapprove of their actions. Being a responsible government, we must express our attitude. [There is an attempt to interrupt the premier at this point.] I have not finished yet; we have an agreement.

As the premier of the government and as a Communist party member, I do not intend to hide my opinions, but I am not going to talk about them here. I will discuss them at an appropriate occasion. Moreover, I have almost stated my views already. If we want to continue to quibble over this question, I believe that it is inappropriate and unreasonable.

Let me say, finally, if you, the students sitting here, cannot influence the action of the others, then let me urge the fasting students, through you, to end the hunger strike as soon as possible and to go to the hospital to get treatment as soon as possible. Once again let me on behalf of the party and government express my cordial solicitude for them and hope that they will accept this very simple and urgent request from the government.

WU'ER KAIXI: I'm very sorry. Just now I wrote you a note. Now I want to remind you! You just mentioned quibbling. We the students are merely trying to solve the problem on a humanitarian basis; we do not want to quibble.

Another point: The key to resolving the problem is not to convince us who are present here. The question is how to persuade the fasting students to leave. The conditions for their leaving I have already made abundantly clear. They will leave on only one condition, and that is an objective fact. Even if one student refuses to leave and continues the hunger strike, then we cannot guarantee that the rest of the thousands of people will leave.

Moreover, with regard to the Red Cross, I beseech Premier Li to discuss it with the other comrades to see if it is feasible. There is no need to quibble, that is also my view. Quickly reply to our conditions; our comrades on the Square are starving. If there is no answer, then we assume that the government is not sincere in trying to resolve the problem. There is no point for us representatives to continue talking here.

WANG DAN: If Premier Li believes that the turmoil in society, or any other bad influences, [are due to the student demonstrations], then I could say as a representative of the students that the responsibility for this lies with the government.

XIONG YAN: Dear comrade, Li Peng just raised a point that there are signs of turmoil in society. I want to speak about the relationship between the student demonstrations and turmoil. There is no relationship between the demonstrations and the turmoil. I hope the problem can be solved quickly.

YAN MINGFU: [Reads a note.] The hunger strikers' union asks the student representatives to return quickly.

[At this point Wu'er Kaixi collapses. Medical personnel come in to administer aid.]

YAN MINGFU: In this dialogue today, you have expressed your views to the Party Central Committee and the State Council. Comrade Li Peng, representing the Party Central Committee and the State Council, has presented the official point of view. The most urgent question is how to get the fasting students with the aid of the Red Cross to the hospital to be treated. The remaining questions can be decided upon at another time. The dialogue is concluded at this point.

WANG ZHIXIN: This is not a dialogue, just a meeting.

YAN MINGFU: Yes, a meeting.

3

The Hardliners

All Must Do Good Work on the Students

We Still Have the Army

*Report on Checking the Turmoil and Quelling the
Counter-Revolutionary Rebellion*

The Four Cardinal Principles

All Must Do Good Work on the Students
General Yang Shangkun's Speech to the Enlarged Emergency
Central Military Commission
24 May 1989

*[The demonstrations on Tiananmen Square not only drew
worldwide attention to China's problems, they caused dissension
within the party leadership. This confidential speech by Yang
Shangkun, state president and vice-chairman of the Central Military
Commission, gives a detailed account of the power struggle, pitting
party General Secretary Zhao Ziyang, who advocated a softer position
toward the students, against Li Peng, Deng Xiaoping, and other
members of the Standing Committee of the Politburo who wanted to
suppress the movement. Though Yang's interpretation of the events is
understandably one-sided, it nonetheless provides a fascinating
account of the inner machinations of party politics.*

*Yang's speech clearly indicates that the hardline faction
consolidated its power after this bitter struggle. Yang urges his
audience to resolutely back the editorial of 26 April, saying that the
student demonstrations threatened the existence of the socialist state
and all of its accomplishments of the past forty years.*

*Yang also epitomizes the traditional Chinese attitude regarding
political power, saying that only the senior leaders can decide how to
handle the situation. What gives them that right is their lifelong
service and dedication to the party. They are the ones who are best
qualified to save the nation at this crucial moment. This is the clearest
statement of the outlook of this gerontocracy.]*

The Military Commission has decided to convene this emergency
enlarged session and has asked the leader of every unit to participate.
It is most important that we share some information.

The situation in Beijing is still in a state of chaos. Although martial
law has been declared, in fact some of the martial law measures have
not been implemented and some of the measures have been obstructed.
In order to forestall a direct confrontation, we have not used force to
implement the order. Having made some efforts, most of our troops
are deployed at their designated places. A few days ago, the situation
was more chaotic. None of the military vehicles have yet been able to
pass. How can this situation not be called a turmoil?

The situation in the capital is precisely a turmoil, and this turmoil is not coming to an end. During the past month or so, the student movement has had high points and low points but, generally speaking, it has been escalating. From the time of Hu Yaobang's death until now, the slogans being yelled on the streets have undergone many changes. Following Hu Yaobang's death, the only slogan was "Reassess Hu Yaobang." Shortly thereafter, we heard "Down with the Communist party," "Down with government bureaucracy," and "Down with corruption." At that time there was no widespread slogan saying "Down with Deng Xiaoping," except in a few instances.

On 26 April 1989, an editorial in the *People's Daily* called "Clearly Oppose Turmoil" appeared. After the appearance of this editorial, the students changed their slogans from "Down with the government" and "Down with the Communist party" to "Eliminate corruption," "Down with bureaucratism ," "Support the correct Chinese Communist party," and "Support the Four Cardinal Principles."

After 4 May 1989, suddenly some of our comrades started saying that the movement is patriotic and reasonable. This immediately stimulated another high point in the movement and led to the hunger strike. Of these conditions Comrade Li Ximing has made a very detailed analysis, of which the Party Central Committee has already circulated a copy. Please look at your materials; I will not go into it here.

The Party Central Committee has always wanted to soothe the emotions of the people, to defuse the situation. But the situation has become worse and worse; it has become such that Beijing has lost control. At the same time, in other parts of the country, following a period of relative quiet, the demonstrations became more intense. Now almost every [major] city in the provinces has been struck by demonstrations. Generally speaking, every time time we retreat, they advance.

The slogan at the moment is "Down with Li Peng." This is what they themselves have decided internally, and they have abandoned the other slogans. Their objective is to overthrow the Communist party, to overthrow the government. As soon as there is a moment of peace, if someone from Central Committee says something or any article appears, it starts up again. In the end, it has escalated to the point where Beijing has had no alternative but to impose martial law.

How could this situation have come about? Why did the situation get out of control? Demonstrations are occurring throughout the whole nation, and the slogans are aimed directly at the State Council. Why? Not too long ago, a few of our most honored old comrades—Comrade Chen Yun, Comrade (Li) Xiannian, Comrade Peng Zhen, Comrade (Deng) Xiaoping, Comrade Wang Zhen, and "big sister" Deng (Yingchao)—were all deeply aggrieved by this situation. How could it have reached this point?

After analyzing the development of events, we have come to this conclusion: Although this situation is taking place among the students, the root cause of it lies in the party. That is to say, in the Standing Committee of the Politburo there were two different voices; or, as Comrade Xiannian summed the situation up, there were two commanders. Originally, the spirit of the editorial of 26 April was to steadfastly oppose the turmoil. This was decided after discussion in the Standing Committee of the Politburo. It also had the approval of Comrade Deng Xiaoping. At the time, Comrade Zhao Ziyang was not in Beijing; he was in Korea. The Standing Committee's decision and Deng Xiaoping's approval were forwarded to Comrade Zhao Ziyang by telephone. His answer by telegraph was that he agreed and completely supported it. But, upon his return on 29 April, he immediately suggested that the tone of the editorial was too severe and that the nature of the editorial was not correct.

The editorial opposed the turmoil; it pointed out that the turmoil was organized and preplanned, and that the aim of the turmoil was to negate socialism and communism. But Comrade Zhao Ziyang believed that it was a patriotic student movement; he did not admit that it was a turmoil. Upon his return, he wanted the Party Central Committee to accept and publicize his view that this editorial was a mistake. Among the five Standing Committee members another opinion had emerged.

Soon afterwards, he again voiced his views several times. The first time was on 3 May, at the celebration of the May Fourth Movement, [though] it was not so obvious at the time. He said that China cannot experience a turmoil (this was all good). But there were a few instances in his speech where he nonetheless said the student movements were patriotic.

The clearest example of his position occurred when he received the Board of Directors of the Asian Development Bank. This speech you should study very closely. He said that the students' actions are patriotic and understandable. Then he raised the point that we do have many signs of corruption. [With these statements,] he sided with the students. He continued by saying that we will take care of these problems through democratic means and laws. He never said whether the editorial of 26 April was correct or not. This speech of Zhao Ziyang's is a turning point. He completely exposed the differing points of view within the Central Standing Committee to the students. The students then became more aroused, began to support Zhao Ziyang, and wanted to oust Deng Xiaoping and Li Peng.

At this time, there were numerous meetings of the Standing Committee of the Politburo insisting that there could not be any changes in our position. But Zhao maintained his position. Even in front of Deng Xiaoping, he persisted in espousing his views. He said if he could not maintain a stance on the character of the students' movement that was in agreement with that of Comrade Deng and other Standing Committee members, he would raise the question of his resignation, saying that he could not go on.

Afterwards, I advised him that this question was very important. If we changed our stand, everything would topple. The universities would fall. The professors, the school presidents, the activist students would all get slapped in the face; they would not have a position.

At this time, the students were proposing that they establish new student associations to oppose the original associations. Moreover, they wanted to choose (the leaders) themselves. In Beijing, a few things of this kind happened, which were similar to the Cultural Revolution. Beijing University students set the pattern by capturing the student radio station and smashing the signs for the student association. Many universities experienced struggles over their radio stations, even to the point that some were broken into through the windows.

Now the problem was that the differing voices within the party were being completely exposed to society. Because the students felt that there were people within the party supporting them, they became more and more vigorous. They demanded an emergency meeting of the Standing Committee of the People's Congress, and an emergency meeting of the entire People's Congress. Their purpose was clearly to use these organizations to issue a resolution that would retract the editorial of 26 April. According to their line of reasoning, the student movement was a spontaneous patriotic movement. Think, all of you: If the People's Congress issued this kind of resolution, wouldn't that be the equivalent of retracting the previous editorial?

Now they are actively escalating their work; they are launching a signature drive. Looking at this situation, what are we to do? Comrades Xiannian and Chen Yun came back to Beijing urgently demanding that a meeting be held to decide on a direction and a plan of action. Of course there were other old comrades, like Peng Zhen, Wang Zhen, "big sister" Deng, and two other generals who were very concerned about the situation—they all want to know whether to back off or to hold firm. If we back off, it would be admitting that they are right; if we do not retreat and do not waver, we will be reaffirming the 26 April editorial.

For many years now, we octogenarians have never sat down together to discuss important affairs. This is the first time. Xiaoping, Chen Yun, Peng Zhen, "big sister" Deng, and Old Wang all feel that there are no alternatives. If we retreat from our position, it will mean the end of us. It will also be the end of the People's Republic [of China].

A communist nation that fails would amount to the restoration of capitalism. This is what the former U.S. Secretary of State Foster Dulles hoped for—that after a few generations, our socialism would be transformed into a free society. Comrade Chen Yun said something that is very important: namely, that this is no less than the complete destruction of decades of struggle to achieve the People's Republic [of China] , wasting the blood of thousands of revolutionary martyrs. It amounts to the negation of the Chinese Communist Party.

Our comrades in Beijing could see clearly that, on the morning of 19 May, Comrade Zhao Ziyang went to Tiananmen Square and visited the hunger strikers. You heard what he said. Anybody with half a mind could see he was talking nonsense. First, he said we came too late; then he began to cry. Second, he said the situation was very complex and that there were many things that could not be resolved, but that after a period of time they will be settled. [He told the students:] "You are young and still have a long road ahead of you; we are old, so it doesn't matter." In talking this way, his tone was very sad; he expressed feelings of guilt as if there were many grievances he could not express. Many cadres in Beijing seeing him speak that way said this person has completely lost control of himself, he is too undisciplined.

That evening, cadres from the Beijing Municipal Communist Party, the municipal government, and the military had an important meeting.

Originally, he [Zhao] was scheduled to attend, but when the meeting was to begin, he didn't show up. In a meeting of such importance, if the party secretary does not participate, everybody immediately knows that there is a problem. He had been scheduled to speak but didn't go. Everybody was waiting for him. At this time, the military had already started moving toward Beijing.

It had originally been decided that the declaration of martial law would begin at zero hour on the twentieth, because without martial law the situation was intolerable.... Originally I had not been scheduled to speak, but under the circumstances I had to say something because the military vehicles were stuck there. How could I not say a few words about this? So I said that military vehicles were arriving to ensure public security and that they certainly were not going to move against the students—if you do not believe me you can wait and see.

Out in the community, some materials from a research institute have been circulating. They are counterfeits of the *People's Daily* and discuss five questions. These things have been given out for everyone to see. The material says that everything suggested by Comrade Zhao Ziyang has been completely rejected by the Standing Committee of the Politburo. Nothing like this has happened. For example, if from now on we adopt the laws and conventions of a democratic system to solve our problems, everybody would approve. We are making preparations to hold a session of the People's Congress upon the return of Comrade Wan Li. In the past month, everyone has been doing Zhao Ziyang's work, declaring that we cannot retract the 26 April editorial. If we retract it then we have no place to stand. But he would not listen. And when Comrade Deng Xiaoping and we old comrades decided that we could not retreat, he then wrote a letter to Comrade Deng saying, "I cannot do it. My thinking and yours are not the same. My thinking cannot keep pace. If I participate in this Standing Committee meeting, I will hinder the ideas of my old comrades, including those of Chairman Deng."

But at the time he agreed that to have a resolution is better than to have no resolution. This is most important: Whether we retreat or not, we definitely need a decision. Comrade Xiaoping and several of his old comrades had already decided that we could not retreat, so he [Zhao] indicated that it was better to have a resolution than not to have one. Second, [he agreed that] the minority should follow the majority.

Comrade Xiaoping said this was correct; it is an organizational principle of the party. But, in the end, he [Zhao] rejected it. So, we can say that the root of the problem is in the party.

Comrade Xiaoping already spoke twice in regard to this problem. One time he said that we have incurred economic disharmony, inflation, overheating of the economy, and such phenomena. This has already developed over the last five years;over the last three years it has become especially serious. We have not adopted measures to prevent it. Another occasion was a speech on 25 April, in which he said there are different voices within the party. In opposing bourgeois liberalization, he pointed out Zhao as an example of someone who agrees with Hu Yaobang. If we had completely implemented the policy of opposing bourgeois liberalization, then we would not have had the current situation. Especially in regard to opposing spiritual pollution, we only opposed it for twenty days, then stopped. This matter is related to the failure to completely oppose liberalization and spiritual pollution. So it could be said that Comrade Zhao Ziyang's disposition not to oppose liberalization was the same as Comrade Hu Yaobang's. This was the crux of his speech.

On one other occasion, Comrade Xiaoping was talking with some foreigners and said that in the Third Plenum of the Eleventh Party Congress, our biggest failure in these ten years was that we did not pay enough attention to education. He then said that, in regard to the thinking behind the opening up of China, we did not work hard enough—we have not glorified our excellent tradition of diligent struggle. He spoke of two matters: One is education; the other is spiritual cultivation. He did not only talk about educational appropriations not being enough. Comrade Xiaoping's thoughts are consistent and hold fast to the Four Cardinal Principles.

Now, as to how to resolve that which has been placed in front of us. Today I would like to acknowledge the comrades of the major military units. After thoroughly analyzing the situation, it is necessary for the Central Committee to calm down the leadership. Because [Zhao] has not been able to carry out the orders of the Central Committee, he is up to something else. [Zhao] wants to go through this legislative procedure to achieve his purpose. Because, out of the whole party and the government, the majority does not agree with him, and in the Standing Committee he is only one vote, Zhao Ziyang wants the news of his being dismissed to reach the outside.

Right now outside there is a rumor going around asking how a bunch of eighty-year-olds can solve these problems. I say this question is very easy to answer. This is a decision by the majority of the members of the Standing Committee of the Politburo. These few old cadres have the most prestige, their history is the longest; moreover, their contribution to the party and nation has been especially great. There is no need to mention Comrade Xiaoping; and Li Xiannian, Chen Yun, Xu Shuo, Nie Shuo, "big sister" Deng, Peng Zhen, and Wang Lao all have made great contributions. In this critical point for our party and our nation, how could they not come out and speak? How could they just stand and watch as the nation verges on disaster? This is a responsibility which every Communist party member must bear.

Right now there are people spreading word that the party is not making any decisions, that it is only the decision of one man. This is completely wrong. This matter was handled by the majority of the Politburo; the Standing Committee and Party Central made this correct decision. Chen Yun, Xiannian, Comrade Xiaoping, and the other members of this older generation of revolutionary leaders have completely supported this correct decision.

When Gorbachev came to China, Zhao Ziyang told him of Deng Xiaoping's place in history, which was completely proper. But during the news briefing he immediately mentioned this question of the student demonstrations and spoke at great length about how all important questions were decided by Deng Xiaoping. Anybody with a little brains would know that he was putting the blame on someone else. He was placing Comrade Xiaoping out front and indicating that all the mistakes that were made were his. Recently there has been a series of things of this sort. I think you all have some views about this.

Right now the whole party must be thoroughly united with one heart and one mind in the spirit of the 26 April editorial. We can only advance and not retreat. Today I am just here to greet you and give you psychological preparation. What is especially important is that the military must be consolidated at all cost. Is the military all of one mind? We will depend on you to do your work. I think that there is no problem with the comrades at the division level, but are there problems among the lower level officers? Now there are still people who say that the Military Commission has three chairmen. Why is Deng Xiaoping alone able to sign and execute the order for the movement of military troops under martial law? These people absolutely do not understand the military; they are only fooling the students. The system of responsibility of the military hierarchy is that the chairman makes the decision and that we all assist the chairman in his work. We are in an advisory capacity. When he makes a decision, he not only seeks me out but also Xuezhi, Huaqing, and minister Qin.

We have asked everybody to come in order to work on these tasks. First, we want you to know where we stand. No matter what has happened, we wanted to clarify the Central Committee's position. Second, when you return to hold meetings of the Standing Committee, the message must be clear that the military and the cadres are united. Unity is very important. Third, Party Committee members must be uniform in their thinking. No matter what, it must be in line with the thinking of the Politburo. This is especially true for the military. If orders are not executed, military law will be of no use to the situation. Fourth, all of you should pay attention to the military schools; their cadres, their department heads, and their professors must all do good work on the students. The military academy absolutely cannot participate in marches or demonstrations or give moral support. Fifth, right now, those troops that are supposed to reach their designated places should get settled immediately to ensure that they are properly rested. We are going to mobilize them, and the lowest level cadre must understand clearly what is going on.

Just as I came, Chairmen Deng gave us a suggestion that we organize the cadres to work on the students and the citizens. We must explain to them what we are to do here. Today already is the fifth day of martial law. For five days we have not fired a single shot, we have not beaten a single person. The people are clear about this. We must strive to do our propaganda work well. There are also some retired comrades; we must give them the message. This is very important. We have to do a good job with the retired cadres. After our party committee meeting is over, we will see what the situation is. In a few days you can make a simple report on the entire situation. Through our work, the spirit of the decision of the Party Central Committee will be thoroughly carried out.

We Still Have the Army
Deng Xiaoping's Speech on 9 June.

*[Deng Xiaoping's appearance before the troops marked his return
to the public arena after some weeks in which his whereabouts were
unknown. This speech served several purposes, but it is mostly an
attempt to show his vigor and vitality in leading the country. Typically
for a master of behind-the-scenes manipulation, he takes no
responsibility for what has occurred. He says that the conflict was
inevitable and that it was "independent of man's will." He reiterates
the line set in the 26 April editorial: that a handful of people were set
on toppling the Communist party and the socialist state.*

*Deng also gives a suggestion of his vision of China's future. He
indicates that the people will be subject to intense "re-education"
programs on adherence to the party line, and more generally with
regard to living a pure and simple life.*

*Deng also tries to reassure the people that the country's economic
policies will remain unchanged. He refers to "one center and two
basic points," the "one center" meaning a focus on economic
construction, and the two "basic points" calling for a continuation of
the open door policy and adherence to the Four Cardinal Principles
(see selection later in this chapter.)*

*Deng admits that in the past these policies had not been
implemented correctly. Such self-effacement, however, is probably
more tactical than it is genuine.]*

You comrades have been working hard.

First of all, I'd like to express my heartfelt condolences to the
comrades in the People's Liberation Army, the armed police, and the
police who died in the struggle; my sincere sympathy and solicitude to
the comrades in the army, the armed police, and the police who were
wounded in the struggle; and my sincere regards to all the army,
armed police, and police personnel who participated in the struggle.

I suggest that all of us stand and pay a silent tribute to the martyrs.

I'd like to take this opportunity to say a few words. This storm was
bound to happen sooner or later. As determined by the international
and domestic climate, it was bound to happen and was independent of
man's will. It was just a matter of time and scale. It has turned out in
our favor, for we still have a large group of veterans who have

experienced many storms and have a thorough understanding of things. They were on the side of taking resolute action to counter the turmoil. Although some comrades may not understand this now, they will understand eventually and will support the decision of the Central Committee.

The 26 April editorial of the *People's Daily* classified the problem as turmoil. The word was appropriate, but some people objected to the word and tried to amend it. But what has happened shows that this verdict was right. It was also inevitable that the turmoil would develop into a counter-revolutionary rebellion.

We still have a group of senior comrades who are alive, we still have the army, and we still have a group of core cadres who took part in the revolution at various times. That is why it has been relatively easy for us to handle the present matter. The main difficulty in handling this matter has lain in that we have never experienced such a situation before, in which a small minority of bad people mixed with so many young students and onlookers. We did not have a clear picture of the situation, and this prevented us from taking some actions that we should have taken earlier.

It would have been difficult for us to understand the nature of the matter had we not had the support of so many senior comrades. Some comrades didn't understand this point. They thought it was simply a matter of how to treat the masses. Actually, what we faced was not just some ordinary people who were misguided, but also a rebellious clique and a large quantity of the dregs of society. The key point is that they wanted to overthrow our state and the party. Failing to understand this means failing to understand the nature of the matter. I believe that after serious work we can win the support of the great majority of comrades within the party.

The nature of the the matter became clear soon after it erupted. They had two main slogans: to overthrow the Communist party and to topple the socialist system. Their goal was to establish a bourgeois republic entirely dependent on the West. Of course, we accept people's demands for combatting corruption. We are even ready to listen to some persons with ulterior motives when they raise the slogan about fighting corruption. However, such slogans were just a front. Their real aim was to overthrow the Communist party and to topple the socialist system.

During the course of quelling the rebellion, many of our comrades were wounded or even sacrificed their lives. Some of their weapons were also taken from them by the rioters. Why? Because bad people mingled with the good, which made it difficult for us to take the firm measures that were necessary.

Handling this matter amounted to a severe political test for our army, and what happened shows that our People's Liberation Army [(PLA)] passed muster. If tanks were used to roll over people, this would have created confusion between right and wrong among the people nationwide. That is why I have to thank the PLA officers and men for using this approach to the rebellion.

PLA losses were great, but this enabled us to win the support of the people, and made those who can't tell right from wrong change their viewpoint. They can see what kind of people the PLA are, whether there was bloodshed at Tiananmen, and who were those that shed blood.

Once this question is made clear, we can take the initiative. Although it is very saddening that so many comrades were sacrificed, if the event is analyzed objectively, people cannot but recognize that the PLA consists of the sons and brothers of the people. This will also help people understand the measures we used in the course of the struggle. In the future, whenever the PLA faces problems and takes measures, it will gain the support of the people. By the way, I would say that in the future, we must make sure that our weapons are not taken away from us.

In a word, this was a test, and we passed. Even though there are not so many veteran comrades in the army and the soldiers are for the most part little more than eighteen, nineteen, or twenty years of age, they are still true soldiers of the people. Facing danger, they did not forget the people, the teachings of the party, and the interest of the country. They kept a resolute stand in the face of death. They fully deserve the saying that they met death and sacrificed themselves with generosity and without fear.

When I talked about passing muster, I was referring to the fact that the army is still the people's army. This army retains the traditions of the old Red Army. What it crossed this time was truly a political barrier, a threshold of life and death. This is by no means easy. This shows that the People's [Liberation] Army is truly a great wall of iron and steel of the party and country. This shows that no matter how heavy the losses we suffer and no matter how generations change, this army of ours is forever an army under the leadership of the party, forever the defender of the country, forever the defender of socialism, forever the defender of the public interest, and the most beloved of the people.

At the same time, we should never forget how cruel our enemies are. For them we should not have an iota of forgiveness.

The outbreak of the rebellion is worth thinking about. It prompts us to calmly think about the past and consider the future. Perhaps this bad thing will enable us to go ahead with reform and the open door policy at a more steady, better, even a faster pace. Also it will enable us to more speedily correct our mistakes and better develop our strong points.

The first question is: Are the line, goals, and policies laid down by the Third Plenum of the Eleventh Central Committee ... correct? Is it the case that because this riot took place there is some question about the correctness of the line, goals, and policies we laid down? Are our goals "leftist?" Should we continue to use them for our struggle in the future? These significant questions should be given clear and definite answers.

The question is this: Is the general conclusion of the Thirteenth Party Congress of "one center, two basic points" correct? Are the two basic points—upholding the Four Cardinal Principles and persisting in the open policy and reforms—wrong?

In recent days I have pondered these two points. No, we haven't been wrong. There's nothing wrong with the Four Cardinal Principles. If there is anything amiss, it's that these principles haven't been thoroughly implemented—they haven't been used as the basic concept to educate the people, the students, and all the cadres and party members.

The crux of the current incident was basically the confrontation between the Four Cardinal Principles and bourgeois liberalization. It isn't that we have not talked about such things as the Four Cardinal Principles, worked on political concepts, and opposed bourgeois liberalization and spiritual pollution. What we haven't done is maintain continuity in these talks—there has been no action and sometimes hardly any talk.

The fault does not lie in the Four Cardinal Principles themselves but in wavering in upholding these principles, and in the very poor work done to persist in political work and education.

Promoting plain living must be a major objective of education, and this should be the keynote for the next sixty to seventy years. The more prosperous our country becomes, the more important it is to keep hold of the enterprising spirit. The promotion of this spirit and plain living will also be helpful for overcoming decay.

When the People's Republic [of China] was founded, we promoted plain living. Later on, when life became a little better, we promoted spending more, leading to wastage everywhere. This, in addition to lapses in theoretical work and an incomplete legal system, resulted in backsliding.

I once told foreigners that our worst omission of the past ten years was in education. What I meant was political education, and this doesn't apply to schools and students alone but to the masses as a whole. And we have not said much about plain living and the enterprising spirit, about what kind of a country China is and how it is going to turn out. This is our biggest omission.

Is there anything wrong in the basic concept of reforms and openness? No. Without reforms and openness how could we have what we have today? There has been a fairly satisfactory rise in the standard of living, and it may be said that we have moved one stage further. The positive result of ten years of reforms must be properly assessed, even though there have emerged such problems as inflation. Naturally, in reform and in adopting the open policy, we run the risk of importing evil influences from the West, and we have never underestimated such influences.

Looking back, it appears that there were obvious inadequacies—there hasn't been proper coordination. Being reminded of these inadequacies will help us formulate future policies. Further, we must persist in the coordination between a planned economy and a market economy. There cannot be any change.

What is important is that we should never change China back into a closed country. Such a policy would be most detrimental. We don't even have a good flow of information. Nowadays, are we not talking about the importance of information? Certainly, it is important. If one who is involved in management doesn't possess information, he is no better than a man whose nose is blocked and whose ears and eyes are shut. Again, we should never go back to the old days of trampling the economy to death. I put forward this proposal for the consideration of the Standing Committee. This is also an urgent problem, a problem we'll have to deal with sooner or later.

What We Have Achieved

In brief, this is what we have achieved in the past decade: Generally, our basic proposals, ranging from a developing strategy to policies, including reforms and openness, are correct. If there is any inadequacy, then I should say our reforms and openness have not proceeded adequately enough. The problems we face in implementing reforms are far greater than those we encounter in opening our country. In political reforms, we can affirm one point: We have to insist on implementing the system of the National People's Congress and not the U.S. system of the separation of three powers. The United States berates us for suppressing students. But when they handled domestic student unrest and turmoil, didn't they send out police and troops, arrest people, and shed blood? They were suppressing students and the people, but we are putting down counter-revolutionary rebellion. What qualification do they have to criticize us? From now on, however, we should pay attention to such problems. We should never allow them to spread.

What do we do from now on? I would say that we should continue to persist in implementing our planned basic line, direction, and policy. Except where there is a need to alter a word or phrase here and there, there should be no change in the basic line or basic policy. Now that I have raised this question, I would like you all to consider it thoroughly. As to how to implement these policies, such as in the areas of investment, the manipulation of capital, etc., I am in favor of putting the emphasis on capital, industry, and agriculture.

We have to firmly implement the series of policies formulated since the Third Plenary Session of the Eleventh Central Committee. We must conscientiously sum up our experiences, persevere in what is right, correct what is wrong, and do a bit more where we lag behind. In short, we should sum up the experiences of the present and look forward to the future.

That's all I have to say on this occasion.

Report on Checking the Turmoil and Quelling the Counter-Revolutionary Rebellion
Chen Xitong, mayor of Beijing and state councillor
30 June, National Central Committee of the Communist Party

[The mayor's lengthy account, which is excerpted here, is a surprisingly frank and revealing account that unwittingly reveals how widespread the discontent and turmoil was in China in the late 1980s. In effect, it undermines the government's contention that the disaffection was the work of a "handful of organizers and instigators." The section below reflects the conspiracy mentality that permeates the thinking of the hardliners and which allows them to blame other nations and overseas organizations for China's problems.

Note: A translation of the entire report by Chen Xitong is included in the appendix. For the moment, it is the single, most comprehensive account of the student movement from its beginning to its tragic conclusion. The reader, of course, should be aware of the perspective of the report's author.]

Chairman, vice-chairman, and committee members, during late spring and early summer, namely from mid-April to early June 1989, a tiny handful of people exploited the student unrest to launch a planned, organized, political turmoil that later developed into a counter-revolutionary rebellion in Beijing, the capital. Their purpose was to overthrow the leadership of the Chinese Communist Party and to subvert the socialist People's Republic of China. The outbreak and development of the turmoil and the counter-revolutionary rebellion had an extensive international background and social basis at home.

One: The Turmoil was Premeditated and Prepared for a Long Time Before it Happened

Some political forces in the West have always attempted to make the socialist countries, including China, give up the socialist road, to eventually bring these countries under the rule of international monopoly capital, and to put them on the course of capitalism. This is their long-term, fundamental strategy. In recent years, they have stepped up the implementation of this strategy by making use of some policy mistakes and temporary economic difficulties in socialist countries.

In our country, there was a tiny handful of people both inside and outside the party who stubbornly clung to their position of bourgeois liberlization and went in for political conspiracy. Echoing the strategy of Western countries, they colluded with foreign forces, ganged up at home, and for years made ideological and organizational preparations to stir up tormoil in China, overthrow the leadership by the Communist party, and subvert the socialist People's Republic [of China].

What deserves special attention is that, after Comrade Zhao Ziyang's meeting with a U.S. "ultraliberal economist" on 19 September last year, some Hong Kong newspapers and journals that were said to have close ties with Zhao Ziyang's "brain trust," gave enormous publicity to this and spread the political message that "Beijing is using Hong Kong mass media to topple Deng and protect Zhao...."

Collaboration between forces at home and abroad intensified toward the end of last year and early 1990. Political assemblies, joint petitions, big- and small-character posters and other activities emerged, expressing fully erroneous or even reactionary viewpoints.

For instance, a big seminar on the "Future of China and the World" was sponsored by the Beijing University Future Studies Society on 7 December 1989. Jin Guantao, deputy chief editor of the "Towards the Future" book series and advisor to the society, said in his speech that "attempts at socialism and their failure constitute one of the two major legacies of the twentieth century." Ge Yang, chief editor of the fortnightly *New Observer,* immediately stood up to "provide evidence," in the name of "the eldest" among the participants and a party member of dozens of years' standing, saying "Jin's negation of socialism is not harsh enough, but a bit too polite."

On 28 January 1990, Su Shaozhi [a research fellow at the Institute of Marxism-Leninism-Mao Zedong Thought under the Chinese Academy of Social Sciences], Fang Lizhi, and the like organized a so-called "neo-enlightenment saloon" at the Dule bookstore in Beijing that was attended by more than one hundred people, among them Beijing-based U.S., French, and Italian correspondents as well as Chinese. Fang described this gathering as "smelling of strong gunpowder" and ... professed to "take to the street after holding three sessions in a row...."

At a press conference he gave for foreign correspondents on 16 February, Chen Jun [of the Chinese Alliance for Democracy] handed out Fang Lizhi's letter ... calling for amnesty and the release of Wei Jingsheng and other so-called political prisoners, who had gravely violated the criminal law.

On 26 February, Zhang Xianyang [a research fellow at the Institute of Marxism-Leninism and Mao Zedong Thought], Bao Zhunxin [an associate research fellow at the Institute of Chinese History], Ge Yang, and thirty-eight others jointly wrote a letter to the Communist Party Congress Central Committee calling for the release of so-called political prisoners.

Afterwards, a vast number of big- and small-letter character posters[1] and assemblies attacking the Communist party and the socialist system came out on the campuses of some universities in Beijing. On 1 March, for example, a big-character poster titled "Denunciation of Deng Xiaoping—a Letter to the Nation" was put up at Qinghua University and Beijing University simultaneously. The poster uttered such nonsense as "the politics of the Communist party consist of empty talk, coercive power, autocratic rule, and arbitrary decision," and openly demanded "dismantling parties and abandoning the Four Cardinal Principles." A small-character poster titled "Deplore the Chinese" turned up in Beijing University on 2 March, demanding the overthrow of "totalitarianism" and "autocracy."

On 3 March, there appeared in Qinghua University and other universities and colleges a "letter to the mass of students" signed by the Preparatory Committee of the China Democratic Youth Patriotic Association and urging students to join in the "turbulent current for democracy, freedom, and human rights under the leadership of the patriotic democratic fighter, Fang Lizhi...."

The big-character poster "Call of the Times" that came out in Beijing University on 6 April questioned in a way of complete negation "whether there is any rationale now for socialism to exist" and "whether Marxism-Leninism fits the realities of China after all."

On 13 April, the Beijing Institute of Post and Telecommunications and some other school received a "message to the nation's college students" signed by the Guangxi University Students' Union that called on students to "hold high the portrait of Hu Yaobang and the great banner of democracy, freedom, dignity, and rule by law in celebration of the May Fourth Youth Day...."

Two: Student Unrest was Exploited from the Very Beginning by Organizers of the Turmoil

Comrade Hu Yaobang's death on 15 April prompted an early outbreak of the long-brewing student unrest and turmoil. The students and broad masses mourned Comrade Hu Yaobang and expressed their profound grief. Universities and colleges provided facilities for the mourning on the part of the students. However, a small number of people took advantage of this to oppose the leadership of the Communist party and the socialist system under the pretext of "mourning."

Some so-called elitists in academic circles ... organized a variety of forums during the period and indulged in unbridled propaganda through the press. Most outstanding among the activities was a forum sponsored by the *World Economic Herald* and the *New Observer* in Beijing on 19 April. The forum was chaired by Ge Yang, and its participants included Yan Jiaqi, Su Shaozhi, Chen Ziming [director of the Beijing Institute of Socioeconomic Science], and Liu Ruishao [head of Hong Kong Wen Hui Pao's Beijing office]. There were two main topics: One was to "rehabilitate" Hu Yaobang; the other was to "reverse" the verdict on the fight against liberalization. They expressed unequivocal support for the student demonstrations, saying that they saw from there "China's future and hope...."

Rumor mongering greatly sharpened students' antagonism toward the government....This led to a serious situation in which sixty thousand university students boycotted classes in Beijing, with many students in other parts of China following suit. The student unrest escalated and the turmoil expanded.

This turmoil was marked by another characteristic: that is, it was no longer confined to institutions of higher learning or the Beijing area; it spread to the whole of society and to all parts of China....A number of people went to contact middle schools, factories, shops, and villages, made speeches in the streets, handed out leaflets, put up slogans, and raised money, doing everything possible to make the situation worse.... Students from Beijing were seen in universities and colleges in Nanjing, Wuhan, Xian, Changsha, Shanghai, and Harbin, while students from Tianjin, Hefei, Anhui, and Zhejiang took part in demonstrations in Beijing. Criminal activities of beating, smashing, looting, and burning took place in Changsha and Xian.

Reactionary political forces in Hong Kong, Taiwan, the United States and other Western countries were also involved in the turmoil through various channels and by various means. Western news agencies showed unusual zeal. The Voice of America, in particular, aired news on three frequencies beamed to the Chinese mainland for a total of more than ten hours every day, spreading rumors, stirring up trouble, and adding fuel to the turmoil.

Facts listed above show that we were confronted not with student unrest in its normal sense, but with a planned, organized, and premeditated political turmoil designed to negate the Communist party leadership and the socialist system.

[Most of Chen's speech is devoted to rehashing the party line on the demonstrations and the crackdown, blaming Zhao Ziyang, the "small number of people," and various foreign governments and organizations. The following section, however, demonstrates how low the government's reputation had sunk during the demonstrations. Chen details the government's extensive effort to provide relief for the hunger strikers but admits that these measures met no success. It is an indirect acknowledgment of the government's credibility problem, which has a long history in Chinese culture.]

The Hunger Strike was Used as Coercion to Escalate the Turmoil

Good, kindhearted people asked if the government's lack of understanding, consideration, and concession had brought about the students' behavior. The facts are just the opposite.

From the very beginning of the turmoil, the party and government fully acknowledged the students' patriotism and their concern about the country and people. Their demands to promote democracy, promote reform, punish official profiteers, and fight corruption were acknowledged as identical with the aspirations of the party and government, which also expressed the hope to solve the problems through normal democratic and legal procedures.

But these good intentions failed to win a positive response. The government proposed to increase understanding and to reach a consensus through dialogues on various levels and in different formats.... The illegal student organization, however, put forward very strict conditions as terms of the dialogue. They demanded that their partners to the dialogues "be people holding positions at or above membership in the Standing Committee of the Politburo of the Party Central Committee, or vice-chairman of the National People's Congress Standing Committee and vice-premier...." This was nothing like a dialogue; it was more like setting the stage for political negotiations with the party and government.

On the morning of 13 May, the Bureau for Letters and Visits of the general offices of the Party Central Committee, the State Council, and the National People's Congress Standing Committee again notified them of the decision to hold a dialogue with students on 15 May. Despite their agreement, the students began maneuvering for the number of participants in the dialogue. After the government agreed to their first proposed list of twenty people, they then demanded that the number be raised to two hundred.

Without waiting for further discussion, they accused "the government of insincerity in wanting to hold a dialogue." Then, just four hours after they had been informed of the dialogue, the students hastily made public their long-prepared "hunger strike declaration," launching a seven-day fast that involved more than three thousand people and a long occupation of Tiananmen Square. Thirteen May was chosen as the starting date of the hunger strike "to put pressure on them [the government] during Gorbachev's China visit," said Wang Dan, the leader of the Beijing Federation.

During the hunger strike, the party and government maintained an attitude of utmost restraint and did everything they could in various aspects:

1. First of all, staff members of various universities, leading officials at all levels, and even party and state leaders went to Tiananmen Square to see the fasting students on many occasions and to reason with them.

2. Second, efforts were made to help the Red Cross and to mobilize more than one hundred ambulances and several hundred medical workers to keep watch at the fasting site day and night. Fifty-two hospitals were asked to have some two thousand beds ready so that students who suffered shock or illness because of the hunger strike could get first-aid and timely treatment.

3. All sorts of materials were provided to alleviate the suffering of the fasting students and to ensure their safety.

4. The Beijing Municipal Party Committee and people's government mobilized cadres, workers, and vehicles to provide the fasting students

day and night with drinking water, edible salt, and sugar via the Red Cross.

5. The Municipal Environment Sanitation Bureau sent sprinklers and offered basins and towels for the fasting students.

6. Adequate supplies of medicine preventing sunstroke, cold, and diarrhea were provided by pharmaceutical companies and distributed by the Red Cross.

7. The Provisions Department sent a large amount of soft drinks and bread to be used during the emergency rescue of the students.

8. A total of six thousand straw hats was provided by commercial units, and one thousand quilts were sent by the Beijing Military Area Command in response to the city authorities' request to protect the fasting students from heat in the day and cold at night.

9. To keep the hunger strike site clean, makeshift flush toilets were set up and sanitation workers cleaned the site at midnight. Before the torrential rain of 19 May, seventy-eight coaches from the Public Transport Company and four hundred thick boards from the Materials Bureau were sent to protect the fasting students from rain and dampness. No fasting student died in the seven-day hunger strike.

But all this failed to get any positive response.

Under these circumstances, the fasting students were put "on the back of the tiger and found it difficult to get off." Many parents of the students and teachers wrote to or called top government agencies, press organizations, and radio and television stations, asking them not to force the fasting students onto the path of death, to save the children, and to stop this form of "killing by public opinion." But this did not work.

The students' hunger strike and the Beijing citizens' demonstrations threw Beijing into chaos and seriously disrupted the Sino-Soviet summit that was closely followed worldwide. These events forced some changes in the agenda, and some activities were even cancelled.

The Four Cardinal Principles

[This speech is the central document in the development of China in the aftermath of Mao Zedong. Since Deng Xiaoping delivered it in March 1979, the "Four Cardinal Principles" have been the guiding principles for China's reform effort, exercising far-reaching influence on virtually all of its leaders, including the hardliners presented in this chapter and the liberals presented in chapter 4. An analysis of this speech and its consequences on the restructuring of the Chinese political landscape is contained in chapter 8 of this volume, "Deng Xiaoping and the Student Movement of 1989."]

What I want to talk about now is ideological and political questions. The Central Committee maintains that, to carry out China's Four Modernizations [advances in defense, industry, agriculture, and science and technology], we must uphold the Four Cardinal Principles ideologically and politically. This is the basic prerequisite for achieving modernization. The four principles are:

1.   We must keep to the socialist road;
2.   We must uphold the dictatorship of the proletariat;
3.   We must uphold the leadership of the Communist party; and,
4.   We must uphold Marxism-Leninism and Mao Zedong Thought.

As we all know, far from being new, these Four Cardinal Principles have long been upheld by our party. The Central Committee has been adhering to these principles in all its guidelines and policies adopted since the Gang of Four, and especially since the Third Plenary Session of the Eleventh Central Committee.

First, we must keep to the socialist road. Some people are now openly saying that socialism is inferior to capitalism. We must demolish this contention. In the first place, socialism and socialism alone can save China—this is the unshakable historical conclusion that the Chinese people have drawn from their own experience in the sixty years since the May Fourth [1919] Movement. Deviate from socialism and China will inevitably retrogress to semifeudalism and semicolonialism. The overwhelming majority of the Chinese people will never allow such retrogression.

In the second place, although it is a fact that China lags behind the developed capitalist countries in its economy, technology, and culture, this is not due to the socialist system but basically to China's historical development before liberation; it is the result of imperialism and feudalism. The socialist revolution has greatly narrowed the gap in economic development between China and the advanced capitalist countries. Despite our errors, in the past three decades we have made progress on a scale that old China could not achieve in hundreds or even thousands of years. Our economy has attained a fairly high rate of growth. Now that we have summed up experience and corrected errors, it will undoubtedly develop more rapidly than the economy of any capitalist country, and the development will be steady and sustained. Of course, it will take a considerable period of time for the value of our national output per capita to catch up with and surpass that of the developed capitalist countries.

In the third place, let's ask: Which is better, the socialist system or the capitalist system? Of course the socialist system is better. In certain circumstances, a socialist country may make serious errors and even experience such major setbacks as the havoc created by Lin Biao and the Gang of Four. Naturally, this has its subjective causes, but basically it is due to influences inherited from the old society with its long history, influences that cannot be swept away overnight. Capitalist countries with a long feudal history—such as Britain, France, Germany, Japan, and Italy—all experienced major setbacks and reversals at different times. But relying on the socialist system and our own strength, we toppled Lin Biao and the Gang of Four without too much difficulty and quickly set our country back on the road to stability, unity, and healthy development. The socialist economy is based on public ownership, and socialist production is designed to meet the material and cultural needs of the people to the maximum extent possible—not to exploit them. These characteristics of the socialist system make it possible for the people of our country to share common political, economic, and social ideals and moral standards. All this can never happen in a capitalist society. There is no way capitalism can ever eliminate the extraction of superprofits by its millionaires or ever get rid of exploitation, plundering, and economic crisis. It can never generate common ideals and moral standards or free itself from appalling crimes, moral degradation, and despair.

On the other hand, capitalism already has a history of several hundred years, and we have to learn from the peoples of the capitalist countries. We must make use of the science and technology they have developed and of those elements in their accumulated knowledge and experience that can be adapted to our use. While we will import advanced technology and other things useful to us from the capitalist countries—selectively and according to plan—we will never learn from or import the capitalist system itself, nor anything repellent or decadent. If the developed capitalist countries were to rid themselves of the capitalist system, their economy and culture would certainly make greater progress. That is why the progressive political forces in the capitalist countries are trying to study and propagate socialism, and are fighting to eliminate the injustices and irrational phenomena endemic in capitalist society and to carry our socialist revolution. We should introduce to our people, and particularly to our youth, whatever is progressive and useful in the capitalist countries, and we should criticize whatever is reactionary and decadent.

Second, we must uphold the dictatorship of the proletariat. We have conducted a lot of propaganda explaining that the dictatorship of the proletariat means socialist democracy for the people, democracy enjoyed by the workers, peasant, intellectuals, and other working people, the broadest democracy that has ever existed in history. In the past, we did not practice democracy enough and we made mistakes. Lin Biao and the Gang of Four, while boosting their so-called "all-round dictatorship," exercised a feudal fascist dictatorship over the people. We have smashed this dictatorship, which had nothing in common with the dictatorship of the proletariat but was its diametric opposite. Now we have corrected the past mistakes and adopted many measures to constantly expand democracy in the party and among the people. Without democracy there can be no socialism and no socialist modernization.

Of course, democratization, like modernization must advance step by step. The more socialism develops, the more must democracy develop. This is beyond all doubt. However, the development of socialist democracy in no way means that we can dispense with the proletarian dictatorship over forces hostile to socialism. We are opposed to broadening the scope of class struggle. We do not believe that there is bourgeoisie within the party, nor do we believe that under the socialist system a bourgeoisie or any other exploiting class will reemerge after class exploitation and the conditions of exploitation have really been eliminated. But we must recognize that in our socialist society there are still counter-revolutionaries, enemy agents, criminals, and other bad elements of all kinds who undermine socialist public order, as well as new exploiters who engage in corruption, embezzlement, speculation, and profiteering. And we must also recognize that such phenomena cannot be eliminated for a long time to come. The struggle against these individuals is different from the struggle of one class against another, which occurred in the past (these individuals cannot form a cohesive and overt class). However, it is still a special form of class struggle or a special form of leftover, under socialist conditions, of the class struggles of past history. It is still necessary to exercise dictatorship over all these antisocialist elements, and socialist democracy is impossible without it. This dictatorship is an internal struggle and in some cases an international struggle as well; in fact, the two aspects are inseparable. Therefore, so long as class struggle exists and so long as imperialism and hegemony exist, it is inconceivable that the dictatorial function of the state should wither away, that the standing army, public security organs, courts, and prisons should wither away. Their existence is not in contradiction with the democratization of the socialist state, for their correct and effective work ensures, rather than hampers, such democratization. The fact of the matter is that socialism cannot be defended or built up without the dictatorship of the proletariat.

Third, we must uphold the leadership of the Communist party. Since the inception of the international communist movement, it has been demonstrated that the movement's survival is impossible without the political parties of the proletariat. Moreover, since the October Revolution it has been clear that, without the leadership of a Communist party, the socialist revolution, the dictatorship of the proletariat, and socialist construction would all be impossible. Lenin said: "The dictatorship of the proletariat is a persistent struggle—bloody and bloodless, violent and peaceful, military and economic, educational and administrative—against the forces and traditions of the old society. Without an iron party tempered in the struggle, without a party enjoying the confidence of all that is honest in the given class, without a party capable of watching and influencing the mood of the masses, it is impossible to conduct such a struggle successfully." This truth enunciated by Lenin remains valid today. In our country, in the sixty years since the May Fourth Movement, no political party other than the Communist Party of China has integrated itself with the masses of the working people in the way described by Lenin. Without the Chinese Communist Party there would be no socialist New China. The misdeeds of Lin Biao and the Gang of Four aroused the resolute opposition of the whole Chinese people as well as of the whole party precisely because Lin Biao and the Gang cast aside the Chinese Communist Party, the long-tested leading force that maintains flesh-and-blood ties with the masses. And if the party's prestige among the people throughout has been enhanced since the downfall of the Gang of Four, and particularly since the Third Plenary Session of the Eleventh Central Committee, it is precisely because the entire nation pins all of its hopes for the future on leadership by the party. Although the mass movement of 1976 that culminated in the incident at Tiananmen Square where the people gathered to mourn Premier Zhou Enlai was not led by the party organizationally, it staunchly supported the party's leadership and opposed the Gang of Four. The revolutionary consciousness of the masses in that movement was inseparable from the education given by the party over the years, and it was precisely members of the party and the Communist Youth League who were the principal activists among them. Hence we must on no account consider the mass movement at Tiananmen Square to have been a purely spontaneous one like the May Fourth Movement, which had no connection with party leadership. In reality, without the Chinese Communist Party, who would organize the socialist economy, politics, military affairs, and culture of China, and who would organize the Four Modernizations? In the China of today we can never dispense with leadership by the party and extol spontaneity of the masses. Party leadership, of course, is not infallible, and the problems of how the party can maintain close links with the masses and exercise correct and effective leadership is still one that we must seriously study and try to solve. But this can never be made a pretext for demanding the weakening or liquidation of the party's leadership. Our party has made many errors, but each time the errors were corrected by relying on the party organization, not by discarding it. The present Central Committee is persistent in promoting democracy in the party and among the people and is determined to correct past errors. Under these circumstances, it would be all the more intolerable to the masses of our people to demand the liquidation or even the weakening of leadership by the party. In fact, bowing to this demand would only lead to anarchism and the disruption and ruin of the socialist cause.

Fourth, we must uphold Marxism-Leninism and Mao Zedong Thought. One of the key points of our struggle against Lin Biao and the Gang of Four was opposition to their falsification, doctoring, and fragmenting of Marxism-Leninism and Mao Zedong Thought. Since the smashing of the Gang, we have restored the scientific character of Marxism-Leninism and Mao Zedong Thought and have guided ourselves by them. This is a resounding victory for the whole party and people. But a few individuals think otherwise. Either they openly oppose the basic tenets of Marxism-Leninism, or else they uphold Marxism-Leninism in word only while in deed opposing Mao Zedong Thought, which represent the integration of the universal truth of Marxism-Leninism with the practice of the Chinese revolution. We must oppose these erroneous trends of thought. Some comrades say that we should uphold "correct Mao Zedong Thought" but not "erroneous Mao Zedong Thought." This kind of statement is also wrong. What we consistently take as our guide to action are the basic tenets of Marxism-Leninism and Mao Zedong Thought or, to put it another way, the scientific system formed by these tenets. When it comes to individual theses, neither Marx and Lenin nor Comrade Mao could be immune from misjudgments of one sort or another. But these do not belong to the scientific system formed by the basic tenets of Marxism-Leninism and Mao Zedong Thought.

Now I want to talk at some length about Mao Zedong Thought. China's anti-imperialist revolution and antifeudal revolution went through innumerable cruel defeats. Was it not Mao Zedong Thought that enabled the Chinese people—about a quarter of the world's population—to find the correct road for their revolution, achieve nationwide liberation in 1949, and basically accomplish socialist transformation by 1956? This succession of splendid victories changed not only China's destiny but the world situation as well. From the international point of view, Mao Zedong Thought is inseparably linked with the struggle against hegemony; and the practice of hegemony under the banner of socialism is a most obvious betrayal of socialist principles on the part of a Marxist-Leninist party after it has come to power. As I have already mentioned, in the evening of his life Comrade Mao Zedong formulated the strategy of differentiating the three worlds and personally ushered in a new state in Sino-American and Sino-Japanese relations. By so doing he created new conditions for the development of the worldwide struggle against hegemony and for the future of world politics. While conducting our modernization program in the present international environment, we cannot help recalling Comrade Mao's contributions. Comrade Mao, like any other man, had his defects and made errors. But how can these errors in his illustrious life be put on a par with his immortal contributions to the people? In analyzing his defects and errors, we certainly should recognize his personal responsibility, but what is more important is to analyze their complicated historical background. That is the only just and scientific—that is, Marxist—way to assess history and historical figures. Anyone who departs from Marxism on so serious a question will be censured by the party and the masses. Isn't that natural?

Mao Zedong Thought has been the banner of the Chinese revolution. It is and always will be the banner of China's socialist cause and of the antihegemonist cause. In our forward march we will always hold the banner of Mao Zedong Thought high.

The cause and the thought of Comrade Mao Zedong are not his alone; they are likewise those of his comrades-in-arms: the party and the people. His thought is the crystallization of the experience of the Chinese people's revolutionary struggle over half a century. The case of Karl Marx was similar. In his estimation of Marx, Frederick Engels said that it was only thanks to Marx that the contemporary proletariat became conscious for the first time of its own position and demands and of the conditions necessary for its own liberation. Does this mean that history is made by any one individual? History is made by the people, but this does not preclude the people's respecting an outstanding individual. Of course, this respect must not turn into blind worship. No man should be looked upon as a demigod.

To sum up, in order to achieve the Four Modernizations we must keep to the socialist road, uphold the dictatorship of the proletariat, uphold the leadership of the Communist party, and uphold Marxism-Leninism and Mao Zedong Thought. The Central Committee considers that we must now repeatedly emphasize the necessity of upholding these Four Cardinal Principles, because certain people (even if only a handful) are attempting to undermine them. In no way can such attempts be tolerated. No party member and, needless to say, no party ideological or theoretical worker, must ever waver in the slightest on this basic stand. To undermine any of the Four Cardinal

Principles is to undermine the whole cause of socialism in China, the whole cause of modernization.

Notes

1   The big- and small-letter character posters are uniquely Chinese forms of political expression which are inexpensive and require only a piece of paper, brush, and ink. They are used generally for criticisms and denunciations. They may be signed or unsigned.

4

The Intellectuals

16 May Declaration—The Intellectuals Speak Out

17 May Declaration

The Intellectuals Go On Hunger Strikes

Human Rights in China

Patriotism and Global Citizenship

Does Chinese Culture Have a Future?

The [Yellow] River Elegy

16 May Declaration—The Intellectuals Speak Out

[Intellectuals had been providing behind-the-scenes support for the students, but this support was announced publicly with this statement. Among the intellectuals who formulated and signed it were the political scientist Yan Jiaqi, Marxist theoretician Su Shaozhi, and reportage writer and famous television documentary "Heshang" (The [Yellow] River Elegy) coauthor Su Xiaokang, all widely recognized in and outside China now.

With the intellectuals joining forces with the students, the movement became more complex but at the same time gained greater articulateness and sophistication. The statement attempts to frame the debate in terms of adherence to the Constitution rather than to the party line. It also identifies corruption as the cause of the student protests and voices a strong demand for democracy as a means of ending corruption. It begins by referring to the 16 May Notice, which announced the beginning of the Cultural Revolution in 1966, thus adding a historical dimension to the occasion. The intellectuals were also aware that they were at a turning point in history.]

The 16 May Notice of 1966 undoubtedly symbolizes dictatorship and darkness to the heart of the Chinese people. Now, twenty-three years later, we have strongly felt the yearning for democracy and the hope for a bright future. History has finally reached a turning point. At present, a patriotic democracy movement, with the students in the vanguard, has spread throughout the country. Within less than a month, in Beijing and all over China, demonstrations have erupted, surging forward like a great tidal wave. Hundreds of thousands of students have taken to the streets to denounce corruption, calling for democracy and the rule of law. Their call expresses the will of the workers, peasants, soldiers, cadres, intellectuals, and working people of every field. This is a national awakening that has carried forward to new heights the spirit of the May Fourth Movement. This is a great historical moment that will determine the fate of China.

Since the Third Plenary Session of the Eleventh Congress of the Chinese Communist Party, China has embarked on a path of national renaissance and modernization. It is to be regretted, however, that the ineffectual efforts at reform of the political structure have brought severe setbacks to the initial successes of the economic reforms.

Corruption grows worse by the day; social conflicts have grown even sharper. The entire reform movement, in which the people have placed so much hope, now faces a crisis. China is at a critical point. At this time when the fate of the people, of the country, and of the ruling party is at stake, we intellectuals in or outside of China who have signed this statement on this day of 16 May 1989 do solemnly proclaim our stand and principles:

1. We feel that the party and government have not been very wise in dealing with the student movement. Not long ago, there were even signs of attempts by the authorities to deal with the students by force. History's lessons should not be forgotten. All attempts by dictators to suppress the student movement with violence, whether it be the Beijing government in 1919, the Kuomintang of the 1930s and 1940s, or the Gang of Four in the late 1970s, have all been shamefully recorded in the pages of China's history. History has proven that all those who try to suppress student movements will come to a bad end. Recently, the party and government have started to show welcome signs of becoming more reasonable, and the situation has therefore improved a little. If the government would continue by following the principles of modern democratic processes, respecting the will of the people and joining the popular tide, China can emerge as a stable and democratic nation. Otherwise, a country that has been so full of hope can be driven into the abyss of real civil turmoil.

2. If the present political crisis is to be handled according to democratic political principles, one precondition is that the legality of the independent student organization, which was born out of the democratic processes of the student movement, must be recognized. Otherwise it would be in conflict with the Constitution of the People's Republic of China, which guarantees freedom of assembly and association. The attempts once made by the government to brand the independent students' union as illegal can only sharpen the conflict and deepen the crisis.

3. The direct cause of the present political crisis is widespread corruption, which the young students have firmly opposed during the patriotic democratic movement. The biggest mistake of the past ten years of reform is not in the field of education but rather in neglecting to reform the political structure. [Deng Xiaoping had told a foreign dignitary before the student movement that the biggest mistake in China's reform effort had been the neglect of education.] It is because of the bureaucracy, which has never really been dealt with, and the feudal-

style special privileges, which have been introduced and gained an unobstructed foothold in our economic life, that corruption has developed.... This has not only swallowed up the fruits of the economic reform but has shaken the people's faith in the party and the government. The party and government should draw profound lessons from this, and, according to the wishes of the people, push forward the reform of the political structure, do away with all special privileges, investigate and forbid "official profiteering," and uproot corruption.

4. During the student movement, the news media, as represented by the *People's Daily* and the Xinhua News Agency, for a time withheld the true facts about the student movement and stripped the citizens of their right to know [of it.] The Shanghai Municipal Party Committee has fired Qin Benli, editor-in-chief of the *World Economic Herald*. These totally illegal acts are a gross violation of the Constitution. Freedom of the press is an effective means to uproot corruption, maintain national stability, and promote social development. Absolute power unchecked and unsupervised will definitely lead to absolute corruption. Without freedom of the press, without independent newspapers, all hopes and aspirations about reform and the open policy will remain empty talk.

5. It is wrong to brand this student movement an antiparty, antisocialist political turmoil. The basic meaning of freedom of speech is to recognize and protect the citizens' right to express different political views. Actually, ever since Liberation [1949], every political campaign launched by the authorities has been to suppress and strike blows at different political views. A society that allows only one voice cannot be a stable society. The party and government should learn a lesson from all the past movements, such as the "Oppose Hu Feng Movement," the "Anti-Rightist Campaign," the "Cultural Revolution," the campaign against "spiritual pollution," and the campaign against "bourgeois liberalization." They should, instead, establish a dialogue with the people, the students, and the intellectuals, and altogether discuss the problems of the nation. Only in this way can a united and stable political situation be truly established in China.

6. It is wrong to rant about needing to isolate "a handful of instigators" and "a small clique of bearded ones" who are allegedly the "behind-the-scenes plotters." All Chinese citizens, no matter what age, have equal political status, and all have the political right to discuss political matters and to participate in them. Freedom, democracy, and rule by law have never been bestowed on anyone. All those who seek truth and love freedom should struggle tirelessly to make the guarantees in the Constitution come true: freedom of thought, freedom of speech,

freedom of the press, freedom to publish, freedom of assembly, freedom to hold public meetings, and freedom to demonstrate.

We have come to a historic turning point. Our long-suffering nation cannot afford losing more opportunities and cannot turn back.

We Chinese intellectuals, who have a tradition of patriotism and are always concerned about the nation, should become conscious of our unshirkable historic duty. We should stand up and push forward the movement for democracy. Let us struggle to build a politically democratic, economically developed, modern state! Long live the people! Long live a free, democratic, socialist motherland!

17 May Declaration

Yan Jiaqi, Bao Zuenxin, Li Nanyou, etc.

[On 16 May, Zhao Ziyang told the visiting Soviet leader Mikhail Gorbachev that Deng Xiaoping was still in charge. The remark was interpreted as an attempt to separate himself from more conservative members of the Politburo and curry support with the students. The intellectuals immediately responded with this statement, issued just one day after they had openly come out in favor of the students. This statement is a harsh attack on Deng, made all the more severe by its directness.]

Since the afternoon of 16 May, more than three thousand students have gone on a hunger strike at Tiananmen Square that has lasted over one hundred hours. Over seven hundred of them have now fainted from it. This is an unprecedented tragedy in our nation's history. The students demand that the 26 April editorial of the *People's Daily* be retracted and a live dialogue between government officials and the students be conducted. As the sons and daughters of our nation are falling one after another, their justified demands are being ignored, which is the reason that the hunger strike could not come to an end. Today, our nation's problem is that, because the dictator holds unlimited power, the government has lost its sense of responsibility and has lost its humanity. Such a government is not one of the republic but one under the absolute power of a dictator.

Seventy-six years have passed since the Qing dynasty [1644-1911] fell. Yet China continues to have an emperor, though without that title—an elderly, doddering dictator. On the afternoon of 17 May, Secretary Zhao Ziyang publicly declared that all major decisions have to be approved by this aging dictator. Without the approval of this dictator, the 26 April *People's Daily* editorial cannot be retracted. Now that the students have persisted in a hunger strike of over one hundred hours, there is no other choice. The Chinese people can no longer wait for the dictator to admit his mistakes. Now it is up to the students, up to the people. Today, we declare before all China, before the whole world, that the hundred-hour hunger strike of the students has won a great victory. The students have used their own actions to declare that this student movement is not a riot, but a great patriotic movement to finally, and at last, bury the dictators in China, bury the system of monarchy. Let us all cheer for the victory of the hunger strikers! Long live the spirit of nonviolent struggle!

Down with the dictators! Dictators will come to no good end!

The Intellectuals Go On Hunger Strikes
2 June 1989—Liu Xiaobo, Zhou Tuo, Hou Derchien, and Gao Xin

[Contrast this declaration by the intellectuals with the earlier declaration by the youthful students. This statement tends to be much more theoretical in defining what democracy is, how it works, and how the students have misused democratic concepts in their attempts to seek democratic change. Liu Xiaobo, who was trained in philosophy and studied in the West, is much more knowledgeable about the workings of democracy and democratic procedures. He has essentially set down succinctly the basic principles of participatory democracy and has made incisive criticisms of the weaknesses of the students. Liu Xiaobo is calling for the creation of a new political culture—a democratic culture. In this new political culture, the citizens must be instilled with a sense of political responsibility.]

Today we have decided to go on a hunger strike. Our purpose is to protest, appeal, and confess.

We are not looking for death, but for a real life. In the face of the mounting pressure of military violence by the Li Peng government, which has lost its ability to reason, Chinese intellectuals must end our "osteomalacia," which we inherited from the ancestors of our ancestors over thousands of years. We have indulged ourselves more in talking than in doing. Now we are taking action to protest martial law, to call for the birth of a new political culture, and to confess the mistakes we made in the past because of our "weak knees." We are all responsible for China's being left behind by the rest of the world.

This democratic movement, unprecedented in Chinese history, has been using legal, peaceful, and rational means in an attempt to achieve freedom, democracy, and human rights. However, the Li Peng government moved hundreds and thousands of troops to suppress the students and civilians, who did not have a single inch of iron in their hands. Therefore, our strike is no longer intended as a petition. Ours is a protest against the government's martial law. Although we prefer the peaceful ways of democratic progress to violence of any form, we are not afraid of violence. We will show through peaceful demonstrations how much potential strength lies in the people's support for democracy. We want to break the iron order that has been maintained by lies and bayonets. To employ troops and martial law in order to crack down on the peaceful petitioners was an absurd and stupid decision that has already become a stain on China's history. It resulted in great humiliation for the Communist party, the government, and the People's Army, and it destroyed the achievements that we made during ten years of openness and reform.

Chinese history, which covers several thousand years, is filled with instances of pacifism replaced by violence. In recent times, hostility among people is still a problem in social relations. Since 1949, the slogan "Class struggle is the key link" has represented the extreme form of this traditional hostility and the violent overthrow of dynasties. The current martial law is also part of the political class struggle culture. The purpose of our fasting is to appeal to the people to cast off the hostility among us and to abandon the idea of class struggle. We must learn that hatred can only lead to violence and dictatorship. Chinese democracy must be built on the basis of tolerance and cooperation. Democracy is a political form excluding enemies and hatred; it requires mutual respect, forgiveness, and cooperation in making its decisions after discussion and voting. Li Peng made serious mistakes in the office of the premier; he should step down according to democratic procedures.

However, Li Peng should not be considered our enemy. When he is out of office, he will enjoy the rights that a citizen does. He can, if he chooses, hold on to his wrong political ideas. We call upon every citizen from the government level to the grass roots to abandon the old political culture. We want the government to stop martial law immediately and to resume talks between the students and the government in order to resolve the conflict.

The student demonstration has received support and understanding from Chinese people of all walks of life. The exercise of martial law has in fact turned the movement into a nationwide democratic undertaking. But we have noticed that a lot of support came from people's dissatisfaction with the government and from their sympathy for the students. The people lack the concept of political responsibility. We therefore want to gradually raise their awareness of citizenship and help them give up their status as onlookers or sympathizers.

Citizenship means, first, political equality for everyone. Everybody should know that his rights are the same as those of the premier. Second, citizenship means not only justice and sympathy, but rational involvement in politics, that is, political obligation. It is not enough for the individual to express his sympathy and support. He should join in the building of democracy for China. A good political structure in a society comes from the participation of everybody living in it. Likewise, all the people share the responsibility for a bad political structure in their society. A citizen has the divine responsibility to take part in social politics. The Chinese people must know that in the democratic process of politics, everybody is first and foremost a citizen, then a student, teacher, worker, cadre, or officer.

For thousands of years, Chinese society has been circling from one emperor to another. We overthrew the old emperor only to establish the crown of another. History has proven that the replacement of an unpopular ruler by a popular ruler does not resolve China's political problems. What we need is not a perfect savior but a good democratic system. Therefore, we appeal for the establishment of independent organizations by the people at all levels so as to form a political force to work with the government in policy making. Since at the center of democracy is this equilibrium, we would rather have ten contending devils than one omnipotent angel. We also appeal for a solid, workable system of discharging officials who makes serious mistakes in office. We understand that it is not important who comes into power, but how he gets there. Nondemocratic designations and dismissals can only lead to the concentration of power in the hands of a dictator.

During this movement, both the government and the students have made mistakes. The problem with the government was that it was controlled by the old "class struggle" theory and took a stand against the students. That theory led the conflict from bad to worse. The problem with the students was their lack of structure and thought. In the course of their fight for democracy, antidemocratic elements appeared in their words and deeds. Therefore, we appeal to the government and the students for calm examinations of the past few weeks. On the whole, we consider the government responsible for the severity of the whole situation. Demonstrations and hunger strikes were democratic ways for people to express their wills. They were consistent with the Constitution and should not be seen as "turmoil." The government ignored the citizens' basic rights guaranteed by the Constitution and wantonly determined that the student movement was a "turmoil." As a result of a series of wrong policies issued by the government, the demonstration escalated again and again, and the conflict worsened. We may well say that the "turmoil" was actually incited by the government; its consequences are no better than those of the Cultural Revolution. Because the students and civilians held themselves back, and because many of the important people from society appealed very strongly for nonviolence, large-scale bloodshed has been avoided so far. The government must admit and acknowledge these mistakes. We think it is not yet too late for the government to do so. The government should learn an important lesson from this democratic movement and listen to the people's voices. They should also get used to the people's using their constitutional rights to express their wishes and govern the country through democratic procedures. The nationwide democratic movement is teaching the government how to do these things.

The students' problem was in the confusion of the organizational structure and the lack of efficiency and democratic procedures. They used nondemocratic means to fight for democracy. They announced democracy as their ideal, but they did not use it in coping with day-to-day routines. They lacked the spirit of cooperation, so their strength was wasted in conflict. Their decisions were temporary and inconsistent. The student leaders did not know how to manage money and materials. They were more emotional than rational and more involved in exercising their individual power than in practicing the democratic ideal of equality.

For about a hundred years, the Chinese people's democratic movement focused mainly on ideological concepts and slogans. It engaged itself in discussing the basic ideas of democracy and its goals but seldom had actual experience in the procedures and methods of democracy. We think that democratic politics is realized by democratizing government operations and procedures. Therefore, we appeal to the Chinese people to switch from empty talk of democracy at the level of enlightening to the solid study and practice of building a working democracy. We must begin this with every little job we are doing now. The students may want to start this examination with their demonstrators in the Square.

One of the big mistakes that the government made was its use of the term "a handful." We want to tell the world through fasting that this "handful" is not students but civilians who, driven by their political obligations as citizens, took part in the student democratic movement.

What they did was reasonable and legal. They want to use their wit and energy to force the government to realize, acknowledge, and correct its mistakes in politics, in the exercise of justice, and in personality cultivation. They wish that the student independent organizations would gradually complete their own structures in the light of democracy and law.

We must acknowledge that the practice of democracy in Chinese politics from the central government level is new to every Chinese citizen. Therefore, the people as well as the top leaders must start the lessons from the beginning. Mistakes cannot be avoided during the learning process. The key to success lies in the willingness to learn from our mistakes and to correct them as soon as possible. In that way, we can turn mistakes into precious experience and master the democratic operation of our country.

Our basic tenets:

1.   We have no enemies! Do not allow hatred and violence to poison our wit and hamper the progress of the democratization of China.
2.   We need to reexamine the past. Everybody is responsible for the underdevelopment of this country.
3.   We are, above all, citizens.
4.   We are not looking for death but for a real life.

The details of our hunger strike:

1.   Place: the Monument to the People's Heroes at Tiananmen Square.
2.   Time: seventy-two hours, from 4:00 P.M. 2 June to 4:00 P.M. 5 June 1989. (Note: Because Hou Derchien will be going to Hong Kong on a business appointment regarding the production of his records in six days, his hunger strike will end at 4:00 P.M. 4 June.)
3.   Regulations: except water, no food or drinks of nutritious liquid, such as those containing sugar, starch, protein, or fat, are allowed.

Names of hunger strikers:

LIU XIAOBO: Ph.D. in literature, lecturer in Chinese literature department, Beijing Normal University.
ZHOU TUO: former lecturer at the Sociology Research Institute of Beijing University, now director of General Planning and Development of SiTong Group, Inc.

HOU DERCHIEN: well-known composer and songwriter from Taiwan.

GAO XIN: former chief editor of *Beijing Normal Weekly*, Chinese Communist Party member.

Human Rights in China
Fang Lizhi (From a telephone conversation 22 March 1989)
22 March 1989

[Fang Lizhi, one of China's most famous dissidents, was the ousted vice-president of the Chinese University of Science and Technology in Anhui province. An outstanding astrophysicist in his own right, Fang is the l'enfant terrible in his outspoken criticism of the government. He has become the thorn in the government's side. In his criticism of the government, he has said that Marxism is obsolete, and, as for modernization, he has maintained that "there should not exist a Chinese-styled modernization or a Western type of modernization. Modernization is modernization and that's it." Fang Lizhi has made human rights his special issue and is considered by some to be China's Sakharov. In this telephone interview on 22 March 1989, he speaks specifically about human rights in China and argues in an almost scientific manner about the indispensability of human rights in the creation of a democratic society. He adds further that not only is human rights necessary domestically but also on the international level for the furtherance of world peace.]

I am very happy to have the opportunity to talk about my views on human rights in China. For a long time there was no mention of the term "human rights" in the political life of China. On the international level, it has been the same. This has given people the impression that human rights are not appropriate for China. Some even say that human rights should only be discussed where cultural circumstances are appropriate.

From my point of view, recent events have proven that this theory is mistaken. The concept of human rights is a very simple one. It is just as the International Declaration of Human Rights has pointed out: anyone regardless of his or her skin color, race, language, religion, or political belief should enjoy these rights. The concept of human rights should not be any different whether it is in the East or West. Human rights should be the same everywhere. Even if the concept of human rights is very rarely mentioned in China, the problem is still the same.

Human rights in China during the time of Mao Zedong was very similar to that during the time of Stalin in the Soviet Union. The two socialist countries were both propagating the idea of class struggle, and the results were similar. For example, during the antirightist movement in 1957, approximately half a million people received punishment of various sorts. Some lost their jobs; some were sent to labor reform camps. I admit that in the past ten years, after ten years of reform, there has been some improvement regarding the question of human rights. But the problem is still there. Many serious human rights violations are still happening in China, the most notorious case being the suppression of the democracy wall in 1979. Following that there was the antispiritual pollution campaign of 1983, then the suppression of the student demonstrations in 1986-87 and the antibourgeois liberalism campaign. These movements clearly indicate that the idea of class struggle is still being used to violate the people's fundamental rights.

Until now, even though certain articles of the Chinese Constitution specify certain rights, such as freedom of speech, these rights have not actually been implemented. For instance, the Chinese government still has not given support to the International Declaration of Human Rights and has not accepted the conditions of the Declaration. Other human rights matters have no direct relation to politics, such as international academic exchange, and yet have often encountered interference from the government. Sometimes natural science or technological reports have been withdrawn or expurgated for political reasons. These all indicate that there are many instances of human rights violation in China. Therefore, in my view, one of the most important goals of reform at the present is to improve and protect the fundamental rights of the intellectuals and the ordinary citizen. In my view, the most important items at the present time are freedom of speech, news and information, assembly, and belief.

Recently I have seen that many people in China have reacted strongly to the the question of releasing political prisoners. This is another test of the respect for human rights. People feel that this year, on the eve of the fortieth anniversary of the establishment of socialism in China, is an especially good opportunity for the government to take some concrete steps. But, up to this point, the government has not taken any. For this reason, we still need to make more effort.

Here I want to make one point clear: the demand for human rights is actually not opposed to reform but is closely tied to reform. For example, the protection of human rights is essential to economic reform. Economic reform and development similarly require that the people have individual economic rights and equal rights in the economic system. These two kinds of rights are inseparable. From my point of view, the increase in corruption in recent years, especially corruption in certain agencies within our leaders' departments, proves that without democracy and human rights it is impossible to create an environment that is beneficial to economic development. Therefore, economic development and human rights are inseparable.

Another point is that the protection of human rights is necessary for a stable society. Recently, some have said that the demand for human rights and democracy will lead to instability. In fact this is not so. The Great Cultural Revolution was a period of great disorder, and many people suffered various degrees of violation of their human rights. Everyone remembers these events just like they happened yesterday. These were not the result of having democracy and human rights; rather they were brought about because there was no regard for human rights and democracy. This proves that democracy and human rights are the ingredients necessary to bring about a stable society.

Still another point: I believe that in matters regional or global in nature, human rights are a key ingredient in maintaining peace. If a government cannot respect human rights in handling its internal affairs, then people would have a hard time believing that it will respect the principle of peace in handling international affairs. Domestic and international affairs are closely linked. The demand for human rights in China today is actually an indispensable step in China's modernization program. If the provisions for human rights are not improved, then China cannot modernize.

The international situation is relatively calm and peaceful at this time, and the attention to human rights has become a worldwide trend. In Asia and the rest of the world we have been hearing the greatest outcry for human rights. In this regard, China has joined the rest of the world. Now, the development of China is closely linked with the development of the rest of the world. The struggle for human rights in China is not an isolated undertaking, it is in step with the worldwide human rights movement. If we are successful, then we will be making a great contribution to the world. At the same time, we will be benefiting from the progress made in the rest of the world because we have already become an important part of this worldwide trend. This is why I dare say tonight that I have full confidence in the development of human rights in China.

I will only speak on these points. Thank you.

Patriotism and Global Citizenship
Fang Lizhi
25 February 1989

[In this talk on patriotism and global citizenship, Fang Lizhi warns against a narrow-minded interpretation of patriotism that can be exploited for political purposes. He also speaks, in his ebullient manner, about global issues such as the population problem, environmental pollution, energy, and global citizenship. He maintains logically that a narrow view of patriotism not only could be politically exploited but also would not be helpful in solving these global problems. The idea of the global citizen he borrows from Einstein, obviously one of his heroes.]

Yesterday I attended a meeting of the History of Science Society regarding commemorative ceremonies for the seventieth anniversary of the May Fourth Movement. Current plans for commemorating May Fourth do not include the theme of science and democracy. Of course, the student groups would like to talk about science and democracy, but it seems that they will be forced to use patriotism as a substitute. Patriotism is a slogan one hears quite often right now. My name probably won't be allowed on the list of official speakers, but I do have a few things to say about patriotism.

Patriotism is a big problem in this country. Criticize someone for being unpatriotic and it will shut them right up. But in my opinion, and I want to say this very clearly, patriotism should not be our guiding principle. Let me be a little more specific. The word patriotism can carry a range of implications from the purest of emotions to the dirtiest of politics, so the word itself is not too clearly defined. In part, certainly, it refers to deep feelings for your homeland, your mother, your kith and kin. In this sense patriotism is a fine thing, and we can respect it. But the use of the word patriotism these days by no means carries such a simple meaning. Particularly when you emphasize the "ism" part, it comes to mean that what you love is the nation-state.

In my younger days, I used to join in on the criticism of our poor old teachers, who would always defend themselves by saying "at least I'm patriotic; at least I love my country." Our standard reply was "But what country do you love? A communist country or a Kuomintang country?" Of course, what we were implying was that they really weren't patriotic at all. In this context, patriotism obviously does not mean loving your native place, its land and rivers and people; it means loving the state. Such a sentiment clearly can't serve as our guiding principle. After all, what is the state? According to standard Marxist-Leninist teachings, the state is the instrument of repression! The most important tools of the state are the police, the courts, the prisons, and the army. Does that mean that if we love our country we must love the police, the courts, the prisons, and the army? Clearly, such patriotism is not a lofty principle at all but only an emotion being exploited for political purposes.

The first opposition to this kind of nationalist patriotism that I know about came during the First World War. (Of course, there were probably even earlier examples, but this one concerns physics and I'm a physicist.) Though Germany and England were at war, the German and British physics communities continued to cooperate. Many felt that nationalistic patriotism was wrong. At that time, Einstein was setting out General Relativity, and his theoretical predictions were being confirmed by the experimental observations of British scientists. This was an outstanding act of cooperation. Why shouldn't we revere the same sentiments in China? Certainly there is no way that patriotism, as in "loving the instrument of the state," should be exalted as the first principle of the May Fourth commemoration. That is one point I want to make.

A second point is that even very pure feelings of love for one's homeland have their limits. They can be quite parochial and not constitute absolute criteria on which to base our judgments. Of course you should love your mother and the land of your origins. But when you encounter something new, should you automatically assume that it's good because it originates from your homeland, or that it's bad because it does not? Such an attitude is the source of serious problems in China, and we need to rethink it very carefully. Einstein was a good model here, as well. Although he was a Jew, he did not feel compelled under every circumstance to speak as Jew, but only as a human being.

In science, we approach a situation by asking if a statement is correct or incorrect, if a new theory is an improvement over an old one. These are our criteria. We do not ask if a thing originates with our race or nationality. This is extraordinarily clear in the natural sciences: There is no Jewish physics or German physics. There is only physics that gives good answers and physics that doesn't. Where it comes from is irrelevant. There are no national boundaries in scientific thought, and science is not the exclusive property of any race or nation.

I think that many scientists have a perspective that transcends their own particular culture. Local cultures should of course by respected, but not as some immutable principle that must be defended to the bitter end. In China, as well as in the West, there has long been a saying to the effect that "I love my teacher, but I love the truth more." You should love and respect your teachers, but their ideas shouldn't displace your own judgment and convictions. You have to love the truth more, you simply have to. Whether something is or isn't Chinese is not the issue. You can't go tip-toeing around for fear of challenging anything that is labelled Chinese. This is not the nature of real knowledge. The issue is whether a thing is true or false, not whether or not it's Chinese.

Things are more difficult in the social realm than in natural science, but I think humanity has been slowly evolving in this area as well. As time goes on, we arrive at concepts that are more and more universal in their application. Certainly science was the first such domain. The laws of natural science apply everywhere. But I personally feel that in the domain of the social sciences, in society itself, we are also arriving at increasingly universal concepts. As in science, these truths are not a function of skin color, religion, or nationality. They transcend such boundaries.

Human rights are an example of such a concept. Human rights are not the property of a particular race or nationality. Every human being is born with the right to live, to think, to speak, to find a mate. These are fundamental freedoms, and everyone on the face of the earth should have them, regardless of what country they live in. I think humanity is slowly coming to recognize this. Such ideas are actually fairly recent in human history; in Lincoln's time, only a century past, it was just being acknowledged in the United States that black and white people should enjoy the same rights. But such an issue is just what we are confronting now in China. The validity of human rights does not depend on the particular culture involved. Cultural biases are fine if you are not asking questions of right and wrong. You may like whatever kind of food you want to, and so may I. This is a question of preference, not of truth. Taste can be altogether a function of a particular place. But truth cannot. Truth doesn't distinguish between localities.

Of course, when you start asking detailed questions about democracy, such as whether to have a multiparty system, these are things that can differ from place to place. The specific framework of democracy in Britain is a constitutional monarchy, in France a republic, and so forth. These can differ. But they all start with the acknowledgment of human rights and are built on this foundation. In this sense, every place is equal and China is no exception.

The reason we should oppose patriotism is that it seems to become more narrow-minded as time goes on, while even the purest of patriotic sentiments is too parochial for the world we now live in. Humanity is faced with a very new kind of reality. A century or two ago, a country could be quite isolated from the outside world. Relationships based on common interests between nations were rare in those days. But if we look from the vantage point of science, the interests of the whole earth have become inseparable. We increasingly face common problems, such as those of energy and the environment. There are environmental issues of a global scale, involving the oceans, the atmosphere, and outer space. Population is another global issue. These are truly collective problems, and no nation can go off by itself and solve them. It simply can't be done. If Asia is turned into a desert, the United States will suffer. You can't run away from it, not even all the way across the Pacific Ocean. These are global issues, and they demand to be looked at from a global perspective.

In this regard, I would have to say that I personally have been guilty of something common to many scientists, which is believing that science inevitably leads to progress. In fact, you have to acknowledge that science has played a major role in creating many large-scale problems. With the advance of medical science came overpopulation, with the development of technology came energy problems, and so on. But at any rate, how you do you deal with such problems? I believe that they require a holistic approach, looking at every aspect, including the scientific and technological. Moreover, they demand that we create a truly global civilization.

Patriotism has little to contribute to solving problems of this nature. It is a throwback to an earlier state of history. To restrict your love and concern to your own country at this point in time is completely misguided. We must face up to this. Our activities are now intimately linked to developments in the rest of the world.

You know, the earth is really very, very, small. To those of us who work in astronomy, it is clear how small it is. People think that the atmosphere and the oceans are so vast that polluting them is of no consequence, but in fact if humanity continues on its course the earth will not be able to withstand it. Under such circumstances, it is very dangerous not to have a mutual, balanced management of the world's affairs. We need to develop a world culture. National boundaries need to be weakened, not strengthened.

So one might speak of what China achieved all by itself a millennium or two ago, but in the next century this won't be possible. Progress in China depends on progress in the rest of the world. There are those who speak of the twenty-first century as being the "Chinese Century," but I find this unlikely. At least in the sense of China overcoming all her problems entirely on her own, it is not very likely, because the problems we face today don't only involve China.

Einstein's concept of world citizenship was profound. Of course, many of his ideas were poorly received while he was alive. Many critics called his work on a unified field theory, on which he spent the last thirty years of his life, a dead end. Marxist-Leninists blasted his work as philosophical idealism. He had surprisingly few students. But time has shown the true profundity of Einstein's scientific thought. His ideas about world citizenship were also severely criticized at the time; they were labelled cosmopolitanism. But in the years ahead, the human race will have to come to grips with this idea as well. It is in this vein that I say that patriotism is not of primary importance. I would even call it narrow-minded.

[Transcribed by G.K. Sun and translated by James H. Williams.]

Does Chinese Culture Have a Future?
Liu Xiaobo

[Liu Xiaobo, known as something of a maverick philosopher and literary critic, had just been invited to give a series of lectures at Columbia University when he decided that he would like to return to Beijing to join his compatriots in the democracy movement. He was moved to tears after watching on television the determination and ardor of the students in their struggle against the government. In his thirties, Liu Xiaobo was both a passionate scholar and a man of action. After arriving in China, he became an adviser to the students and participated in the last hunger strike—on 2 June on Tiananmen Square.

In this essay, which is an afterword to one of his many books, Liu Xiaobo expresses the profound sense of disillusionment that many Chinese felt in comparing their culture to the West—a comparison that went beyond the material to the intellectual and spiritual level. He expresses the "moral burden" of the Chinese intellectual, feeling that he faces a dilemma in being an intellectual in China currently visiting the West , where his new environment has given him this radically new perspective on life. His critical evaluation of traditional Chinese culture has given him a severe inferiority complex. He compares himself to Lu Xun in his denunciation of traditional Chinese culture. At the same time he feels an emptiness that gives him no choice but him to take an existential leap of faith.

After 4 June, Liu was arrested and detained at Qincheng prison.]

My tragedy may be likened to that of Lu Xun's [in the 1920s and 1930s] in that we have no transcendent values. Ours is the tragedy of having no God. Lu Xun's sense of tragedy as expressed in his [collection of prose poems] *Yecao* (Wild Grass) shows a profound internal disintegration that is in desperate need of transcendental values. In this feeling of hopelessness in [having no alternative but to] face the grave, there is the need of a God to point the way. During Lu Xun's *Yecao* period, no earthly value could help him. In his criticism of Chinese culture, Lu Xun moved from his clear-headed criticism and disappointment with Chinese realities to a hopelessness within himself. If he had not had any transcendental absolute value system as a standard, then Lu Xun, even if he were at the height of his creative powers during the writing of *Yecao*, would have only been digging his own grave.

In fact this was the case; after *Yecao*, Lu Xun could no longer bear his inner loneliness, isolation, and hopelessness. Even when he escaped from the his internal struggles, he would sink again into the vulgarities of the actual world and engage himself in meaningless battles with unworthy men who were not his equal. As a result of his battles with those mediocre people, he became one of them. Lu Xun was unable to bear facing an unknown world and was afraid to face the graveyard. He was unwilling to carry on a transcendental dialogue with his own soul under the eyes of God. The utilitarian character of the traditional Chinese literati once again came alive in Lu Xun. Having no God to save him, Lu Xun could only degenerate.

I believe the vision of the educated Chinese is too narrow; they are only concerned with China's problems. The Chinese people's thinking is too practical, they are only concerned with practical matters of livelihood. Chinese intellectuals lack transcendental drive; they lack the courage to face a totally unfamiliar world, an unknown world, and lack a combative spirit to fight loneliness and isolation and to use an individual's life to combat the forces of society. They could only live in a society they are familiar with and where the applause of the ignorant masses cheers them on. They are very reluctant to abandon their fame and good name and to begin from zero in a strange land. It is precisely this kind of feeling that causes the Chinese men of culture to grasp tightly to the straw of patriotism.

However, as I reflected on my utilization of Western culture to help me criticize Chinese culture, suddenly I found myself at a total loss. I have fallen into an awkward situation where I could not advance or back out. Suddenly I realized that I was using an already old implement to criticize a worn out culture; I am a cripple making fun of an invalid.

As I found myself actually living in an open society, I suddenly found out that I am neither a philosopher nor a famous personality, but just an ordinary person who needs to start out from ground zero. In China, the general ignorance [around me] was able to buoy up my intellectual standing, and my natural stupidity gave me good health. Now in the West, I am no longer in ignorant surroundings, and consequently my intellectual superiority no longer exists. Now that my natural surroundings have changed, I have become a sick man with illnesses all over my body. Furthermore, I am surrounded by sick people.

In China, for the sake of an empty name, I kept my worthless body alive. Only in the West have I for the first time encountered life for the first time, and the cruel decisions of life. As a person falls from an illusory high peak into an actual abyss, only then does he discover that he was not on a high peak at all and that he has only been struggling in an abyss. This kind of hopelessness that comes from having just awakened from a dream made me hesitate, made me uncertain, and made me stealthily desire to return to the country that I know so well. If it were not for the Metropolitan Museum, I really would have made my pact with ignorance again.

My wife wrote to me once saying,

Xiaobo, on the surface you are a famous rebel in our society, but in fact you have a profound identification with this society. This society is able to to accept you, to forgive you, to excuse you, and even to indulge you though they oppose your views. You are this society's reverse ornament and decoration.

But as for me, I am a completely unknown person. I am not worthy to demand anything from this society. I do not even think about reprimanding this society. I am totally cut off from this society. Even you cannot imagine the degree of my isolation. Even you cannot accept me.

At first, I had no reaction at all to what she said, but now I see that she hit the mark. I am grateful to her. She is not only my wife but also my most perceptive critic. Under her scrutiny, I have no place to hide.

There is no retreat. I either jump over the abyss or fall, to be smashed to bits. If you want freedom, then you must sink into a dead alley.

The [Yellow] River Elegy

Su Xiaokang, Wang Luxiang, et al.

[These excerpts, taken principally from the first episode of a controversial six-part television documentary, reflect a new wave of interest and concern with China's cultural past. The series created a "River Elegy craze" across the country after its initial showing on national television in June 1988. Su Xiaokang, using the powerful cultural symbols of the Yellow River, the Great Wall, and the dragon, makes a sweeping critical reevaluation of the whole of Chinese civilization from the ancient past to the present time.

In spite of some historical inaccuracies and oversimplifications, the television series created, through the medium of television, a powerful argument for reform and openness. The bottom line is that the Chinese civilization that had its origins in the yellow earth cannot give rise to scientific knowledge and the democratic spirit. For these, China must turn to the West. In spite of its many abstract and complex ideas, the documentary's reception was overwhelmingly positive. A more detailed discussion of this documentary is presented in chapter 9.]

Where are the roots of the Chinese people? Every yellow-skinned Chinese knows that the Chinese people were raised and nourished by the Yellow River. In that case, how did this great river mold our national character? How did it determine our cultural fate? Perhaps many of us have not given these questions much thought.

This river is indeed a most unusual river. It flows from the snow-capped mountains of the Bajan Kara Mountains and, after cutting through the high plains of yellow earth, it becomes a yellow-colored muddy river. And it just happens that this Yellow River raised and nourished a yellow-skinned people. Again by coincidence, the Chinese people call their earliest ancestor the Yellow Emperor, and now, on our globe today, one out every five people is a descendant of the Yellow Emperor.

The yellow water, yellow earth, and yellow-skinned people—how mysterious is this natural relationship! It is as if someone wanted the people to believe that the skin of the yellow people had actually been dyed yellow by the waters of the Yellow river.

Indeed, between heaven and earth there is no other natural force that has had the Yellow River's inestimable effect on shaping Chinese civilization. We do not need to do extensive archaeological research; we have proof of it from looking at a most commonly seen and most respected and feared image [of the dragon].

It can be said that the dragon is the symbol of our people, of our nation. But have our people ever thought about why we should worship such a violent and ferocious-looking monster? ...

It is said that our ancestors once observed a grand scene of a huge, two-headed snake emerging from a rainbow that stretched between heaven and earth and took a drink from the [waters of the] earth. Others have said that our ancestors observed a flash of lightning between the break in the clouds and saw a golden snake dancing wildly in rhythm with the wind and rain. From this, the people fashioned the image of the dragon. This is the imagination characteristic of a great river culture.

The reason dragon worship had its origin in the Yellow River valley is that the people of the valley feared and respected the great river that gave them life. Without question, the Yellow River is one of the most violent, cruel, and stubborn of all the great rivers of the world.

Some say that Chinese culture shows great tolerance toward tyrannical forces; others say that the Chinese national character has a fatal weakness of being overly pragmatic, submitting passively to fate, and accepting punishment as the natural course of things. Now, these characteristics are not accidental. For a large agricultural country with a long history, the lifeline of that country is water. But the water is controlled by the Dragon King. Therefore, the people of that culture both love and hate him, praise and curse him. This very complex feeling is just what the Chinese feel toward the dragon.

Zheng Yi, a Shanxi writer, said:

Three years ago, I rode my bicycle from the border of Shanxi and Inner Mongolia to Henan. I traveled the whole of the valley of Shanxi and Shenxi. I passed through tens of villages and tens of districts and covered over ten thousand *li*. This was a very significant experience for me. This was the first time I had direct contact with the Yellow River, and only then did I understand why the Yellow River is the symbol of our people.

The region that I traveled through was, according to tradition, the region where the sage emperors Yao, Shun, and Yu had lived in hoary antiquity. Later in this same region, the drama of Chinese history took place scene by scene. This trip changed my whole outlook toward literature.

I heard a story in a little village. Once there was a village in which the villagers depended on the Yellow River for their livelihood. Later, because trade declined and the land became infertile, they had no means of livelihood. The government moved them to another place, gave them land, and built them a house. After a few years, these people, for no apparent reason, one by one, moved back to the banks of the Yellow River, found their old cave dwellings, and settled down again. There was no way that I could understand why. After a long time, I finally understood the people's emotional ties with the land, a kind of blood relationship that could never be fully explained.

This story better expressed what I had in mind. As soon as I saw the Yellow River and traveled along it, I realized what I should write about. For the past few years I have been searching and searching, for what, I did not know. But as soon as I saw the Yellow River, I knew I wanted to write about the Yellow River.

Chinese civilization is not strange or unusual. Its longevity symbolizes the final struggle of the entire old world for its very survival. Asia has met its challenge; Europe is challenging the whole world.

Precisely because of the longevity of their civilization the psychological burden of the Chinese people is especially heavy. As Chinese civilization, like Egyptian and Indian civilizations, begins its decline, the soul of the Chinese people become particularly sorrowful and painful.

Why is it that a once powerful nation that made Marco Polo sigh with admiration, that inspired the European rulers to create the myth about the yellow peril, that caused the great Napoleon to warn the world not to awaken the sleeping lion, became so backward that it was about to be cut up by the world? Why is it that after just having escaped the disaster [of the Cultural Revolution], China suddenly felt that it had become tremendously strong and powerful again?

In our emotional make-up there seems to be a blind spot: It appears that the humiliations we have suffered in the past one hundred years appear to be only temporary setbacks in our glorious history. From 1840 on, there have always been people who have taken our ancient glory and greatness to cover up our recent poverty and backwardness. It is as if we always need an ancient tranquilizer from the distant past to relieve ourselves from the pain of the past one hundred years. Every time a great archaeological discovery is made, it seems like we find great comfort and satisfaction.

But our civilization is declining. The richness of our history and the longevity of our civilization are of the past. No matter how plentiful our archaeological finds, no matter how fine our ancient relics, no matter how far back we trace the origin of our civilization, isn't this simply our ancestors playing a joke on us, on us of the later generations? Aren't they trying to make us feel more regretful, guilty, and shameful? ...

This great land of the yellow earth cannot give us the real scientific spirit. This tyrannical Yellow River cannot give us the real democratic spirit. This Yellow River and yellow earth can no longer nourish and support our spiraling population, our new culture. It does not have the nutrients or the energy.

Confucianism had various kinds of ancient and effective "gimmicks." But in the several thousand years of its history it did not produce a forward-looking spirit, a system of rule by law, a mechanism for cultural renewal. On the contrary, in its decline, it developed a mechanism for national suicide. It continuously destroys the best of its culture, it kills those elements that are most spirited, and it puts to rest generation after generation of its best people. In spite of the fact that it has had thousands of years of the best, what cannot be avoided today is that everything will go up in flames.

The characteristics of despotism are secrecy, autocracy, and arbitrary rule. The characteristics of democracy should be transparency, popular will, and science. We are just now in the process of moving from opacity to transparency. We have already moved from enclosure to openness.

The Yellow River is destined to cut across the loess plateau. The Yellow River will ultimately enter the azure ocean.

The anguish of the Yellow River, the hope of the Yellow River, contribute to the Yellow River's greatness. The greatness of the Yellow River perhaps rests on its creation of a strip of central plain between the loess plateau and the ocean.

The Yellow River has arrived at the mouth of the ocean—a magnificent but painful juncture. It is here that the mud and silt carried turbulently along for thousands of miles will be deposited to form a new mainland. It is here that the surging waves and the Yellow River will collide together. The Yellow River must cleanse itself of its terror of the ocean. The Yellow River must keep the indomitable will and vigor that came with it from the high plateau.

The life-giving water comes from the ocean and returns to the ocean.

After thousands of years of solitude, the Yellow River finally catches sight of the azure sea.

5

The Reformers

China Will Not Sink into Turmoil

Sorry, We Have Come Too Late

We Should Use Discretion in Handling Matters Concerning People

The Primary Stage of Socialism

All Knowledge Contains Truths

Key to Understanding China

Young People Are the Hope of Humanity

The Crisis of Marxism in China

China Will Not Sink into Turmoil
Zhao Ziyang's Speech at the Asian Development Bank

[The reformist faction in the party was led by Zhao Ziyang, premier of China during most of the 1980s but party general secretary after Hu Yaobang's removal in 1987. Zhao's reformist tendencies are suggested in this 4 May speech, which hardliners would later label a "turning point for the escalation of the turmoil." Zhao expresses sympathy with the students and refers to them as "patriotic." He reassures the delegates of the Asian Development Bank that "China will not sink into turmoil." This is contrary to the spirit of the 26 April editorial in the People's Daily. Zhao's sympathetic attitude was interpreted as a softening of the government's position and an encouragement to the students to continue their demonstrations and protests, culminating in the hunger strike of 13 May.]

All of you who have come to China probably know that recently some students have taken to the streets. Does this mean that China's political situation is not stable?

Here I want to emphasize that the basic slogans of the marching students are "Support the Communist party," "Support socialism," "Support the Constitution," "Uphold the reforms," "Push forward democracy," and "Oppose corruption." I believe that this reflects the basic attitude of the majority of the marching students toward the party and government—namely, they are both satisfied and dissatisfied. They are by no means opposed to our basic system. What they want is that we eliminate the defects in our work. They are very satisfied with the accomplishments of the past ten years of reconstruction and reform, and with the progress and development of our country. But they are very dissatisfied with the mistakes we have made in our work. They want us to correct our mistakes and improve our work, which happens to be the stand of the party and government as well. We also aim to affirm the accomplishments, correct our mistakes, and move further toward progress.

Are there people who have tried to use and are still using the students? China is such a big country. Of course, this is difficult to avoid. There are always some people who want to see us in turmoil.

There are always people who are ready to make use [of the student movement]. It is unimaginable that they are not going to make use of it. While such people belong to a tiny minority, we must always be on guard against them. I believe the majority of the students understand this point as well. At this point, some students in Beijing and in some other cities are still demonstrating. But I firmly believe that the situation will gradually quiet down. China will not sink into turmoil. I have complete confidence in this.

[As to the questions raised by the students,] I think we should solve them according to the rule of democracy and law. We should solve these problems through reform and in a reasonable and orderly way. If we analyze the specific situation, we will understand it more clearly. At present, the students' main dissatisfaction is with the phenomena of embezzlement and corruption. This is a problem the party and government have been trying to solve in recent years.

But why do we still have so many people who are still dissatisfied, and so strongly dissatisfied? There are two reasons for this: First, we lack a sound legal system and democratic supervision to the extent that some cases of corruption that certainly exist are not being revealed and dealt with in a timely manner. Second, due to the lack of openness and transparency [(the Chinese word for *glasnost*)], some rumors are either completely misrepresented, unduly exaggerated, or purely fabricated. In fact, the majority of our party and government office workers live on low salaries, and they do not have sources of income other than their fixed salaries, let alone special privileges accorded them by law. We do have some people who are engaged in violating the law, seeking special rights and special privileges. But there are not as many as rumored, and their cases are not as serious either. Of course the question of corruption has to be resolved, but that can be done only in the course of reform by improving the legal system and democratic supervision, and by expanding transparency.

Since last year, we have experimented in some urban and rural areas by opening up the working process of local governments, publicizing the results of such working processes, encouraging the masses to supervise [government officials], and establishing supervision centers for people to report any misconduct of government officials. In this way, we have combined the punishment of corruption with the construction of democracy and law. We are now learning from such experiments, and we are going to apply them gradually at higher levels on a large scale.

[In terms of how to deal with the student demonstrations], I believe they have to be solved according to the rule of democracy and law and in the atmosphere of reason and order. At present, we need to hold extensive and consultative dialogues with the students, with workers, with intellectuals, with various democratic parties, and with people in all fields. We must exchange ideas and promote understanding [between different sectors of society] under the rule of democracy and law and in the atmosphere of reason and order; in this way, we will work together to solve the questions of common concern.

What is most needed now, however, is soberness, reason, restraint, and order. We must solve the problems according to the rule of democracy and law. The party and government are ready to do so. I believe that the student and other individuals will also agree to work in this way. If everybody works in this way, then we can certainly achieve our goal of maintaining order and stability. I believe that this will mean a new unity on a higher level. On the basis of stability and unity, China's political and economic reforms and our socialist, modernized construction will undoubtedly move forward more smoothly. I am very optimistic about China's political stability and the future of reforms. China's investment climate will continue to improve. I hope that my explanation of the situation will help in your understanding of China.

Sorry, We Have Come Too Late
Zhao Ziyang's Farewell Speech at Tiananmen

[Zhao Ziyang met with the students for the last time at 4:40 AM on 19 May after he was fully aware that his position as general secretary of the party was at end. He made an emotional and personal appeal to the students to end their hunger strike, even though he knew that whether or not they continued their hunger strike would not affect his position. This fact made his appeal that much more meaningful and significant. Obviously moved by the occasion, Zhao spoke informally with the students for about twenty minutes, his hands shaking and his eyes filled with tears. His sympathy for the students was judged to be genuine and sincere.]

Students, I want to say a few words to you. We are sorry we've come too late. It is right that you should blame us and criticize us. But I am here now not to ask for your forgiveness. I just want to say that your bodies are very weak now. You have been on a hunger strike for seven days; you must not go on like this. If you continue refusing to eat, the effects on your health could be permanent. It can endanger your lives. What is most important now is that I hope you will stop your hunger strike as soon as possible. I know that you are on a hunger strike because you want the party and government to give you satisfactory answers to your demands. But you have been on a hunger strike for seven days. Do you really want to proceed to the eighth, the ninth, or the tenth day? Many problems could be solved eventually, and the channel for dialogue is still open; the door of dialogue will never be closed. But some problems need some time before they can be fully resolved. I feel that the substantive questions you have raised could eventually be solved, and we could eventually reach a consensus in solving these problems. But you should understand that, in resolving any question, the situation is always complicated and more time is still needed.

With your hunger strike reaching the seventh day, you must not persist in the strike until satisfactory answers are given. It won't help. By that time, it will be too late and you will never be able to make up for the damage to your health. You are still young and have a long way to go. You must live on in good health, live to the days when China finally realizes the Four Modernizations. You are not like us.

We are getting old and it doesn't matter what happens to us. It has not been easy for the state and your parents to raise you and send you to college. You're only eighteen, nineteen, or twenty years old. Are you going to give up your lives like this? I think about it in a more rational way.

I have not come to hold a dialogue with you. I just want to urge you to think more rationally about the situation you are facing. You know that the party and government are very worried about you. The entire society is worried, everybody in Beijing is talking about you. Also you know that Beijing is the capital. The situation is getting worse every day. It cannot go on like this. Your comrades all mean well, you mean well for our country, but if this situation continues and gets out of control, the consequences could be very serious.

I think that is what I want to tell you. If you stop your hunger strike, the government will not thereby close the doors to further dialogue. It will definitely not do that. We will continue to study the issues you have raised. It is true that we have been slow in solving some of the problems, but our views on some questions are gradually coming closer to each other.

I have come today mainly to see you students and tell you what I feel. I hope you students and the organizers of the hunger strike will think about this question [of stopping the hunger strike] very calmly and coolly. It will be very hard to think clearly about this question when you're not in a rational state of mind. As young people, it is understandable that you are all bursting with passion. I know that. We all used to be young. We also have taken to the streets; some of us have even been across railroad tracks to stop trains. At that time, we also never thought about what would happen afterwards.

Students, please think about the question calmly. Many problems could be resolved gradually. I do hope that you will stop your hunger strike very soon. Thank you, comrades.

We Should Use Discretion in Handling Matters Concerning People
Zhao Ziyang

[Zhao's attitude toward the students was not surprising,
considering some of the comments he had made prior to the
demonstrations. While Zhao considered himself to be a dedicated
socialist, this passage from a 1987 speech to the National People's
Congress suggests that he sees the battle between socialism and
"bourgeois liberalization" as requiring persuasion rather than
coercion. He also sees this struggle as strictly a party matter,
indicating that he believes that a party capable of resolving its
conflicts without bitterness will have wider appeal.]

Combatting bourgeois liberalization is a difficult, complicated, and long-term struggle. It demands, on the one hand, that we take a clear-cut stand and not give up halfway, and, on the other, that we apply correct policies and methods and throughout the struggle convince people by reasoning things out. We must learn from our previous experience and refrain from launching another political campaign or repeating the "leftist" mistakes of the past [during the Cultural Revolution]. In the last few months, the Central Committee has adopted and made known a series of correct principles and policies in this struggle that can be summed up as follows:

1. The struggle against bourgeois liberalization will be strictly confined within the Chinese Communist Party and conducted chiefly in the political-ideological domain. It will emphasize solving the problems of basic political principles and orientation and will not concern itself with policies of economic reform, rural politics, scientific and technological research, exploration of literary and artistic styles and techniques, or the everyday life of the people.
2. It will not be conducted in rural areas, and in enterprises and institutions there will only be education by positive example.
3. No attempt will be made to ferret out exponents of bourgeois liberalization at various levels, to implicate people at higher or lower levels, or to have everybody make self-criticisms.
4. We shall adhere to the principle of uniting with the overwhelming majority of people and draw a strict line of demarcation between the

tiny handful who are wedded to bourgeois liberalization and who do not stubbornly cling to their own opinions and respect discipline.

5. We shall draw a strict line of demarcation between non-Marxist academic views, writings containing ordinary mistakes, and faults in academic exploration on the one hand and bourgeois liberalization on the other.

6. Differing ideas on academic theories and on culture and art are to be approached through continued, normal, and free discussion, criticism, and countercriticism, in accordance with the relevant provisions of the Constitution. We should use discretion in matters concerning people. As far as those who have made the mistake of bourgeois liberalization are concerned, we should help them through serious criticism and give them adequate time to ponder over the problem; their self-criticisms are welcome. As for people who have made erroneous viewpoints or written erroneous articles under the influence of bourgeois liberalization, the main thing is to encourage them to increase their understanding through study and practice. Even when a few individuals who stubbornly cling to bourgeois liberalization are dismissed from their posts, they should be assigned suitable jobs so as to turn their professional skills to good account and enable them to contribute to society.

The Primary Stage of Socialism
Zhao Ziyang

[Given Zhao's dedication to socialism, how far do his democratic tendencies go? An October 1987 report titled "Advance along the Road of Socialism with Chinese Characteristics" lays out his ideas on political reform and makes a cogent analysis of China's problems in developing itself and at the same time in trying to avoid Western influence. He declares that China is in the "primary stage of socialism" but, because of its unique circumstances, must seek its own path in developing its own brand of socialism. He proposes mechanisms that seem vaguely democratic, although he rejects capitalism and other aspects of Western democracy and remains bound to the idea of one-party rule. Like many Chinese leaders, he is struggling with the contradictions inherent in the need for stability, development, and the desire to maintain a distinctly Chinese identity.]

Building socialism in a big, backward, eastern country like China is something new in the history of the development of Marxism. We are not in the situation envisaged by the founders of Marxism, in which socialism is built on the basis of highly developed capitalism, nor are we exactly in the same situation as other socialist countries. So we cannot blindly follow what the books say, nor can we mechanically imitate the examples of other countries. Rather, proceeding from China's actual conditions and integrating the basic principles of Marxism with those conditions, we must find a way to build socialism with Chinese characteristics through practice.

We must endeavor to build democracy on the basis of stability and unity. In a socialist society there should be a high degree of democracy, a comprehensive legal system, and a stable social environment. In the primary stage, as there are many factors making for instability, the maintenance of stability and unity is of special importance. We must correctly handle the contradictions among the people. The people's democratic dictatorship should not be weakened. Because feudal autocratic influence is still strong, it is particularly urgent to build socialist democracy. But, in view of the restrictions imposed by historical and social conditions, that can only be done step by step and in an orderly way ...

Adherence to the Four Cardinal Principles—that is, (1) keeping to the socialist road, (2) upholding the people's democratic dictatorship, (3) leadership by the Communist party, and (4) Marxism and Leninism and Mao Zedong Thought—is the foundation underlying all our efforts to build the country. Adherence to the general principle of reform and the open policy has been a new development in our party's line since the Third Plenary Session of the Eleventh Central Committee, and it has added to the Four Cardinal Principles new content appropriate to our time. The two basic points—adherence to the Four Cardinal Principles and adherence to reform and the open policy—are interrelated and mutually dependent, and they are integrated in the practice of building socialism with Chinese characteristics. We must not interpret the Four Cardinal Principles as something rigid lest we come to doubt or even reject the general principle of reform and opening to the outside world. Neither can we interpret reform and the open policy as something bourgeois liberal lest we deviate from the path of socialism. In the primary stage, when the country is still underdeveloped, the tendency toward bourgeois liberalization, which rejects the socialism system in favor of capitalism, will persist for a long time. Unless we overcome hidebound thinking and pursue reform and the open policy, we will not be able to demonstrate convincingly the superiority of socialism and to enhance its appeal, and this failure will encourage the spread of bourgeois liberalization....

Like the development of a socialist commodity economy, the building of a socialist democracy is a gradual, cumulative process. Confronted as we are with the complicated contradictions that arise in the drive for modernization, we need a peaceful social and political environment. We shall never again allow the kind of "great democracy" [(as seen in the Cultural Revolution)] that undermines state law and social stability. The system of people's congresses, the system of multiparty cooperation and political consultation under the leadership of the Communist party, and the principle of democratic centralism are the characteristics and advantages of our system. We shall never abandon them by introducing a Western system of separation of the three powers and of different parties ruling the country in turn. In the reform of the political structure, we must handle properly the relationship between democracy and stability and between democracy and efficiency.

To correctly handle contradictions and reconcile various social interests is an important task in a socialist society. Only when the leading bodies at all levels listen attentively to the view of the masses can they gear their work to actual conditions and avoid mistakes. And only when they let the people know what they are doing and what difficulties there are can they secure the people's understanding. There should be channels through which the voices and demands of the people can be easily and frequently transmitted to the leading bodies, and there should be places where the people can offer suggestions or pour out any grievances they may have. Different groups of people may have different interests and views, and they too need opportunities and channels for the exchange of ideas. It is therefore imperative to develop a system of consultation and dialogue so that what is going on at higher levels can be promptly and accurately made known to lower levels and vice versa without impediment, thus enabling people at all levels to understand each other.

In the past few years, China's elections have become more and more democratic. However, an electoral system has not been fully and effectively implemented and needs to be improved. We should respect the will of the voters and ensure that they have more options in elections. We should continue the practice of holding elections with more candidates than posts, as prescribed by law, and improve procedures for nominating candidates and methods of publicizing them. For instance, the present practice of setting rigid quotas for different geographical areas when nominating candidates for the elections of deputies to congresses at various levels tends to prevent the election from fully reflecting the will of the voters. In order to have candidates who represent broader sections of the people, therefore, we shall introduce the practice of electing deputies not only from geographical areas, as is done at present, but also from different walks of life.

All Knowledge Contains Truths
Hu Yaobang
On the Centenary Commemoration of the Death of Karl Marx

*[Hu Yaobang, the beloved general secretary of the party from 1981
to 1987 whose death triggered the student movement of 1989, was a
strong advocate of the importance of knowledge and of the central
role that intellectuals ought to play in China's modernization
program. This statement by the general secretary gives long overdue
credit to the intellectuals who had been most viciously attacked during
the Cultural Revolution. Hu, who was loved and respected by
intellectuals, writers, and artists, did much to rehabilitate them in the
post-Mao era and to improve their lives.]*

Comrades and friends, what lessons should we draw from the past
twists and turns on the question of knowledge and intellectuals? And
what truly revolutionary and scientific Marxist concepts should we
establish in light of them?

First, it is imperative that we fight against the incorrect tendency of
isolating Marxism from the cultural achievements of mankind and
setting it against the latter, that we establish the correct concept of
valuing scientific and general knowledge, and that we mobilize the
whole party and the whole people to strive to acquire knowledge of
modern science and culture.

Where does Marxism come from? Fundamentally, it is no doubt the
product of contradictions and of the workers' movements in capitalist
society; at the same time it is the result of absorbing human
knowledge accumulated over several thousand years. If the cultural
achievements of mankind had not been applied to the scientific
discovery of the laws governing historical development and to the
definition of the fundamental and the long-term interests of the
working class, the movement of the workers could only have given
rise to various kinds of theories such as syndicalism, economism,
reformism, and anarchism, but not to Marxism. Moreover, our
comrades have all learned through personal experience that to study
Marxism one has to have a certain amount of knowledge. Simple class
feeling can make one receptive to some isolated Marxist concepts but
is inadequate for a systematic understanding and good command of
Marxism. In order to build a new world under the guidance of

Marxism, apply and develop it in the great cause of China's modernization, and use it to educate all the builders of socialism, it is all the more necessary that we make sustained efforts to critically assimilate new knowledge and the new achievements of modern science and culture. "Knowledge is power." It should be part of the fine qualities of us Communists and all builders of the future to value knowledge, embrace it, thirst after it, and turn it into immense power for building a new world.

A fallacy that prevailed during the Cultural Revolution was that "the more learned one becomes, the more reactionary he will be." It must be pointed out explicitly that human knowledge—that is, the knowledge of natural sciences, of production and technology, of history and geography, of different branches of modern social sciences studied under the guidance of Marxism, and of operation and management as a reflection of the laws governing mass social production, as well as various other kinds of knowledge embodying the progress of mankind and the progressive classes in history—all such knowledge contains truths accumulated by mankind in the long process of understanding and changing the world, is the product of its hard labor, and can be a weapon in its fight for freedom. The more knowledge people acquire, the better they will be able to know the world and to change it. This is a sign of social progress. Even certain things that played an important role in history but are imbued with the prejudices of the reactionary classes should be critically analyzed by Marxists so that whatever is useful in them can be assimilated. What really matters is the standpoint, views, and methods people apply in regard to knowledge. In general, it is always better to have more knowledge than less, and it definitely must not be said that "the more learned one becomes the more reactionary he will be." ...

Second, it is imperative that we oppose the erroneous tendency of separating intellectuals from the working class, counterposing them to the workers, and regarding them as an "alien force"; that we confirm the correct concept of intellectuals as a part of the working class and that we strengthen a hundredfold the unity between workers and peasants on the one hand and intellectuals on the other.

We must respect and rely on the intellectuals as much as we respect and rely on the workers and peasants in the great cause of socialist construction. In the Marxist view, intellectuals do not constitute an independent class. Before the founding of New China, ours was a semicolonial and semifeudal society. Although intellectuals were for the most part linked to the bourgeoisie or the petty bourgeoisie in their social status, the overwhelming majority of them were at the same time oppressed by imperialism and by the Kuomintang reactionaries. Therefore, a number joined the revolution directly, others sympathized with it, and a great many cherished anti-imperialist and patriotic aspirations. Those reactionary intellectuals who did obdurately range themselves against the revolutionary people and served the ruling classes were of course a force alien to the proletariat, but they were very few in number. When our socialist society was built, the conditions of China's intellectuals underwent a fundamental change. The overwhelming majority of them coming over from the old society have been working energetically for socialism and have been educated in Marxism and tempered and tested over a long period since the founding of New China. Moreover, over 90 percent of our intellectuals today have been trained in the new society and, in their overwhelming majority, come from worker, peasant, or intellectual families. Although major differences in their form of labor still exist between intellectuals, this does not keep us from stating that, in terms of their means of living and whom they serve, on the whole the intellectuals in our country have definitely become a part of the working class. This change is a great achievement in the history of Chinese revolution and in our socialist development.

In the new period of socialist modernization, intellectuals have a particularly important role to play. In the Marxist view, and judging from the latest trend in the development of science and industry, essential differences between manual and mental labor will gradually diminish and eventually disappear, and there will be successive generations of new people in whom labor is integrated with mental labor on an even higher level. But this is a long-range perspective and will not happen right away. In other words, for a fairly long time to come, scientific and cultural knowledge and mental work will continue to be relatively concentrated among one section of the population—the intellectuals. Therefore, the intellectuals, who possess the trained mental power indispensable to socialist modernization, are a valuable asset to our country. In our society, we must create an atmosphere in which knowledge and intellectuals are valued, and we must take effective steps to improve their working and living conditions. This should be taken as "capital construction," and of the most essential kind at that....

Third, it is imperative that we oppose the erroneous tendency of divorcing party leadership from expert leadership or setting the former against the latter, that we implant the correct concept that all leading personnel must strive to be experts, and that we ensure that our cadres become better educated and more professionally competent on the basis of becoming more revolutionary-minded.

That our socialist modernization needs knowledge and intellectuals is a guiding idea that must be embodied, first and foremost, in the reform of the leading organs at all levels and departments so that our cadres will be younger, better educated, and more professionally competent on the basis of becoming more revolutionary-minded. People may ask: Didn't we win our revolutionary wars even though the educational level of our cadres wasn't very high? True, due to the protracted rural guerilla fighting, our party cadres lacked knowledge of modern science and culture during the war years.... The situation today is radically different from that in the past. Socialist modernization, being an entirely new task, is much broader in scale and far more complex in nature, involving many more branches of learning than the tasks we faced before. Military work, too, has become more specialized. Under these circumstances, to rely merely on past knowledge and experience is far from adequate. It is a pressing necessity of the current struggle to master modern science, technology, and culture. Is it not, then, entirely correct, necessary, and in conformity with the requirements of historical development for now to set higher demands of training between educated and more professionally competent cadres.

Key to Understanding China
Hu Yaobang

[Hu Yaobang's vague democratic ideas are discernable, as seen in this 1986 speech. It should be noted, however, that it was given at the British Royal Institute of International Affairs in June of 1986, so it is possible that he toned down some of the rhetoric for the benefit of his foreign audience.

In the speech, Hu introduces them to various aspects of China's reform effort and foreign policy. He shows some understanding of the importance of having broad-based input and support for national policy, if not full-fledged democratic mechanisms for determining it.]

China may appear to be an inscrutable country to some of our friends in the Western world. This is because a vast distance separates us, and our cultures, languages, and customs are quite different. Furthermore, we have followed different courses of social development in modern history. China was long closed to the outside world; it waged a titanic struggle for liberation over the last century; and since the founding of New China more than three decades ago, while great progress has been achieved, there have also been many twists and turns. All this has added to the sense of mystery.

Where is China headed? I submit that China's basic national policy in this century and the next boils down to two goals: First, to promote a sustained and steady growth of China's economy by following a policy of reform and openness to the outside world; and second, to ensure that China concentrates on uninterrupted development by pursuing an independent foreign policy of peace. If these points are grasped, one will have grasped the key to understanding China's trend of development. Now allow me to use this key to open the door to understanding China and to dwell on the following four questions.

The First Question: China's Reform and Openness to the Outside World

Having made a detour, we came to realize that, after the establishment of a new social system, our fundamental task is to develop the productive forces and gradually to improve the people's material well-being and cultural life. In order to ensure a sustained and steady growth of the national economy, it is imperative to be open to the outside world, to reform the rigid and highly centralized structure in which administrative means are used to manage the economy, and to develop a planned socialist commodity based on public ownership. So, in the past six to seven years, while pursuing a policy of openness to the outside world, we boldly explored reform. The reform that first began in the rural areas is in full swing today, covering economic, scientific-technological, and educational structures as well as the political realm. It is being carried out in material, cultural, and ideological fields. The all-round, speedy, and steady growth of China's economy, and the marked improvement in the material and cultural well-being of the people in the past few years have all shown that the reform and the openness to the outside world have yielded initial success and the people are pleased with it....

The Second Question: China's Foreign Policy

Some friends have asked: What are the basic points of China's independent foreign policy of peace? Will this foreign policy be adhered to in the long run?

With regard to the main content of China's foreign policy, Premier Zhao Ziyang, in the recent Fourth Session of the Sixth National People's Congress, summarized the ten aspects that, briefly speaking, comprise the following three basic points:

First, we support everything that is in the interests of world peace and stability. We oppose all acts of hegemony, no matter who practises them and what form they take.

Second, China will never attach itself to any superpower, nor will it enter into alliance with either side. China is willing to develop friendly relations with all countries of the world on the basis of the Five Principles of Peaceful Coexistence.

Third, China firmly sides with third world countries and stands for fairness and justice....

The Third Question: the Relationship between National Defense and Economic Development

Economic development requires huge investments while expansion of military strength needs increased funds. The two are mutually exclusive and it is hardly possible to lay equal stress on both....

The Fourth Question: Whether or not China's Basic State Policies will be Changed

Now that I have briefed you on China's basic state policies, someone may ask: Who can guarantee that you will adhere to your basic state policies over the next several decades? This is indeed an important issue that has a bearing on the direction of China's future development. It is also an issue we have tried to resolve over the past few years. I can say in all seriousness that China's basic state policies have struck deep roots and are full of vitality mainly for the following four reasons:

First, our current policies have already brought the people substantial benefits and have thus won the wholehearted endorsement and support of the overwhelming majority of the Chinese people. These policies are deeply rooted in the masses and have been grasped by them. No one can in the true sense abandon them, for to do so would be to violate the will of the people. Of course, no specific policies are free from the limitations of the times, and they must develop along with the march of events. If you call this development a "change," then our policies will only change for the better.

Second, the entire set of major policy decisions currently in force in China was established on the basis of an earnest summing up of past experience, an extensive solicitation of opinions from all quarters, and consultations with various democratic and nonparty personages and people from all walks of life. True, leaders of the older generation have been at the helm. However, our policies are not determined by a certain individual but are the crystallization of collective wisdom.

Third, we are also determined to further develop socialist democracy and to make it institutionalized and legalized so as to bring into play the people's initiating their own affairs to and ensure their democratic rights and effective supervision in political, economic, cultural, and social activities. In so doing, we will be able to effect the sustained and steady implementation of correct policies and guidelines on the track of a socialist democracy and legal system.

Finally, over the past few years, we have achieved gratifying successes in our efforts to promote younger people to posts of leadership at various levels, from the central authorities to the grass roots. Now, a big contingent of energetic, competent, and enterprising young people have taken up leading posts. This is of great importance to the vitality of our cause and the continuity of our policies and guidelines.

With the above four points of understanding, we have reason to believe that our basic state policies will not change when changes in our leadership occur. China will follow the present correct orientation in its successful march toward the twenty-first century.

Young People Are the Hope of Humanity

Hu Yaobang

[Students held Hu Yaobang in especially high esteem because he refused to crack down on their demonstrations in 1986-87. The following brief excerpt from a rally for Japanese youth in November 1983 gives a suggestion of his empathy for young people.]

Frankly speaking, I have a special feeling of closeness to young people. It is not just because I, like other elders, have had the experience of youth but, more importantly, because I have engaged in youth work for twenty years. Long years of experience have convinced me that young people are the future of the nation and the hope of humanity, as well as the masters of the destiny and future of the state. This is a truth. Mankind will invariably advance from one generation to another, and the young people will also make constant advances through the generations. I sincerely hope you will look to the future and contribute your best to the peaceful development of your country and to the worthy cause of preserving world peace and promoting the progress of humanity.

The Crisis of Marxism in China

Su Shaozhi

[Su Shaozhi, formerly the director of the Marxist-Leninist-Mao Zedong Thought Institute under the Chinese Academy of the Social Sciences in Beijing, was one of the chief Marxist theoreticians in China. As early as 1983, Su had argued for the need to observe the changes in the contemporary world. He asserts in this essay, written shortly before the demonstrations on Tiananmen Square began, that Marxism in the form that has been applied in China is in some degree outmoded and a reevaluation should be made, and he goes on to maintain that socialism and even capitalism need to be reevaluated and the proper adjustments made. Su was removed from his post in 1987 during the Antibourgeois Liberalization Campaign and is now a visiting scholar at the Bradley Institute, Marquette University.]

In October 1976, the Gang of Four met its well-deserved end. However, the mistakes made by Mao Zedong in his later years were not exposed and criticized. Instead, they were propagated under the slogan the "two whatevers"; that is, "we firmly uphold whatever policy and directions Chairman Mao made and we unswervingly adhere to whatever instructions Chairman Mao gave." The "two whatevers" upheld "the theory of continuous revolution under the dictatorship of the proletariat," "taking class struggle as the key link," and "putting politics in command" and the "ultraleft" line. As a result, Marxism lost its once high reputation in China, causing a "crisis of faith" among the Chinese.

The reform movement was initiated after the Third Plenum of the Eleventh Central Committee of the Chinese Communist Party. Reform not only combated "leftism" but threw to the winds whatever obstructed modernization. In fact, those conventions were closely tied to some individuals' personal interests. Different interest groups and different trends of thought would emerge in the reform movement. This is reflected in the uninterrupted struggle and ideological discord, even after the fall of the Maoist extremists.

Two most vehement criticism campaigns (in the post-Mao period) were the "Antispiritual Pollution" (1983) and "Antibourgeois Liberalization" (1987). Except for the two years 1982 and 1984, 1986 and 1988 were the ideologically active years.

Some important issues have been raised over the years regarding the future of Marxism among Chinese academics:

1. Marxism should be reunderstood. It is necessary to study Marxism in a practical, evolutionary, creative, critical, and liberal way, recognizing that it is outmoded to some degree.
2. Capitalism should be reevaluated. We should differentiate contemporary capitalism from traditional capitalism. Although capitalism cannot resolve its innate contradictions, it has changed a great deal, evidencing new leeway for increased productivity and showing more adaptability and flexibility. Therefore, capitalism is required to revise some of Marx's theses.
3. Socialism should be reinterpreted. Contemporary socialism should be distinguished from traditional socialism. It is essential for us to develop a new theory of socialism that is different from socialism in the 1930s and 1940s. We must recognize the flaws of that socialism and accept the necessity for pluralistic socialism, which is compatible with different forms of ownership. In fact, the socialist economy should be a planned market economy and the socialist political system a democratic system. The Communist party should be remodeled and brought into line with a multiple party system.
4. Human values and humanism need to be taken more fully into account. We should point out that human beings are the starting point of Marxism, and that the emancipation of man is its final goal. Thus, human values are the basis upon which socialism should be built.

In spite of many difficulties, Marxism was evolving in a creative way in China thanks to the reform movement, the open door policy, and the liberation of people's minds. Marxism was in ascension in China.... In June 1989, condemning the democratic movement as counter-revolutionary, [the government officials] cracked down on it with military force. After this, they will no doubt go back to "taking class struggle as the key link," and to stressing political education, willpower, and rigid Stalinism. Once again, Marxism has fallen into a purposefully aggravated crisis.

Part II

Essays on the Student Movement

Interlude

Steven Mark

China is a Mess

In the Chinese language, there is a word, *fuza,* that English speakers who learn Chinese and Chinese who learn English commonly translate as "confused." Unlike many high falutin' Chinese words and phrases, *fuza* is an ordinary word that ordinary people use.

During a trip I took through China with my family in late 1988 and early 1989, this word, *fuza,* surfaced constantly in conversations with Chinese. Like a drill in Chinese class, the phrase *Qingkuang hen fuza,* (the situation is very confused) became embedded in my mind.

One day in Beijing, I was talking about China with a young Chinese named Michael. Michael was distantly related to us but had treated us as if we were close members of the family. He was one of those Chinese youths whom Westerners would proudly describe as Westernized. He spoke English well, sported jeans and a ski jacket, and worked for a trading company where he often dealt with Westerners. But he also was very interested and knowledgeable about Chinese history and culture.

That day, we were speaking in a peculiar pidgin of English and Chinese, throwing Chinese words into English sentences and vice versa. I found myself repeating a now-familiar phrase, only with an unusual syntax: "The situation now seems to be very *fuza.*"

Michael was unimpressed. With a tone of irritation in his voice, he retorted, "*Fuza* is not bad enough! China is a mess right now!"

143

Five months later, China erupted in demonstrations, marches, conflict—and bloodshed. Tiananmen Square was China's attempt to clean up the "mess" that it had become. The students, the government, the people wanted it done, but finally the army stepped in to do the job in its ugly, brutal way.

The following chapters will deal with many aspects of the demonstrations and the mess that caused them. They will provide an in-depth look at China's troubles, from its political structure to the spiritual malaise expressed by its artists. They will give insights into the demonstrations from a variety of perspectives—the social, psychological, historical, and others.

This brief introductory chapter will not delve into such weighty topics; rather, it is intended to give a hint of the tension that was evident on the surface of Chinese society before it erupted on Tiananmen Square. It is simply a compilation of observations and anecdotes from my trip, but they describe a China at unease with itself. This mood may be of some surprise to those who assumed that liberalization—in the economy and, to a lesser degree, in society and politics—would automatically bring happiness to the Chinese. Therefore, it is hoped that this chapter can provide some background on China and can answer a question that is both simple but nonetheless pertinent to the events on Tiananmen Square: What was China like in the late 1980s?

A Farmer's Lament

We had stopped outside of Xian, the ancient capital of China, to take a look at a "typical" village. We were being escorted by an acquaintance of the family, the head of one of the major research institutes in Xian. As was customary, he had virtually forced us to allow him to be our host and guide.

Pulling into this village in his black, Soviet-made Beretta, a model commonly assigned to officials, must have given us the aura of VIPs, I thought. If it did, the villagers didn't show it. The children, of course, were curious, but some citizens we met seemed only marginally friendly. They were hard at work building furniture, having converted a two-story, concrete-slab home into a workshop. The newness of the building identified this village as a fairly prosperous one.

Finally, we were confronted by a sturdy, middle-aged man dressed in a tattered Chinese costume, his skin tanned to a coffee-brown and his hair tousled in a disheveled mess. Reeling slightly as he approached, he greeted us with, "So! You're here to interview us, right?" He had taken us for government officials—and he was ready to give us a piece of his mind. He launched into a diatribe, most of it in a dialect that was all but incomprehensible to me, about the trials of life on the farm.

One of his pet peeves, as I learned later, concerned inflation, which had reached an annual rate of close to 30 percent and was causing major unrest in society. But his was an unusual complaint. It went something like this: He knew that if he could hold onto his produce as long as possible, he could earn more from it, since the price would inevitably rise. But the villagers had no storage capacity, no refrigeration, no grain silos. Their only preservative was the sun. As in ancient times, the villagers put their produce on the roofs of their homes to dry. There were mounds of corncobs piled up there from the fall harvest.

The lack of storage meant that the farmer had to take his goods to market as soon as they were harvested, which often meant competition from other farmers—and lower profits. In essence, this man was complaining about inflation, but not in the conventional sense of rising prices. He was angry that he could not take advantage of inflation to make more money. It was difficult to figure out whether he thought inflation was good or bad.

The Burden of History

Shu-shu, or "Uncle," is an electrical engineer for a state-owned construction company in a medium-size city. He is the Chinese equivalent of what Americans would call a "doer." I will never forget how he obtained a berth on a train for me. It was a special express that wasn't on the regular schedule, so we had to go to the train station to get information about it. When we arrived, there was, as usual, a huge mob of people packed in front of the ticket window.

In about five minutes, Shu-shu had shoved his way to the front of the line. He yelled a few words at the window, jotted down a note, and came back satisfied. There was indeed a train, he said, but no tickets could be purchased here.

I was to depart the next day. Shu-shu accompanied me to the train station again and managed to talk us past an official who is supposed to let only ticketed passengers on the boarding platform. When the train arrived, Shu-shu sprinted the length of the train to find the conductor and avalanched him with words. Suddenly, I found myself with a berth on the train.

Earlier, Shu-shu had complained bitterly about his job. It was not just that there was no inspiration, no incentive to do good work—there was just no work. Shu-shu spent most of his day reading the newspaper. But as an engineer, he spent some time tinkering with various electronic devices and had come up with an invention. He had even secured a patent for it and been paid 10,000 *yuan*, about $1,300—a tidy sum.

But he didn't stop there. He'd gone on to improve and refine his device, and had received a second patent. But he wasn't telling anything about this one, though he dreamed of running a factory that manufactured his device.

Why was he being so secretive? He was worried that his superiors, once they learned of the probability that more accolades were coming his way, would try to undermine him. Not that they would fire him, since that would be too blatant and possibly illegal, or even reduce his salary, since the money was insignificant, but they might shunt him to a lesser position, taking away the perquisites that are the real reward for a Chinese worker.

Thinking that perhaps his superiors were the vain, power-hungry types that one can find in any country, I asked what made him think they would do this. His answer referred not to his company, not to the government, not even to the Communist party or its ideology. "Chinese people just do this kind of thing," he said. He went on to describe an incident from ancient Chinese history in which some lowly official who had enjoyed personal success was quashed by the emperor. To Shu-shu, the inherent character of the Chinese would cause his bosses to do likewise.

At that moment, I understood the barriers that history has placed in the Chinese mind. Over the course of five thousand years, there has been both good and evil in China. But the evil seems to lie within easy reach of the mind, ready to surface at a moment's notice to snuff out China's talent and energy.

The Entrepreneurial Spirit

If Shu-shu was not willing to take a chance on capitalism, there were plenty of others who were. Everywhere in China, one encountered money-making schemes, from the busy night markets in the cities to the children selling tea eggs at school.

On a train to Chengdu, I met a man of about twenty-five who knew the thrill of making money. He was on his way there to close a deal on the sale of lighting fixtures. He explained to me how he had worked out the contract, borrowing money to buy the fixtures. arranging for transportation, working out the sales agreement. The Chinese who listened along with me, most of whom were well-established in their jobs, were fascinated by the inner workings of the capitalist system and amazed at the 7,000 *yuan* he would earn as a result—several times their annual salary.

He had spent a few months at his state-assigned job as a janitor before trying his hand at business. It was a classic story: a person unhappy with his lot in life, striking out on his own and working hard to make a success out of himself.

But he wasn't very happy. Without an assigned job, he had a difficult time trying to find a reasonable place to live. He had to stay with friends or family, which made business difficult to conduct. The inefficient transportation system, the untrustworthy communication system, and bureaucratic red tape made it a nightmare at times. He had only managed to make it onto this train by bribing the conductor with ten *yuan* and a cigarette.

He pulled a paperback book from his bag and said maybe I would be interested in it. It was a book of Western poetry—Carl Sandburg, Robert Frost, W.B. Yates, all translated into Chinese. "I want to be a writer," he said. "Maybe for films, maybe in television. It won't be as much money, but it will be more interesting." He had come to the conclusion that money can't buy everything.

A Night at the Opera

While entrepreneurs were finding only superficial satisfaction from making money, their success was nonetheless making established society extremely edgy. Most Chinese I met were uncomfortable with China's nouveau riche, partly out of jealousy—a frequent comment was that "they only go into business because they can't get a real job"—but perhaps more because they were dismayed by the power that money had.

Early in our trip, we paid a visit to the Beijing opera. The evening's feature was a nineteen-year-old girl performing a difficult "triple"— three scenes from three operas, each stressing major aspects of opera performance: singing, acting, and martial arts. To my untrained eye, the show was very impressive, especially the martial arts performance.

Our host that evening was a well-known opera star, an award winner herself in the martial arts performance. The next day we had lunch with her, and she asked my opinion of the show. I said I was impressed, but since I was no expert, I preferred knowing her views.

She did not say much about the quality of the performance. Instead, she talked about how the girl's father was a high-ranking military officer who had spent a lot of money hiring top instructors for her training. He had even paid the band and rented the theater for her performances. This obviously bothered our host, who thought it unjust that money should dictate who is groomed for stage stardom.

Her attitude reflected a growing concern stemming from China's "one child" policy. Chinese parents, allowed to have only one child or else be punished financially or socially, were spoiling these children rotten. They had begun to be called "Little Emperors" and "Little Empresses" because of their demanding ways.

Nonetheless, I couldn't see what was wrong with a parent's indulging his daughter's interest, as long as opera was what she wanted to do. Parents everywhere, in the West as well as in China, want to provide for their children as best they can. It was somewhat disturbing to see our host advocate what amounted to the old communist system, especially considering the dreary proletarian art produced under more reactionary times.

The Generation Gap

The two young lovers had bid each other tearful goodbyes before the young man climbed aboard the train and sat in the berth across from me. He was soft-spoken and sensitive. When someone nearby started smoking, he asked if I smoked, and when I said I didn't, he went over to the man and pointed out that we were sitting in the nonsmoking section. I never saw anybody else in China do that again.

He was an engineering student and obviously very intelligent. He had been accepted at a university in the Soviet Union, an opportunity made possible by the increasing ties between the world's largest communist nations. His departure had been delayed, probably by some bureaucratic red tape, so he had had some time to spend with his girlfriend.

A middle-aged gentlemen sitting nearby overheard us talking. "Young people like this are the hope of China," he said. "China has so many problems, but with ability like this we can go very far."

The student, however, was not so optimistic. "The worst thing is that when I get back I probably won't be able to use much of anything I've learned," he said. "This may be the important and worthwhile thing in my life, but it won't amount to anything."

The two of them continued on in this vein for some time, discussing the future of their country. It amounted to a polite argument, and my presence put the older man, an economist by profession, in a difficult position. He was trying to give me an accurate picture of China's difficulties and yet not be too discouraging to the student. But the student seemed to know all too well what China's failures were.

The Question of Freedom

"Freedom, such as you have in the United States, wouldn't work in China." Having been raised in the tradition that worships freedom as the root of America's strength, I suppose I should have strenuously disputed this statement when an old friend of the family said it. But after spending some time in China, I was neither surprised to hear it, nor could I completely disagree.

He was talking specifically about freedom of movement and the problems it would cause in China. There was a conflict between the needs of society and the demands of the culture, in that the Chinese always respected scholarship and would go to great lengths to obtain a good education.

"Everybody would move to Beijing because of the schools," he said. "Chinese want their children to get the best education, and the best schools are all there."

Beijing certainly didn't need any more students—or any other kind of people. The city already was overflowing, with new public and private housing projects going up everywhere. The city of 8 million people already was encircled by three ring roads, the farthest extending more than five miles out from the center of the city. Construction already had begun on a fourth circle, and plans for a fifth were underway.

I thought that the government could conceivably enact programs to encourage people to move elsewhere. Maybe it could even establish a new city, complete with incentives such as good jobs and a major university.

That wouldn't work, our friend said, because the Chinese are accustomed to hardship but not to taking chances. "They would rather suffer in Beijing than try someplace new," he said.

The Hair Trigger

The Chinese temper surprised me. The pushing and shoving to get aboard trains and buses usually did not amount to many confrontations, but on other occasions fights broke out over nothing.

We had stopped at the burial site of Qin Shihuang outside Xian. Qin Shihuang had been the first emperor of a unified China, a tyrant of a man who burned books and imprisoned intellectuals during his brief reign. Only now that his grave sites were pulling thousands of tourists to China every year were the Chinese willing to grant him some respect for his place in history.

In what was to become an all-too-frequent occurrence, a scrappy-looking youngster approached me and asked if I had any money to exchange—any kind: U.S., Japanese, even Taiwanese currency. I decided against it and got into the car, but he kept after me, tapping against the window to get my attention.

Our driver flew into a rage at his prize being touched this way. He began chewing out the money exchanger, who promptly told him off. For several minutes, the two hurled insults at each other, throwing in some choice cuss words. Finally, our driver opened the door and stepped out. He and the money exchanger were rolling up their sleeves when our guide threw his arms around the driver and pulled him inside the car. "Country people," he said.

A few weeks later, we were eating lunch at a cafe in Shanghai. It was a popular establishment, so patrons had to wait in a long line. Suddenly an argument broke out between a man and a woman. The man had apparently taken a table that the woman had considered hers.

Their argument was long, loud, and bitter, their shouts becoming even more heated as everyone in the restaurant quieted down to watch. It ended as suddenly as it started.

Both of these incidents had begun over seemingly trivial matters and had escalated into loud and angry disputes. None of the protagonists showed the slightest concern about "losing face" in front of onlookers. It occurred to me later that it might have been a loss of face to back down.

One other incident was especially shocking. Just outside the gateway to People's University in Beijing, I caught a glimpse of a woman peddling a cart furiously up the road, carrying a man slumped over behind her. A knife was sticking out his back.

Tiananmen Square

It had been an exhilarating, but rather depressing trip. The mood of the people was evident in the small posters of the snakes that were seen on doors of homes. It was too early for these posters to be put out, since it was still the year of the dragon and the Chinese New Year was still two months away. They had posted them in hopes of bringing the luck of a New Year a little sooner.

We spent one of our last days in China in and around Tiananmen Square. The Square embodies the cultural hodgepodge that China has become. It is one of the few places in China where it is forbidden to spit. To the north sits the Forbidden City, for centuries the palatial playground of the Chinese emperors. On its southern wall, facing the Square, sits a huge portrait of Mao Zedong, his placid face overlooking the huge expanse of stone-cut bricks where he once held rallies for a million people at a time. He stares across the Square, seeming to look beyond the Monument to the People's Heroes to the classic proletarian building where his body lies in state. A short distance further, to the west, is the largest Kentucky Fried Chicken restaurant in the world.

Just behind Mao's mausoleum sits a typical statue depicting the glory of "Liberation," as the founding of the People's Republic of China in 1949 is called. Etched into the gray stone are the smiling, fresh-looking faces of People's Liberation Army soldiers.

We had gone to the Square with a young Chinese couple. They were by all standards a success, with good jobs, a comfortable apartment, and family to help them take care of their energetic five-year-old son. Still, they had been very downbeat about China's situation.

As we looked at the statues, reading some of the old Maoist slogans from days gone by, they suddenly looked at each other and began laughing a nervous, embarrassed laugh. "What are you laughing at?" I asked. "Nothing," came the reply. "We have nothing to laugh at, but we can still do it, so we do."

6

Civil Disobedience and Dissent against the Party-State: An Eyewitness Account of the 1989 Chinese Student Movement

King K. Tsao

For days, the loudspeakers posted outside the gates of Beijing University had blared out the news about the student occupation of Tiananmen Square. With the domestic news media coming firmly under the control of the hardline leaders by late May, and overseas broadcasts of the Voice of America and the British Broadcasting Service being jammed, this was one of many methods for the students to get their message across to the public at large.

On 3 June, a particularly ominous bit of information was broadcast. There was no way to determine whether it was true but, given the anxiety that had developed since the declaration of martial law two weeks earlier, many seemed willing to believe it. According to the report, several street-cleaning vehicles were parked close to the National Library of China near the Purple Bamboo Garden. When pressed by students and citizens as to what they were doing there, the drivers said they had been ordered there and to ready themselves in case their services were needed. The invasion of Tiananmen Square was only hours away.

Student Activism Takes Shape

In retrospect, the confrontation between the students and the regime had been building for a long time. Students, like all social groups in China, had been affected by the problems and dilemmas brought by Deng Xiaoping's reform program. Students and intellectuals in particular were sensitive to the new ideas that had been imported from abroad; they also had expectations and high aspirations about the direction the country should go. However, they believed that something was wrong with the existing political structure of the regime and something had to be done about it..

There was growing evidence that the economic reforms were failing. Official profiteering, rampant corruption, and the high inflation rate (amounting to 30% in 1988 and 1989), had lowered the standard of living of the intellectuals, students, and government workers on fixed incomes.

With the economy—and society in general—spinning out of control, student activism became commonplace. The student demonstrations in late 1986 and early 1987 that erupted in many cities and finally led to the ouster and downfall of former Party Secretary Hu Yaobang are well known, but only because of their supposedly "prodemocratic" tilt. In fact, students had found other causes around which to rally. At Beijing University (Beida), students demonstrated after consecutive world championship victories by the Chinese women's volleyball team in 1984, reflecting a resurgence of nationalistic pride in a society where spirits were sagging as awareness of China's relative weakness in the world grew. This awareness was one of the consequences of Deng's "Open Door Policy."

In September 1985, students organized a boycott of Japanese goods, expressing resentment against the economic "invasion" of a powerful and threatening neighbor country that had in some instances dominated the markets of nascent national industries with visible quantities of imported Japanese goods. The murder of a graduate student, Chai Qingfeng, by hooligans in May 1988 also caused student unrest and subsequent marches to the Square, and in December 1988 there had been protests over an incident involving African students at Chinese universities. These protests were an indication that the students were unhappy over their status, which both materially and spiritually had failed to keep pace with other economic reforms.

Although there were no student demonstrations in the early part of 1989, political ferment was still brewing. In particular, the formation of discussion groups, later called "democracy salons," provided the forum to exchange ideas, thoughts, and contacts among students and intellectuals. The basis for the salons, besides shared interests, was mutual trust and friendship. The forums were to provide a loose framework for organizing and mobilizing student activities. For example, the democratic salon at Beida was first formed by a few students in the department of history, including Wang Dan, Yang Tao, and others. It had held several meetings before the death of Hu Yaobang, and it was this organization that was later to provide important leadership for the student movement.

The year 1989 held special significance in China. It marked the fortieth anniversary of the founding of the People's Republic of China, the bicentennial anniversary of the French Revolution, and the seventieth anniversary of the May Fourth Movement. The sentiments incited by these historic events aroused the youths' enthusiasm and patriotism, instilling in them a desire to create a force within civil society that would pay attention to the issues, problems, and ills of society and urge the continuation of reforms. With such emotions running high among students, there was a general perception that soon they would leave campuses and take to the streets, especially around the May Fourth period.

The Death of Hu Yaobang

The death of Hu on 15 April sent a tremor of activism through the campuses in Beijing. At Beida, People's University, Beijing Normal University, Beijing Politics and Law University, and others, big-character posters were posted to commemorate Hu as an enlightened Communist who had advocated a more relaxed political environment during his tenure as party secretary. In addition, essays and poems were written, speeches were made, and students collected money for memorials to Hu. They organized a march on 17 April to Tiananmen Square and Xinhuamen (Chinese Communist Party headquarters) of the Zhongnanhai (State Council headquarters) to commemorate him.

These, however, were only the most visible manifestations of student activity. Behind the scenes, an effort was underway to organize and expand the movement to offer a constructive response to the situation. In this effort, a meeting of the democratic salon at Beida on 19 April evening proved to be crucial.

Usually, the salon met outside the dormitories for the foreign students and scholars, or inside one of the campus buildings. This meeting, however, was held in *sanjiaodi*, a "triangular zone" that was the hub of campus activity. When I first arrived there that evening, the atmosphere was surprisingly casual. Most people were chatting amicably or looking around for friends. Eventually, more than a thousand students were packed in that area—a much greater number than ordinarily participated in the salon meetings. Those who wanted to have a better view climbed up to the top of the walls that were supporting the bulletin boards.

At around 9:45 P.M., the salon was declared open and a sense of urgency quickly developed. The key members of the salon, including Wang Dan, led the discussion, focusing first on the supposed agenda of the meeting—Hu Yaobang's contributions to the country and the party, and the restoration of this reputation. The discussion then shifted to the broader topic of the causes of the failure of the 1986-87 student movement, and the lack of an independent organization to put forward the students' goals. The leaders also discussed how the government had been able to use the students' weaknesses to put down the movement.

The audience listened intently, but only a few dared to speak up over these sensitive issues. It took tremendous courage to speak up in the meeting. It was widely believed, even at the time, that agents from the National Security Bureau were there and that photographs and tapes were being made of the event. Thus, when someone dared to stick out his neck to address the audience, a wave of applause immediately followed. It was only in the preliminary stage of the movement, yet everyone knew that the risks were unusually high.

The discussion went on for about two hours when suddenly some students reported that several hundred Qinghua University students had gathered outside of Beida but were not being allowed to enter the campus. The Qinghua students wanted to join Beida students to go to Xinhuamen (the Chinese Communist Party Headquarters) together, where several hundred students, mostly from Beijing Normal University, were staging a sit-in.

Opinions were divided as to whether the meeting should be continued or dissolved. It was a particularly crucial moment, because the group sensed that a certain momentum had developed. Dissolving the meeting without some kind of formal action would be counterproductive. A quick decision by the organizers favored continuation of the meeting and further discussion on the setting up of a preparatory committee. This committee was later to lead to the formation of an independent student organization. Some representatives were sent to explain the situation to the Qinghua students and to ask for their patience.

That night, fewer than ten students spoke up, including Wang Dan, Xiong Yan, Yang Tao, Feng Congde, and Ding Xiaoping. Having dared to speak up in public, these students were automatically included in a committee that would lay the groundwork for the establishment of an autonomous student union. Ding was also elected by the members as the coordinator of this committee. The meeting finally ended at midnight. Some students met the Qinghua students and continued their discussion until early in the morning.

Ironically, the demonstration at Xinhuamen, which most of the Beida and Qinghua students missed that evening in order to continue their organizational meeting, would become one of the major events of the evening. As we learned the next day, police had attacked students at Xinhuamen, beating them severely and even reportedly killing one. When word of the beatings got out, the students were really mad.

Still, the forum played a significant role in the course of the demonstrations. From a political perspective, the students had essentially negated the official Beida student union as their legitimate representative. The students realized that the organization had contributed to their previous failures. There had been no intercampus student organization to coordinate their efforts and thus no unity. It was felt that an autonomous association, out of the control of government authorities, would be able to address this problem.

In addition, the forum had served as a learning process for formulating strategy. Rather than responding completely spontaneously, the organizing committee was made responsible for analyzing the current political situation and for developing a position on major issues, such as freedom of the press. The students realized that their previous failures could be attributed to insufficient support from other social groups, and they decided to address this issue.

The fruits of this effort were seen immediately. The students had learned to play the official game and to use its rules to their own advantage. They believed that by following the authorities' prescribed rules, the authorities could not find any pretext to suppress them. This sometimes resulted in some rather provocative actions. For example, the authorities had declared Changan Boulevard and the Square closed for the morning of 22 April. However, the students went to the Square and occupied it in the middle of the night, before the curfew came into effect. Thus, when the memorial service for Hu Yaobang was held, the students, although not admitted to the service, were on the Square, three of them kneeling on the steps of the Great Hall of the People in a dramatic attempt to speak to the authorities.

The Students and Turmoil

On 26 April, the *People's Daily* published a front-page editorial called "Resolutely Oppose Turmoil." It asserted that the disturbances were due to "a small minority of people with ulterior motives" whose goal was to "poison people's minds, create national turmoil, and sabotage the nation's political stability."

This reaction from the government was expected. It was not the first time that the officials had characterized the students' dissent as subversive and harmful. The students recognized immediately that the government's strategy would be to accuse a small number of "bad elements" of instigating social turmoil while neutralizing the great majority of the people.

Even though the students were expecting it, the editorial became the turning point of the whole movement and set the stage for further confrontation. At the *sanjiaodi*, students immediately responded with big-character posters and speech making, all denouncing the editorial. There seemed to be a massive and complete rejection of it. Some of the speakers chose specific phrases and wrote essays criticizing it; others rebuked it point-by-point. After every speech there was enthusiastic applause.

Instead of sowing dissension and dividing the students, the government had incited fear and antagonism in the great majority of the students, thus uniting them. The government had raised the stakes for students, suggesting that they would face severe punishment if they participated in the movement. This strategy had worked in the past, but it did not work this time because so many students were participating in the movement. All of them regarded the movement as patriotic and believed that they were widely supported.

It was now that the efforts to organize the students bore the most fruit. The Temporary United Association of Beijing Universities and Colleges (*Beijing gaoxiao linshi lianhehui*) established on 19 April had evolved into the Autonomous Student Union of Beijing Universities and Colleges (*Beijing gaoxiao xuesheng zizhilianhui*, or *Beigaolian* for short) on or about 26 April. Its emergence signified the coordination and the unification of various campus activities by this student union. Individual and independent student unions were also set up on each campus, alongside the official student unions. These nonofficial student unions organized the demonstrations on 27 April.

The demonstration built upon the previous experience of marching and parading. Many students had participated in demonstrations before and some of them had been in the Square many times. There had been important lessons to learn in the 21 April demonstration, in which tens of thousands of students marched to Tiananmen Square, and the occupation of the Square during Hu's funeral the following day.

Meanwhile, the authorities were putting tremendous psychological pressure on the students. The editorial was broadcast frequently on the school's radio station as a warning to students. The government also announced that the Square and Changan Boulevard would be closed on 27 April and declared rallies and demonstrations illegal. It mentioned the presence of the Thirty-Eighth Army in the capital. Student party members were warned not to participate in the demonstrations; teachers were mobilized to convince their students not to engage in the march.

The students realized that the cost of participating in the march was high; some Beida students even wrote letters to their parents containing their wills, in case they were killed in the process of demonstrating.

27 April

Regardless of these threats and dangers, the students marched from their campuses on 27 April. The memory of observing this dauntless and defiant rally is indelible. At Beida, it began with the playing of the "Internationale" on the Beida campus radio station. A group of students, from the philosophy department, was the first to gather at the *sanjiaodi*, its department flag hoisted. More students came to *sanjiaodi* from all directions. School authorities constantly broadcast the official warning not to march. This was totally ignored.

The students walked from the triangular zone to the road leading to the Southern Gate, and gathered there according to their departments. They then grouped themselves according to classes. School flags, department flags, and placards were raised. They all received cheers and applause from onlookers and finally left Beida at around 8:45 A.M.

When they left the campus and turned into the junction with Haidian Road, they came to a halt. Students from other campuses also were stopped there. Seven to eight rows of policeman, several hundred of them, were lined up at the intersection. The students could not move forward.

Thousands of people were on the sidewalks of this main road, watching the situation (*guanwang*), some even standing between the policemen and the students. They clapped their hands to welcome the students, and shouted "*rangkai*" (get out of the way) to the policemen. The situation was tense, and neither side showed any sign of yielding. It seemed that the popular and strong support from the people had an effect on the policemen. After only a few minutes, they stepped aside and let the students pass.

The march moved ahead again. The Beida students were in front, followed by the students from the Institute of International Relations, Beijing University of Agriculture, Qinghua University, and the Chinese Academy of Sciences. Students sang the national anthem song and the "Internationale." Slogans filled the air: "Eradicate official profiteering," "Down with corrupt officials," "Long live understanding," "Peaceful petition, not turmoil," "Long live the motherland," "Patriotism is not wrong," "Long live the people," "Freedom of the press," "Nonsense with the *Beijing Daily*," "*People's Daily* lies to the people," "Long live democracy," and "Long live liberty." There were also many placards expressing a wide range of grievances, from dissatisfaction with the official press to condemnation of society's ills; from criticism of the government's use of violence and brutality toward the students at Xinhuamen to condemnation of the Shanghai Municipal Party in shutting down the *World Economic Herald*.

The scene was a heroic, emotional, and joyful one. People clapped their hands, applauded the students, and shouted: "Long live the students."

Once the policemen let the students through the first intersection, the blockades at other parts of the march route offered only token resistance. More students, coming from the People's University, the Beijing Institute of Foreign Languages, the Beijing University of Science and Technology, the Institute of Minorities, and many others in the Haidian district, joined in and formed a sea of people flowing toward the center of the city. They made the blockades close to the Friendship Hotel and *Baishiqiao* (White Stone Bridge) ineffective. The parade took about ninety minutes to pass the Fuxingmen Bridge before it turned onto Changan Boulevard, where even more students who had used different routes joined in.

This whole demonstration line, as it marched along what was called the western route, was well protected by "pickets," i.e., students who stood guard along the route of the march to keep out infiltrators. Many people and citizens either walked or cycled in front of the column, helping the students clear the way along the route.

There were incidents that would be profoundly prophetic during this march. At Fuxingmen Bridge, many people were waiting for demonstrators from the western route. Fifteen military trucks, packed with soldiers from the Thirty-Eighth Army, suddenly appeared, driving toward the Square along Changan Boulevard. As they passed by, people hissed at the soldiers.

As the students were coming to Fuxingmen Bridge, construction workers left their job and climbed down from the work site to welcome the students. When the students chanted "Long live the workers," the workers and other people replied by shouting "Long live the students."

Students received cash donations from the people. I will never forget an old woman, about sixty years old, donating ten *yuan* to the students at the junction of Haidian Road. That was about one-tenth of a worker's monthly salary, and it meant plenty to an old lady who was already retired and depended on others for support. She was furious toward the authorities, and constantly criticized them for being *tai guofen* (going too far) and *bu xianghua* (simply outrageous) in their treatment of the students.

The students finally formed a wall of bodies more than ten kilometers long marching along Changan Boulevard toward the

Square. More than two hundred thousand students participated in the march. More than a million people were lined up on the route to welcome the students. It was a highly organized demonstration.

The soldiers had retreated from the Square and the demonstration continued. But the students did not occupy the Square during all this time; instead, they passed by the government-owned New China News Agency and other news organizations to protest the distorted reports on the student activities. Then, they took a different route back to their respective campuses. The demonstration lasted the whole day.

That night, the Beida students came back to the campus at about midnight and were given a heroes' welcome by teachers, staff, and students at the Southern Gate. Fireworks were set off and traditional drums greeted them. They were exhausted but their spirits were high. The school authorities even permitted the canteens to serve the students at this unusual hour. Finally, the teachers, staff, and students all gathered at *sanjiaodi* to celebrate the successful march. All were overwhelmed by the authorities' promise to dialogue with the students, but were cautious about the difficulties still lying ahead. This meeting finally ended with the playing of the "Internationale" from the broadcasting station.

Conciliation and Concession

The government's response to the march on 27 April appeared conciliatory. It agreed to dialogue with the students, and Party Secretary Zhao Ziyang and a member of the Standing Committee of the Politburo, Hu Qili, also gave signals that the authorities were willing to compromise. None of these tactics, however, mollified the students. A dialogue held on 29 April was widely criticized because the government did not allow representatives from the autonomous student unions to participate. In addition, no substantial issues, such as the problem of official profiteering and the lack of educational funds, were addressed to the satisfaction of students.

Zhao Ziyang also attempted to signal a change in the official attitude toward the student movement at a meeting of the Asian Development Bank on 4 May. He called for "calm, reason, restraint and order," and that the reasonable demands from the students "be met through democratic and legal means." Also, when Hu Qili met representatives of the press, he suggested that the mass media had reached a point of *fei gaige buxing* (urgent need for reform), and implied that it was on the agenda.

There was widespread speculation about the apparent change in Zhao's attitudes at the time. Even now, his speech seems ambiguous to me. Although there was a general consensus in favor of Zhao's speech because it appeared to take a milder stance toward the movement, very few students, if any, interpreted it as an indication that Zhao had a voice independent of Deng's. It was known that Zhao was part of the reform clique, so that some believed he was merely trying to safeguard his personal power.

In fact, Zhao had been subject to widespread criticism for his economic policies and his two sons' participation in illegal speculative ventures. Some students and intellectuals believed that Zhao knew he was going to be forced out after Gorbachev's visit. They were suspicious that he was siding with the students in order to strengthen his own political power base.

For a while, however, the tension on campus subsided. The students were overwhelmed by their success in forcing the authorities to dialogue with them. Although a demonstration on 4 May garnered widespread attention, the number of students participating was much smaller than that of 27 April. Also, most of the students, except at Beida and Beijing Normal University, stopped boycotting classes. For much of the next week, the Beida campus was quiet.

The Hunger Strike

Personally, I did not feel that the hunger strike, which three thousand students launched on 13 May, would last that long. It was clearly aimed at gaining the attention of the international media, which had gathered by the hundreds in Beijing to cover the Sino-Soviet summit. A couple of students I talked to said they were expecting the authorities to clear them from Tiananmen Square before the arrival of Soviet leader Mikhail Gorbachev. If they could stay on the Square for a couple of days, they would regard the hunger strike as successful.

But the authorities did not clear the students away. Instead, Gorbachev was diverted from the Square on the first day and, subsequently, for his entire visit.

Paradoxically, this may have worked to the disadvantage of the students. Their hunger strike garnered a tremendous amount of sympathy, as tens of thousands of citizens came to Tiananmen Square to express their support. If previous student movements had lacked popular support, this one had galvanized virtually the entire populace behind it and against the government. The students' fighting spirit, endurance, and courageous acts had gained the hearts and souls of Beijing citizens and people all over the world. Many locals not involved at the beginning, especially the workers, state bureaucrats, and other social groups, now went out to support the students. They simply could not let these young and idealistic youths die of hunger and fatigue.

But this sympathy merely reinforced the students' convictions. They became even more convinced of the justness of their cause and the correctness of their tactics. And as a result, they became less flexible.

This attitude had developed considerable momentum when Zhao Ziyang dropped a bombshell during Gorbachev's visit. On the afternoon of 16 May, when Zhao met Gorbachev, he disclosed that the party, in the Thirteenth National Party Congress in 1987, had passed a resolution declaring that Deng "still steers the way" on all important matters. Immediately, his remark was interpreted by the students and intellectuals as blaming Deng for the government's hardline approach in dealing with the student movement. It was clear that Zhao was trying to betray Deng in public.

The response to Zhao's public comments revealed the strength of public sentiment against the hardline stance. On 17 May, more than 1 million people, consisting of Chinese from all walks of life as well as students, demonstrated and demanded Deng's retirement and resignation. For the first time, slogans in great numbers were directed at Deng.

This demonstration was noticeably different than previous large-scale demonstrations, such as the 27 April one. Even at that emotionally charged demonstration, I do not recall any slogans being directed toward Deng. Deng had a very high position and a good reputation as the leader of the reform movement. Moreover, the students knew that if they singled Deng out for blame, that would turn the demonstration into a confrontational situation. By 17 May, these sentiments had all changed.

Zhao's isolation became even clearer in the few days following 17 May. In the early morning of 18 May, Zhao with three other Standing

Committee members, went to the hospital to visit the student hunger strikers. Li Peng met the representatives of the student hunger strikers at noon on the same day. On 19 May, a few hours after the Standing Committee convened and planned a crackdown of the movement, Zhao went to the Square in the early morning to visit the students for the last time. Later, on the same day, four of Zhao's advisors issued a statement concerning the situation at hand and asked for a nonmilitary solution to the crisis by convening an emergency meeting of the People's Congress. On the same night, Li Peng, flanked by three Politburo Standing Committee members, declared that martial law would be enacted on 20 May. Zhao was absent, a clear sign of his loss of power in the political rift with Deng and Li.

As we were soon to find out, Zhao apparently had been maneuvering behind the scenes to bolster the position he had hinted at in his 4 May speech. According to a document circulated by some of his aides, on 13 May Zhao suggested to the Standing Committee of the Politburo that the 26 April editorial be repudiated, but his proposal was rejected by the four other members. On 15 May, Zhao wanted to go to the Square to announce his personal opinion but was stopped on the grounds that he would be violating party discipline. On 16 May, at the meeting of the Standing Committee of the Politburo, in the presence of Deng, Zhao proposed five items including repudiation of the 26 April editorial and going to the Square to meet the students, but his five-point proposal was rejected. The division in leadership was clear to all.

Martial Law

Once the decision was made to impose martial law in Beijing and to send thousands of troops to the capital to carry out the orders, the use of force became a matter of time. The students did not have many strategic options, but they managed to mobilize citizens to blockade the soldiers. They tried to persuade soldiers not to enter the city by explaining to them the real circumstances of the movement. They went to the street to give lectures and talks to the masses about their cause and to ask their help to stop the entrance of the soldiers into the city.

Hopes were raised for a brief moment when Wan Li was recalled from his North American trip. It was believed that his return would enable the People's Congress to convene and resolve the political crisis. An emergency session was urged to convene in order to deal with this crisis. Many Beida professors who were members of the National Congress signed a petition calling for such a meeting. However, instead of going back to Beijing directly from the United States, Wan Li stopped in Shanghai, claiming that he needed to be hospitalized for a while. The dream of settling the matter was gone.

The situation was particularly tense for the first few days of martial law. Many people did not go to the Square, particularly foreigners. After a while, however, martial law became part of life and the threat seemed to disappear. A few demonstrations were launched in the city, and the students made one last attempt to gain worldwide attention by unveiling the Goddess of Democracy in Tiananmen Square on 31 May.

On the Beida campus, the attitude of defiance continued. A young English Department faculty member at Beida, Zhu Li, posted a big-character poster shortly after the imposition of martial law on 20 May, condemning the Yang-Li clique [President Yang Shangkun and Premier Li Peng] and declaring her withdrawal from the party, which she had belonged to for twelve years. She risked a lot by publicly denouncing the party and flagrantly condemning the leaders. She was the only teacher and faculty member at Beida to publicly give up her party ties during this month-long student demonstration, although there were a few students who gave up their membership in the Chinese Communist Youth League during this period.

The reception to her small yet explosive big-character poster reflected the people's intense opposition to the government, attracting widespread attention and praise from students. Many of her students wrote comments on her poster, all of them remaining anonymous. I still remember vividly some of the comments. "Teacher: You are good, and I respect you a lot," wrote one student. Another said, "Teacher: you are courageous indeed. I highly appreciate you." A student from Shanghai put down, "[We] welcome your resignation from the Communist party, and we invite you to join the people's party"—the latter term being the designated name of the student movement. Her action was even reported in the student-run newspaper *Xinwen Daobao* (News Herald) as well as in other places.

The students' organizing activities continued. On the Square, the Hunger Strike Headquarters was changed to the Square Headquarters, since the hunger strike had ended. Also, there was the Autonomous

Student Union of Non-Beijing Universities and Colleges (*Waigaolian*) that took charge of and was responsible for all the students from outside of Beijing. A workers' organization, the Beijing Autonomous Workers' Union (Gongzilian) was formed, and the workers participated in the movement on a small scale. But there was little that the students could do. They had committed themselves to using peaceful means, and largely confined their actions to the rules and laws of the Constitution.

By early June, the situation was deteriorating rapidly. Without any other tactics to fall back on, the students could rely only on getting the information out to the people. This effort was undertaken every night by "information promoters," who would tell the citizens about the movement of the soldiers and the dangers that their entrance into the city presented. Every night around 7:00 P.M., these students would be dispatched every thirty minutes from the *sanjiaodi*, gathering in groups of up to fifteen volunteers in front of Building 29. With a hero's send-off, they would cycle away, a flag held by one of the students flying in the wind.

Out of habit, more and more people, sometimes totalling more than one thousand, were coming to the *sanjiaodi* after dinner. Even more gathered outside the Southern Gate and the area designated as the school cinema, listening to the school's broadcasting station.

The situation became especially tense by 3 June. Earlier that afternoon, there had been reports of a conflict between the students and the public security men in Muxidi, which I learned later was caused by an accident involving an army truck. The broadcast station, after calling for information promoters, turned the microphone over to Xiong Yan, who was later arrested by the Chinese government as one of the twenty-one most-wanted students. Speaking in a heavy Hunanese accent, he gave a long and eloquent speech on the strategies and goals of the student movement.

Xiong had always received enthusiastic applause from the audience as he spoke. This time, however, some people interrupted and urged him to stop, while others wanted him to continue. As I reflect on the matter now, it seems unlikely that he was interrupted by agents of the public security unit. Possibly his address had disturbed those in the audience who no longer were interested in "democracy" and wanted to have an immediate solution to the threatening situation.

It was quite usual at these forums held at the *sanjiaodi* for people to show their immediate approval by applause, and to show disapproval by hissing and booing. However, as a rule, the speaker always had a chance to have his say, although at times he needed to cut short his talk. The rules were that the speakers had the right to express their personal opinions and the right to finish their talks. In spite of the inadequate broadcasting facilities, the rules were generally complied with. The aim was to put into practice the ideas of "democracy."

But it seemed that, while democracy was no doubt one of the many slogans and goals advocated by the movement, it was not the only or even the most important one. At the grass-roots level, the students at Beida were not primarily driven by the idea of democracy. What they regarded as democracy at the time was in part the need to respect the rights of the individual guaranteed by the state Constitution. In fact, they had adopted the term "democracy" from the heritage derived from the May Fourth Movement of 1919. This had nothing to do with a multiparty system or a system of checks and balances as commonly identified by the West.

Although there was a dilemma between reforming the economy, on the one hand, and keeping the political system unchanged, on the other, the movement did not receive active support from China's newly emerging entrepreneurial class. It was supposed that the emergence of private entrepreneurs would generate demands that would change the political system. But most Chinese entrepreneurs did not engage in any political activities. They were not the engine of change in the movement of 1989, although some entrepreneurs did funnel money and give tacit support to the movement.

Finally, Xiong Yan had to stop. There was an announcement that there were hundreds of thousands of people in Tiananmen Square and along Changan Boulevard, and hence no more "information promoters" were needed to publicize the circumstances. Instead, the broadcast urged all the students to stay on campus and to protect the campus against possible encirclement by the soldiers.

It was then that the announcement about the street-cleaning vehicles was made.

4 June

It was about 2:00 A.M. on 4 June when I received a phone call from my brother in the United States. We had talked frequently since the demonstrations began, but I was aware that most of the school phones were bugged and was therefore careful about what I said.

It was from my brother that I first learned that the army was firing on the people along Changan Boulevard and around Tiananmen Square. It was a tremendous shock. Like everyone else, I had not believed that the government would use brutal force to suppress the students. The students had been so intoxicated by their power that they believed that almost anything was possible. One professor, recently returned to China, had been quite optimistic even after the declaration of martial law. He believed that at most only a few student leaders would get in trouble, since it was clear that the movement had gained overwhelming support from almost every sector of society.

After the phone conversation, I hurried out of my room toward the *sanjiaodi* to find out more. There, I met a French student who said she had just returned from Tiananmen Square and had heard gunfire on the north side of the Monument to the People's Heroes. She had been urged to leave the Square because "it was not deserving for a foreigner, like me, to die in this kind of situation."

The school broadcast station was blaring mourning music. An announcer came on and announced the names of more than twenty students who had been killed and whose bodies were in Fuxing Hospital. They had been killed at Muxidi and other places. I was later to find out that these deaths had occurred even before the final assault on Tiananmen Square. About fifty students had gathered at the *sanjiaodi*—some were weeping and crying, others screaming in anger.

In the morning, the *sanjiaodi* was quickly lined with big-character posters denouncing the massacre. A banner was suspended across one building with the words, in red ink, "This bloody debt must be repaid with blood." Students surrounded a classmate who had just returned from the downtown area. He was displaying a machine gun bullet, two rifle bullets, an empty teargas cannister, a cudgel, a helmet, and a rifle tripod. The students took pictures of these items.

I met a friend who had been horrified over what he had seen at Muxidi. The army, he said, had fired at the crowd at random. With two other students, he had stood up and waved a flag, shouting, "We are students, please do not fire on us." The soldiers answered with a volley of gunfire. His mates fell to the ground beside him, and it was only then that he realized that the army was using real bullets. As he ran for cover, gunfire rained on him, not only from the back, but from the roofs of nearby buildings as well. According to many accounts, the attacks on Muxidi and Liubukou were far more brutal and extensive than on Tiananmen Square.

For the next day, until I managed to leave the Beida campus, such accounts were widespread among students and professors. Like many students, I went through moments of anxiety as I searched for friends who had been on the Square the previous evening. Like them, I felt tremendous relief when they were located.

A complete account of everything that occurred during those hectic days would be endless and repetitive. But as I reflect on the movement now, its weaknesses are apparent. Strategically, it lacked long-term objectives and definite alternative courses. Most of its measures were adopted to respond immediately to the needs and threats of the situation, which were beyond the control of the students.

There were organizational weaknesses as well, in spite of the students' efforts to present a strong and united front. With the exception of the student organizations that had sprung up at the beginning, none of the organizations had many core members. Most of the other organizations, such as the Workers' Autonomous Union, were formed only after the introduction of martial law in Beijing, and they did not exert that much influence, in comparison with the students, to the whole political situation. There were no strikes organized by the workers to support the movement.

Psychologically, the organizers and participants were not prepared for the worst outcome that they might encounter. In addition, they were intoxicated by their widely praised actions and glorious deeds and, hence, underestimated the implications of their actions on the regime.

Theoretically, they were not ready to entertain the idea of power sharing with the dominant party—not even minimally—not to mention the alternative of replacing it.

In short, the fundamental problem lies in the fact that all these students and intellectuals believed that they were merely engaging in civil disobedience and in dissent against the party-state. They were not aware of the significance of their actions and hence did not search out ways to reorganize the state or to implement their ideals and goals. Additionally, the students were naive in believing that simple patriotism was enough to win their cause. Therefore, it is hard to say that China, if there is another large-scale student movement in the near future, will move toward democracy. In fact, I am more inclined to believe that China, at this moment, is not quite ready for democracy.

But, despite all these weakness and mistakes of the movement, the movement rightly deserves high praise. The students had shown courage, determination, and the willingness to sacrifice themselves for a cause. People will not forget those who participated in the movement, and those who were killed or wounded. Previous student movements have propelled the progress of modern Chinese history. The stirring memory of the rally on 27 April, the first large-scale demonstration that I and undoubtedly millions of other Chinese had ever witnessed, is enough to give me hope that the students' noble ideals will someday be fulfilled in China.

[This chapter is a revised and adapted version of a more technical article submitted originally for this project but was subsequently revised to fulfill the requirements of this book. Special thanks are due Steven Mark for his invaluable editorial assistance.]

7

Deng Xiaoping and the 1989 Tiananmen Square Incident

Peter Nan-shong Lee

In the four decades of the People's Republic of China, the Tiananmen Square incident was unprecedented as a spontaneous, grass-roots movement that gained popular sympathy and massive support. The incident can be easily analyzed, from a socio-psychological perspective, as a form of collective behavior.[1] However, this perspective is not quite adequate to account for the political characteristics of the incident. It cannot explain the incident in terms of the party-state's basis for dealing with the student movement, its changing ideologies and interests, the main issues, and the crisis of legitimacy that confronted the party.

As a Leninist, Deng Xiaoping sees the party-state as having—in the words of Antonio Gramsci, the founder of the Italian Communist Party—a "positive-educative" role in society. This view is anchored in Lenin's definition of the revolutionary party as the vanguard and the most conscious sector of the proletariat. Therefore, for a proletarian party to ride on the high tide of historical transformation, not only does it need to exercise dictatorship through the use of coercive and compulsory power, it must also exercise "leadership" by building the "active consent" of the populace.

Deng is a Leninist to the extent that he regards the party-state as having a dual role as both an organizer of active consent and as an apparatus of power (specifically, coercive power). According to Christine Buci-Glucksmann, the former is what Gramsci calls "hegemony," and is built upon the cultural, political, and economic leadership of the party-state; the latter is taken as "dominance which relies heavily upon the apparatus of coercion, including the army, police, courts, and the bureaucracy."[2] She cites Gramsci to support her analysis:

> The state is the entire complex of practical and theoretical activities with which the ruling class not only justifies and maintains its dominance, but manages to win the active consent of those over whom it rules.[3]

In an ideal situation, an "integral state" can be built, in Gramsci's view, through the marriage of moral and intellectual leadership, i.e., hegemony, with coercion as armor.[4] In this situation, every element of hegemony, according to Buci-Glucksmann, is necessarily an educational relationship,[5] and, therefore, the use of violence is perhaps required in the political arena but can be reduced to a minimal level.

Conversely, the question arises as to what form the political regime will take if it has lost its educational function, if it can no longer exercise its moral and intellectual leadership, and if it is not sustained by the "active consent" of society. In Anne S. Sassoon's interpretation of Gramsci's position, without the element of "active consent" the socialist state will degenerate into a "statolatry state," i.e., a government by functionaries; democratic centralism into a bureaucratic centralism.[6] Under these circumstances, a revolutionary party, according to Sassoon, undertakes what Gramsci calls "passive revolution," and "merely reproduces a traditional relationship between the state and the mass of the population, even in different forms."[7]

It is noteworthy that once Deng gained power, he fought hard to prevent the degeneration of the party-state into a "statolatry state." Starting in 1978, Deng engineered a restructuring of the party-state, a move made necessary by the devastation caused by the radical politics of the previous two decades.

This very restructuring process, however, created destabilizing political consequences and produced a crisis of legitimacy for the party-state during the reform era. Although Deng had stressed the educational ingredient of the party-state, this ingredient was premised on an ideological renewal of the Chinese Communist Party, which he failed to accomplish. Thus, the Chinese Communist regime found it more difficult than ever to defend itself when its legitimate foundation eroded, and therefore became increasingly prone to use coercion to maintain its dominance, as witnessed in the Tiananmen Square incident.

The Tiananmen Square incident took place on the fringes of the party-state, marking the limits of state power and the rise of spontaneous sociopolitical forces within a relatively short time span. Despite the magnitude of these forces, however, it is evident that the parameters and direction of events were defined more by the Leninist regime than by the masses of the students and people; it was the regime and its established ideology and policies that led to both the escalation and eventual suppression of the movement. The incident therefore provides one of the best illustrations of how a Leninist regime acts in a political confrontation at a societal level.

Deng Xiaoping and the Leninist Legacy

In retrospect, the outcome of the Tiananmen Square incident should not be a surprise, considering the consistency of Deng Xiaoping's position on the subject of political confrontation. This position can be derived from the Leninist stand on the purposes, sources, and structure of power, and the relationship of the party-state to society. In this regard, Deng resembled Mao Zedong, but he was also confronting the political realities of the post-Mao era.

Leninism as an organizational principle represents the design of the vanguard socialist party in its task of seizing and maintaining state power. It is characterized by its emphasis on ideological conviction, elitism, the revolutionary party apparatus, combat orientation, agitation, and mobilization.[8]

The Chinese Communist party-state differed somewhat from the classic Leninist model in that it was infused with a radical ideology associated with Mao Zedong, especially from 1957 to 1976. The radical politics of those two decades mirrored the tension between a populist ingredient in Maoism and the Leninist emphasis on organizational discipline (i.e. party discipline). In fact, during the height of radicalism in the Cultural Revolution, Mao had to take an explicit stand in favor of the return to the Leninist legacy of the predominant role of the party. This was illustrated by Mao's serious reservations over the formula of the Shanghai Commune in the spring of 1967, an idea derived from early Marx.[9]

The aforementioned tension demonstrates the incompatibility between the role of a vanguard party in its revolutionary seizure of power and its role as a governing party administering the economy. Lenin had laid the theoretical foundation for both, unifying them under one epistemological core known as "the infallibility of the ruling elite." This notion of the infallible ruling elite creates the ideological, political, and institutional climate for the Chinese population to accept the omniscient and omnipotent role of the party leadership in society, whether in the form of the charismatic leadership in the revolutionary struggle or, alternately, the planner's sovereignty in the design and implementation of the command economy.[10]

With this framework in mind, one can examine Deng Xiaoping's basic attitude toward democratic tendencies. It became discernable in the late 1970s and remained relatively stable for approximately one decade, from 1979 to 1989. Upon the confirmation of his hegemony in the second half of 1978 and early 1979, Deng began to make policy statements concerning the overall problems of the Chinese Communist regime, as is evident in an often-cited speech titled "Uphold the Four Cardinal Principles." The four principles attempt to address four aspects of a political problem that the Chinese Communist party-state confronted in the post-Mao era: (1) the nature of the economic institutions and policy orientation, to be defined by "the socialist road"; (2) the characteristics of a regime shaped by "the proletarian dictatorship"; (3) the role and nature of the political leadership, to be defined by the principle of "the Communist party leadership"; and finally (4) the sources of political and institutional legitimacy derived from Marxism, Leninism, and Mao's thought.[11]

The "Four Cardinal Principles" are more than rhetoric, for they offer an abstract formulation of some concrete political problems that had developed as a result of the radical politics of Mao during the Cultural Revolution. One decade later, in 1989, these problems would still mark the salient features of the regime's response to the prodemocratic tendencies.

What problems do the Four Cardinal Principles address? Deng's statements of early 1979 make this clear:

To sum up, in order to achieve the Four Modernizations we must keep to the socialist road, uphold the dictatorship of the proletariat, uphold the leadership of the Communist party, and uphold Marxism-Leninism and Mao Zedong thought. The Central Committee considers that we must now repeatedly emphasize the necessity of upholding these four cardinal principles, because certain people (even if only a handful) are attempting to undermine us. In no way can such attempts be tolerated.

Recently, a small number of persons have provoked incidents in some places. Instead of accepting the guidance, advice, and explanations of leading officials of the party and government, certain bad elements have raised sundry demands that cannot be met at present or are altogether unreasonable. They have provoked or tricked some of the masses into raiding party and government organizations, occupying offices, holding sit-downs and hunger strikes, and obstructing traffic, thereby seriously disrupting production … and public order.

Moreover … there is a so-called "China Human Rights Group," which has gone so far as to put up big-character posters requesting that the president of the United States "show concern" for human rights in China. Can we permit such an open call for intervention in China's internal affairs?[12] [Emphasis added]

Citing Lenin's view to support his thesis, Deng explains that even the 1976 mass movement commemorating Premier Zhou Enlai at Tiananmen Square could not be treated strictly as a spontaneous mass movement unrelated to the party's leadership. In spite of its spontaneity, the 1976 Tiananmen Square movement, with its demonstrated "political consciousness," was "inseparable from the education of the party for many years in the past." Deng continued to emphasize the point that the spontaneity of the masses should not be extolled at the expense of the party's leadership. Political participation by the masses, according to Deng, is impermissible, even under the guise of socialist democracy.

Deng Xiaoping on Socialist Democracy

There is no lack of mention of "democracy" in Deng's views of the Chinese political system, but close analysis of them reveals that the term as he uses it does not carry the same meaning as it does in the West, i.e., an institutional safeguard for popular control of government. "Democracy," as used in the Chinese Communist party-state, does carry the meaning of popular sovereignty—or "of the people" in Abraham Lincoln's expression—and it refers to the policies made in the interest of the people—or "for the people," in Lincoln's words. However, "democracy" in Deng's sense does not have quite the same meaning of Lincoln's phrase "by the people," that is, controlled by and accountable to the people. In fact, Deng's views of "democracy" are fully congruent with the party's tough stand against the student movement, which, with its call for "dialogue," was demanding a degree of accountability from the government.

Deng talked about "democracy" extensively upon the conclusion of the Work Conference of the Central Committee preceding the Third Plenum of the Eleventh Party Congress in December 1978. He even expressed some views that appear "liberal." He said that, in light of the experience of the Cultural Revolution, it was undesirable to have excessive "taboos" and "forbidden zones" (lack of freedom of speech and thought) as well as too much "democratic centralism" and overconcentration of power within the party.[13]

In addition, Deng advocated some aspects of "immunity" similar to the Western notion of liberty, for instance, respect for the rights of party members in accordance with the party charter, and the rights of citizens in accordance with the Constitution. He was willing to create more room for the "liberation of thought" and more legal protection for the people. Moreover, Deng referred to the "initiative" and "autonomy" that the people should enjoy.

However, Deng's intention in allowing this kind of "democracy" is clearly not to permit political participation in the Western sense; it is to share power in the administrative, economic, and managerial contexts. Examples of the latter include consultation on the implementation of policy, the delegation of power from the central to the local work unit and individual levels, and giving autonomy to the management of factories and production brigades.[14]

These views are intended as fresh political alternatives to what Mao and the Gang of Four had offered during the Cultural Revolution. However, they still fall short of the expectations of those who support true democratic reform in China. It is not too far-fetched to draw a parallel between the conception of the "bird cage economy," an idea of Deng's ally Chen Yun, and what can be attributed to Deng as "bird cage democracy." To put it another way, the sovereign planner constitutes a systematic component in the "bird cage economy" as much as the infallible party leadership does in the "bird cage democracy."

From an institutional perspective, Deng's notion of "democracy" means an institution "under the guidance of centralism." Furthermore, unlike pluralism, in which the individual's interest has a legitimacy unto itself, socialist democracy can only accommodate the individual's interest according to the overall interest of the party-state. In Deng's words:

> Democratic centralism is an integral part of the socialist system. Under this system, personal interest[s] must be subordinate to the collective one; the interest[s] of the part to that of the whole, and immediate to long-term interests.[15]

In retrospect, Mao placed more stress on the populist aspect of Leninism, while Deng was willing to strengthen its organizational dimension. Mao tended to talk more often about the "mass line"; Deng was inclined to pay greater attention to "democratic centralism." Deng consistently gave Mao a "positive evaluation" during the reform era. This cannot be taken as tactical maneuvering to bypass Mao as a political controversy, or as an enlightened strategy to protect the legitimate foundation of the regime, but a genuine belief in the relevance of Leninism to the seizure and maintenance of state power in the Chinese context. Deng cited Mao's oft-repeated ideal of the *Yanan* way, which refers to decentralized political structures that were responsive to local needs, when describing the political and institutional manifestations of democratic centralism:

> This is precisely why Comrade Mao Zedong said that our aim is to create a political situation in which we have both centralism and democracy, both discipline and freedom, both unity of will and personal ease of mind and liveliness. This is the political situation that exists when there is true socialist democracy—the situation we must strive to create today and in the years to come.[16]

In Deng's view, the Chinese Communist Party could make a mistake, but only the party, rather than any spontaneous political force, can be a legitimate channel to correct the mistake. To put it another way, the party is still infallible to the extent that it is the only entity able to correct its own mistakes.

In essence, Deng suggests that the party is still the depository of truth, and it should function as a self-correcting mechanism:

Our party has made many errors, but each time the errors were corrected by relying on the party organization, not by discarding it. The present Central Committee is persistent in promoting democracy in the party and among the people and is determined to correct past errors. Under these circumstances, it would be all the more intolerable to the masses of our people to demand the liquidation or even the weakening of leadership by the party. In fact, bowing to this demand would only lead to anarchism and the disruption and ruin of the socialist cause.[17]

It is worth noting that the guiding principles and design of the Leninist regime evolved during the long revolutionary struggle from 1921 to 1949 and during the political takeover and consolidation in the early years of the People's Republic of China. It does not seem that any spontaneity, autonomy, and initiative from the grass-roots level can be accommodated within the existing political framework. Deng does not think that any political group or individual has the right to discover the truth or to substitute for the party's role in identifying and defining the truth. For him, democratic tendencies not sponsored by the party should not be tolerated. In this light, the attitude and policy of Deng and his associates toward the Tiananmen Square demonstrations should be regarded as fairly consistent with their system of values.

The Party-State Restructured in the Reform Era

In Professor Tsou Tang's view, the Chinese communist movement was a response to a total crisis at the level of the political community, and was organized and led by a Leninist type of revolutionary party.[18] The movement went through two stages of "revolution": the "new democracy" stage and the "socialist revolutionary" stage. The former was aimed at the seizure of state power on the basis of a "national democratic" platform; the latter intended to implement the socialist system of production and distribution within the framework of central planning and public ownership.[19] Of course, the latter entails a broader scope than the former in terms of state intervention in the economic arena and a further expansion of the party's political control over society.

Since the founding of the People's Republic of China in 1949, the Leninist party apparatus and the administered economy reinforced each other, and this produced a species of totalitarianism. Within this system, the Communist party-state wielded coercive, political, administrative, and economic powers and intended to maximize its total control over the entire society. However, this totalitarian system tended to result in unintended consequences due to a variety of factors inherent in the political structure itself, as well as those derived from the society in which it operated.

Reconstructed from Deng Xiaoping's perspective, this totalitarian system constitutes two hemispheres. The first hemisphere, representing the establishment, can be further divided into two echelons: the upper echelon, which embraces the top leadership within the government and party at both the central and local levels; and the lower echelon, which comprises the basic units of production and other institutions. Political relations within the upper echelon generally are handled through consensus building with the code of civility and an atmosphere of comradeship. Nevertheless, these have been marked by tensions and conflicts at specific moments in history. The relationship between the upper and lower echelons is defined mainly by economic, organizational, and managerial means, and to a lesser extent it features a patron-client network as well.

The second hemisphere includes the masses of industrial workers, peasants, and soldiers. The category of the masses is always to be led and guided by the party, and therefore the masses do not have independent political status other than what is prescribed by the party. The masses cannot be taken as citizens in the Western sense, enjoying the institutional sanctions and legal foundations that ensure their immunity and protection as well as political participation and initiative.[20] Since a Leninist regime does not normally accommodate spontaneity from the masses, the masses could readily be taken as alien social forces if they move into an orbit outside the party leadership. On the whole, the allocation of power within the first hemisphere is taken with patience and tolerance, but the relationship between the first and second hemispheres is marked by rigidity, impersonality, and often a high-handed approach.

During the decade from 1979 to 1989, Deng was able to forge a new political coalition on the basis of the platform of the Four Modernizations. This coalition was sustained not only by an ideology—the belief in improving industry, defense, agriculture, science, and technology—but also by the shared material interests of those involved. In other words, Deng was successful in rebuilding a hegemony with its leadership component on top of its dominating and controlling component. The demonstrations on Tiananmen Square, however, are indicative that students and intellectuals in particular had begun to feel that the dominating component had prevailed. They sensed that the party-state could only passively maintain its control over society, but had lost its ability to lead the nation.

At the initial stage of the reform era, Deng Xiaoping was able to ride on the tide of the "reversal of verdicts" of both the leaders at the top and intelligentsia at the middle level. In spite of Deng's common ideological ground with Mao, Deng relied upon most of the top leaders who fell from Mao's favor, cultivating his potential supporters from those who had been alienated by the radical politics of the previous two decades. Deng took advantage of the grievances and discontent created by the Cultural Revolution and the initial round of campaigns against the Gang of Four.

At the top level, Chen Yun, Peng Zheng, Yang Shangkun, Bo Yibo, Xi Zhongsun, and many more were able to return to the political arena. Hu Yaobang, in his capacity as the head of the Organization Department of the Central Committee, was instrumental in the rehabilitation of numerous disgraced high cadres. In addition, many institutions of the party and the government were restored not only to accommodate Deng's allies, but also to carry out his pragmatic policies. This led to the creation of such entities as the Secretariat of the Central Committee, the Central Disciplinary Inspection Committee, the State Economic Commission, etc.

The relationship between the upper and lower echelons of the first hemisphere was fortified through the introduction of "readjustment, reform, rectification, and improvement." In essence, the purpose of these policies was to streamline the managerial and economic relationship between the party-state and the basic units; to delegate more managerial power to the latter; and, in the meantime, to make material concessions in order to ensure their compliance. In sharp contrast to Mao, Deng tended to build up his political support among the "power-holders," the intellectuals, and the senior rank stratum within the lower echelon of the establishment.

Under Chen Yun, Deng Xiaoping, Li Xiannian, and later Zhao Ziyang, the so-called "readjustment, reform, rectification, and improvement" program attempted to rebuild the economy through a number of remedial measures mainly experimented with in the late 1950s and 1960s. For example, central local revenue-sharing schemes, first introduced in the late 1950s, were restored with some amendments, starting in February 1980.[21] In the rural sector, price support was given to grain procurement from 1979 on. This was followed by the abolition of the People's Communes, the introduction of the agricultural responsibility system, the encouragement of rural sideline businesses and small enterprises, and the expansion of the rural market.[22] In the industrial sector, state-owned enterprises were allowed to take part in a variety of profit-sharing schemes, such as the "enterprise fund" scheme, the profit-retention system, the "taxation to substitute for profit-remittance" program, and the "industrial economic responsibility" (contractual responsibility) system.[23]

The Four Modernizations coalition built by Deng was anchored on a wider sharing of economic power as well as an effort for continuous policy innovations, first under the guise of recovering from the Cultural Revolution and then as part of the reform and the "open door" policy. In the eyes of the people at the time at least, this was a form of hegemony achieved not only through the application of remunerative measures,[24] but also through the promotion of inspiring policies and workable programs.

The Fall of the Cultural Fortress

According to Max Weber, political dominance can be maintained either by exercising power or authority, or a combination of both.[25] However, power and authority differ from each other in the sense that the former refers to the application of reward and punishment, whereas the latter is concerned with compliance on the basis of acceptance of the regime and its policies on ethical grounds. In other words, the latter has to do with an evaluative and critical ingredient, asking what is right or wrong, just or unjust, good or evil.

The foregoing analysis has suggested that during the reform era the restructured party-state was considerably strengthened owing to its ability to provide ideas and direction for change as well as the exercise of economic power, e.g., the wider sharing of managerial power and material benefits at all levels of the party and government hierarchy and at the basic unit level. Therefore, there was much less need to resort to coercive power. However, the party-state was subsequently weakened insofar as its legitimate foundation was concerned, for reasons to be given later.

Antonio Gramsci understands well that political dominance needs to be maintained by a mixture of power and authority. He suggests that in many instances naked power is exercised only after the legitimate foundation of the regime has eroded. The apparatus that defends the authority of the regime is taken by Gramsci as the "ethical state" or "cultural state."[26] Using the offense and defense in modern warfare as a metaphor, Gramsci states that, in order to maintain political dominance, the first line of defense tends to concentrate on the defense of the "cultural fortress," that is, the safeguarding of the legitimate ground of the regime.[27]

The Chinese communist movement emerged partly as the result of ideological developments starting with the May Fourth Movement. After the successful seizure of state power in 1949, the Chinese Communist Party relied heavily upon ideological appeals to perpetuate its existence and to initiate the social and political transformation of China. These appeals were largely the work of a group of people identified as "establishment intellectuals"[28] positioned at the lower echelon of the power hierarchy (or the first hemisphere). This group is directly relevant to the Tiananmen Square incident.

In the Chinese context, the term "intellectuals" (zhishifenzi) refers to a category of people who normally have a background of high education and who work in cultural and educational institutions in a wide variety of professions, such as arts and literature, teaching and research, mass media, and science and technology. In what Ludwig Wittgenstein calls "family resemblances,"[29] the intellectuals are grouped under one category because of their common role in the process of knowing and working with ideas, know-how, culture, symbols, language, and media. They are expected to contribute to the functioning of the party-state by providing professional know-how (for example, Li Xiu-guang, the former minister of geology) and as the vehicle of ideology (for instance, Zhou Yang and Hu Qiaomu.)

Traces of information confirm the views of Timothy Cheek and Carol Lee Harmin that, although the "establishment intellectuals" are not often related to one another at the horizontal level, they are sometimes associated with the top party leaders in a patron-client network and in an informal and formal working relationship.[30] For instance, Wu Han and Ma Hong were closely related to Deng Xiaoping; Xue Muqiao worked as a subordinate to Chen Yun in the financial and economic field in the 1950s; Yang Xianzhen and Deng Tuo are identified as having been associated with Peng Zhen.

Some of these intellectuals might have had stature of their own because of their seniority and contributions within the party. Sun Yefeng, for instance, established himself due to his study in the Soviet Union in the prewar period and earned his name in the theoretical reformulation of the socialist economy in the late 1950s.[31] Similarly, Hu Qiaomu, who had a close working relationship with Mao, played an important role in the ideological transition from the middle 1970s to the early 1980s. In many instances, they were called upon to form a team of scholars (*xiucaibanzi*) to draft policy papers. During the reform era, they often formed a think tank or acted as policy advisors.

Both establishment and nonestablishment intellectuals were devastated during the radical politics of 1957 to 1976. Deng tried very hard to undo the damage of the Hundred Flowers Campaign and to rehabilitate those accused of being "rightists." The rehabilitation of many artists and writers came hand in hand with the restoration of their professional associations. Furthermore, Deng's interest in those practical subjects such as law, economics, and other social science subjects created an encouraging tendency to strengthen research facilities and activities in the universities and the policy-making units of the party and government.[32]

There were some unintended results of Deng's policy toward the intellectuals. First, Deng had allowed the rehabilitation of literary and cultural circles, partly to contain and eliminate the residual influence of the Gang of Four, and partly due to his conviction that the "forbidden zone" needed to be opened up and "liberal thought" allowed. But the reassessment of Mao Zedong as well as the Cultural Revolution tended to lead to the reevaluation of the legitimate foundation of the Chinese Communist party-state. Deng himself recognized the possibility of this occurring, as shown in his remarks on 1980-81 drafts of "Resolution on Certain Questions in the History of Our Party since the Founding of the People's Republic of China":

When we write about his mistakes, we should not exaggerate, for otherwise we shall be discrediting Comrade Mao Zedong, and this would mean discrediting our party and state. An exaggeration of his mistakes would be at variance with the historical facts.[33]

At about this time, literary works began referring to the Cultural Revolution and became a vehicle for criticizing the socialist political system. These led to deep reflections on its moral and philosophical foundations. In search of an answer to the excesses and distortions caused during Mao's era, authors could not account for how Marxism resulted in the violation of humanism. One philosophical formulation even suggested that there was a continuous process of alienation inherent in the socialist system as much as in the capitalist system. This formulation resulted in the questioning of the infallibility of the vanguard party and thereby posed a challenge to the dictatorship of the proletariat and the party's leadership. It is no wonder that Deng moved to the forefront to defend the regime in the "spiritual pollution" campaign in 1983, as he stated:

A number of theorists are indifferent to the major theoretical questions raised by socialist modernization.... They have engaged in discussions of the value of the human being, humanism, and alienation and have only been interested in criticizing socialism, not capitalism.... Rather, they allege that alienation exists under socialism and can be found in the economic, political, and ideological realms, that in the course of its development socialism constantly gives rise to a force of alienation, as a result of the activities of the main body of the society.[34]

Literary and artistic works were not the only way in which the socialist system was critiqued. Deng's approach of "seeking truth from the fact" logically led to an emphasis on the study of practical subjects. With Deng himself saying that "for many years we have neglected the study of political science, law, sociology, and world politics, and now we must hurry to make up our deficiencies in these subjects,"[35] the study of social sciences, management, as well as science and technology was promoted and encouraged.

These empirical studies encouraged inquiries into the viability of central planning and public ownership, in essence questioning the workability of the socialist system. In their endeavor to reassess the socialist economic system, the establishment intellectuals went further than the top leaders wanted in identifying the fundamental weaknesses of the system. For example, Hu Qiaomu's policy paper "Observe the Economic Laws and Speed Up the Four Modernizations," published in October 1978, discussed the sizable and ever-existing sector of a half-planned and nonplanned economy in the socialist framework as well as its fundamental causes. Hu's paper implies that the socialist economy has neither brought about the macrorationality nor microrationality as promised originally.

Three months later, in January 1979, the official diagnosis made in the communiqué of the Third Plenum of the Eleventh Party Congress avoided raising the question of the legitimacy of the socialist system in administering the economy. The communiqué instead stated that the key problem of the Chinese economy is overconcentration of managerial power, and therefore by implication no change of a fundamental nature is warranted.[36]

So in the aftermath of Mao, the establishment intellectuals, who were depended on to refute the ideas of the Gang of Four on many key ideological and policy issues, instead began developing some critical views and reservations about the socialist state. After all, socialism had yet to deliver its promises after forty years of experimentation in China.

But if it was bad that the establishment intellectuals lost their enthusiasm for the task of renewing Leninist ideology and defending it on ethical grounds, worse still, in Deng's view, was that those intellectuals, especially middle-aged ones, would have adverse influence over the younger generation. With the advantage of hindsight after the 4 June incident, Deng's worry concerning ideological problems associated with the movie script "Unrequited Love" on an earlier occasion was not entirely groundless:

But we must admit that among them—and among some middle-aged writers too—there are also bad tendencies that have an adverse influence on some young readers, listeners, and viewers. Our veteran writers who stick to the socialist position have responsibility to unite and give proper guidance to the new generation. Otherwise, it won't be able to advance on the right path. If we don't do a good job in this respect, contradiction may intensify and result in major disruptions.[37]

Of course, the entire cultural and educational establishment was demoralized by the sudden economic deterioration from 1987 to 1989 after one decade of steady improvement. Above all, the hegemony of the Leninist regime became substantially weakened when the cultural fortress had been taken on both moral and practical grounds. The party-state could simply no longer defend why it should claim a monopoly on power. As a result, the party-state was left naked, without protection, and open to challenge.

The Party-State and Society: Major Cleavages

During the reform era, Deng Xiaoping identified three major cleavages between the party-state and society. They were: (1) the aggregate of antisocial elements in society; (2) people alienated by the abuses of public power, such as official privileges and corruption; and (3) those intellectuals, including students, who were inclined to entertain alternative ideologies and systems. In fact, Deng perceived that he needed to confront these groups as early as the late 1970s, and his views on the student movement of 1989 are clearly rooted in these early perceptions.

Deng's assessment of the student movement as "turmoil" was based on the first cleavage: the aggregate of antisocial elements. Commenting on the "Democracy Wall" incident of 1979, Deng identified at least several "destabilizing elements," such as the residues of the Gang of Four, power cliques (new and old), criminal gangs, counter-revolutionaries with foreign connections, "prodemocracy factions," "anarchists," and so on.[38] "All these destabilizing elements," Deng said, "could be combined together and could form a destructive force to cause considerable turmoil and damage under certain circumstances, although they are different kinds of people."[39] Deng prophesied that, since this had occurred the previous year (in 1979), this "could happen again in the future."[40] Deng subsequently made similar observations on other occasions.[41]

The second major cleavage concerned the discontent and alienation caused by the abuse of public power, especially at the institutional level. Deng's policies and comments provided hints of his concern about this problem. As soon as the Central Disciplinary Inspection Committee of the Chinese Communist Party was reestablished in early 1979, its task shifted quickly from the combat against the residual influence of the Gang of Four to the problems of privileges among the high party cadres. Deng spoke of the decisive importance of correcting cadres' work habits during the moment of transition in 1979:

The masses of people (including the party members and cadres) are dissatisfied with the widespread phenomenon of privilege seeking (including "back door" practices). Some people with ulterior motives have tried to exploit this to make trouble.[42] ... If leading cadres in the party do not set strict standards for themselves and observe party discipline and the laws of the state, how can they be expected to help reform standards of conduct at the societal level [*shehui fengqi*]?[43]

In addition, at the end of 1979, the Central Committee and the State Council promulgated "Several Regulations on the Material Benefits of Senior Cadres" in order to curtail privileges and abuses, such as excessive housing benefits and nepotism.[44] As Deng noted, these complaints were aired in big-character posters on "Democracy Wall."[45]

But from 1980 on, there was a phenomenal increase in corruption. This was associated with the legitimizing of pecuniary pursuit, the drastic delegation of power, the rapid expansion of the market economy, as well as slowness in the introduction of new legislation and regulatory mechanisms. Visible and continuous efforts were made to fight corruption, and alternative approaches (such as party disciplinary exercises, legal approaches, organizational rectification, financial inspections, and so on) had been tried up to the eve of the Tiananmen Square incident.

Another element of the discontent with official corruption and privileges was the broader issue of the shortcomings in the leadership and cadre system of the party-state. Deng considered these shortcomings to be "bureaucratism, overconcentration of power, paternalism, and the lifelong job tenure of the leading cadres."[46] Deng felt that such problems, if allowed to continue, would be equally alienating:

At present, there are still some cadres, who, regarding themselves as master rather than servants of the people, use their positions to seek personal privileges. This practice has aroused strong resentment among the masses and tarnished the party's credibility.[47]

The third major cleavage, in Deng's view, was the most dangerous to the regime, because the groups involved were the most articulate citizens in society. These groups included the nonpartisan dissidents. As Deng put it:

Nor can we take too lightly the so-called democrats and other persons with ulterior motives who flagrantly oppose the socialist system and

Communist leadership. Their position is clear. Although they sometimes claim to support the chairman and the party, they are essentially opposed to party leadership and socialism. In reality, these people think that capitalism is better than socialism and that Taiwan is better than the mainland.[48]

The third cleavage, in Deng's view, was associated with the tendency of "bourgeois liberalization" and deviated from the socialist orbit and the party's leadership. He explained that "its social and historical background can be traced mainly to the ten-year turmoil of the Cultural Revolution; it is also connected with corrosion by bourgeois ideology from abroad."[49] In fact, since 1979, Deng had been confronting an increasingly articulate sector of the population who, after serious reflection, could not be convinced that socialism was the right alternative for China's future and that the party's leadership was infallible.

From the early 1980s onward, Deng believed that "bourgeois liberalization" was due mainly to the inadequacy of ideological work. He attempted to reverse this situation, stating on at least two occasions that the party members should argue the case of socialism assertively, partly out of his conviction of the viability of socialism in the long run, and partly for the need to draw clearly the limit of the Chinese Communist Party's tolerance toward defiance. With reference to the student unrest at the end of 1986, Deng spoke of this conviction:

It is no simple thing to introduce reform and modernize our country.... I am convinced that our future accomplishment will be a further demonstration of the correctness of our present line, principles, and policies. Problems will be solved naturally. So long as we go on developing in the way we have during the last eight years, and try to overcome interference from any side, we can continue to grow and advance steadily and to raise the people's living standard.[50]

Deng believes that the students who took part in the 1986 turmoil should be educated as to what is at stake in terms of "what serves the fundamental interest of the country and what damages [it] ... By what is right and what is wrong, I mean, what helps us to achieve the basic socialist objectives we have set for the century and the next and what hinders us from doing so."[51]

In the same speech, he suggested that the party leaders should not be afraid of damaging their reputation abroad in order to take appropriate measures against it and to use the instrument of dictatorship when necessary. "If we take no action and back down, we shall only have more trouble down the road,"[52] he said.

> Dealing with the student disturbances is a serious matter. Leading cadres should take a clear-cut stand.... The fact that the leading cadres take an unequivocal stand encourages those who are firmly opposed to disturbances and helps persuade those who are undecided on the matter. Disturbances can be checked if the leaders take a strong stand.[53]

With hindsight, one should not be surprised at the top Chinese Communist Party leaders' response to the Tiananmen Square demonstrations, judging from what Deng had said about student unrest on previous occasions.

In recent years, the third cleavage became enlarged due to the increasing exposure of the younger generation of the intellectuals to the outside world. Because of Deng's "open door policy," they have come to expect not only Western living standards and lifestyles but also Western ideas and methods for handling the practical problems that confront the country. Although well-intended, the young intellectuals did not have a sense of selectivity and critical perspective when they first came into contact with Western ideas, cultures, practices, and institutions. Understandably, they would not be patient with the progress that China was making up to 4 June 1989. There is an ingredient of truth in Deng's comment on the open door policy, though it might not be shared by young intellectuals:

> It would be foolish to keep our doors closed and persist in the same old ways, if we want to learn from capitalist countries and take advantage of such advances in science, technology, management, and other areas as may be useful to us. But in learning things in the cultural realm, we must adopt a Marxist approach, analyzing them, distinguishing the good from the bad, and making a critical judgment about their ideological content and artistic form.[54]

There are good reasons for Deng to find that "this corruption of young people by the decadent bourgeois culture of the West is no longer tolerable,"[55] partly because of the competing political alternatives that the West could offer. University students felt that the country had been falling behind in the last several decades, and, after the introduction of the open door policy, the perceived inadequacy had grown as China was compared unfavorably with the West and the newly industrialized countries.

The root of the Tiananmen Square incident of 1989 is therefore cultural and ideological, for it is a symptom of the failure of the party-state to play its role of ideological renewal and to perform its "positive-educative" function, both of which are essential to the maintenance of its hegemony.

Conclusion

This essay has documented that over one decade, from 1979 to 1989, Deng Xiaoping was fully aware of the broad tendency of ideological and political disintegration of which the 1989 Tiananmen Square incident was one manifestation. This tendency includes an aggregate of social elements, among which the intellectuals were the most articulate sector. The incident concluded with the application of coercive instruments, demonstrating that it had lost its capacity to offer ideological renewal, which its performance gap as contrasted with other developed countries had made clear.

Deng does not differ from Mao substantially with reference to the importance of the ideological role of the party-state. Deng foresaw that failure on this account would invite unrest, turmoil, and disturbances, but he was not able to make positive contributions to deter adverse developments along this line. He repeatedly alerted his colleagues to the paralysis in the party's ideological work starting from 1979. In January 1987, when speaking of the need to uphold the Four Cardinal Principles, Deng stated:

> We must conduct education in these principles among our people. In the past few years we have witnessed the emergence of bourgeois liberalization, an ideological trend that has not been effectively countered. Although I have warned against this trend on many occasions, our party has failed to provide adequate leadership in combatting it. This is a major mistake made by Comrade Hu Yaobong.[56]

Deng Xiaoping has come very close to Gramsci's view that the modern state has an important function, that is, its positive-educative function "to raise the great mass of the population to a particular cultural and moral level, a level (or type) that corresponds to the needs of the productive forces for development and hence to the interest of the ruling class."[57] Failing in this, as suggested by Gramsci, the crisis of authority (or the crisis of legitimacy) will take place where the ruling elite will no longer be "leading" but "dominating," with the exercise of coercive force necessary to maintain the political regime. His observation, although generalized, is pertinent to the Tiananmen Square incident: "This means precisely that the great masses have become detached from their traditional ideologies, and no longer believe what they used to believe."[58]

Notes

1   The case can be interpreted from Neil J. Smelser's formulation of "strains" as well as "generalized beliefs" developed at the levels of facilities, roles, norms, and values (for example, the anxiety over China's material backwardness, incompetence, and abuse of officials, and perceived inadequacy of institutions and socialism as a guiding principle). See Neil J. Smelser, *Theory of Collective Behavior* (New York: Free Press, 1962). The incident can also be treated as an aggregate-psychological response to "relative deprivation" (or its subcategory, "aspirational deprivation") with reference to the enlarging distance of China from the advanced standards of the world. See Ted Robert Gurr, *Why Men Rebel* (Princeton: Princeton University Press, 1970).

2   Christine Buci-Glucksmann, *Gramsci and the State* (London: Lawrence and Wishart, 1980), pp. 91-93.

3   Originally in Antonio Gramsci's *Prison Notebooks,* as cited by Buci-Glucksmann 1980, p. 93.

4   Buci-Glucksmann, p. 91.

5   Ibid., p. 285.

6   Anne Showstack Sassoon, *Gramsci's Politics* (London: Croom Helm, 1980), p. 172.

7   Ibid., p. 157

8   Ken Jowitt, "Soviet Neotraditionalism: The Political Corruption of a Leninist Regime," *Soviet Studies* 25(3) (July 1983): 275-97.

9   Mao Zedong, "Dui Shanghai wenhua degeming de zhishi," in *Mao Zedong sixiang wansui* (n.p.: 1969), pp. 667-72.

10   Peter Nan-shong Lee, "The Chinese Industrial State in Historical Perspective: From Totalitarianism to Corporatism," a paper presented to the conference "Contemporary Chinese Politics in Historical Perspective," organized to celebrate Professor Tsou Tang's seventieth birthday and retirement on 17 December 1988. Pages 4-8

11   Deng Xiaoping, "Uphold The Four Cardinal Principles," in Deng Xiaoping, *Selected Works of Deng Xiaoping, 1975-1982* (Beijing: Foreign Language Press, 1984), pp. 166-91

12   Ibid., pp. 180-1.
13   Deng, "Emancipate the Mind, Seek Truth from Facts, and Unite as One in Looking to the Future," in Deng 1984, pp. 130-4.
14   Ibid., pp. 134-7.
15   Deng, "Uphold Four Cardinal Principles," in Deng 1984, pp. 161-2.
16   Ibid., p. 183.
17   Ibid., p. 178.
18   Chalmers Johnson, "The Two Chinese Revolutions," *The China Quarterly* 39 (July-September 1969): 12-29; Mao Tse-tung, "On New Democracy," in Mao Tse-tung, *Selected Works of Mao Tse-tung*, vol. 2 (Beijing: Foreign Language Press, 1967), pp. 339-430.
19   Tang Tsou, *The Cultural Revolution and Post-Mao Reforms: A Historical Perspective* (Chicago and London: The University of Chicago Press, 1987), pp. 259-334.
20   Tang Tsou, "Twentieth-Century Chinese Politics and Western Political Science," *PS* (or *APSA*) 2 (Spring 1987): 327-33.
21   Xing Hua, "Yijiubaling nian kaishi de caizheng tizhi zhongyao gaige" (The Major Reforms of the Financial System Beginning in 1980), parts 1 and 2, *Caizheng* (Finance) 12:8-10 and 1:13-5.
22   Kathleen Hartford, "Socialist Agriculture is Dead; Long Live Socialist Agriculture! Organizational Transformation in Rural China," in Elizabeth J. Perry and Christine Wong (eds.), *The Political Economy of Reform in Post-Mao China* (Cambridge, Mass. and London: The Council on East Asian Studies, 1985), pp. 32-61.
23   Peter Nan-shong Lee, *Industrial Management and Economic Reform in China, 1949-1984* (Hong Kong, London, and New York: Oxford University Press, 1987), pp. 170-211.
24   Amitai Etzioni. *A Comparative Analysis of Complex Organizations* (New York: The Free Press, 1961); George William Skinner and Edwin Winkler, "Compliance Succession in Rural Communist China, A Cyclical Theory," in Amitai Etzioni (ed.), *A Sociological Reader in Complex Organizations*, 2nd ed. (New York: Holt, Rinhart and Winston, 1969).
25   S. N. Eisentadt, ed., *Max Weber on Chrisma and Institution Building* (Chicago and London: The University of Chicago Press, 1968), pp. 11-17.
26   Quintin Hoare and Geoffery Nowell Smith, eds., *Selections from the Prison Notebooks of Antonio Gramsci* (New York: International Publishers, 1971), pp. 257-64.
27   Ibid., pp. 229-39.
28   Carol Lee Harmin and Timothy Cheek, *China's Establishment Intellectuals* (Armonk, New York and London: M. E. Sharpe, Inc., 1986), pp. 2-20.
29   Renford Rambrough, "Universals and Family Resemblances," in George Pitcher (ed.), *Wittgenstein: The Philosophical Investigations, A Collection of Critical Essays* (Garden City, New York: Anchor Books,

1966), pp. 168-204.
30 Harmin and Cheek 1986, pp. 13-7.
31 Ibid., pp. 124-54.
32 Deng 1984, pp. 161-5, 188-9.
33 Deng, "Remarks on Successive Drafts of the Resolution on Certain Questions in the History of Our Party Since the Founding of the People's Republic of China," in Deng 1984, p. 287.
34 Deng, "The Party's Urgent Task on the Organizational and Ideological Fronts," in Deng Xiaoping, *Deng Xiaoping Fundamental Issues in Present-Day China* (Beijing: Foreign Languages press, 1987), pp. 30-1.
35 Deng 1984, pp. 161-5.
36 Lee 1987, pp. 172-8.
37 Deng, "Concerning Problems on the Ideological Front," in Deng 1984, pp. 369-70.
38 Deng, "The Present Situation and Tasks," Deng 1984, pp. 237-42.
39 Ibid., pp. 238-9.
40 Ibid.
41 Deng 1987 , pp. 24-40; Deng, "Take A Clear-Cut Stand Against Bourgeois Liberalization," in Deng 1987, pp. 161-6; Deng. "Clear Away Obstacles and Adhere to the Policies of Reform and of Opening to the Outside World," in Deng 1987, pp. 161-70.
42 Deng, "Senior Cadres Should Take the Lead in Maintaining and Enriching the Party's Fine Traditions," in Deng 1987, p. 201.
43 Ibid., p. 210.
44 Ibid., p. 208.
45 Ibid., p. 209.
46 Deng, "On the Reform of the System of the Party and State Leadership," in Deng 1984, p. 309.
47 Ibid., p. 315.
48 Ibid., p. 237.
49 Ibid., p. 368.
50 Deng 1987, pp. 168-9.
51 Ibid., p. 169.
52 Ibid., p. 164.
53 Ibid., pp. 165-6.
54 Ibid., p. 34.
55 Ibid., p. 35.
56 Deng, "Promote Education in the Four Cardinal Principles and Adhere to the Policies of Reform and of Opening to the Outside World," in Deng 1987, p. 171.
57 Hoare and Smith, p. 258.
58 Ibid., pp. 275-6.

8

Conformity and Defiance on Tiananmen Square: A Social Psychological Perspective

Chung-fang Yang

[This chapter uses several Chinese terms, which have been integrated along with their definitions into the text. In addition, there is a glossary at the end of this essay for easy reference.]

Many observers who watched the student movement on Tiananmen Square unfold in the spring of 1989 were struck by two characteristics. One was the defiance exhibited by a massive number of presumably conforming citizens against their own autocratic government; the other was the order and solidarity manifested in the mass rallies and the self-sacrifice displayed by the people who participated in them.

The movement started out as a student protest triggered by the death of a popular leader, Hu Yaobang. As the movement continued, the students demanded freedom and democracy. The scene was not particularly unusual, as can be seen by recent events in several Eastern European countries. It became unusual, however, when millions of Beijing citizens united with the students to fight against their own government in a peaceful but emotional manner. This aspect of the movement was especially interesting to political scientists and social psychologists. What made ordinary citizens from a culture that emphasizes harmony and order, living in a country that is tightly controlled by its autocratic government, become defiant and confrontational? What made them convert their defiance into mass action?

Historically, the Chinese citizens have shown little interest in forming political or social organizations for a cause;[1] moreover, since the beginning of the People's Republic of China, no one has even been allowed to form an independent political organization. With most channels of communication controlled by the government, no experience in organizing and coordinating peaceful protests, and no formal civil or political organizations to lead the emotional crowds, the mass rallies conceivably could have become chaotic and violent. However, the rallies went smoothly, one after another, showing order and efficiency. How was this possible?

In this chapter, I plan to provide a social psychological explanation regarding the questions raised here. I shall analyze the demonstrations as a social psychological drama involving three major parties: the government, the students, and ordinary Beijing citizens. This drama evolved into a kind of competition in which the government and the students vied for the support of the citizens. The citizens sided with the students, escalating the drama into an all-out emotional act against the government.

My analysis is based on three indigenous Chinese concepts that denote emotions in regard to interpersonal relationships: *qing* (pronounced like ching), meaning human feeling among individuals; *fu* (foo), a sense of trust or dependence; and *xia* (shya), a sense of righteousness that motivates one to right a wrong. These three terms will be explained and analyzed at length in the first section of this essay.

I will then demonstrate how these emotional forces came into play at Tiananmen Square. I shall argue that the release and exchange of these emotions became the major thrust of the student movement and overwhelmed its significance as a political or social movement. The students' original demands for more freedom and democracy were largely forgotten, never to be converted into realistic terms that could be used in bargaining with the government. The emotional release continued until the government finally lost patience, resulting in regress, rather than progress, in the course of the country's democratic development.

There are two points put forth in this chapter that are the antithesis of prevalent Western belief. One is that, in a "societalistic" (often called collectivistic) culture like China's,[2] conformity or submission to authority is neither an inherited trait nor a personality characteristic of its people. Rather, gaining conformity requires that the authority earn legitimacy by fulfilling its obligations to the people, just as the authority in more individualistic cultures does. Exactly what is required of the authority to earn legitimacy, of course, may differ among cultures. In addition, the basis for defiance and revolt are the same, i.e., social injustice.[3] But here again, the exact conditions and manner in which the people rebel against a government may differ from culture to culture.

My second point is that, despite cultural values that de-emphasize and even discourage the outward display of emotion and in certain situations regard the non-display of emotions as a virtue,[4] the real motivating force for Chinese behavior is still based on emotion. However, the cognitive reasonings and appraisals that cause various emotional states and the conditions under which they are expressed are quite different from what is expected in the West. This makes the study of emotions in Chinese culture, using an actual event like the 1989 prodemocracy movement, important not only to the understanding of its people and their behavior, but to that of human emotions in general.

Qing, Fu, and Xia in Chinese Culture

The Concept of Qing

Lin Yutang has defined the Chinese concept *qing* as "sentiment, passion, love, sympathy, friendly feeling." He has further elaborated on the concept by referring specifically to a basic human emotion, *renqing*, as follows:

> To be able to understand people or the human heart is "to know *renqing* or human sentiments." Any man who is inhuman, who is over-austere, or who is an ascetic is said to be *bujin renqing*, or "to have departed from human nature or human sentiments." Any philosophy which has departed from human sentiments is a false philosophy, and any political regime that goes against one's natural human instincts, religious, sexual, or social, is doomed to fall.... A man who is cold or hard-hearted or disloyal is said to be *wuqing*, or "to have no heart."[5]

Within this general concept of emotion among human beings, Hsien Chin Hu distinguished two specific kinds: the real and the assumed.[6]

The former denotes a spontaneous and genuine feeling toward a particular person; the latter denotes a prescribed or obligatory emotion toward another human being, as required by social norms.

Francis K.L. Hsu has illustrated the same concept, using "eros" to denote real emotion and "affect" to denote assumed emotion. He elaborated on the relationship between them as follows:

> Eros can combine with affect in whole (rare for men, more common for women) or in part; eros and affect can be irrelevant to each other; or affect (a particular kind) can reign so supreme that it eliminates everything else, including eros. But there is no need to deny the existence of eros to mobilize affect.[7]

This notion of real and assumed emotion is surprisingly consistent with Confucian ideology, the blueprint for Chinese society. An overview of this ideology suggests how it developed and flourished.

The central concept of Confucianism is to maintain harmony in society through moral conduct in all social relationships.[8] To this end, Confucius conceived of a hierarchical structure that used role relationships as the framework for society. He prescribed specific kinds of behavior, embedded in a code of conduct called *li* that were to be applied in the various kinds of human dyadic relationships designated in his framework. His five cardinal relationships, and their corresponding prescribed behaviors, are: righteousness between emperor and subject; affection between parent and child; order between brother and brother; duty between husband and wife; and loyalty between friend and friend.[9]

In the ideal Confucian world, the prescribed behavior, as encompassed in *li*, would always be performed with real emotion. There would be no distinction between real and assumed emotion; in effect, there would be no assumed emotion at all. According to Donald J. Munro, "It is desirable that there be a correspondence between the knowledge of certain duties and certain feelings. A knowledge of filial duties should be accompanied by filial feelings; a knowledge of public duties by humane feelings."[10] In addition, the performance of the prescribed behavior can be taken as an indication that the genuine emotion exists.

In actuality, however, the Chinese sometimes perform the prescribed behavior in ritualistic fashion without evoking genuine feelings. An assumed emotion is applied on these occasions.

Confucius himself stated that he abhorred the type of person who practiced *li* without the real accompanying emotions. This indicates that, in his time, there were people who performed prescribed behavior without attaching genuine feelings to them.

It seems inevitable that the Confucian emphasis on the prescribed behavior, as opposed to behavior based on genuine emotions, would give rise to a separation of real and assumed emotions. Both Lin Yutang and Francis Hsu attributed it to the escalation of another important concept valued in Chinese society, i.e., the concept of *pao*, the norm of reciprocity.[11] Hsu states:

> The network of *pao* or reciprocity can extend itself widely over large territories and sizable populations as well as between societies. But it tends to become more and more a matter of pure business exchange without sentiment. The central focus will be the correct thing to do, since *pao* is socially required and its standard is culturally determined. It is inevitable that, in time, the correct thing to do tends to substitute for true sentiment on the part of the individual.[12]

Hsu further states that this obligatory reciprocity often compels one to take the assumed feelings over real feelings: "Where there was a conflict, eros [real emotion] must be sacrificed in favor of affect [assumed emotion] within the primary kinship grouping."[13]

With these two levels of emotion (*qing*) operating in interpersonal interactions among the Chinese, people usually treat others with real emotion, or real *qing*, when they think others treat them with real *qing*; they treat others with assumed *qing* when they think others treat them with assumed *qing*. Both levels of *qing* flow parallel to each other, each serving its function.[14] The assumed *qing* keeps society running harmoniously; people engaging in such interactions do not expect real emotions from each other. Social interaction involving real emotion serves the individual's needs for love, safety, and security. This type of real emotion at first is shared only among family members, and they can gradually operate under other types of dyadic relations as well.[15]

Although Chinese culture emphasizes the importance of attaching real emotions to prescribed behaviors, the priority is on performing the prescribed behavior. The assumed emotions therefore take precedence over the personal needs for real emotional comfort. Real emotions are not denied, as Hsu states, but their expression is not supposed to interfere with that of the assumed emotions.

The assumed emotion hence becomes what the Chinese culture requires as a minimum in a social situation to keep interpersonal interactions running smoothly; it is the baseline for a human being living in society.

Assumed Qing Between the Ruler and the Ruled

In the Chinese political arena, the Confucian theory of "government by goodness" was the dominant ideology that prescribed the relationship between the ruler and the ruled.

This political philosophy has not changed very much; neither has the prescribed relationship.[16] The theory still prevails under the Communist government.[17] According to the traditional political philosophy, the ruler, represented by the emperor, is to love his subjects like his own sons, in exchange for their genuine affection and loyalty.

Of course, this was too idealistic in that it unrealistically demanded that the ruler invest real emotion in his interactions with his subjects. The all-embracing power bestowed on the ruler by the Chinese political structure often obscured the fact that the ruler depended on his subjects while the subjects did not expect real emotions to come from their ruler. In reality, both sides seemed happy if the assumed emotions (assumed qing) were operating. The ruler needed to show at least this in order to gain assumed loyalty from his subjects. The ruler was supposed to appreciate the interdependent nature of the relationship between himself and his subjects, as represented in Xunzi's observation that "subjects are like water in a river; it can float a boat but it can also sink a boat."

If this bottom-line obligation was not fulfilled by the emperor, he was considered to be without the appropriate feeling or wuqing. Hence, his subordinates would feel no obligation to show their assumed qing in return. With righteousness on their side, they had the right to overthrow the ruler and seek someone who would follow the prescribed behavior of a ruler. This tense relationship between the ruler and the ruled prompted Hsu to say that "the relationship between Chinese emperors and their subjects was always a negative one."[18]

The present-day relationship between the government and its people is not much different from the traditional one. Chinese subordinates are still trained and encouraged to follow prescribed behavior; i.e., to conform to the orders of the authority and to show the assumed emotion (assumed *qing*) to the authority. And it is required that the authority show at least a minimum of concern for its people.

The Concept of Fu

Fu as a noun denotes "a body posture of kneeling or lying with the face down close to the ground," a posture of surrender or submission. As a verb, it means "to reign over someone or something"; as an adjective, "a state of adhering or clinging flat to someone or something." The character often combines with other characters to form words with similar meanings, such as *fuwu*, to serve or to do one's duty, and *fucong*, the act of conformity, or to obey.

As an adjective referring to emotion, *fu* often refers to a feeling of trust and dependence one has for another person such that he is willing to follow the orders or steps of that person.[19] The other person can be an equal or a person with a higher or sometimes (but rarely) lower position or status. The other person can also be an abstract entity, like the ruler, the government, or a particular organization.

As with other emotional states, there is both real and assumed *fu*. When one is responding to a person in a higher position, i.e., an authority figure, the conforming behavior is sometimes accompanied by a genuine feeling of trust, or *xinfu*, which literally means *fu* "from the heart." There also can be conformity with no such real emotion, called *koufu*, a *fu* "from the mouth," or lip service. This is demonstrated by making no protest to the authority, but doing little to heed its orders.

The real emotion of trust and dependence toward another person is derived first from a recognition of this person's ability or competence. In performing a group task together, one who has a trusting feeling toward another person believes that this person's leadership ability will lead to accomplishing the task faster and easier.

While competence is necessary, however, it is not sufficient for a real feeling of trust and dependence to occur in a situation involving two people or more working together toward a common goal. To evoke a real emotion of trust (*xinfu*), it is required that one perceives the other as someone who will work toward the goal for the group's benefit and will not use the power to work only for his own interest. One must also perceive that the person is willing to sacrifice his personal interest for the group interest, if necessary.

Group members do not necessarily think that submission to another person's orders is in any way a sign of inferiority. Instead, they take the view that, if someone is a more competent leader and if following his orders can bring the group to the goal faster and more efficiently than working individually or as a leaderless collective, then they are willing to follow his orders. Meanwhile, they feel that they contribute as much as the leader because they have forfeited their autonomy (a self-sacrifice) for the sake of the group. This general belief—that a group needs a leader but that the group must listen only to one toward whom it has a feeling of trust—leads Lucian W. Pye to the conclusion that the Chinese value and are thus dependent on authority without being authoritarian.[20]

Fu Between the Ruler and the Ruled

Throughout the history of Chinese politics, the authority of a government or the ruler was always established by force. Conformity from subordinates was always achieved by coercion, or *qufu*. The heart-felt trust (*xinfu*) always came later, if it came at all, after the authority had convinced its subordinates that it could improve the lives of the people, that it had the interests of the country at heart, and that it placed the country and its people's interests ahead of its own.

Chinese history further tells us that the genuine emotions carefully and painfully cultivated at the beginning of a dynasty often diminished gradually toward the end of the dynasty when a weak ruler could not control his selfish and corrupt officials. Inefficiency and corruption led to the deterioration of people's lives and resulted in revolt and a new dynasty.

Francis Hsu points out that one of the reasons for this recurring result in one dynasty after another was the distant relationship between the Chinese ruler and his subjects. The distance let the ruler and his officials operate unchecked as long as they let the subjects run their lives without too much control and taxes; this distance also enabled the regime to avoid having to crush oppression. Hsu proposes that the distance allowed the ruler to be autocratic but never totalitarian.[21]

This illustrates that the relationship between the rule and the ruled in Chinese society was—and still is—often casual and remote. Both sides are content with maintaining a relationship based on assumed emotion (assumed *qing*). As long as the ruler maintains the assumed emotion toward his subjects by attempting to make his subjects' lives stable and prosperous, the ruled often are indifferent about who is ruler and happy to show at least assumed conformity (assumed *fu*) to whomever it is.

Genuine conformity to one's orders, that is, obedience and real emotion, is not something that the ruler can win by simply climbing to the position of ruler. It can be earned only through showing real emotion (*qing*) to the people. In this sense, H.G. Creel was quite correct when he stated that genuine conformity is harder to achieve in a conformist society like China's than it is in an individualistic society like that of the United States because it requires the ruler to invest private and genuine emotions.[22]

Sometimes, however, a mistrustful feeling, or *bufu*, arises when the ruler cannot provide a decent livelihood for his subjects. This negative emotion crystallizes when it is perceived that the authority is working for its own interests and that it is unwilling to give up its interests for those of the people.

In most situations, the mistrustful sentiment is suppressed, or expressed only in idle gossip, but one can do several things to openly display *bufu*. When the authority is watching, one can obey orders with no enthusiasm; when the authority is not watching, one can do nothing at all; or, one can do just the opposite of what is demanded in an effort to undermine the command. The Chinese often refer to these tactics as passive resistance or rebellion.[23]

When people's mistrust has been aroused but is not dealt with properly or at all, the intensity and the spread of this feeling can result in violent revolt. Inarticulate and inexperienced in political action, the people resort to violence to release their mistrust when it has reached the point of being intolerable, or *ren wu ke ren*. Chaos and further suffering follow. This leads Francis Hsu to say that in China there was only revolt but no revolution before 1912.[24]

Fu and Bufu in the People's Republic of China

By the eve of the 1989 student demonstrations, the government was no longer enjoying the real trust that the people had bestowed on it in the early 1950s. After the founding of the People's Republic of China in 1949, the people gave their trust to the government because its policies brought stability and prosperity, which in turn greatly improved the livelihood of the oppressed and poverty-stricken masses. That feeling of trust diminished in the late 1950s when the government made a series of serious policy errors and organized several unpopular mass campaigns to enforce them. The campaigns brought the people to the verge of starvation, causing the popularity and the prestige of the government to slip.

The government attempted to recapture the real emotional support of the people by using a variety of appeals. First, it resorted to the traditional and familiar concept of reciprocity (*pao*). It came up with a campaign called *yiku sitian* (enjoying the sweet present while remembering the bitter past) that reminded the people of the party's good deeds in bringing them out from under poverty and misery. In return for this peace and prosperity, the people were urged to collaborate with the government to fight the adversity of bad times.

A second campaign tried to elicit feelings of nationalism and patriotism. The themes in the campaigns to "support Vietnam, oppose U.S. imperialism" and "learn from Lei Feng" reminded the people that they needed to be unselfish for the national cause and should commit themselves to self-sacrifice for the sake of the country.

During the Cultural Revolution, the feeling of trust was channeled to the establishment of a cult for the worship of one person, Mao Zedong. Mao granted auditions and meetings to the people, demonstrating that he was a leader who not only could bring the country to the right path, but who loved the people and followed their demands. The feelings of genuine trust and dependence (*fu*) established toward Mao swept the country; his commands, whatever they were, were carried out enthusiastically.

But Deng Xiaoping's open door policy, adopted since the purge of the Gang of Four, had a detrimental impact on the feeling of trust. For the first time since 1949, people had a glimpse of life in Western countries, and, to their surprise, they found that people living in these countries fared much better than they did. This was quite a shock to people who had been told since they were young that they were the saviors of this two-thirds of mankind, which had been said to be suffering "in deep waters and hot fires." The feeling of trust toward the government slipped even lower.

The widespread corruption of government officials in the 1980s not only exacerbated the downfall of *fu*, it gave rise to a genuine feeling of mistrust (*bufu*) toward the government. The people were able to tolerate policy errors and political misdemeanors, but they had little patience with corrupt officials who looked out only for their own interests at the expense of the country. The fact that the government could not stop the corruption despite many highly publicized attempts indicated that it was not working with the people for the prosperity of the country. The people would not have minded living in adverse conditions as long as the government was in the same boat. When they found that this clearly was not the case, the positive feelings toward the government evaporated and the feeling of *bufu* began to grow.

The Concept of Xia

The feeling of *xia* carries a connotation of altruism and chivalry and compels a person to right a wrong, regardless of the adverse consequences that may result from this action. Xia is a prompter for moral action. When one has a feeling of *xia*, one does not hesitate to act out of this feeling of injustice. It compels a person to take an unjust matter originally not involving him as his own; therefore, he expects no reward from the party he is helping. Moreover, he feels that it is his own moral responsibility to correct the wrong with full force.

When *xia* is used as a noun, it denotes a class of people in ancient China during the Warring States Period (475-222 B.C.) called the knights-errant (*youxia*). They were professional fighters who travelled about offering their services to feudal lords. Fung Yulan quotes a passage in *Shiji* (Historical Memoirs by Sima Qian) that describes the knights-errant:

> Their words were always sincere and trustworthy, and their actions quick and decisive. They are always true to what they have promised. Without regard to their own persons, they will rush into dangers that threaten others.[25]

Lien-sheng Yang states that, even though the knights-errant were curtailed after China became a unified empire under the Qin and Han dynasties (221 B.C.-A.D. 220), they persisted and

> were known for their absolute reliability, pugnaciousness, and transgression of prohibitions.... The chivalrous spirit of the ancient knights-errant ... did not die. The celebrated models recorded in the Historical Memoirs never failed to inspire later generations.[26]

Although this *xia* feeling is a celebrated part of Chinese culture, it is not readily taken on by Chinese people. Most people who witness unjust behavior do not take any action; they just suffer through it or ignore it. Certain conditions have to be met for their tolerance to be transformed into action. The unjust behavior must be used by someone strong and powerful against someone weak and powerless; and the transgressor must repeat his unjust behavior, raising the sense of injustice to the point of becoming intolerable (*ren wu ke ren*).

While Chinese themselves do not frequently act out of a feeling of *xia*, they have always placed this feeling and those who act out of it in high esteem. In present-day Taiwan, Hong Kong, and the People's Republic of China, stories and movies about the knights-errant inciting the feeling of *xia* are very popular and always bring cheers from adults and youngsters alike.

These knights-errant fascinate the Chinese for several reasons. Their absolute reliability and high ethical standards in troubled times are especially admired. Their ability to generalize their concern to total strangers and to empathize with these people makes them appear to be on a higher moral plane that most people, who care about only those close to them.[27]

In addition, they are admired for their ability to act out their feelings. Most Chinese people, being generally more inclined to "take the middle way," tend to be restrained when it comes to acting out their feelings. Therefore, the feeling of catharsis, *tongkuai* or "the pleasure of releasing one's emotion" is always elicited when people see the knights-errant behave out of a feeling of *xia*.

Injustice Involving the Ruler

A central feature of the Chinese concept of social justice is *zhengming*, the "rectification of names," which means that the "name" must correspond to the "actual." Zhengming requires the ruler to act with righteousness toward his subjects, as dictated by Confucius's five cardinal principles. If the ruler—the name—is to live up to being a "true" ruler—the actual—he must be benevolent and righteous; he must set a living example for his subordinates to follow. His government must be a government of virtue. The state must not only be merely a formal organization of political, economic, and military activities, but also a community in which moral ideals may be realized by way of these organized activities.[28]

Additionally, the ruler has the responsibility of seeing that his subjects are able to fulfill their proper roles in society. As stated by

Fung in this description of the Confucian diagnosis and prescription of a state in turmoil:

> It was Confucius's belief that the degeneration of political and social states originates from the top....Confucius believed that under these circumstances the only way to restore order would be to arrange affairs so that the emperor would continue to be emperor, the nobles to be nobles, the ministers to be ministers, the common people to be common people.[29]

With the state having these responsibilities in society, the Chinese people consider one of its obligations to be a willingness to hear them out. The government should listen to their grievances and their appeals; otherwise, they have the right of rebellion. Munro states that "the ruler had his proper function, so that his doing otherwise absolved his subordinates from their normal duty to obey him."[30]

When the government is seen as not fulfilling its obligation to listen to the people, this is not just seen as mere insensitivity, it is seen as an injustice. When people are being victimized by the government, the sense of injustice becomes even stronger, even among people who are not directly involved.

When this sense of injustice has been prolonged for a long period of time and has become widespread among the people, it can prompt individual and mass action to right the wrong. The *xia* feeling is elicited among people who feel it is their moral obligation to take action against the government. Historically speaking, this type of *xia* action, individual or mass, often leads to violent and destructive results.

Qing, Fu, and Xia at Tiananmen Square

The Citizens as Observers, 15-26 April
During the period between the death of Hu Yaobang on 15 April and the appearance of the editorial in the *People's Daily* on 26 April, the citizens participated in the demonstrations only as bystanders. They were generally sympathetic with the students because, as stated earlier, sentiment was quite antigovernment at the time.[31] It did not come as a surprise to them that students would use the death of a beloved political figure, Hu Yaobang, as an occasion to express negative feelings against the government. Under ordinary conditions, these feelings would have been kept private or discussed only among

acquaintances, but the demonstrations following the death of Zhou Enlai in 1976 had set a precedent. The success of overturning the Gang of Four following that protest rally raised the hope that a protest this time might bring similar results.

Many students wrote emotional and insinuating poems saying that the "wrong person" had died. Hu was remembered as someone who had had the respect of intellectuals and was instrumental in improving the life of academics. Hu had been unfairly sacked and the students regretted not having protested stronger when he was removed from his post, and they grieved over his premature death. A long banner hung over the Tomb of the Unknown Heroes on 17 April, and it brought the emotions of grief over Hu and dissatisfaction with the government to a climax.

During this period, the citizens witnessed several events that crystallized their mistrustful attitude (*bufu*) toward the government, turning them into sympathizers of the students. The government forbade the students to participate in the farewell ceremony set for Hu on 22 April, a move that was perceived by the citizens as being inhumane (*wuqing*). It was only natural to allow people to attend funeral rites to show their respect for someone who has died, let alone someone they loved and respected. The citizens realized that the government did not have the "heart" to grant even this small expression of human compassion (*renqing*) to its people.

Likewise, the seven-point petition made to the Standing Committee of the National People's Congress was considered reasonable by most of the citizens (see chapter 1). Even though the citizens might not have thought the student protest would produce any concrete results, the fact that the requests fell on deaf ears[32] indicated to the citizens that the government was not fulfilling its duties, i.e., to show concern for the people. It had not performed even the assumed emotion, let alone the real emotion.

On 20 April, a clash broke out between the police and students, who were demanding to see Premier Li Peng in front of Xinhuamen. Some students and Hong Kong reporters were beaten. The students for the first time were seen as victims of police brutality.

The most crucial drama during this "bystanders period" was when three students kneeled in front of the Great Hall of the People on 22 April, pleading for a meeting with Li Peng or any of the government dignitaries attending Hu's funeral inside. The students got no response and broke into tears with disappointment.

The event had a great emotional impact on the citizens. The citizens, who still considered the students "children" and believed that one should not be too harsh with them, perceived the government's unresponsiveness as extremely cruel, especially after the students humbled themselves to the point of acting like subjects in Imperial China. Many citizens cried with the students.

The students' decision to boycott classes on 23 April and the establishment of the Temporary Beijing Student Association on 25 April were unwelcome from the citizens' point of view. They viewed them with apprehension; the memories of the chaos of the Cultural Revolution were still fresh in their minds.

However, the editorial in the *People's Daily* on 26 April erased any doubts the citizens had. The editorial confirmed the students' predictions about what would be done to them. The government, in its effort to pacify the students, had repeatedly stated that the students' protests and requests came from their patriotic desires and thus would not be labeled as "turmoil." The last assurance had been given only hours before the editorial appeared. But the editorial verified that the students were right in their assertions that the government would resort to the same old tricks to suppress differences of opinion and expressions of discontent.

Furthermore, it aroused moral outrage among the students and the citizens that the government had not kept the promises it had made in public. The breach of promise was perceived once more as evidence that the government could not be trusted. As a result, the citizens' generally passive feelings of discontent and dissatisfaction with the government were transformed into an active mistrust (*bufu*) that now intensified.

The Citizens Become Supporters, 27 April-19 May

Disregarding warnings issued by the government not to participate, 1 million citizens took to the streets on 27 April to support a peaceful protest attended by over one hundred thousand students from forty or more universities. This rally signified that the citizens had taken the students' side in demanding government action. However, even though they were more active in their support, they still did not participate directly in the antigovernment actions. They limited themselves to donating money and food and to voicing their feelings openly. It was not until the declaration of martial law on 19 May that the citizens became full participants in the movement.

The period from 27 April to 19 May can be considered a period in which the students actively attempted to consolidate the support they had already gained from the citizens in the previous period in an attempt to force the government to deal with their demands. The students shifted their attitude from pleading and compromise to defiance and confrontation, demanding an immediate retraction of the 26 April editorial. They knew that if their rallies were classified officially as "turmoil," severe punishment and retaliation would follow.

The students wanted to convert popular support into power to use in a showdown with the government. They wanted to tell the government that it no longer had the support of the people and that therefore it had better take a negotiating attitude toward the students. At this stage, the students had very little to lose by taking a tough stand. Even if the government refused the students' demands, they would have succeeded in making the government appear powerful but heartless to the citizens.

Two emotional responses developed during this period that indeed made the students the winners. With the exchanges between the students and the government taking place right in front of their eyes, the citizens gradually developed a feeling of trust and confidence (*fu*) toward the students. They believed that the latter's desire for a dialogue with the government was sincere and well-intended, and saw that the students were willing to sacrifice themselves for the sake of the country. Meanwhile, a strong sense of injustice that had to be righted (*xia*) evolved when the citizens saw the government employing schemes to forestall the students' requests and to portray them as being manipulated by conspirators to launch a counter-revolution.

The development of these emotional responses coalesced around the ill-fated attempts to begin substantive dialogues. To quell the public outrage caused by the 26 April editorial, and to forestall the student rally celebrating the May Fourth Movement, the government arranged a meeting between forty-five students from sixteen schools and the State Council spokesman Yuan Mu on 29 April. However, the majority of students chosen to attend this meeting were representatives of officially approved student organizations, which were suspected of spying for the government. The students on the Square were outraged, further deepening the rift with the government.

To the citizens, the Yuan Mu meeting made the government look manipulative and insincere in dealing with the students and in trying to solve the nation's pressing problems. The students were beginning to be perceived as righteous underdogs, victimized by a powerful and inhumane government.

On 2 May, the vice-chairman of the National Commission for Education, He Dongchang, refused to recognize the Beijing College Students' Autonomous Union as a legitimate student body and declined to talk with representatives from that organization. Meetings with other government officials brought no progress, mainly for similar reasons.[33] Neither side had gotten to substantive issues; both had gotten caught up in formalities and procedures.

The frustration derived from these meetings triggered another round of pleas for dialogue on 2 May. The students upped their demands, setting twelve preconditions this time, and pressed the government to give a reply within two days or a demonstration would follow. (A celebration commemorating the seventieth anniversary of the May Fourth Movement was already planned.) At this juncture, a violent confrontation erupted, resulting in the police using force to drive the students away. Many students were brutally beaten, but the government accused the students of inciting the incident. The beating again made the government the transgressor and the students the victims. The government then rejected the students' "plea for dialogue" and singled out, for the first time, Professor Fang Lizhi as one of the culprits behind the student demonstrations.

As a result, five hundred thousand citizens joined the rally for the May Fourth Movement. May Fourth symbolized the participation of Chinese students and intellectuals in modern patriotic movements seeking political modernization; for the students, it was a day to commemorate the historic event and consolidate their own sense of responsibility to the country.

Many intellectuals, some of them working for government agencies and research institutes, and the tightly controlled news organizations joined the rally, resonating the patriotic mood of the original May Fourth Movement and protesting the way the students were being treated by the government. Citizens joined in as well because they were moved by the students' determined efforts to fight the government and their strong desire to transform China into a prosperous and modernized nation. The citizens considered the students to be a group that really cared about the country and was sincerely willing to work with the government.

In the early weeks of this period, only one dialogue was granted—but it was not for students. On 12 May, some newsmen and writers were granted a dialogue, and they were joined by students and celebrity intellectuals pleading for freedom of the press. No dialogue, however, was granted to students.

With the government being seen as increasingly intransigent, even the students' growing defiance did not bother the citizens, who instead were impressed by the students' willingness to sacrifice themselves. Just before the Beijing Normal University students prepared to march from their campus, student leader Wu'er Kaixi read a will to his mother expressing his determination to die for democracy and freedom. This "letter to mother" format was later used by both students and government workers.[34] To the citizens who had been all along treating the students as "children," these dramatic letters were very effective in winning their heart-felt support. It struck an emotional chord for every Chinese. The wills indicated that their determination to die was sincere, their self-sacrifice genuine and noble.

Frustrated by the government's refusal to talk with the student delegation, the students started a hunger strike on 13 May. The strike idea was suggested by some Hong Kong students who had gone to Beijing to support the Beijing College Students' Autonomous Union. The original plan was to have it for twenty-four hours, as often was the case of hunger strikes in the Western countries, where it was meant to make a point, not a threat.

The action and its effect, however, took an unusual turn at the Square.[35] The hunger strikers did not stop after their symbolic and strategic point had been made, presumably to emphasize the government's unwillingness to negotiate. Rather, the students decided to die if their request was not granted. They wanted to make the point that they would not tolerate the government's labelling them as unpatriotic creators of turmoil.

In the long run, this tactic would be seen as counterproductive. However, the students were overcome by anger and frustration; they wanted to use self-sacrifice as a final protest against the government, to cause the government to lose face in front of the people.[36]

The fact that the students were willing to sacrifice their lives for their cause, however, manifested to most Chinese that they possessed genuine concern (real *qing*) for their country and were sincere in what they were doing. Tens of thousands of citizens went to the Square to support the striking students.

The government, meanwhile, was unsuccessful in its attempts to convince the citizens otherwise. It used the news media to blacken the image of the student movement, the most dramatic example occurring when leaders of the Beijing College Students' Autonomous Union were filmed eating at a restaurant, the subsequent broadcast intimating that they were violating their own hunger strike.[37] This effort got just the opposite result. From then on, the government was viewed as devious and as for using its powerful security machinery to spy on the students.

The withdrawal of traffic and security police on 17 May was an attempt to define the student demonstrations as a disruptive force. It did indeed produce chaos for awhile, but order was soon restored when the students took on the policemen's responsibility.

During this period, many citizens went to the Square to visit and to give support to the students. What they saw moved them greatly: hungry and exhausted students tortured by the blazing sun during the day and by the cold wind at night. Many students could have suffered irreversible damage to their health, or died. Citizens were moved to tears, blaming the government for the students' suffering. This was another stage in the development of a *xia* feeling. A weakened party was being victimized by the authorities, a wrong that should be righted.

The *xia* feeling was reinforced in other ways. On 15 May, the students reduced their demands for ending the strike to two: a dialogue between equals and negotiations on the 26 April editorial. The demands were not granted. Meanwhile, rumors spread that at any minute the government was going to take over the Square by force. Fear and anxiety were heightened by the sound of sirens as ambulances delivered failing students to the hospital. This had a great impact on the onlooking citizens, who thought the government had been inhumane and unrighteous (*buren buyi*) in allowing the students to suffer when it was within its power to change the situation.

On the fifth day of the strike, a million citizens, including people from all walks of life, attended a mass rally supporting the students.

The unyielding attitude adopted by the government illustrated to the citizens that it had neither compassion nor a sense of justice (*wuqing wuyi*). It had not even demonstrated the assumed emotion it was supposed to have, nor had it shown the minimum human emotion basic to any interpersonal relationship. Antigovernment slogans were common in this rally, a clear sign that a feeling of injustice had been transformed into a feeling of righteousness (*xia*).

The nationally televised dialogue granted by Li Peng on 18 May (see chapter 2) only further justified feelings of mistrust toward the government. The students, who already had won the hearts of the citizens, now confronted Li with a strong negative attitude; Li's arrogant, recalcitrant, and unsmiling face further exacerbated the situation. Though nobody expected Li to say or do any better than he did, the event only emphasized the sentiment that the government was neither trustworthy nor righteous.

The appearance of Zhao Ziyang on Tiananmen Square in the early hours of 19 May offered too little too late. He could do no more than offer an oral guarantee that the students would not be punished; yet, in a televised talk with Gorbachev, he had hinted that he was not the person who could change the 26 April editorial, saying that all major decisions were referred to Deng. The students knew this. However, Zhao's tears and apologetic statements were perceived as genuine emotion (real *qing*) toward the people; he immediately received genuine emotion in return. He was heartily applauded after his informal talk. From then on, he was singled out from the larger entity, the government, and was treated as a compassionate person.

A few hours later, when Li Peng announced martial law, twenty thousand students joined in the hunger strike. Many bottles, signifying Deng Xiaoping ("xiaoping" is pronounced the same as "little bottle") were thrown out of the windows of student dormitories; it was a Chinese way of expressing emotion and resentment both indirectly and symbolically.[38]

At this point, the citizens could no longer be just spectators or supporters; they had to act against this extreme instance of injustice. Li Peng's announcement finally crystallized the righteous feeling (*xia*) among them because the wrongs of the government against the students had gone beyond what the citizens could accept as spectators or sympathizers. They had become self-involved, and considered the matter their own, requiring action to right the wrong.

The students had won the full-hearted support of the citizens, gaining their trust and dependence (*fu*). Moreover, the students had led the people in expressing their antigovernment feelings. The hunger strike had pushed the drama of an unsympathetic and unrighteous government mistreating its people to a climax. The feeling that this situation could no longer by tolerated was converted from a sense of injustice to a feeling of *xia*. The citizens were ready to take the role of the knights-errant and to act out their feelings toward the transgressor.

Citizens as Knights-Errant, 20 May–4 June

After the announcement by Li Peng, the students stopped the hunger strike but refused to leave the Square. At the beginning of this period, more than two hundred thousand students stationed were at the Square, and most of them had come from other provinces just to support the movement. Guarding the Square and stopping the army from reaching the Square became the dominant goal of the students. They were prepared to pay any price to achieve this common goal.

The citizens joined the students and they became one group. One million people participated in a rally on 23 May demanding the impeachment of Li Peng and the lifting of martial law. The students from the outside provinces and the citizens from all walks of life added many new faces to the Square, making the task of keeping order very difficult. Many soldiers and plainclothes policemen infiltrated the crowd. Disputes, confusion, and accidents occurred, and the sanitary conditions on the Square deteriorated to the point of endangering the lives of the students.

But the citizens, fulfilling the role of knights-errant, took up the responsibility of protecting the students and restoring order. They formed watch groups to help maintain peace and order. They organized "dare-to-die" brigades to protect the students from being hurt by the army or the police. They were willing to die to protect the students, feeling that the students could do more for the common good than they could.

The citizens trusted and depended on the students, obeying their orders. With genuine emotion toward the students running high, the students were allowed to fill the gap left by the absence of police and other authorities. Showing a student identification card allowed a student to stop a fight, settle a dispute, direct traffic, and recruit manpower.

The most notable efforts of the citizens in their capacity as knights-errant occurred when they went to the suburbs around Beijing and tried to persuade the army not to go to the Square. They used genuine emotion (real *fu*) to appeal to the soldiers, not only forming a human wall around them but also delivering food and water to them. They tried to convince the soldiers that the army and the people are united and that "the army loves the people; the people love the army." They resorted to moral arguments to persuade the soldiers, saying that they should not kill the people they were supposed to protect and that armed soldiers do not kill unarmed people.

The sharing of emotions was immense among the crowd. The feeling of being able to convert their genuine emotions into actions was a cathartic "letting out of pent up emotions" (*tongkuai*). This was not an experience that the Chinese people experience very often, especially concerning politics.

This feeling of release was also elicited by the fact that their behavior was no longer bound by a set of rules they had been taught and persuaded to follow all their lives. They became defiant, ignoring martial law conditions and doing what they thought was right. These actions also set the students free from the frustrations that had accumulated since the movement started. It set the citizens free from the sense of frustration of not being able to do anything to improve their condition.

The release of emotions reinforced more defiant actions, and more defiant actions brought more relaxation of tension. One result of this was the unexpected appearance of literary and musical activity. Moving poems, essays, and songs were written and performed on the Square, creating an almost festive atmosphere. The students and citizens also displayed their sense of humor, rarely seen under ordinary circumstances. In one instance, they organized a masked parade mimicking some of the antiturmoil rallies orchestrated by the government to counteract the student demonstrations.

The strong sense of sharing of emotions also included the sharing of a romantic optimism. The euphoric mood permeating the air of the city made the citizens feel they could stop the army simply because justice was on their side. Feeling the responsibility of a million people's lives on their shoulders, the students were calmer and worked out an evacuation plan. They anticipated that they would be driven from the Square; they never expected that the People's Liberation Army would fire real bullets at their own totally unarmed people.

Conclusion

The prodemocracy movement of 1989 started with the students openly challenging the authorities' orders forbidding them to attend former Party Secretary Hu Yaobang's funeral ceremony. The act annoyed the government, putting it into a confrontational mode with the students. This poisoned the atmosphere between the government and the students, making both parties extraordinarily sensitive to perceived slights and offenses by the other.

Historically, this has occurred in many political and interpersonal conflicts among the Chinese. Overemphasis on harmony in interpersonal relationships often leaves them little alternative but to avoid conflict at all costs. They suppress—but do not repress, as noted by Hsu[39]—their genuine emotions and resort to indirect means for expression. Negotiations are conducted not on face value but on the underlying or symbolic emotion.

In dealing with conflict, the Chinese are unaccustomed to a direct, open approach and prefer to settle differences in a manner that shows harmony and unanimity on the surface. Deviation from this preferred conflict management style, such as a demonstration, is received with resentment and hostility. Therefore, open bargaining for positions, as was the case when Li Peng met students on 18 May, becomes a situation in which positions are rigidly held by both sides and each sees any concession as losing face or compromising principle.[40] Any action is always seen as a symbol of an underlying emotion. The action followed is always a response to an emotion, assumed or real, rather than the substance of the matter. Both sides become more defensive and more committed as the bargaining process continues.[41] As a result, the conflict often escalates to an uncontrollable emotional bout and turns to violence for a solution.

The student movement of 1989 can be seen as such a conflict. The events were symbolic of an emotional exchange designed to expose the other side as without feeling or righteousness (*wuqing wuyi*), and therefore undeserving of the people's support. In this battle of emotions, victory was on the side of the powerless, unarmed students;

but the ultimate winner was the strong and powerful government. The substance of the students' demands—democracy and freedom—became almost immaterial as the movement progressed. They had been sacrificed with the determination of the students to sacrifice themselves.

Glossary of Chinese Terms

bufu: mistrust, disloyalty, unwillingness to rely on someone or something. (see *fu*)

bujin renqing: "to depart from human feelings"; to be unsympathetic to other people. (see *qing*)

buren buyi: literally, "neither humane nor righteous." Can also mean cruel, cold, unsympathetic.

fu: conveys a feeling of trust, dependence, relying on someone or something. Also carries a connotation of obedience, conformity to orders or commands.

fucong: obedience, conformity to commands.

fuwu: to serve, to perform one's duty.

koufu: "trust from the mouth," to express trust without feeling it; i.e., "lip service."

li: Chinese traditional code of proper behavior in interpersonal relations. Similar to etiquette except much broader in application. *Li* includes proper use of language, performance of proper rituals, and, ideally, a feeling of the proper emotion.

qing: emotion, sentiment, feelings, sympathy.

qufu: to bring about *fu* through coercion; to conquer or force one into submission. (see *fu*)

renqing: human emotions, feelings for other people, sympathy. (see *qing*)

renwu keren: to be intolerable or insufferable.

tongkuai: the feeling after pent-up emotions have been released; catharsis.

wuqing wuyi: "without *qing* and without righteousness"; to be both unsympathetic and cruel.

wuqing: "without *qing*," i.e., unfeeling, cold, unsympathetic.

xia: a sense of righteousness and altruism that motivates one to act to try to correct a wrong. Goes beyond passive feeling of injustice in that it elicits action.

xinfu: "*fu* from the heart," i.e. sincere feelings of trust, loyalty, and dependence. (see *fu*)

yiku sitian: "enjoying the sweet present while remembering the past." Refers to campaign in China in the 1950s telling the people that they would have to suffer some in order to improve their lives.

youxia: knights-errant in Chinese history who acted out of *xia* feeling. Considered heroic figures to the Chinese for their willingness to help people in need.

zhengming: "rectification of names," a traditional concept meaning that a person's behavior should be brought into line with his position in

222 Culture and Politics in China

society; i.e., a king should behave like a king, a general should behave
like a general, etc.

*[The author would like to thank misses Candice Yee and Shu-chun
Chan for their help in preparing a summary of instances in which
emotional exchanges occurred.]*

Notes

1   Francis L.K. Hsu, "Eros, affect, and *pao*," in F.L.K. Hsu, ed., *Kinship
     and Culture* (Chicago: Aldine Publishing, 1971), pp. 439-475 .
2   The Chinese culture has often been labeled "collectivistic," but I prefer
     to use "societalistic" to accentuate the culture's placing of societal
     interests ahead of that of individual members. I do this because this term
     places the emphasis on the relationship between society and the
     individual member; it thus reflects the essence of the culture better than
     the term "collectivistic."
3   Barrington Moore, Jr., *Injustice: The Social Bases of Obedience and
     Revolt* (London: The Macmillan Press, 1978).
4   Richard H. Solomon, *Mao's Revolution and the Chinese Political
     Culture* (Berkeley: University of California Press, 1971), chapter 4;
     Lucian W. Pye, *The Spirit of Chinese Politics: A Psychocultural Study
     of the Authority Crisis in Political Development* (Cambridge: MIT
     Press, 1968), chapter 6.
5   Lin Yutang, *The Importance of Living*, (Hong Kong: Heinemann
     Educational Books (Asia) LTD., 1977), p. 421.
6   Hsien Chin Hu, "Emotion, Real & Assumed, in Chinese Society,"
     unpublished manuscript on file with Columbia University Research in
     Contemporary Culture, 1949, document no. CH 668.
7   Hsu 1971.
8   James C.F. Wang, *Contemporary Chinese Politics: An Introduction*, 3rd
     ed. (Singapore: Prentice-Hall International, 1989), p. 2.
9   See Hsu 1971, pp. 450-451 for a brief discussion.
10   Donald J. Munro, *The Conception of Man in Contemporary China* (Ann
     Arbor: The University of Michigan Press, 1977) p. 32.
11   Lin Yutang, *My Country and My People* (New York: Reynal and
     Hitchcock, 1935), chapter 6; Hsu 1971, p. 465.
12   Hsu 1971, p. 465
13   Ibid., p. 451.
14   See Fei Xiaotong, *Rural China* (Shanghai: Guan cha she, 1948), p. 88.
15   Kuang-Kuo Hwang, "Face and Favor: The Chinese Power Game,"
     American Journal of Sociology 92 (1987): 944-974.
16   Many people took this point of view, for example H.G. Creel, *Chinese
     Thought from Confucius to Mao Tse-tung* (Chicago: University of
     Chicago Press, 1953).

17 For example, William T. de Bary, "Chinese Despotism and the Confucian Ideal: a Seventeenth-Century View,". In John J. Fairbanks (ed.), *Chinese Thought and Institutions* (Chicago, University of Chicago Press, 1957), p.163.

18 Francis L.K. Hsu, *Americans and Chinese: Passage to Difference*, 3rd ed. (Honolulu: University Press of Hawaii, 1981), p. 196.

19 It sometimes also denotes a feeling of giving up on dealing or arguing with someone for reasons other than one's competence, such as one's stubbornness or one's peculiar behavior beyond normal reasoning.

20 Lucian W. Pye, *The Dynamics of Chinese Politics* (Cambridge, Mass.: Oelgeschlager, Gunn & Hain, Publishers, 1981), p. 187.

21 Hsu 1981, p. 23.

22 Creel 1953, p. 243.

23 For example, Richard Madsen, *Morality and Power in a Chinese Village* (Berkeley: University of California, 1984) reported this type of moral reasoning by villagers living in Chen Village.

24 Hsu 1971, p. 459. Hsu gave a more elaborate explanation in his *Americans and Chinese*, chapters 7 and 8.

25 Fung Yulan, *A History of Chinese Philosophy*, vol. 1 (translated by Derke Bodde) (Princeton: Princeton University Press, 1952), p. 52.

26 Lien-sheng Yang, "The Concept of '*pao*' as a basis for social relations in China," in J.K. Fairbank (ed.), *Chinese Thought and Institutions* (Chicago: University of Chicago Press, 1957), pp. 294-295.

27 Fung Yulan even considered them as having a higher moral standard than that of the sages and the wise because the latter take the *zhong-zhi-dao* (the middle way).

28 Tung-mei Fang, *The Chinese Way of Life: The Philosophy of Comprehensive Harmony* (Hong Kong: The Union Press, 1957), p. 242.

29 Fung 1952, p. 66.

30 Munro 1977, p. 41.

31 The popular journalist Liu Binyan made a similar comment on 18 June in Hong Kong (*Ming Bao*, 19 June, p.2).

32 Under pressure, the Beijing city government did have someone receive the students' seven-point petition, but failed to grant them admission to Hu's funeral ceremony.

33 For instance, one was granted to students at Qinghua University by the State Department, but the students failed to show up because a dispute erupted as to who should represent the students. A second one was granted on 30 April to student representatives to talk with the mayor of Beijing, Chen Xitong, producing no concrete results.

34 For example, on 22 May a letter was printed and circulated on the Square, written by a mother of a college student who participated in the movement. The letter was addressed to the protesting students, asking them to fight on. (Included in *Cry Freedom: A Collection of Original Documents and Materials from the Tiananmen Square Prodemocracy Movement*, compiled by Wen Xun Magazine Publishing Co., 1990.)

35 Gandhi was another example of someone who took a hunger strike as a real weapon, not a symbolic or strategic one, to achieve his goals with peaceful means. He of course had more clout and thus could better afford to do so.

36 Many witness accounts pointed out this irrational mood prevailing at that strike period.

37 Other examples included questioning the academic competence and the ethical and moral standards of student leaders such as Wang Dan, Wu'er Kaixi, and Chai Ling.

38 The present author witnessed such an instance on the eve of 19 May in a teachers' college in Guangzhou.

39 Francis L.K. Hsu, "Suppression Versus Repression: A Limited Psychological Interpretation of Four Cultures," *Psychiatry* 1949:223-242.

40 Lucian Pye, *Chinese Commercial Negotiating Style* (Cambridge, Mass.: Oelgeschlager, Gunn & Hain, Publishers, 1982).

41 Roger Fisher and William Ury gave good discussions of this traditional "positional" negotiation in their book, *Getting to Yes* (New York: Penguin Books, 1983).

9

Social Malaise as Reflected in the Literature of the 1980s

Peter Li

> *A nation with an ancient civilization when encountering ... a Western industrial society faces a severe crisis.... The older the civilization, the greater the crisis. And the greater the crisis, the more intense that nation's search for roots.*[1]

In the decade and a half of the post-Mao era (1976-90), China saw enormous changes in the political, economic, and cultural realm. In spite of repeated efforts by the government to quell the rising tide of liberalization and openness, developments went ahead apparently unabated until the brutal crackdown of 4 June 1989.

This chapter will examine the developments in the cultural realm, especially in literature and film. These works form a literary and artistic movement that reveals a deepening sense of cultural crisis from 1978 to 1989. It began with the appearance of the "literature of the wounded" movement in 1978, evolved into the "literature of reform" and the "literature of critical reflection *(fansi wenxue)*" movements, and finished with the "search for cultural roots" movement, which included both literature and film. This last movement concluded in 1988 with the controversial television documentary "Heshang" (The [Yellow] River Elegy), which shifted the "search for roots" movement to a sweeping, critical evaluation of the whole of Chinese civilization, from its very origins to its manifestation in the present day.

This literary movement in the post-Mao reform era is interesting not only as the development of an artistic expression but as a reflection of an ever-growing sense of cultural consciousness and psychological malaise. Most experts agree that following the conclusion of the Cultural Revolution (1966-76) and the subsequent opening up to the West, China found itself plunging headlong from the pinnacle of revolutionary euphoria into a cultural abyss.[2] The consequent feeling of cultural loss, the confusion, and the painful choices that each individual had to make in facing the forces of modernization brought China back to a stage of development it had faced seventy years previously, during the May Fourth Movement of 1919.

This period was the final shock to consciousness for China. Defeat by Great Britain of the Opium War in 1839-42 had jolted China from a deep sleep into an agitated slumber, and since then it had struggled with the problem of transforming a weak and backward nation into a strong and powerful state. By 1919, China was in the midst of the tumultuous warlord era. It was an iconoclastic period in which the classical values of Confucianism were attacked and rejected, becoming known as "totalistic iconoclasm" or "radical iconoclasm."[3] Confucius and Confucianism took the blame for China's poverty and backwardness, its inability to modernize. The motto of the day was "Down with Confucius and Sons!"

This tendency to criticize the most venerated of Chinese figures naturally led Chinese intellectuals to examine the defects in the Chinese national character and their causes. The foremost critic of traditional Chinese culture and the Chinese character was Lu Xun (1881-1936), who wrote extensively about the Chinese character and the "backwardness" of Chinese society. His most famous tract was "The True Story of Ah Q," which has become a classic of modern Chinese literature. Through the character of Ah Q, a lowly and miserable peasant handyman, Lu Xun exposes several weaknesses in the Chinese national character: his refusal to face reality, his rationalizations for spiritual victory and superiority in the face of physical defeat, his illusions of grandeur when facing the reality of his wretchedness, and so on.

The May Fourth Movement produced not only critiques of Chinese culture but some preliminary analyses of the West. Intellectuals studied the works of Marx, Nietszche, Darwin, Spencer, Mill, Dewey, and Russell and the literary writings of Dickens, Walter Scott, Arthur Conan Doyle, Ibsen, and Romain Rolland, hoping to find secrets for building a strong and wealthy nation. This resulted in the determination by the intellectuals that science and democracy were the secrets of Western civilization's success. Therefore, the May Fourth students and intellectuals raised high the banner of "Mr. Science" and "Mr. Democracy" as the saviors of China.

This past history of the May Fourth Movement demonstrates how important literary developments are to political and social events in China. In China, as in other cultures, literature does not reflect measurable or quantifiable developments but deals with less tangible aspects of society—its psychological and spiritual dimension.

But, in comparison to the West, Chinese writers and intellectuals probably have a much more important role and perhaps much greater influence on society. Literature in China is less likely to be taken as pure entertainment than in the West, serving instead as a political barometer of society. Chinese writers play a dual role as both artist and intellectual. The former implies creativity and freedom; the latter gives a moral responsibility and an obligation to help educate the people and serve society. Books are truly prized possessions in China; to realize this, one only has to go to a local bookstore to see people poring over works that they are unable to buy. Therefore, cultural consciousness and awareness in the literary context can be of great significance to society as a whole. Literature reflects the concerns of society; in turn, literature influences society.

Sixty years after the May Fourth Movement, the literary developments of the reform period, which would become known as the Literature of the New Era, began. As in most every aspect of Chinese society after the end of the Cultural Revolution, change and development in Chinese literature was rapid and seminal. Not only were the works written quickly and in great quantity, the style and content changed at a breathtaking pace. It is unlike the situation with *The Dream of the Red Chamber* or Flaubert's *Madame Bovary,* which were caressed and shaped to the authors' content over a long period of time. There was a kind of urgency in this new literature. The writers were bursting with ideas that had been pent up for decades during the Cultural Revolution or since the antirightist campaign.

The Literature of the Wounded

The literary awakening of the post-Maoist period began in 1977 with the appearance of a rather ordinary short story, "The Teacher," by a thirty-five-year-old writer, Liu Xinwu (b. 1942), who had been a schoolteacher himself.[4] This story was epoch-making in that it broke the ten-year-long literary silence that the revolutionary politics of the Cultural Revolution had imposed on writers. The protagonists are two high school students: one a juvenile delinquent often involved in violent gang fights, the other a model female student who lives in an intellectual straitjacket. The author blames their problems on the radical politics of the Cultural Revolution. He accuses the Gang of Four of duplicity in creating this situation, writing that

> Zhang's [the teacher's] disgust with the Gang of Four burst forth more violently than ever. Never before had so many people been fooled by reactionary policies disguised as true revolutionary "logic" as during the period of their reign.[5]

Although this story was hailed, it did not exhibit highly developed literary skills. It does not provide much psychological subtlety in its characters or much plot development. At the time, of course, the urgency of condemning the Gang of Four was uppermost on the minds of China's leadership and its writers. Liu Xinwu openly and boldly attacked the Gang of Four, which was a courageous act. The Gang of Four had just been arrested the year before, and the policy of the party was still unclear. There were no celebrations in the streets over the arrest of Jiang Qing and her cohorts, although stores were reporting that their stock of liquors and wines was suddenly diminishing; apparently, the people of Beijing were secretly celebrating the end of the bloody reign of the Gang of Four in their homes.

Liu Xinwu's "The Teacher" was the opening shot of a new literary movement in China and the beginning of a new openness in the literary and cultural realm. This story was followed by a plethora of stories condemning the effect of the policies of the Cultural Revolution on youth and the future of China.

A year later there appeared a second story that touched off another round of soul-searching. The heart strings of the people were touched by Lu Xinhua's short story "The Wound," published in 1978. The writer was a young man of twenty-five, and his story first appeared on the wall posters of his department at Fudan University in Shanghai. It immediately aroused much interest and was subsequently published in a Shanghai newspaper, *Literary Gazette* (Wenhuibao). Within a period of three months, the *Gazette* received over nine hundred letters, the majority enthusiastically responding to the story.[6]

Lu Xinhua went much further than political condemnation; he showed how the policies of the Cultural Revolution had destroyed the most sacred of human relations, that between mother and child. In his story, sixteen-year-old Wang Xiaohua severs relations with her mother when she finds out that during the Cultural Revolution her mother had been labeled a traitor to the revolution: "It was nine years ago," Xiaohua painfully recalled.

> At the time, she suppressed her intense hatred against her "renegade mother," left school without graduating, and applied to work in the countryside. She could not imagine that her mother, who had served the revolution for all those years, could actually be like the character Dai Yu in [the novel] *The Song of Youth* and crawled out of the same dog hole as Dai Yu the enemy. She read *The Song of Youth*[7] and found Dai Yu utterly disgusting.[8]

The girl had made a clean break with her mother, which was what was required of her if she was to have any respect from her friends and companions. But nine years later, when her mother is on her deathbed and it is too late for the daughter to see her mother for the last time, she eternally regrets this failure.

"The Wound" showed a more developed approach to the tragedy of the Cultural Revolution in shifting from straight political criticism to descriptions of the inner conflict in the mind of the protagonist. Feelings of love, hate, regret, and remorse are examined. This shift in the narrator's point of view from the external to the internal is significant as the first step in the beginning of a more extensive and profound reflection on the effect of the communist revolution on the people and the nation.

Lu Xinhua's story was significant in another sense. It was the first time since the Cultural Revolution that a story was written about love and tragedy. These were previously taboo areas. Tragedy was taboo because theoretically it could not exist in a socialist society; love, because it was considered "bourgeois."

The Literature of Critical Reflection

From the end of 1979 to the beginning of 1980, the Literature of the New Era began its second phase, a phase of moral and long-range historical reflection. It is significant that the emphasis shifted away from the immediate past, i.e., the psychological trauma suffered by youth during the Cultural Revolution. Instead, the literary movement focused on the suffering of middle-aged and older people, who had lived through decades of Communist rule.

These people, the new literary phase suggested, had been deprived of their right to love and happiness because their morality had been politicized. It referred to the party's longstanding policy, implemented since it gained control in 1949, of "socialist realism" in literature and the arts. The avowed purpose of socialist realism was to serve politics and sing the praises of the Communist party and the new society (*gede*). Literature was not to expose the defects of society (*quede*).

During the turmoil of Mao's era, the literature of socialist realism became politicized to such an extent that it became dehumanized and amoral. Emotions such as love or sadness, right or wrong, simply became means of expressing adherence to the ideology of the state. But the new literature regarded love and morality as a basic element of human existence, and therefore formed a striking contrast, infusing the new literature with human feeling.

Zhang Jie's short story "Love is Not to be Forgotten" is a prime example of the revival of this new humanist literature.[9] The protagonist is a middle-aged woman who is married and has a child, but is married to a man whom she does not really love, posing a moral dilemma. The man she really loves is married to another woman whom he felt obligated to marry because of a debt of gratitude. Such a bourgeois situation—that someone is married to someone while loving someone else—would have been inconceivable a few years previously.

In the story, the love-forsaken woman dies, but her diary is found and read by her daughter, who is faced with a similar choice: either to marry a handsome young man to whom she is attracted but does not love, or to find another partner; the author chooses not to tell what she decides. Thus, the story contrasts the past, when a person's actions had been dictated by circumstances beyond his or her control, to the present, where individual choice seems plausible, if not possible. The ultimate moral of the story is not that one should always follow love's dictates but that "love should not be forgotten."

Another story that emphasizes long-range disappointments in China is "Li Shunda Builds a House" by Gao Xiaosheng.[10] What is markedly different in this story is that the protagonist is an older man reflecting on his past. A quaintly heroic figure, Li Shunda has lived through the forty years of Communist rule, witnessing and experiencing excessive shifts in policy through Mao's political campaigns. He saves his money to build a house and purchases the construction materials. But, responding to the call of the Great Leap Forward, he decides to donate them to the commune backyard furnace project. After the failure of that campaign, he again saves his money to build a house. But, to avoid drawing attention to his plans, he holds off on purchasing the materials. Eventually, during the Cultural Revolution, his savings are discovered. Instead of allowing himself to be accused of being a capitalist roader[11], he hands over his savings to the government official.

Many other stories, poems, and plays in this vein were written during this period. A controversial play by the writer Bai Hua called "Unrequited Love" (Kulian) might be mentioned in passing because the criticism of this play marked a tightening of political control since the beginning of this period of openness. The criticism of Bai Hua's play may be considered a precursor to the "antispiritual pollution" campaign that began in 1983. It was one of Deng Xiaoping's early attempts to curb the rising tide of Westernization in China since the reforms.

A Nation in Culture Fever

From 1985 to 1987, the Literature of the New Era took perhaps its most significant step—the "search for cultural roots." The movement was felt in both literature and in society as a whole. China was said to be suffering from "culture fever" (wenhua re). In this process of searching for roots, the Chinese writers and intellectuals reflected long and hard on the predicament of the Chinese nation over the preceding forty years.

"Culture fever" can be seen as the growing pains of a nation in the throes of rapid modernization. The self-confidence, boldness, and optimism of the early stages of socialist reconstruction in the 1950s and 1960s had given way to introspection, self-doubt, and masochistic self-criticism. The lack of confidence and the desperate search for solutions to China's backwardness more than just coincidentally resembled the intellectual, social, and political crisis of the May Fourth Period seventy years ago.

The writers of this movement are pedantically pessimistic. One of the important writers in the "roots" tradition, Zheng Yi, who wrote "Old Well," a love story that uses a village's arduous search for water as an allegory for the hardships of life in China, said this about his own writing:

> Man's life is worse than that of a dog? I don't understand. I have always believed in "history," "progress," "civilization," and other such terms. I have never doubted the "success" of mankind in some sense of the word, nor would I ever demean mankind, myself included, to such an extent as to say that my life is worse than that of a dog. But why is it that I have found instances of a man's life actually being worse than that of a dog's life? I leave the problem to the theoreticians; I deal with only the emotions and feelings. Thereupon, I will sing a shepherd's song from the Taihang Mountains about man's stubborn will to live and be free.[12]

According to Han Shaogong, one of the founders of the "search for roots" school,

> one should not misunderstand this school to mean that all we want to do is hide ourselves from the present and stick our heads in the past and thus escape from the present. The "search for roots" movement has a patriotic motive: Don't think that the search for roots is merely sticking yourself into a mud hole and then you will become a root.... The search for roots is not to build up a new national essence, or to glorify a region or a locale, but to rebuild an Eastern culture ... to establish a new person, a new attitude, a new spirit, a new mode of thinking, and a new sense of beauty, and to contribute to the Chinese nation's rapid development.[13]

The development of this attitude—the need to reevaluate Chinese culture and to create a "new Chinese culture"—was a logical development in the literary movement of the reform era. Even before the release of "River Elegy" in 1988, it was clear that the movement had taken on a life of its own. Taboos had been lifted, and writers and intellectuals were probing deeper and deeper into the Chinese condition, each phase of reflection becoming more extensive and creating greater criticism of the fundamental "Chinese character."

They examined the traditional basic human relationships (*renlun* between mother and daughter, mother and son, father and son, etc.) and began tentative explorations of the relationship between love and friendship and love and lust. They extended this discussion to bold exploration of such topics as the relationship between sexual impotence and political abuse.

The Search for Cultural Roots

The works in the "search for cultural roots" movement represented a change in geographical focus in Chinese literature. Attention moved away from the prosperous, more modernized, and well-developed coastal regions and the cities to the more backward, primitive conditions in the heartland of China. It seemed that the reasons for China's backwardness could not be found easily in the coastal cities of China.

Writers such as Jia Pingwa, Zheng Yi, and Gu Hua went inland to the less prosperous heartland of China, where Chinese culture and civilization had its origins. There, in the backwaters of the loess plateau of Shanxi, Shenxi, and Henan—the heart of the Yellow River valley—writers, and now film makers, discovered a new strength: the primitive power of the Chinese people and the traditions of the Chinese nation (*minzu*, a complex socio-political-cultural concept). For example, films and stories such as "The Yellow Earth" and "Old Well" are all set in the barren heartland of China along the Yellow River.

Additionally, writers traced China's problems deeper into its history, beyond the communist era and the early turmoil of the republic. In "The Yellow Earth," which was produced in 1984, the story goes back to the pre-Liberation days of the 1930s, when an idealistic young soldier of the Red Army comes to a backward village in search of folk songs. The film explores the shocking backwardness and hopelessness of the hard life there. Through conversation with the young soldier, the young girl of one of the villagers, fated to be married off, learns of another world outside the village and tries to run away to the liberated area. Unfortunately, her attempt is unsuccessful and she drowns in the waters of the Yellow River.

Another major film, "Red Sorghum," also goes back to pre-Second World War days, before the Japanese invasion. Among the scenes portrayed in the film are a traditional wedding ceremony in which the bride is subject to the brutality of the villagers and is later raped by one of the peasants; the peasants worshipping a dragon king who brings rain to the parched yellow earth; and, finally, the primitive unleashing of their pent-up hatred of the Japanese in a guerrilla-type surprise attack. The message therefore is that the peasants are crude and uncultivated and yet also strong, patriotic, and able to bear great hardship.

In "Old Well," the author addresses the long-unsolved difficulty of living on the central China plain, which suffers from chronic shortages of water. As the setting for his complex, passionate love story, the author cites a historical record that extends back some three hundred years. These records indicate that in a village called Old Well in Shaanxi province, 127 attempts had been made to drill a well deep enough to obtain water in times of drought. Finally, in 1983, the villagers succeed in drilling a well over 250 meters deep, which guaranteed them water. This long history of hardship, endurance, determination, and pure stubbornness is indicative of the strength of the Chinese people, which is part of the Chinese national character.

The Yellow River Elegy

On 11 June 1988, when the six-part television documentary "The Yellow River Elegy" was first shown on the Central Television Station in Beijing, the response was unexpectedly intense. The station received more than a thousand letters from viewers requesting that the series be shown again. When the Shanghai Television Station ran the series, it was shown on six consecutive nights during prime time—from eight to nine o'clock in the evening. One of the authors of the commentary, Zhang Gang, who was also the director of the liaison office of the Chinese Research Institute for Reform of the Economic System, said:

> After looking at dozens of letters from the general public ... I was deeply moved. Every one of them, from retired cadres all the way down to primary school students, from leaders of the party, the government, and the military to ordinary workers, showed a strong reaction, and none was negative. From reading these letters, I felt that the hearts of our people are full of hope.[14]

Interest in the series was not limited to the Chinese people. After the fourth episode, the U.S. consulate in Beijing asked if it could borrow the tape for a private viewing. It soon became obvious that there was a "Heshang" *re* (River Elegy craze) going on around the country.

The popularity of the series soon incurred the wrath of arch-conservatives in the Standing Committee of the Politburo. One such committee member, Wang Zhen, lashed out at the documentary as unpatriotic. Hu Qili, another member in charge of ideological work in the party, took a milder stance and tentatively tried to curb discussions of the series in the newspapers. But some newspapers, such as the *Guangming Daily, China Youth Daily, Economic Daily*, and *Wenhui Daily*, continued to print discussions on the series in spite of the warning.[15]

Just what is the "Elegy" all about? Seen from the point of view of the "search for cultural roots" movement begun in 1985, it is an inevitable development. Films like "The Yellow Earth," "Red Sorghum," and "Old Well" had already carried the search for cultural roots much farther back than any previous works. The history of the Old Well Village dates back to the Yongzheng Period (1723-35) of the Qing dynasty.

The documentary carried the "search for roots" analysis one step further. Life along the Yellow River had already been explored in stories and films, revealing extreme poverty and hardship. Since the Yellow River is the cradle of Chinese civilization, the question the film asks can be seen as: What influence did it have on the nature of Chinese civilization?

The answer that "Elegy" gives is resoundingly negative, but it is not a wholesale condemnation of Chinese culture and tradition. It does harshly criticize Chinese culture, one of the the most severe criticisms being reflected in this passage:

Perhaps Confucianism had many ancient "gimmicks," but in its several thousand years of history it has not created a forward looking national spirit, a nation with a legal system, a mechanism for cultural renewal. On the contrary, it has gone in the direction of decline and created a frightening kind of suicidal mechanism, continually destroying its own best and most talented people, killing those elements that have the greatest vitality, stifling generation after generation of the best minds of our nation. This has led inevitably to the destruction of what is best in our culture.[16]

The authors of "Elegy" do not deny the greatness or the past glory of Chinese civilization. They even suggest that Chinese culture is capable of change. But they insist that it is on the decline, and that the hope of China depends on turning to the West; otherwise, it will face certain death. They insist that the time has come for China to face reality:

> Now, the most important thing is that we not fool ourselves any longer. When a civilization has declined, there is no need to grieve. All the great river valley civilizations without exception have declined. The English historian Toynbee once pointed out that twenty-one civilizations have appeared in human history. Among them fourteen are already extinct; six are in the process of decay. Only the ancient Greek civilization transformed itself into an industrial civilization and engulfed the whole [Western] world.[17]

The most poignant message of "The Yellow River Elegy" is contained in the last episode. It expresses grief, a sense of mission, a sense that China is standing at the moment of decision, and that after centuries of suffering, of bitterness, of humiliation, and of hardship, China must make the proper choice. The documentary is not meant to be demeaning, sarcastic, or ironic, nor critical of communism. But it is powerful because the Yellow River has become the personification of the Chinese people. Like the Chinese people, the river is strong, violent, and nourishing, but its ultimate fate is to flow into the deep blue sea:

> It is fated that the Yellow River will cross the plateau of the yellow earth.
> Ultimately the Yellow River will merge into the deep blue ocean.
> The suffering of the Yellow River, and the hope of the Yellow River are what give the Yellow River its greatness.
> The greatness of the Yellow River lies in its having created the great plain between the ocean and the high plateau.
> The Yellow River has finally arrived at the painful juncture of entering the ocean.
> The thousands of miles of mud and sand are about to be deposited to form a new continent.
> The wildly tossing waves are crashing against the waters of the Yellow River.
> The Yellow River ought to rid its fear of the great ocean.

The Yellow River ought to maintain its undaunted determination and vigor.
The water of life comes from the great ocean and flows back to the ocean.
The isolated Yellow River that has been alone for thousands of years finally sees the deep blue sea.[18]

"The Yellow River Elegy" ends with this final incantation. It is a cry of desperation from the Chinese people, the Chinese nation, and the Chinese race. The Yellow River has suffered like the Chinese people. The Yellow River has accomplished great things like the Chinese people. As the Yellow River faces the great ocean, it must not be afraid; likewise, the Chinese people as they face the challenge of the West. Their fates are intertwined.

Aside from this overwhelmingly pessimistic tone, the documentary does refer to areas where China has excelled. This commentary, however, is framed as a call for openness, which is the larger import of the documentary. At one point, Professor Ye Lang of Beijing University (director of the research and teaching section of the Department of Philosophy) is interviewed as saying:

The vitality of Tang culture is closely related to its degree of openness.... A very important aspect of the self-confidence, vitality, and creativity of a nation lies in its interaction with foreign cultures: Does it shut itself off or does it openly receive it? ... My study of Tang culture has inspired me with these two observations: (1) an outstanding feature of a culture is that if it is really open then it does not follow any pattern or any tune of development; it has various shadings of color, it is not monotonous or uniform. (2) How did this vitality and flourishing ["letting the hundred flowers bloom"] arise? A very important ingredient is openness to outside influence. Nourishment from an outside culture, stimulation from an outside culture, create a flourishing culture within. Without absorbing nourishment from the outside it is impossible to create a flourishing culture from within.[19]

The documentary discusses the recent development along China's coast in a positive light. It says the establishment of the Shenzhen special economic zone "announced to the world that the several thousand years of inland culture has finally reached the edge of the ocean." Regarding the 1988 formation of Hainan Province, it announced that its short-term goal was to challenge the Four Little Dragons of Asia. The ancient continent of Asia has finally let down its pretense.... If the Hainan experiment is successful, then together with the other fourteen cities along the Pacific coast it would become the giant economic dragon [of Asia]. This historical movement would totally change the countenance of Chinese culture.[20]

The effect of the series, as has been suggested previously, was enormous. Its message was powerful because of the visual imagery and the impact of personifying a commonly identifiable cultural symbol like the Yellow River. There are few other objects or symbols in China that could produce the same kind of emotional response; perhaps only the Great Wall and the dragon carry the same weight as a spiritual anchor for the Chinese people. The power of television brought its message into ordinary people's homes and compelled them to watch it. No one can remain unmoved as the powerful, rampaging Yellow River rounds its bends and flows toward the ocean, or the windblown, erosion-carved, barren loess highlands flash across the screen.

The reactions to the documentary came generally in two strains. As mentioned previously, many responded positively to its message. The opposite reaction was that the series not only destroyed the Chinese people's self-confidence but also destroyed their sense of dignity and self-respect. Wang Zhen was supposed to have said: "This series not only goes counter to our culture but is also a self-humiliating, historical, nihilist document. It poses a serious danger to our thinking."[21]

A television documentary on the Yellow River is in itself a worthwhile task because the Yellow River has special significance to the Chinese people. The producer of the series, Su Xiaokang, did not want to give simply a tourist's view of the Yellow River. He expressed the seriousness of the subject in this way:

> The Yellow River is a huge topic that extends ten thousand *li* from east to west, spans a time period of over four thousand years, and encompasses millions of people along both its banks. The Yellow River is closely related to the origin of the Chinese race, its history, culture, and development. In addition, [it is] closely related to East Asian culture and the whole of global culture. We believe that to put the Yellow River on the television screen is a much different matter than with the Yangzi River, or the Grand Canal. Its peculiar weightiness and rich content is something much worthier than the Silk Road or the Yangzi River....

If we were to use traditional thinking, methods, and style to present the Yellow River, it would result in showing its glorious sights but would not be able to express the seriousness of the subject. Moreover, since we are presenting the Yellow River just at a time when we are promoting reform and openness, we must give this topic a clear and powerful message that reflects the [concern of the] times.... It must critically examine the history, culture, and fate of our nation. Only in this way can the program about the Yellow River justify the seriousness of the subject and the answer to the requirement of the time.[22]

Perhaps it was precisely statements of this kind that caused some speculation that "The Yellow River Elegy" was actually a project engineered by Zhao Ziyang through the office of the Research Institute for Reform of the Economic System, which he had established under the State Council. There was at least one obvious connection: Zhang Gang, one of the narrators in the tape, was a Liaison Office director in the Research Institute.

It was also said that, after the documentary was aired, a ten-point critique was penned in October 1988, but that allegedly Zhao Ziyang forbade its publication. Interestingly enough, the critique was finally published on 19 July 1989, six weeks after 4 June, when the hardliners had clearly consolidated their power. The points in the critique were predictable: that "Elegy" was a funeral song to the whole of traditional Chinese culture; that it did not use materialism to interpret Chinese history, instead using ideology, geography, and the environment to explain Chinese history; that it ridiculed and indiscriminately attacked everything yellow—Yellow River, yellow earth, yellow soy bean, and yellow skin; that it attacked China's cohesion and questioned all China's attempts at unity; that it distorted history by neglecting all the heroic efforts of the working people to resist foreign encroachments on China, lumping them altogether as disruptive and destructive; that it did not give any credit to the Chinese Communist Party, and regarded the socialist road as a total failure; that it sang endless praise of Western and European culture at the expense of Chinese culture, totally neglecting the fact that it was Western imperialism that invaded and plundered China, killing its people; that the ideas of reform advocated in "Elegy" were diametrically opposed to the reforms advocated by Deng Xiaoping, of socialist reform with Chinese characteristics; that it criticized the intellectuals as not having enough backbone to stand up for their ideas (although the documentary itself was proof that there are intellectuals strong enough to stand up for their ideas) whereas there are many young intellectuals who are working under the leadership of the Communist party; and that it was not a serious work and was carelessly put together with many inaccuracies and mistakes.[23]

Whether these criticism are valid or not, "Yellow River Elegy" was viewed as an extremely powerful, well-articulated plea for reform. It probably was precisely because of its power that the conservative government authorities in Beijing were frightened into censoring it, thus alienating Zhao Ziyang even more from the hardliners.

Another important contribution of this series is that it introduced the thinking of the foremost intellectuals in China today to the people as a whole. This had never been possible before because television had not been available. Now, television is available even in the countryside. The documentary dealt with complex ideas, concepts, and concerns in a way that even the common people understood, even though they could not articulate them, and it effectively encouraged people to ponder the future of their country. Even peasants from remote parts of the country joined in the discussion about the future of China.

Historically there had always been a gap between the common people and the intellectuals. Now, for the first time in Chinese history, this gap was bridged, even if only momentarily. Since 4 June 1989, the authorities have been very careful about what messages are portrayed on Chinese television.

Conclusion

The literature of the past decade, the Literature of the New Era, reflected both the concerns of the people and the problems of society, and at the same time this literature influenced the thinking and behavior of the people. As we trace the development of the literature of these past ten years, we find the self-confidence of the past has gone. Critical reflection on Chinese society led deeper and deeper into the human condition, reaching back in time, delving further and further into the cultural roots and the Chinese national character that is grounded in these roots.

This exploration into the cultural roots and the national character is reminiscent of the May Fourth Period seventy years earlier, when China faced another crisis. At that time, China was also facing questions about whether to Westernize totally or partially, whether Chinese civilization was culturally superior to Western civilization, and whether science and technology could be used only to materially modernize China while it retained a basically Chinese essence. Lu Xun was the harshest in-house critic of Chinese civilization at the time, demanding the abandonment of all of Chinese culture for Western culture. But his critique did not have the depth and the soul-searching quality of "River Elegy"; its desperation and pain is much greater than Lu Xun's.

During the seventy years between Lu Xun and "Yellow River Elegy," China experienced much pain. What was significantly different was that much of that pain since 1949 China had inflicted on itself. The search for China's cultural roots and a resolution to the dilemmas it poses for the question of modernization have therefore become much more urgent. Unfortunately, this search was cut short by the intervention of the government's long arm. But the questions it raised and forcefully articulated reached a fundamental point; what's more, these questions were aired before the common people and received positively. This indicates that in the next phase the search may find answers.

Notes

1 Su Xiaokang, et al., *Heshang* (Hong Kong: China Books Press, 1988), p. 10.

2 Ji Hongzhen, "Lishide mingti yu shidai jueze'zhongde yishu shanbian" (The Artistic Changes Which were Determined by History and the Times), *Dangdai zuojia pinglun* January 1989:15.

3 Lin Yu-sheng, *The Crisis of Chinese Consciousness* (Madison: University of Wisconsin Press, 1979), pp. 6, 10-55.

4 *Prize-Winning Stories from China, 1978-1979* (Beijing: Foreign Languages Press, 1981), pp. 3-26 gives an English translation of the story that first appeared in *People's Literature* (November 1977).

5 Ibid., p. 18.

6 *Xin shinian zhengyi zuopin xuan, 1976-1986* (Controversial Works of the Past Ten Years, 1976-1986) (Guangxi: Lijiang Press, 1987), p.48.

7 This is an autobiographical novel written by a woman writer in the 1950s about a young woman's intellectual evolution from an idealistic naive young girl to a seasoned revolutionary. It was condemned during the Cultural Revolution because it expressed sympathy for bourgeois ideas and feelings.

8 *Prize-winning Stories*, p. 109.

242 Culture and Politics in China

9   For an English translation of the story, see Helen F. Siu and Zelda Stern, *Mao's Harvest: Voices from China's New Generation* (New York and Oxford: Oxford University Press, 1983), pp. 92-106.
10   For an English translation of the story, see Gao Xiaosheng, *The Broken Betrothal* (Beijing: Panda Books, 1987), pp. 25-57.
11   The term "Capitalist roader" is a derogatory term used to refer to an enterprising person who tries to earn a little extra money to better his life.
12   Quoted in Ji Hongzhen, *"Lishide mingti yu shidai jueze' zhongde yishu shanbian"* (The Artistic Changes Which were Determined by History and the Times), Dangdai zuojia pinglun January 1989:18.
13   Zhang Zhiying, et al., eds., *Binfende xiaoshuo shijie* (The Riotous Profusion in the World of Fiction) (Shijiazhuang: Huashan wenyi Press, 1988), p. 3.
14   *Zhengmin* September 1988:62.
15   Originally in *Jingbao* (August 1988), see translation in *Inside China Mainland*, 11(1) (January 1989):2.
16   *Heshang*, p. 104.
17   Ibid., p. 21.
18   Ibid., pp. 110-111
19   Ibid., p 47.
20   Ibid., p. 105.
21   "Wang Zhen Tells off *Heshang* and Does a Good Job," *Jiushi niandai* December 1988:92.
22   Su Xiaokang, "A Call for the Entire Nation to Reflect," in *Heshang*, p. 1.
23   *Renmin ribao* (*People's Daily*, overseas edition) 19 July 1989, p. 4.

10

Student Movements in Chinese History and the Future of Democracy in China

Ying-shih Yu

Student movements have a long and celebrated tradition in Chinese history, and the student movement of 1989 was a part of this tradition. But it was also significant as a step toward establishing a democratic government in China. This chapter will offer some observations from a historical perspective on the future of democracy in China and the role that the students and intellectuals can play in its establishment.

The first student movement in the world occurred in China. During the reign of Emperor Ai (6-2 B.C.), a student movement broke out in the city of Changan (present day Xian), which was then the capitol of the Han dynasty. An upright official by the name of Bao Xuan was arrested for offending the prime minister. The students of the Imperial Academy (Taixue), more than one thousand in number, gathered in front of the institution and demanded Bao's immediate release. Bao Xuan already had been given the death sentence, but the students were determined to intervene. They called another mass demonstration and prevented the prime minister's carriage from passing through the main street of Changan.[1] As a result, Bao Xuan received a partial pardon. He was not executed but instead given a lighter sentence. This happened simply because of the students at the Imperial Academy, which was founded in 124 B.C. and was one of the earliest universities in the world.

What is especially interesting about the Imperial Academy in relation to modern times is that Beijing University is its direct successor. Founded in 1898, Beijing University was originally known as Jingshi Daxuetang (The Metropolitan University) and was supposed to revive the institution of the Imperial Academy. This historical dimension gives us a sense of historical depth with regard to the student movement in China today. This historical and cultural tradition helped shape the spirit of protest shown in the demonstrations in Tiananmen Square in 1989.

The next large student movement in Chinese history occurred in the second century A.D. This time it was a protest against the the Imperial Court, which had been corrupted by a clique of eunuches. By the second century A.D., the student body in the Imperial Academy had grown to well over thirty thousand, which even by modern standards is large. Thousands of students formed organizations in support of those political and intellectual leaders in the government who were fighting the eunuches. The eunuches, however, controlled the military forces and imperial guards, and, as a result, many students were killed while others were imprisoned.[2]

Most of the demonstrators became fugitives, running from one place to another. Many were secretly protected by common people sympathetic to their cause. This reminds us very much of the students after the Tiananmen massacre, like Wu'er Kaixi, who fled from Beijing to Canton and finally arrived safely in Hong Kong. According to the historical records of the Han dynasty, after the crackdown numerous student leaders and scholars went into hiding. Everywhere they went they were protected by the local people, including local officials who were total strangers to them. Local people and officials throughout Han China went all out to help these political fugitives, often at the risk of not only their own lives, but in many cases even at the risk of the lives of their whole families and clans. In their eyes, these refugee scholars and students were heroes who stood for justice, integrity and social conscience.

Many other examples can be cited, but perhaps one more will suffice. In the early twelfth century, under the Song dynasty (960-1279), the Jurchens were about to invade China. The Imperial Court was indecisive at this time of grave national crisis. Again, the students in the Imperial Academy rose up under the leadership of a young man, Chen Dong, who even aroused the people and soldiers to support them. He led a group of civilians in a demonstration in Kaifeng, then the capitol of China. The demonstration occurred at what was called Xuandemen (Gate of Manifestation of Virtue), which, like Tiananmen (Gate of Heavenly Peace) today, symbolized imperial power. The people and the soldiers, numbering more than one hundred thousand, all supported the demonstrators. Unfortunately, Chen Dong was sacrificed. He was executed on the order of the emperor, who was influenced by his wicked ministers. But this truly patriotic student movement was fully vindicated by history. Several decades later, Chen Dong was restored to his grave and honored by the court as a national hero.[3]

This brief historical sketch of student movements in Chinese history throws considerable light on the events of April and May of 1989. They did not come out of the blue. Nor can the demonstrations be viewed simply as a "modern" phenomenon growing out of Western influence; on the contrary, they grew out of a Chinese tradition of more than two millennia. Because of the central position they occupied in traditional society, Chinese intellectuals, especially young idealists, developed at a very early date a collective sense of social responsibility, wherein they considered it their calling to protest against political and social injustice.

However, the May Fourth Movement of 1919, which in part served as the inspiration for the student movement of 1989, did take a decidedly modern turn when "Mr. Democracy" and "Mr. Science" came to China from the West. The May Fourth Movement of seventy years ago has been paradigmatic for all the later student movements. It was, first of all, a movement initiated by the students without any external stimulation, in the sense of being manipulated by others. The late Fu Sinian (1895-1950), one of the top student leaders of the May Fourth Movement in 1919, who died during his tenure as president of National Taiwan University remembered that

> many people said that during the May Fourth Movement we students were manipulated by certain politicians in the North. This was definitely nonsense. I was involved centrally in that movement. I know for a fact that nobody manipulated me, nobody asked me to rise against the unpatriotic government that was about to sign the Treaty of Versailles.[4]

Student leaders at Tiananmen Square this year could say the very same thing. They started the demonstration entirely of their own accord and did it in a very orderly way. It was one of the most peaceful, orderly civilian movements that ever occurred in China. In fact, it was more peaceful than the May Fourth Movement of 1919. In the original May Fourth Movement, the students burned down a house and beat up a minister badly. Several dozen students were arrested, and many were beaten by the police.[5] The next day, however, they were all released under the pressure of public opinion. Compared to the warlords of 1919 China, the present regime acted much worse. We normally think of the warlords as unreasonable, uncultured barbarians, but if you look at history you find that there were no students killed on 4 May 1919. Only one student later died of some kind of disease. No one was executed, and no one was gunned down, although some were arrested and then released.

Expectations for the Student Movement

Now, the question is: Where will the student movement of 1989 lead us? Is China any closer to democracy since the movement started last April? Needless to say, it is unrealistic to expect that democracy can be established in the span of a single student movement, given the size and population of China. That is too much to ask. But we have good reason to believe that the movement was not wholly in vain. It has already seen its result, and has bore some kind of fruit. I think Wu'er Kaixi was right when he referred earlier to the people's movement in East Germany as being in some way inspired by the Tiananmen Square demonstrations.[6] The Tiananmen massacre was very much on the minds of the East Germans when they started their own revolution. One of the workers said he did not trust the new leader of the party, Egon Krenz, because he had paid tribute to Deng Xiaoping after the Tiananmen tragedy and had supported the bloody suppression of the student movement in Beijing. Other movements in Eastern European countries are also indirectly linked to the Tiananmen Square Incident as part of a chain reaction in the communist world. It would be an exaggeration, however, to say that what is happening in Eastern Europe would not have happened without Tiananmen Square. But what happened in Tiananmen Square had some bearing on what's happening in Eastern Europe today. In that sense, the blood on Tiananmen Square has not been shed in vain.

What about the future of democracy in China? The future of democracy depends on not just the students, not even just the masses in Beijing, or masses in other major cities like Shanghai, Nanjing, Wuhan, Xian, and Chengdu, which all rose against the regime in May and June of 1989. According to reports, more people may have been killed elsewhere than in Beijing without being covered by the news media.

In considering the prospects for a democratic government in China, we must question the validity of a dominant view concerning the rise of democracy. For instance, Barrington Moore, Jr., in his book, *Social Origins of Dictatorship and Democracy,* states that the Western type of parliamentary democracy is the product of the bourgeois class, the middle class. The implication is: "No bourgeoisie, no democracy."[7] To an extent this is true. You need the bourgeois class to develop preliminary democratic mechanisms. This is what happened in England in 1688. It also happened in France in 1789, with the establishment of the First Republic.

But I do not share Moore's negative, essentially Marxist view about the peasant class. Farmers are also inclined toward democracy in their own way. As a farmer who participated in the American Revolution in 1776 later testified, "We had governed and we always meant to. They (i.e. the British) did not mean that we should."[8] Self-governance has also been a basic principle in the long tradition of rural China. The fact that the peasants care little about voting is no argument against the possibility and the desirability of democracy in a rural society.

If we look at Germany and Japan before the Second World War, we have to admit that they were two capitalistic societies, not lacking in a bourgeois class. And yet neither established a democracy. Instead, Germany developed another form of totalitarianism, Nazism. So one can see that capitalism alone will not necessarily lead to democracy. Democracy needs both economic and social changes along with basic structural changes on the one hand, and an intellectual revolution, a change of mind, on the other.

In addition to the establishment of a bourgeois class, democracy as an idea is important too. I don't think democracy necessarily grows directly out of the capitalist market system. Even if modern democracy was originally related to the bourgeoisie, we must avoid the fallacy of class origins. "Democracy" has already become a most powerful idea and as such it can transcend its class origins.

Today it is generally accepted that democracy (in its various forms) is the most rational and reasonable political system. Like all institutions humanly created, democracy is not perfect. But it is an open-ended system capable of improving and readjusting itself from time to time. On the whole, it has been working well in open Western societies; most liberals in the United States today seem to think so as well. The Marxist view that democracy is false because it protects the class interests of the bourgeoisie has been totally discredited. It would be overoptimistic, however, to go as far as Fukuyama,[9] for instance, to say that we have come to the end of history because liberal ideology is the best we have. But I think the liberal institutions as implemented in the West since the eighteenth century are among the finest human creations.

Since Dr. Sun Yat-sen and the May Fourth Movement of 1919, the idea of democracy has been deeply ingrained in the hearts and minds of the Chinese people. In all the revolutions in China since then, the idea of democracy has generated a power of its own, quite independent of social, economic, and political forces.

Take the situation in Taiwan as an example. Taiwan was not even democratic; it was not even beginning to take the road to democracy until two or three years ago. Even now, democracy in Taiwan is still in an experimental stage. We do not know where it will lead us, but clearly it is a society gradually opening up. This new development is not due to any one force, such as the government or the ruling party, the middle class or working people. The emergence of democracy in Taiwan is to a certain extent related to the economy but not only that. Before the economy took off, liberal ideas already had been very active, and a group of liberal intellectuals had tried to promote democracy. The only liberal magazine, *Free China*, was suspended and closed down by the government. The publisher was later sentenced to a ten-year term in prison.[10]

What was promoted by the *Free China* group was not a simple idea of democracy, but a whole cluster of ideas associated with it, including freedom, equality, social justice, human rights etc. These were the very ideas that had been first disseminated in China during the May Fourth Movement. So the May Fourth Movement, the first Tiananmen Square movement in Chinese history, was far-reaching in its influence.

The various ideas survived from that time on, as if they had lives of their own. These ideas were transmitted from generation to generation through the lives of numerous intellectuals, as well as through publications, meetings, speeches, lectures, and discussions. Today's democratic movement in Taiwan owes a great deal not only to the so-called economic miracle but also to the ideas inherited from the May Fourth period. Although these ideas had their origins on Mainland China, they were brought across the Taiwan straits around 1949.

On the other hand, liberal democratic ideas have not been allowed on the mainland since 1949, especially after the Anti-Rightist Campaign of 1957. Chinese intellectuals have been completely silenced by arbitrary, coercive power—primarily military power.

But even on the mainland, one would be wrong to assume that the Communists really succeeded in suppressing all democratic ideas in their attempt to reform everybody's mind (*gaizao*, as it is called on Mainland China). Nobody's mind can be reformed except by himself or herself. You can only reform when you get enlightenment from within, not when it is forced on you from without. This is why Beida (Peking University) was so important, why it has always played a leading role in student movements, and why Mao Zedong had so many contemptuous remarks to make about Beida, where he once was a library clerk. The intellectual tradition of the May Fourth Movement never died at Beida. Democratic and liberal ideas have been suppressed but not eliminated on its campus. They outlasted one anti-intellectual campaign after another during the 1950s and 1960s. Most of the time these ideas existed at the level of implicit consciousness, but at other times they surfaced in Marxist disguise. Thus, when totalitarian control somewhat loosened, like after 1979, these ideas returned very quickly. They grew like mushrooms after the rain. Now it has reached the point where they can no longer be suppressed or contained. So, if we believe that ideas are also powerful and can change the world when the circumstances are right, then we have reason to be optimistic about the future of democracy in China.

A Cultural Foundation for Chinese Democracy

I wish to stress the point that democracy needs a cultural foundation. Western democracy did not come about overnight and from nowhere. One has to consider the humanistic, secular, and rationalistic culture that developed in the West. The Renaissance, the Reformation, the scientific revolution, the Enlightenment, all contributed, each in its own way, to the growth of modern democracy. At the very center of this new culture was the idea of the dignity of the human person, which began in the Renaissance. Tolerance and freedom has had much to do with religious history since the Reformation. British Puritans migrated to the United States because they were being persecuted by the Anglican Church at home. This eventually led to the building of a new democratic society. In the realm of political thought, the founding fathers of the United States were essentially products of the Enlightenment. This is what I mean by the cultural foundations of democracy.

Democracy is not just about a constitution, parliament, election, etc. Broadly defined, it is also a way of life. Wu'er Kaixi has said that he has been very much impressed by the way children are treated in the United States.[11] This is inherent in the country's democratic culture. When we judge whether a society is sufficiently civilized or not, we begin by looking at the behavior of its people. How do they treat children, women, or the elderly? Democracy has more to do with cultural substance than with political forms. You can have a constitution, you can have a so-called parliament, you can have some kind of nominal voting, but these do not add up to democracy.

A cultural foundation for democracy is exactly what China is lacking at this very moment. Over the last forty years, the Communist party has systematically and consciously demolished all the good aspects of Chinese culture on the one hand, and, unfortunately, has preserved and developed the worst elements in the Chinese tradition on the other. When the Communist party criticizes Chinese tradition, the ideas of Confucius and Mencius are always the first target. This happens to be the essence of Chinese culture. Confucius's idea of humanity and Mencius's idea of tyrannicide (the right of the common people to rise up and kill an evil tyrannical ruler) and the importance of people provide precisely a kind of cultural foundation for modern democracy. Chinese culture is essentially a humanistic and rationalistic one that with some adaptation can go well with democracy. Modernization in the West did not begin with the elimination of Christianity. No one has denounced Jesus Christ and Saint Peter. Some people attacked evil practices and corruption in the church, but not the whole Christian tradition. Many Renaissance humanists and Enlightenment philosophers were themselves still very much Christians. Sir Isaac Newton was very much a true believer in God. He wanted to find out how God created the order of the universe. So he looked at the universe as a machine, like a watch. This view comes from Christian theology.

True, antitraditionalism in China did not begin with the Communists. It is an intellectual cancer traceable to the May Fourth Movement, if not earlier. Since then, we Chinese have always blamed our culture when we are frustrated with modernization. We become more radically antitraditional each time we suffer a new setback in modernization. As a result, the intellectual history of twentieth-century China has become no more than a process of radicalization. Each generation is more radical than the previous one.

Antitraditionalism in modern Chinese thought has been finally crystallized into what may be called the "myth of the clean slate."[12] This refers to the view that, in order to modernize China, we must first sweep away Chinese cultural tradition in its entirety. Only when we have cleaned the slate can we then start again from scratch to build a modern society.

The myth of the clean slate was the guiding principle of the so-called Cultural Revolution (1966-76), in which Chinese radicalism reached its peak. During the Cultural Revolution, everything that was old was to be destroyed. However, I must hasten to add that, while there was some continuity between the antitraditionalism of the May Fourth Movement and that of the Cultural Revolution, the differences between the two are crucial. The former was primarily a spontaneous intellectual discourse initiated by young intellectuals without a hidden agenda, whereas the latter was masterminded by a senile and diabolical revolutionary leader who was determined to regain his personal power by manipulating the discontent of the masses in general and the rebelliousness of the youth in particular.

During the May Fourth Movement, for example, the famous slogan "Down with Confucius and Sons" referred not to the teachings of Confucius and Mencius per se, but to the political and social ideology developed during the imperial age in the name of Confucius. Intellectual leaders of the May Fourth Movement such as Chen Duxiu and Hu Shih still had many good things to say about Confucian humanism. By contrast, during the Cultural Revolution, Confucius and Mencius were bitterly denounced as "spokesmen of the slave-owning class" or "reactionary thinkers whose ideas have poisoned the minds of the Chinese people for over two thousand years." So, under the thirty-year totalitarian rule of the anti-intellectual tyrant Mao Zedong, the Chinese humanistic tradition was systematically demolished and, as a result, China today has been emptied of much of its cultural foundation for democratic reconstruction.

Unfortunately, the myth of the clean slate has outlasted the iconoclasm of the Cultural Revolution and is continuing to haunt Chinese intellectuals in the post-Mao era. Mistaking the Leninist-Stalinist kind of totalitarian control for Chinese tradition, many Chinese intellectuals, including young students, still blame the failure of China's democratization on the latter. They are more convinced than ever that any hope of success for a democratic system in China hinges on whether China can sweep away its cultural tradition. This is precisely the powerful message of the famous television documentary "River Elegy."[13] I am very sympathetic to the intention of the film but cannot agree with its diagnosis and prescription.

I believe it is now high time that we begin to rediscover the Chinese humanistic and rationalistic tradition, which alone can provide the democracy movement in China with a cultural foundation. But, before this rediscovery is possible, we must first rebuild our frame of mind, which has been dominated by the myth of the clean slate for over seven decades. The myth has long trapped us in a vicious circle. On the one hand, we must destroy everything old before we can create something new; on the other hand, the more we destroy the less we are able to create. Thus, the iconoclastic mentality has paralyzed China for any constructive work. To a considerable extent this disease of the mind and heart also stands in the way of a successful democracy movement in China. The philosopher Wang Yang-ming (1472-1529) once said, "It is easy to conquer the rebels in the mountains but difficult to conquer the rebels in our minds and hearts (*po shan zhong zei yi, po xinzhong zei nan)*".[14] Deng Xiaoping and Li Peng are only "rebels in the mountain"; they cannot stop the democratic movement for long. It is rather the clean slate radicalism embodied in an indiscriminate denunciation of Chinese cultural heritage that has long become "the rebels in our minds and hearts." We must conquer this enemy within before we can begin to rediscover and repossess the Chinese humanistic tradition. To those who are dedicated to the cause of democracy in China I would quote Johann Wolfgang von Goethe:

What you have as heritage,
Take now as task;
For thus you will make it your own.

The Future Over the Long and Short Term

Finally, we must ask, where will China go from here? I am a short-term pessimist but a long-term optimist. It seems inevitable that China will experience another political earthquake in the next three to five years when Deng Xiaoping disappears from the scene. The political changes that are almost sure to occur will be more drastic and more basic than those since the death of Mao Zedong.

This observation of mine is based on two important facts: First, Deng Xiaoping is clearly the last "strong man" with some charisma who can hold the various conflicting forces and interest groups within the Communist party together. Charisma, whatever its precise definition, is a product of extraordinary historical situations such as a revolution or religious movement. It was revolution combined with a totalitarian party system that gave Mao Zedong absolute, charismatic power. Given his educational background and administrative ability, Mao would have been very lucky just to climb step by step from the position of clerk to that of curator in the library of Peking University, not to mention national leader. But revolutionary charisma is not something that can be passed on from the first revolutionary generation to the next. Deng Xiaoping belongs to the first generation, and he has created his own charisma primarily through his opposition to the Gang of Four. But his charismatic power is in no way comparable to Mao's. Moreover, he has been losing it steadily in the last three or four years and especially since 4 June 1989. After he is gone, there will be no one in China who can step into his shoes. A charismatic strong man and the totalitarian system depend on each other.

With the disappearance of the last strong man, totalitarian control in China is going to disintegrate rapidly. Jiang Zemin has reportedly been given the additional title of chairman of the Central Military Commission. But how can he possibly be relied upon to exercise effective military authority in time of crisis or emergency? He is even weaker than Malenkov after Stalin or Hua Guofeng after Mao because he is still functioning very much under the shadow of a strong man.

Second, a decentralized China is in the offing. China has been decentralized both politically and economically in the past decade as a result of the implementation of the "opening up" and reform policies. There is already abundant evidence of a growing regionalism in China. Needless to say, decentralization and regionalism go hand in hand. Powers that have been delegated to the provincial and local authorities can no longer be taken back by the central government, especially when the Party Central is steadily weakening. One needs only to compare the membership of the Politburo of the 1950s, 1960s and 1970s to that of today. One will immediately notice the ever-increasing pace at which the process of weakening the center has been taking place. This has now become an irreversible process.

This is not to suggest that warlordism will return to China after Deng's death. What I am saying is only that the immediate prospect in the next three to five years will be in all likelihood a decentralized China with a weakened center. The new regionalism will probably take the form of an alliance between the economic and military forces on a regional basis.

Therefore, it is likely that China will become much worse before it gets any better. This is the price China has to pay in order to rebuild a humane society on the ruins of totalitarianism.

But regionalism has a positive side as well in that it will probably create some breathing space for freedom. Dissident intellectuals, for example, will be able to move from Beijing to Guangzhou or from Nanjing to Shanghai to seek greater freedom of expression. A democratic movement has a better chance under regionalism than under centralized totalitarianism. This is exactly what happened during the May Fourth Movement seventy years ago and during the so-called Warring States period of 475-221 B.C. that witnessed the development of the "Hundred Schools of Thought." The possibility that China will break up into many pieces ought not worry us. Chinese culture has been such a strong adhesive force that it will ultimately hold all parts of China together.

Therefore, the future of China depends very much on the intellectuals, especially the students. The reasons are obvious. In the first place, they alone can provide the rallying point for an organized resistance to totalitarian tyranny. In the past forty years, all the intermediate organizations in traditional China, such as clans, guilds, academia, regional associations, and religious societies have been wiped out. Also wiped out are the well-organized Western-style groups developed by the merchants, workers, and intellectuals in modern times. Communist China today claims to have other "political parties" and "workers' unions," but those organizations are strictly controlled by the Communist party and have no real functions at all.

University and college campuses are therefore the only places where organized resistance can start and grow. In sharp contrast to Europe, organized religion as a tradition has been singularly lacking in China. Solidarity in Poland has its Catholic Church, and opposition forces in East Germany have their Protestant churches. But no such organizational support exists in China. This explains why even in traditional China political protest had to be led primarily by students of the Imperial Academy. It is more so in present-day China.

In the second place, China has been and still is an "elite" society. The masses, especially the peasants, have been politically passive. Nothing is further from the truth than the notion that there is mass participation in China under communism; Mao Zedong's private remarks on this are very revealing. He said, "What is a mass movement? A mass movement is nothing if it is anything other than moving the masses."[15] And in January 1979, Deng Xiaoping told the Central Committee of the Communist party : "During the sixty years since the October Revolution, we haven't done a good job of democracy.... We need to find a way to make the people realize, to make them aware, that they are the true master of the country."[16] Thus, Mao's remark is completely confirmed by Deng's speech. If the masses had been active participants in public affairs, how is it possible that they were still in need of being "made to realize," as late as 1979, that they were the "true masters of the country?"

The simple truth is that the Chinese Communists have been extremely skillful since the beginning of their "revolution" in manipulating the masses. In the 1940s they not only manipulated the Chinese masses well in the name of "patriotism," they also succeeded in deceiving American Foreign Service people in China into believing that they had the full support of the masses. John P. Davis, Jr. for example, reported to the U.S. State Department on 7 November 1944:

Communist growth since 1937 has been almost geometric in progression.... The reason for this phenomenal vitality and strength is simple and fundamental. It is mass support, mass participation. The

Communist governments and armies are the first governments and armies in modern Chinese history to have positive and widespread popular support. They have this support because the governments and armies are genuinely of the people.[17]

In quoting this particular passage I cannot help feeling embarrassed to the extreme.

But Deng is quite right in saying that the Chinese people are in need of being made to realize that they are the "masters of the country." Who can tell and show the people how to exercise their rights as masters of China? Clearly, not the Communist party, which has long established itself as the "new class," with all kinds of privileges. Under present circumstances, only the intellectuals, especially the students, are in a position to assume this responsibility. In view of the long Chinese tradition of students movements, we have reason to believe that Chinese intellectuals today are uniquely qualified to play the role of what Arnold Toynbee calls the "creative minority" and to steer China firmly toward democracy.

[This chapter is a revised edition of a speech delivered on 25 November 1989 at the "Prodemocracy Movement in China" symposium held at Rutgers University.]

Notes

1   Ban Gu, "Biography of Bao Xuan," in *Han Shu* (History of the Han Dynasty) (Beijing: Zhonghua shuju edition, 1962), chapter 72, pp. 3,093-4.

2   Fan Ye, "Biographies of Factionalists," in *Hou Han Shu* (History of the Later Han Dynasty) (Beijing: Zhonghua shuju edition, 1965), chapter 67, pp. 2, 185-90.

3   Huang Xianfan, *Songdai Taixuesheng jiuguo yundong* (Patriotic Student Movements of the Imperial Academy During the Song Dynasty) (Shanghai: Commercial Press, 1937), pp. 12-20.

4   Fu Locheng, *Fu Mengzhen xiansheng nianpu* (A Chronological Biography of Fu Sinian) (Taipei: Biographical Literature Society, 1969), pp. 62-63. For further accounts by participants of the Movement, see Zhou Zezong et al, *Wusi yu Zhongguo* (The May Fourth Movement and China) (Taipei: China Times Publishing Co., 1979), pp. 673-686.

5   For a full factual account of the May Fourth Movement of 1919, see Chow Tse-tsung, *The May Fourth Movement, Intellectual Revolution in Modern China* (Cambridge: Harvard University Press, 1960), chapter 4.

6   Student leader Wu'er Kaixi made this comment in a November 1989 speech at Rutgers University.

7   Barrington Moore, Jr., *Social Origins of Dictatorship and Democracy: Lords and Peasants in the Making of the Modern World* (Boston: Beacon Press, 1966), p. 418.

8   Quoted in Xiao Gongchuan, *Wenxue Jianwang lu* (Memoirs of a Scholar) (Taipei: Biographical Literature Society, 1972), p. 74.

9   Francis Fukuyama, "The End of History?" *The National Interests* 16 (Summer 1989):3-18.

10   I refer to the famous case of Lei Zhen in 1960. See Hu Songping, *Hu Shihzhi xiansheng nianpu changbian chugao* (A Draft Chronological Biography of Hu Shih) (Taipei: Lianjing Press, 1984), vol. 9, pp. 3334-9, 3343-5. For more details, see Lei Zhen, *Lei Zhen huiyilu* (Lei Zhen's Memoirs) (Taipei: Seventies Magazine Society, 1978).

11   Wu'er Kaixi, in his speech in Rutgers University in November 1989, said that the thing that impressed him the most about life in the United States was the schoolbuses "because when the lights flash, everybody stops for the children. Because in this society, children are the most important thing."

12   Stephen Toulmin, *Cosmopolis, The Hidden Agenda of Modernity* (New York: The Free Press, 1990), pp. 175-180.

13   "River Elegy" is a famous television documentary that was broadcast in China in 1988 and 1989 and that was enthusiastically received by Chinese intellectuals and students. One of its chief scriptwriters, Su Xiaokang, was accused of inciting the Tiananmen Square demonstrations.

14   Hou Wailu, ed., *Zhongguo sixiang tongshi* (A General History of Chinese Thought) (Beijing: People's Press, 1960), vol. 4, part 2, p. 875.

15   This information was obtained from Li Shenzhi, vice-president of the Chinese Academy of Social Sciences. Li was present when Mao made this comment.

16   Quoted in Ruan Ming's introduction to his forthcoming book, *Deng's Empire*, pp. 13-14.

17   *The China White Paper, August 1949* (Palo Alto: Stanford University Press, 1967), vol. 2, p. 567.

11

Observing the Observers at Tiananmen Square: Freedom, Democracy, and the News Media in China's Student Movement

Steven Mark

Remember 3 June 1989. A most tragic event happened in the Chinese capital, Beijing. Thousands of people, most of them innocent civilians, were killed by fully armed soldiers when they forced their way into the city. Among the killed are our colleagues at Radio Beijing.

The soldiers were riding on armored vehicles and used machine guns against thousands of local residents and students who tried to block their way. When the army convoys made a breakthrough, soldiers continued to spray their bullets indiscriminately at crowds in the street. Eyewitnesses say some armored vehicles even crushed foot soldiers who hesitated in front of the resting civilians.

Radio Beijing's English Department deeply mourns those who died in the tragic incident and appeals to all its listeners to join our protest for this gross violation of human rights and the most barbarous suppression of the people.

Because of the abnormal situation here in Beijing, there is no other news we could bring you. We sincerely ask for your understanding and thank you for joining us at this most tragic moment.[1]

Thus ended China's short-lived experiment in freedom of the press. This transmission, broadcast the day after the invasion of Tiananmen Square, earned newscaster Li Dan a meeting with government investigators.[2]

The protests and the massacre at Tiananmen Square were the most significant news events to come out of China since the death of Mao and the fall of the Gang of Four. But, unlike the bitterness and anger that marked that era, the demonstrations at Tiananmen Square had an emotional appeal that attracted the support of people around the world. The struggle came to represent the basic components in the human struggle, all expressed in universally recognized symbols: freedom against repression; impetuous youth rejecting old-guard traditionalism; bravery confronting cowardliness; and good vs. evil.

These images and symbols were conveyed in the foreign and domestic news media. In the process, the news media itself became a symbol of the movement's success, serving as a marker of the limits of the leadership's tolerance. For the Chinese press, which covered and joined the demonstrations, there was a brief period of virtually unfettered coverage and commentary on politics and reform. The foreign press got a rare opportunity to view ordinary Chinese citizens openly speaking their minds. And the people of Beijing got an unprecedented experience of life in an open society.

But the brutal crackdown and subsequent events demonstrated that this freedom of the press and of society was only temporary. The brief moment of freedom proved to be little more than an experiment that could be stopped—and was. Since the crackdown, the regime has effectively reclosed Chinese society, regaining control over the domestic press, intimidating the people into quiescence, and even harassing the foreign press.

With the tragic ending of the student movement still in mind, this essay takes a critical view in discussing two themes concerning both the foreign and domestic news media in the Tiananmen Square demonstrations. First, it will show how the news media became part of the chemistry of the student movement. This occurred at different times and for different reasons for the Chinese and the foreign news media but it is important because the commonly accepted ideal for the news media is that it should be more of an observer of events than a catalyst. In addition, since the news media's main function is "to inform the people," this essay also offers some observations on the quality of its coverage, focusing first on cultural bias in the U.S. news media, and then on antigovernment bias in the Chinese press and its implications regarding freedom of the press in China.

In this way, this essay hopes to address some aspects of the movement that might have been overshadowed or misinterpreted in the excitement and tragedy of 4 June, which will be of interest to the general reader. It also raises issues related to the coverage of China, which foreign and domestic journalists, as well as anyone interested in the prospects for democracy in China, might find relevant.

The Chinese Media Sets the Stage

For most of the last forty years, the Chinese news media has existed solely to serve the interests of the state. The Chinese Communist party-state, following a practice from traditional China in which the leader was considered to have the first and the last word, took control of all journalistic (as well as literary) publications and broadcast stations when it gained control over China, and has not allowed the news media much freedom since. As a result, the Chinese news media has come to serve as a kind of political barometer for the people, a way to gauge party tolerance. By reading between the lines of the official media, people can determine the extent to which dissent can be voiced.

By the late 1980s, the official Chinese media had established a climate that seemed to encourage open expression of frustrations and disappointment. It was taking an increasingly aggressive tone, particularly in its coverage of official corruption. This was in line with a government campaign to root out corruption, which had become rampant by the late 1980s. With government encouragement, the Chinese press was inundating the public with tales of official profiteering, coining two terms—*guandao* and *daoye*—to designate the greediest officials.

Even Western journalists were impressed by the coverage. Former *Washington Post* reporter Michael J. Berlin, who taught journalism in China in 1989, wrote that he was "amazed to see a Chinese television reporter, mike in hand, standing outside the private home that a provincial official had allegedly built with government funds and trying to question a family member about the allegation as he emerged, stunned and enraged by the live report."[3]

There was plenty of corruption to cover. Chinese officials reported that 109,000 party members were "expelled or asked to resign" in

1987, most of them due to corruption or disciplinary problems.[4] In 1986, the party felt it necessary to convene a conference on corruption for party cadres and to draw up new guidelines to be used in negotiations with foreign businesses, where the extraction of special treatment was commonplace.

Certainly other discouraging news in China, such as trouble in the economy, was chipping away at the public's confidence in the party. But while stories about economic disarray warned the public of hard times to come, the constant and often sensational tales of corruption appeared to sanction a kind of critical comment about the government that, while indirect, was nonetheless harsh.

An example can be found in the *Beijing Review,* an international weekly. In a rewrite of an investigative report by the *Economic Daily* on official profiteering in fertilizer sales, the *Review* took an aggressive stance in challenging the government:

> Despite the best of government intentions, fertilizer has become even more entrenched with the pork barrel.... Farmers have blasted the government, wanting to know just where that fertilizer—the state-produced, sold, and priced stuff—has gone to. They want to know why there's only the "back door," black market stuff that's sold at much higher prices.... With corruption chewing on China's agricultural policies, the nation waits for its leaders to take measures that will clean up this mess.[5]

With such reporting, the Chinese media not only fanned the people's frustration with government, it gave them the impression that they could criticize the government for its incompetence and greed. This writer, for example, met many people in 1988 who showed no hesitation in voicing their criticisms of the party.

The *Beijing Review* article also revealed an interesting facet of the Chinese media. The magazine reported that, although the *Economic Daily* had not named officials suspected of corruption, it had still provoked an angry outcry from a provincial official who claimed injury to government prestige. This reflects a longstanding but unwritten policy that essentially limited criticism according to the level of the publication. Accordingly, a city newspaper would criticize officials of local government, but not those of the county, and so on. High officials would be subject to the scrutiny of the *People's Daily* or the Xinhua News Agency. Naturally, this placed the top party leaders, especially Deng Xiaoping, above all criticism. The limits of this unwritten policy began to be tested during the protests on Tiananmen Square.

The Chinese Media Becomes the Story

The interaction between the government and the Chinese news media during the early stages of the student demonstrations is a classic example of government blundering and its effect on a social group. In transforming the news media from one of society's many disgruntled groups into one of the most active government critics, the government revealed not only its own lack of savvy in dealing with the press, but the depth of discontent and unhappiness that the students had tapped.

When students began marching in sympathy for the death of former Party Secretary Hu Yaobang, the government ignored their pleas and concentrated its efforts on finding a way to stop the demonstrations. In keeping with its view that the news media should serve the state, the regime decided to use the media to downplay the story and to discredit the students, in hopes that they would go away. This appears to have been the government's only significant strategy through the first week of demonstrations; no other significant response from the government has been noted.

The strategy took shape a few days after Hu Yaobang died, when Politburo member Hu Qili ordered editors of major newspapers not to cover the demonstrations, warning that publicizing them would inflame the situation. However, he apparently did not realize that his order might inflame Chinese journalists; furthermore, his order might not have been necessary. Up until that time, television news appeared to be setting the pace for coverage in giving only passing mention of the demonstrations and describing them in a negative tone. But, in spite of Hu's order, and perhaps because of it, a local newspaper, the *Science and Technology Daily*, published a reasonably complete account of a 22 April protest in which six thousand students marched. The article was the first in a Chinese publication to give full coverage to the demonstrations and was promptly copied and circulated throughout Beijing campuses. The journal's office was swamped with calls praising its coverage.[6]

Soon, another incident in Shanghai angered journalists again. It involved the *World Economic Herald*, a 300,000-circulation weekly that frequently challenged the government on a number of issues. On

19 April, the paper held a forum in which supporters of Hu Yaobang called for a reappraisal of the reformist leader. At the forum, intellectuals such as Yan Jiaqi, former director of the Beijing Academy of Social Sciences, said such provocative things as: "The main problem China has had, up to today, is the lack of democracy. A handful of people can just talk among themselves and put aside the interests of the Chinese people and then reach an unpopular decision."[7] The paper then printed a six-page special section on the forum. But before it could be distributed, Shanghai municipal leaders stopped it and fired the *Herald*'s editor, Qin Benli.

This action touched on a sensitive area for Chinese journalists. The *Herald* was a semiprivate journal linked to the Shanghai Academy of Social Sciences. Many journalists, even those who worked for government publications, thought it improper for government policy to be extended to what was essentially a private publication.

The government's action incensed journalists and, to the party's chagrin, made a hero of Qin; for much of the next seven weeks, the grounds surrounding the *Herald*'s office were filled with students and workers, listening to Voice of America transmissions broadcast on loudspeakers strung up in the yard.

Qin's dismissal came on 26 April, the day of the infamous *People's Daily* editorial, "Resolutely Oppose Turmoil." As has been noted elsewhere, this editorial escalated tensions more than any other event during the protests, and would be a focal point for the demonstrations for the next six weeks. The editorial galvanized opposition to the government and prompted a huge demonstration on 27 April, the largest to date with more than one hundred thousand students marching to the cheers of Beijing citizens. Chinese journalists also were angered by the editorial and responded with their own petition, signed by one hundred reporters and editors from the *People's Daily*.

With the government's worst fears being realized, it abruptly switched its strategy. That day, in a sudden reversal of the previous ban on coverage of the movement, Hu Qili again met with editors from nine major Chinese newspapers and said they could report the "actual state of affairs" in Beijing. This act of "media diplomacy" can be viewed as an attempt to counteract the *People's Daily* editorial and to placate the media's anger over Qin Benli's dismissal.

Hu's action also was an attempt to redefine the significance of the demonstrations and to give them a direction that could be used by the government. He told the editors that the party also wanted to eradicate corruption, as the students were demanding. In later public statements, and even after 4 June, party leaders spoke repeatedly about the need to curb corruption. It is apparent that the party wanted to focus attention on eradicating corruption, hoping to skirt other key issues, namely, the legitimacy of the leadership.

Two days later, after more demonstrations and with a student boycott well underway, the government tried the second phase of its new strategy, and again the media played a role. The government held a televised forum featuring students directing pointed questions at party officials. The forum not only failed to satisfy students, it provided another flashpoint for the nation's journalists. At one point, State Council spokesman Yuan Mu, answering a question concerning freedom of the press, asserted that the press was free in China. "According to the Constitution, the press enjoys freedom, but at the same time, it has to be constrained by the Constitution and the law," he said, apparently not understanding the contradiction in this statement.[8]

From the beginning of the student demonstrations, there had been another force that pushed the media toward the students' side: the students' call for freedom of speech and press. These demands, while they sometimes went to the point of ridiculing the media—such as when slogans like "*People's Daily* lies to the people!" were yelled—formed a perfect counterpoint to the journalists' complaints.

The dismissal of Qin Benli, the censorship of the press, the brazen lies about it, and the appeal of the students did more than arouse the national news media's antipathy for the government. They gave substance to the issue of freedom of the press and created a cause for the Chinese media. In the offices of several Beijing publications, unpublished articles about the protests were pinned up by reporters who could not get them published. Petitions circulated among journalists and eventually were combined into one signed by 1,013 journalists representing thirty top news agencies.[9] The petition demanded the right to cover demonstrations and an apology for the previous ban, the reinstatement of Qin Benli and a reassessment of Yuan Mu's statement.

This petition demonstrated the degree to which the government had alienated its own media. Journalists had won concessions from the government in the 27 April meeting with Hu Qili and had been reporting on the student movement. A demonstration commemorating the seventieth anniversary of the May Fourth Movement—in which some journalists marched with students—received reasonable coverage. For good measure, the government on 6 May again assured newspaper editors that coverage of demonstrations was permitted. But the journalists' petition was delivered on 9 May as an indication of their disenchantment with the government and their growing desire for independence.

The petition was crucial in another way. It represented the first organized effort in support of the students and gave a degree of momentum for them to continue demonstrating. There had been a lull since the rally on 4 May. But as the first wave of demonstrations died down, the journalists provided a link to later events, specifically the one that produced even larger demonstrations and led to the crackdown—the visit by Soviet president Mikhail Gorbachev.

The Foreign News Media is Drawn into the Protests

While Chinese journalists were drawn into the demonstrations as participants, their counterparts in the foreign news media were able to view the demonstrations from the journalist's perspective, as "newsworthy" events. Free from government censorship, they became involved in the protests strictly as observers and reporters. The major story involving the foreign media would come as the demonstrations progressed.

In fact, most of the foreign media did not foresee much of a story coming out of Hu Yaobang's death. The China beat had not yielded much major news since the 1986-87 student demonstrations, and, since then, coverage of China had consisted mostly of stories about communism and capitalism and the troubles in the economy. Political change—the key issue for the U.S. media in coverage of any foreign country—did not appear to be brewing. "The correspondents in Beijing had grown accustomed to repeating the conventional wisdom that the China story had slid way off the front page," wrote John Schidlovsky, the *Baltimore Sun*'s Beijing Bureau chief. "Certainly none of us expected much from China's university students."[10]

There were, however, some suggestions in the U.S. news media that Hu Yaobang's death had come at a particularly critical moment. National Public Radio quoted well-known China writer Orville Schell, just returned from China, as saying that students revered Hu Yaobang and that the situation in China was more confused than he had ever experienced. On 17 April, two days after Hu Yaobang's death, the *New York Times* ran a lengthy report about widespread discontent with Deng Xiaoping. "Some say that Mr. Deng, eighty-four years old, has held onto power too long," the *Times* wrote.

> People often compare him to Mao Zedong of the mid 1970s and say that he should completely retire and leave the stage.... Farmers blame him because they cannot get fertilizer. Workers blame him for the widespread corruption. Intellectuals blame him for ignoring education. And everyone blames him for the rapidly rising prices."[11]

These were the exceptions among the U.S. news media. Many major U.S. news agencies gave only cursory attention to Hu Yaobang's death, with a few mentioning that students were planning demonstrations in his memory. And, once the demonstrations began, they were not considered front-page news.

That all changed on the night of 19 April, when students clashed with police in front of Communist party headquarters at Xinhuamen. Foreign reporters had been at the scene and had made contact with students, and, although they were ordered to leave the area before the struggle ensued, they soon heard that police had severely beaten several students. In the view of the Western news media, which considers violence to be a key aspect of "newsworthiness," this clash immediately raised the tenor of the demonstrations and elevated them to front-page news.

In the next few days, the movement emerged as major news, as the students continued their protests and, to most everyone's surprise, the government restrained itself from taking action. Major coverage was devoted to the dramatic demonstrations and the government's ill-conceived attempts to quell them.

During this period, however, and on through the first two weeks of May, the foreign news media was nothing more than an impartial observer informing its audience of the events in China. Individual students, wary of government surveillance and retribution, spoke cautiously with foreign reporters and often were unwilling to give their names. Aside from yelling a few slogans and marching, they were somewhat reluctant to air their views to foreign correspondents, though print reporters, who were able to operate inconspicuously and offer anonymity, seemed to fare well in their dealings with students. Television crews, however, were received harshly. "In the beginning, the first week, it was very rough," wrote ABC News producer John Reiss in the *Washington Journalism Review*, quoting his bureau chief Todd Carrel. "People would threaten to smash the camera. They wanted the movement to be covered, but they didn't want to be personally identified."[12]

With the demonstrations appearing to reach a stalemate after the first week of May, the Western media for the most part turned its attention to Gorbachev's visit. Although day-by-day coverage continued, the significance of the student demonstrations was considered in the context of the overall desire for reform in the communist world. Many newspapers sent their Soviet reporters to China to accompany Gorbachev for the express purpose of covering this angle.

But Gorbachev's visit was to become much more. It brought together an unusual combination of groups, individuals, and forces— including the newly invigorated domestic news media and the recently expanded foreign press corps—that was to become China's moment of self-revelation.

Gorbachev's Visit as a Media Event

On its face, the visit by Soviet president Mikhail Gorbachev to Beijing should have provided an opportunity for the Chinese regime to recover from the embarrassment caused by the events surrounding Hu Yaobang's death. The visit was a symbol of the rapprochement of the world's two largest Communist nations after thirty years of hostility. It was a political coup for Deng Xiaoping, who hosted the summit as a favor to Gorbachev. Therefore, the summit had tremendous value in building credibility for the Chinese government.

To the students, however, Gorbachev personified the idea of political reform within the socialist framework. His policies of *glasnost* and *perestroika* tapped into their yearnings for greater control over the destiny of their lives and their country.

What the Gorbachev visit really was, however, was a bonanza for both foreign and domestic news media. About twelve hundred foreign reporters were allowed to join the regular Beijing press corps, courtesy of the government's desire for international credibility. The government also had granted extra satellite privileges to the foreign media, permitting live coverage. Chinese journalists, through their petitioning, had secured the right to cover the student movement.

These journalists were greeted by thousands of students, workers, intellectuals, and other citizens protesting the government's response to the student movement. A hunger strike had begun two days before Gorbachev's arrival and garnered worldwide attention. The images of Gorbachev and Deng Xiaoping were overwhelmed by marching youths. Several events planned for Gorbachev had to be rescheduled because protesters jammed Tiananmen Square.

Chinese television became an especially powerful source of information. On 17 May, Chinese television news broadcasted a report of the demonstrations on the Square, listing organizations and groups that supported the students. That was followed by the angry confrontation between Li Peng and several student leaders on 18 May, and Zhao Ziyang's tearful, last-ditch appeal to students the following day. Such scenes of spontaneity, save for one interview that Zhao Ziyang had given in 1987, had never been seen in the past.[13]

The openness in the press was paralleled by a new congeniality among the citizenry toward the news media. People spoke willingly to both the foreign and Chinese press, disputing openly the government's contention that the situation was "turmoil." "The camera became a beacon," wrote John Reiss. "Bringing a camera anywhere, whether to Tiananmen Square or to a back alley, would attract a small throng of boisterous demonstrators, all of whom, it seemed, had something to say."[14]

The Western News Media Transformed

The Gorbachev visit witnessed the transformation of the role of the Western media. Suddenly, it was no longer just an observer, a reporter of events; it became an important catalyst in the chemistry of the student movement. Although this often occurs when a crowd interacts with the news media, at Tiananmen Square it reached an extreme.

The impact of the presence of the foreign news media could immediately be seen in the sudden appearance of a "media savvy" on the part of the students. Conscious of how they were appearing to an international audience, the students began staging formal press conferences and other media events—previously, the news media had

had to guess what the students would do—and using signs and posters in English. Some student groups, such as those from Beijing University, appointed special spokesman to deal with the foreign media.[15] The demonstrators were becoming more preoccupied with the Western news media; one student even asked a *Wall Street Journal* reporter "What kind of coverage is ABC giving us?"

But the presence of the Western news media had a deeper impact. The Western news media is highly respected in China, and, in that it represented a Western audience, it was endowed with a special status: Not only was it disseminating information about the students, it was conferring Western approval on them. This boosted the students' confidence. They knew that the world was watching them; articles from Western newspapers were being faxed to them almost daily and posted up around campus, and some managed to see the television broadcasts from Cable News Network at tourist hotels. Judging from the overwhelmingly positive coverage that they were receiving, they could sense that the Western news media was on their side.

More significant, especially in consideration of the crackdown that was to come later, was that the students believed that the Western media was protecting them. Student leaders were "convinced that the presence of a large international press corps here to cover the visit of Soviet President Mikhail Gorbachev helped restrain hardliners in the government who wanted to use the police to restore order, whatever the cost," reported the *Washington Post*.[16] The students applauded CBS's television cameras when they showed up to cover a rally on 16 May.

They also saw a tactical advantage to being covered by the Western news media. Showing a mentality similar to that of the government— that the news media is a tool—the students began to consider the news media as an instrument to spread their message. They often asked to speak to correspondents from the Voice of America or the British Broadcasting Service, knowing that the former, for example, has an estimated listening audience in China of 60 million.[17] These foreign broadcasts undoubtedly factored into the growth of the demonstrations throughout the country, although of equal or perhaps greater influence was the new freedom being exhibited in the Chinese news media.

The declaration of martial law on 20 May induced the students to retreat only slightly from the Western news media. Although some protesters became more reserved with the media—often refusing to give their full names and asking for anonymity—they still spoke up, as if this was their last opportunity to get their message out. Meanwhile, the security blanket that they believed the foreign media was providing for them was becoming unraveled. The factions involved in the struggle for the leadership of the government had come to appreciate the power of the Western press and tried to bring it under control. On 19 May, on the eve of the imposition of martial law, U.S. audiences experienced government censorship firsthand when CBS and CNN interrupted their broadcast to cover themselves being thrown off the air. The communications link was restored again briefly three days later, suggesting that Zhao Ziyang had gained the upper hand. One day later, however, with the hardline faction consolidating its hold, live television broadcasts were stopped again.

A few days later, the government issued extensive restrictions on all foreign media, including the print media, which were designed to prevent them from interviewing citizens about the student demonstrations.[18] These restrictions were only partly effective; the foreign press was able to evade police surveillance for the most part, though some reporters were detained and harassed. On 3 June, in the midst of the onslaught on Tiananmen Square, reporters were able to circulate freely as long as they did not approach the Square. But, if they sought refuge inside any of the large hotels near Tiananmen Square, they found armed guards there ready to detain them.[19]

In the wake of the assault on the demonstrators, questions were raised about the interaction between the students and the Western news media. Accusations were made that the Western media emboldened the students to continue their struggle. Noted Chinese author Nien Cheng wrote that

China watchers, journalists with cameramen, and writers of world renown flocked to Tiananmen Square to interview the demonstrators. With the world on their side, the students developed a false sense of security. Even when the situation became really ugly and a ruthless crackdown seemed imminent, many remained.[20]

This was at least partly true, though there were other factors involved in the students' decision to stay on the Square. Most students genuinely believed that the army would never fire on the people; others were willing to die for their cause. It appears that there is little the news media could have done, short of ignoring the demonstrations altogether, to keep from being drawn into the demonstrations in this way, since it was the students who gravitated to the reporters and tried to use them.

But there are other instances suggesting how the Western news media encouraged the students. Correspondents have admitted feeling a personal warmth toward the students,[21] who would sense this and gain confidence from it. Since the Western news media is so highly regarded in China, receiving attention from such an esteemed entity had to affect students' egos. One student leader in particular, Wu'er Kaixi, developed what journalists later described as a "swaggering self-assurance" before their very eyes.

Perhaps most harmful, however, was when the news media, stunned at the early success of the students and now deciding to show some expertise, began predicting that the students had "won." These predictions appeared to be based more on the hopeful optimism of a few Western observers than anything factual. During the Gorbachev visit, CBS News quoted a Western diplomat as saying, "They'll never put this genie back in the bottle." One of its expert commentators, Bette Bao Lord, said, "The Great Wall has a crack in it." Even after martial law was declared on 20 May, the predictions continued. It was the consensus opinion of the foreign experts that Li Peng would be ousted when Premier Wan Li was recalled from an official visit to Washington on 25 May. Even after the crackdown, when military units were patrolling Beijing, the foreign media was predicting that civil war was imminent in China. Many correspondents have conceded that this judgment was based as much on rumor as on fact.

If these assessments filtered back to the students—and it seems almost certain that they did—they might have factored into at least some of the students' decision to stay on the Square beyond the point of safety. Their high regard for the Western news media might have led them to believe that what it was saying was true.

What appears to have been missed during this whole period was that the 26 April editorial in the *People's Daily*—the one official declaration of the government's policy toward the students—had never been retracted. The editorial later would become the justification for everything the government did.

Democracy and Cultural Bias in the U.S. Media

The Tiananmen Square Incident produced an unusual kinship between the U.S. people and the Chinese people. At Chinese embassies and consulates around the country, Americans joined visiting Chinese students in protest against the brutal regime. They contributed money to the student movement, and wrote letters of support to newspapers and politicians. U.S. officials, ranging from the liberal New York congressman Steven Solarz to conservative congressman Jesse Helms of North Carolina, called for sanctions against the Communists. New York declared its own Tiananmen Square and Los Angeles erected a Goddess of Democracy.

The reason for this outpouring of support is clear. Americans not only were shocked by the brutality of the massacre, they had come to see themselves in the students. They had been attracted to students chanting slogans from the American Revolution and appealing to the most cherished American values. Americans came to believe that the Chinese wanted a Western, and specifically an American, political system.

Yet, during and after the protests on Tiananmen Square, dozens of editorials, news accounts, commentaries, and other "expert analyses" attempted to refute this view. They pointed out that many if not most students considered themselves loyal Communists and socialists, and that they for the most part were trying to reform the system they had.[22]

How did this apparent contradiction between what the experts were saying and what the American people understood come about? Much of it can be attributed to the U.S. news media, which in its coverage of the demonstrations became fixated on the call for democracy, describing the movement as a "prodemocracy movement,"[23] and playing up the "democracy" angle of the students' demands.

This attachment to "democracy" is a reflection of a bias in the U.S. news media. This bias is not the kind typically attributed to the media—namely, that it is politically liberal and therefore less inclined to scrutinize liberal causes. Rather, it is based on its cultural background as an American entity with American values. Since the news media necessarily shapes its stories to make them accessible to its audience, this kind of cultural bias is understandable, and in that it can help make faraway places relevant to Americans, is not always a bad thing. But in the case of the Tiananmen Square demonstrations, cultural bias caused the news media to gravitate to certain issues and to interpret them in certain ways, and in a way distorted certain aspects of the demonstrations. This left the audience uncertain about what the student movement truly was about.

Television coverage in particular, by using the brief "sound bites" common to its reports, seemed to emphasize the term "democracy" without explaining fully that students, at best, had a superficial knowledge of the term. Television newsmen themselves admit this. Wrote ABC's John Reiss:

> We discovered that the best way to get a coherent sound bite about the movement's goals was to ask, "What do you want?" People inevitably replied: "democracy and freedom of the press." Yet, of the thirty or so people whom I asked, "What do you mean when you say democracy?" only one replied that he wanted the right to vote. Correspondents' descriptions of this were in vain, overwhelmed by the endless sound bites and pictures of people calling for democracy.[24]

Similarly, the news media was fascinated by Chinese reciting, in English, the Declaration of Independence, the Bill of Rights, and other themes from the American Revolution. These images made a convincing argument that it was American-style democracy that the students wanted and created a strong empathy between Americans and Chinese. But presenting them strictly as evidence of a desire for democracy failed to take into account the possibility that at least some of these people, in traditional Chinese fashion, had memorized them simply as preparation for English class. Even the Shanghai Communist Party chief, Jiang Zemin—hardly a democrat, having helped shut down the *World Economic Herald*—was able to recite such passages. Likewise, the slogans "Long live democracy! Long live freedom!" that the students used were probably more reflective of the Chinese penchant for idioms and aphorisms than of a deep understanding of the democratic process.

Cultural bias can also be seen in the U.S. news media's preoccupation with the Westernization of Chinese youths. This is not to say that the influence of the West on Chinese youths was insubstantial—the students clearly were attracted to Western lifestyles, and leaders such as Wang Dan called for political restructuring based on a Western system—but this characterization sometimes went too far. The *San Francisco Chronicle*, for example, described an instance in which a student helped its reporter in an argument with authorities over the reporter's travel plans, suggesting that the Chinese students are normally too meek to do such a thing. Contrary to this somewhat stereotypical view, Chinese do not hesitate to engage in an occasional spat, especially if it is with a minor official.

Aside from focusing on themes that would be attractive and accessible to Western audiences, the cultural bias of the Western news media was reflected in its underestimation of the students' discontent. It seemed to be basing its judgment simply on the tone of the demonstrations; a Reuters dispatch on 18 April, for example, forecast an early end to the demonstrations, quoting a Western diplomat as saying, "This time is different, I do not feel the tension" of demonstrations in previous years. On 4 May, the *Washington Post*, in comparing the Chinese protests with those in Eastern Europe, described the Chinese protests as somewhat light-hearted in comparison to those in Poland.

But the peaceful character of the demonstrations was in a large measure due to a concentrated effort on the part of the students and their supporters to maintain an atmosphere of calm. The student movement loathed the term "turmoil" and wanted to demonstrate that it did not deserve it; the less threatening they appeared, the more likely their chance of success. Their ability to control themselves, therefore, was a testament to the organizational strength of the movement, its commitment, and the breadth of support it enjoyed from other groups. This was more of a threat to the leadership than an angry mob would have been.

One other instance of cultural bias is worth mentioning. On several occasions, the U.S. news media noted with some irony that the protests were happening at a time when China was enjoying unprecedented economic growth and a rise in the standard of living. "Students appreciate Deng's accomplishments. But now they want more," reported the Los Angeles times on 30 April. This reflects a theory commonly applied in U.S. political coverage that puts "pocketbook" issues ahead of all others.

This theory, while relevant to the demonstrations, can be applied only to disappointments that had developed over the short term. On the other hand, Chinese society has long been suffering from a malaise, which has deepened over the past century and specifically the last ten years under the excesses of a changing Chinese leadership. The economic downturn of the late 1980s exacerbated that malaise, particularly among the older generation, who were seeing yet another program go sour, just as the Cultural Revolution and the Great Leap Forward had.

In fairness, it should be said that foreign journalists face a multitude of barriers, political and cultural, in trying to report on China and to present it in an interesting fashion to their audience. Certainly the demonstrations posed special difficulties and complications, and no one could have predicted the series of events that would escalate tensions and lead to confrontation. In general, the Western news media did an admirable job in covering day-to-day events, if not in drawing accurate conclusions from them.

But speaking admittedly from the advantage of hindsight, the U.S. media could have been more conscious of its inherently Western outlook and of its tendency to focus on the short-term situation, especially when problems had been brewing for a long time. The Chinese place a great deal of importance on their long history, and student leaders such as Wang Dan, a history student at Beijing University, tended to view these demonstrations in a historical context. Focusing on political and social developments of only the past ten years did not give an accurate picture of the true problems that Chinese students faced in trying to bring a democratic society to China.

George Orwell once wrote that

> in the case of a word like democracy, not only is there no agreed definition, but the attempt to make one is resisted from all sides. It is almost universally felt that when we call a country democratic we are praising; consequently, the defenders of every kind of regime claim that it is a democracy, fearing that they might have to stop using the word if it were tied to any one meaning. Words of this kind are often used in a consciously dishonest way.

The Chinese government, which defines itself as a "socialist democracy," would be a good example of the regime that Orwell describes. But the the interaction between the student movement and the U.S. news media suggests another situation in which the word "democracy" can be misused. The word brought together a movement looking for support, and the news media looking for an angle on the story. Given Orwell's observation that democracy "resists definition," one could question the dependence on the democracy angle. At the very least, considering the almost biblical significance that the word "democracy" has in the United States, one could question the unqualified use of the term "prodemocracy movement."

Freedom for the Chinese Media: A Service to Democracy?

At a demonstration marking the seventieth anniversary of the May Fourth Movement, Chinese journalists, having been harassed by the government and criticized by the students, joined students in a march on Tiananmen Square. One of their banners said, "Press freedom makes the state stable!"[25] It was an appeal to the basic desire of the Chinese, who are weary from the disorder and unrest that has plagued China for the last one hundred fifty years.

As well-intentioned as this statement is, however, the period of freedom for the Chinese news media clearly did not enhance stability. It created more pressure on the hardliners, who already were feeling on the defensive, and gave them even more reason to believe that a conspiracy was working against them.

For the most part, these perceptions stemmed from the hardliners' own paranoia. However, there were some occasions where the newly liberated Chinese news media gave them reason to feel threatened by a free press. While the reporting by the Chinese news media was, according to many sources, accurate and complete, there were some instances in which its coverage took on a distinct, antigovernment bias. "Some of the stories went to the … extreme of giving short shrift to the official line and distorting actions and statements to make the students look better," wrote Michael Berlin.[26] On one occasion, noted by the *Washington Post*, the Chinese news media "vastly exaggerated" the number of participants in an antigovernment protest.

This bias was indirect but still clearly expressed once martial law was declared on 20 May. With the hardliners moving to consolidate control over the media, Chinese journalists turned to indirect means to express their sentiments. Newscasters on national television sent signals by reading headlines with downcast eyes and the news in gloomy tones; the *People's Daily* featured an article quoting Hungarian leaders as saying they would never order troops to act against civilians. The article was placed conspicuously near articles about the declaration of martial law in Beijing.[27]

This antigovernment bias was understandable, considering the government's attempts to control and censor the press. But it also reflected the partisan mentality of the Chinese news media. In general, there is less emphasis on fair, objective, and accurate coverage in Chinese culture than in the West. In overseas Chinese communities, for example, newspapers have long been identified as "right" or "left" according to whether they are pro-Taiwan or pro-China. The most famous Chinese journalist, Liu Binyan, is known for a style that blends fact and fiction. Chinese journalists told Michael Berlin that freedom of the press means "I can write my ideas instead of the government's."[28]

While bias in the news media is tolerated by most readers, in this instance it may have factored into the decision to crack down on the movement. The coverage clearly exacerbated tensions within the leadership and between the leadership and the people. The sympathetic portrayals of Zhao Ziyang and the students clearly irritated the hardliners, who, as part of the implementation of martial law, ordered troops into the offices of Chinese Central Television , the *People's Daily* and other Beijing publications. They also ordered editors to publish certain articles pushing the hardliners' position.

Even without the hardliners' reaction, however, the overt bias displayed by the Chinese news media raises some fundamental concerns about the press and the role it would play if it had been granted genuine "freedom." Freedom of the press was a major demand of the students, who considered it a means for developing "a democratic consciousness" among the people. It is unclear exactly what they meant by this, but one prevalent viewpoint was that a free press could expose even more official corruption than it had previously.[29]

The students apparently did not think this would be destabilizing or particularly threatening to the government, but it is obvious why the government did. As mentioned previously, the reporting on corruption was already producing outspoken criticism of the party, even though it was the party itself that was encouraging the coverage. A liberated Chinese press certainly would have begun questioning the legitimacy of party supremacy; this already was occurring in literary works and to an extent in journals such as the *World Economic Herald.* Given the Chinese news media's antigovernment bias and its predisposition toward partisan reporting, it might well have considered that attacking the party and the state was its sacred duty as an agent of the free press. Even if the news media concentrated on instilling a "democratic consciousness," which seems to imply that it would be informing the people that they have the right of self-rule, this would inevitably conflict with a party apparatus that historically has awarded government positions according to party loyalty rather than merit.

This is not to say that the students and journalists were wrong to demand freedom of the press, but it does suggest that it was unrealistic to think that press freedom alone would eradicate corruption, create a democratic consciousness in the people, and stabilize society. Unless the students wanted the people to have the right to vote—allowing them to oust officials whom they considered either corrupt or inadequate—freedom of the press could well have destabilized society by emphasizing its problems and the inadequacies of the government in dealing with it.

The Crackdown and the Legacy of the News Media

The crackdown on Tiananmen Square launched the hardliners' final effort to regain control over society. The results of their efforts are well-known: tanks and troops invading the streets, shooting intermittently at crowds of students and citizens, the citizens responding in anger.

The consolidation of the hardliners' power prompted a predictable fate for the news media, which needs only brief mention here. For the Chinese news media, the crackdown marked the complete return of government control, save for the one final transmission on Radio Beijing. Since the crackdown, the propaganda mills have devoted unceasing energy to the party line. Journalists have been arrested for participating in the demonstrations and "re-educated" about the glories of party leadership. The government has targeted the media as a source of its problems, promising a full study on how to better control it.

The Western media fared better, since its reports could not be censored, but its correspondents were restricted, harassed, and in some instances ordered out of the country. Communications capabilities were limited, with jamming of foreign radio broadcasts fully underway, television hookups severed, and security guards keeping an eye on fax lines in and out of China.

The Western news media also suffered the indignity of becoming part of the effort to discredit the protesters, as the government recalled the traditional xenophobia of Chinese culture to denounce the "outside influence" of the foreign media. VOA broadcasts, for example, were cited as examples of U.S. government intervention in China's internal affairs.[30] The U.S. news media also received a bitter lesson in media manipulation when police arrested and beat up a man who had complained about the Chinese government to ABC News. The government had surreptitiously recorded the interview as it was being fed through a satellite linkup to the United States.

These tragic events concluded a trying period for the Chinese and the foreign news media, whose performance and behavior therefore leaves a mixed legacy at Tiananmen Square. For the Chinese news media, it is now clear that it was never able to stray too far from government control. In retrospect, the brief period of freedom it enjoyed seems to be nothing more than a face-saving maneuver by a government that never intended to grant genuine freedom to the press. The Chinese news media also proved itself easily swayed by the appeal of the students, praising them even when it became apparent that they were losing control over their movement.

But in showing a willingness to organize in support of the students, the Chinese news media made perhaps its most significant contribution to the cause of establishing a democratic society in China. This willingness to organize and rally may have greater impact over the long run than the student movement. The students will not remain students for the rest of their lives, and, therefore, the idea of democracy as it relates to their lives is unclear; this is one reason that they could only give vague answers to the question of what democracy meant to them. Journalists, however, know that democratic reforms will have a direct impact on them personally and professionally.

Similarly, the foreign news media, and particularly the U.S. news media, leaves an uneven legacy at Tiananmen Square. It could not remain the "impartial observer" that it strives to be in covering the news; the students, and later the government, would not allow it, and the consequences of this were disastrous.

As an interpreter and prognosticator of events, the news media also receives mixed reviews. Its audience was drawn into the stories, but this writer has encountered many people who expressed confusion about the situation in China. This suggests that the massive coverage by the news media did not inform its audience very well.

The foreign media, however, was key to the development of a new consciousness about China and the Chinese people. It is not too farfetched to say that, prior to Tiananmen Square in 1989, the Chinese people were widely viewed as a faceless, nameless mob. The student movement involved huge masses of people, but viewers did come to recognize and identify with individual Chinese, such as the student leaders Wang Dan, Chai Ling, and Wu'er Kaixi. This development represents a movement by the West toward China, whereas, in the past, China has always been seen as moving toward the West. In the long run, both tendencies are important.

Conclusion

The news media's experience at Tiananmen Square reveals an enduring trait of the Chinese people, whether conservative or liberal, communist or democrat: a practical, utilitarian approach to life that inspires them to find ways to use anything and everything available to achieve their purpose. The news media proved to be a readily available tool for the students and the government, and thus it came to play a major role in the course of events. Eventually, given the ability of the media to communicate with large numbers of people, this became an asset and a liability for the government and the student movement. The students gained support for their movement, but in doing so they embarrassed the government to the extent that it felt it necessary to use brutal force to send a message to anyone considering continuing the movement; the hardliners lost their credibility in the eyes of the world, but succeeded in finding and quelling some of their most active detractors. The regime thus bought some time to try to find a way to reshape society, which is what it has been trying to do for forty years. And, by using tanks and troops in full view of the international media, they convinced the world of their will to go their own way. This desire has always been part of China's struggle to modernize.

The events at Tiananmen Square also show that the news media, in that it was so easily manipulated, has only limited power in changing monolithic cultures such as China's. The students, in turning to the news media for help and protection, were relying on the force of public opinion to either change the hardliners' minds or convince them to abdicate; alternately, they wanted to inspire their sympathizers in the party to turn against the hardliners. As appealing and as just as their arguments were, this ran counter to a major component of Chinese culture, one that ironically has been considered its strength: respect for and reliance on the elders. The spotlight of the news media and the weight of world opinion could not force the Chinese to part with this tradition.

Notes

1   Published in the *Washington Journalism Review* September 1989, p. 37.
2   Ibid.
3   Michael J. Berlin, "Chinese Journalists Cover (And Join) The Revolution," *Washington Journalism Review* September 1989. pg. 32.
4   "CPC [Communist Party Congress] Dismisses Corrupt Members," *Beijing Review* 22 August 1989. The article states that most of those expelled were "involved in smuggling, bribery, embezzlement or violations concerning foreign affairs or foreign nationals," that the number of dismissals was the highest in recent years, and that the number indicated that "the CPC was sincere about enforcing discipline." The government had also set up telephone "hotlines" for citizens to report on corrupt officials.
5   "Patronage Scam Enrages Farmers," *Beijing Review* 10 April, pp. 8-9.
6   This suggests in part that Hu Qili was correct in assessing the influence of news media coverage. However, had reasonable coverage of the protests been allowed in the first place, the impact of the *Science and Technology Daily* article might have been softened. As it was, the students were especially happy to receive even this coverage.
7   Nicholas D. Kristof, "China Bans Pro-Student Newspaper," *The New York Times* 25 April 1989, p. A3.
8   Yi Mu and Mark V. Thompson, *Crisis at Tiananmen: Reform and Reality in Modern China* (San Francisco: China Books & Periodicals, 1989), pp. 127-128.
9   The degree to which Chinese journalists were frustrated can be measured by how much information the Western news media was able to obtain from them. "We saw more than you did, but you published more than we did," one Chinese journalist told *The New York Times* regarding student clashes with police. It seems that, throughout the demonstration period, Chinese journalists kept Western reporters

apprised of their situation at work.

10   John Schidlovsky, "Euphoria And Wu'er Kaixi ... And Then The Killing," *Washington Journalism Review* September 1989, p. 21.

11   Nicholas D. Kristof, "Privately, More and More Chinese Say It's Past Time for Deng to Go," *The New York Times* 17 April 1989, p. A1.

12   John H. Reiss, "The Camera's Red Glare," *Washington Journalism Review* September 1989, p. 28.

13   Mark Hopkins, "Watching China Change," *Columbia Journalism Review* September 1989, pp 35-40.

14   Reiss, p. 28.

15   Comment by Peter Klein, philosophy professor at Rutgers University, who was lecturing at Beijing University in late May.

16   Jim Hoagland, "Blanket Television Coverage Gives Demonstrators a Media Security Blanket," *Washington Post* 19 May 1989.

17   Sheryl WuDunn, "Voice of America Has Won the Ear of China," *The New York Times* 9 May 1989, p. A15.

18   The restrictions declared it illegal for the foreign media to interview or photograph anyone regarding the demonstrations on Tiananmen Square, either on the Square or at other locations, without prior permission.

19   Bruce Kennedy, "Night Scene in Tiananmen Square," *Columbia Journalism Review* September/October 1989:36. Kennedy, a producer for Cable News Network, describes how a CNN reporter was detained at the Beijing Hotel but managed to escape in the confusion. However, a videotape was confiscated by police.

20   Nien Cheng, "China Devours Its Children," *National Review* August 4:30.

21   Reiss, for example, wrote that "it is difficult to explain the kinship one feels with a crowd that embraces one so unconditionally."

22   It is possible, indeed probable, that most people missed this message, which in most cases appeared in analyses and commentaries. But in other cases the view of China specialists were rejected; for example, William Raspberry of *The Washington Post*, who on 5 June wrote that "experts who kept warning uninformed Americans about viewing the demonstrations as (an) attempt to overthrow the Communist rule in favor of Western-style democracy" were mistaken. A few weeks earlier, on 20 April, *The Post* had written on its editorial page, "It is often observed that the democratic spirit is sweeping the world....We hope it's true, but we think that what is really happening in places such as China is the collapse of an arbitrary, cruel, and unworkable political order—communism."

23   The term "prodemocracy movement" appeared in *The Los Angeles Times* on 17 April, and *The New York Times'* s headline on 18 April said, "Chinese Students March for Democracy," but the story qualified the term somewhat in saying that the students "called for a more democratic government." *The Washington Post* kept coverage of the first week's of demonstrations on the back pages, generally describing them as

"antigovernment protesters." On 22 April, it ran the headline "150,000 Chinese March to Demand Democracy" and called the student movement a "prodemocracy movement." Television news almost universally used the term.

24 Reiss, pp. 28-29.
25 Berlin. p. 36.
26 Ibid., p. 34.
27 Daniel Southerland, "Military Group Opposes Martial Law in China," The Washington Post 23 May 1989, p. A18.
28 Berlin, p. 34.
29 This can be seen in Wu'er Kaixi's statement in chapter 1 and in the "May 16 Declaration" in chapter 4 of this volume.
30 For example, "VOA Disgraces Itself," Beijing Daily, reprinted in Beijing Review 26 June 1989, pp. 9-10.

12

Revolution and Counter-Revolution in 1989: Longevity and Legitimacy in Communist States

Irving Louis Horowitz

There can scarcely be any doubt that 1989 is equal to 1789 in its world historic dimensions. Cynics and sophisticates alike recognize that the ubiquitous "people" have spoken. Not a day passes without another startling revelation cracking the mythology of the communist past, or another mass demonstration of disaffection with the communist present. But what exactly links all of these events, and, further, what unites the revolutionary upheavals in every single country from Central Europe to East Asia, in spirit if not in exact consequences, deserves consideration.

In its simplest shorthand terminology, it turns out to be the replacement of the Brezhnev Doctrine with the "Sinatra" Doctrine. Only a short decade ago, the Soviet Union and its satellites were captive to the claim that, once a people accept the blessings of communism, they must forswear all other blessings, especially the blandishments of Western capitalism. In slightly less metaphorical terms: to embrace the communist system was to cross over from the capitalist Styx once and for all.

With the "revolutionary seizure of power," real politics ceased, to be replaced by circuses in the celebration of a new order. The explosiveness of events is partially explained by the absence of routine politics in the communist world soon after the concentration of power in the hands of party officials and government bureaucrats.

Now "iron curtain" figures such as Vytautas Landsbergis, Antanas J. Buracas, and Zigmas Vaisvilla, president of the Lithuanian Reform Movement and members of the Lithuanian Supreme Soviet respectively, visit the Council on Foreign Relations in New York to announce a new doctrine, one based on the principle of Old Blue Eyes, Frank Sinatra. "We will do things our way," they say! One wonders if the comrades from Lithuania concluded their presentation with a chorus of "New York, New York." After all, if you can make it in the Big Apple, you may even be able to make it in Riga.

The Question of Legitimacy

Behind such cultural allegories is a serious comment on the transformation of life under communism. The problem of legitimacy has come of age. More specifically, communist societies are confronting the absence of those elements within a society that bind people together symbolically in the face of troubles and turmoil; and contrariwise, they are faced with the presence of those elements that permit people to employ troubles and turmoil to upset the political and social landscape. In its essential terms, legitimacy means rule with the consent of the governed, or doing things one's own way rather than the way of another power. Furthermore, legitimacy means that, if a policy or a structure does not succeed, one does not have to punish or purge the leaders, or engage in ritualistic self-criticisms within party cells. Instead, one goes to the heart of the matter: change policies, structures, and even cadres.

Legitimate rule is established either through a democratic consensus, as in the evolution of Western democracies; or through a broad-based revolutionary movement, as in the case of the Soviet Union and China. In both of these examples, the appeal to vox populi is based, whether by ballots or by bullets, on a direct sense of having a stake in the running of government. Thus, neither royal abdications in England nor presidential assassinations in the United States remotely rock the political boat. For that matter, major upheavals such as the death of dictators like Stalin in the Soviet Union or Mao Zedong in China did not result in a revolutionary upheaval. Dramatic changes in both sets of systems do occur. But prospects are slim for the overthrow of the present political system in either nation.[1]

In operational terms, this means the slow introduction of the rule of law and parliamentary norms into the lives of ordinary people throughout the communist world, rather than armed struggle or counter-revolution. Among the more remarkable developments through the socialist orbit can be listed the following:

The right of physical movement of citizens without constraint, punishment, and with the right (even the encouragement) of return.

Proposals to permit freedom of the press and prohibition against government censorship or arbitrary removal.

Proposals to permit ownership of private property and retain surpluses owned by small enterprises or farming.

Laws that guarantee workers the right to strike for the first time in communist history since Kronstadt.

Legislation that gives citizens of communist lands the unrestricted right to choose their own religion.

Enabling legislation that permits the establishment of business cooperatives unregulated by the central government.

Enactment of laws requiring that all legislation be submitted to the people in direct referendum before enactment.

These developments, and dozens like them, repudiate the specter of the arbitrary tyranny of the past, and, no less, indicate the parliamentary shape of the future.

But before the issue of the new legitimacy and their implications is addressed, the question of political illegitimacy, or the absence of rule by consent of the governed, needs close scrutiny. It is this element of illegitimacy that links the current upheavals in every nation of Eastern Europe, and which, while understated in the abstract by social and political science, was missed in the concrete in nearly every analyst's prediction about events in Eastern Europe prior to 1990.

Illegitimacy takes many forms. In Rumania (as in North Korea and Cuba), strong elements of dynastic communism emerged. The rule of the people moved quickly to the rule of the party, and then on to the rule of the ruler. Protection of that ruling elite became a family repository, much like a political equivalent of primogeniture. In Poland (under Jaruzelski), the bankruptcy of Communist party rule was blanketed by a direct form of military communism in which the armed forces ruled in the name of the party but exercised authority apart from the party. In Hungary and Yugoslavia, albeit in radically different ways, government agencies ruled apart from party instrumentalities. As a result, the stifling control of the party apparatus was seriously and perhaps permanently eroded. In places like Bulgaria and East Germany, at least until recent events, party rule was absolute. The model of control was a direct outgrowth of Stalinism or, as it is now being called in Sofia at least, a variety of czarist communism.

However, in none of these varieties of communist experience was legitimacy either expressed or countenanced. But they are—or were—so different from each other that the forms of political change in Eastern Europe, while superficially very similar, are in fact radically different from each other. One need only consider ongoing struggles in Czechoslavakia, a nation with a far more democratic past than most places in Eastern Europe, to appreciate the protracted nature of the struggles no less than the distinct characteristics of the outcomes. Thus, the search for unifying elements is neither simple nor as transparent as news headlines tend to assume.

Experts assumed, falsely as it turns out, that longevity and continuity in the rule of individuals, such as with Erich Honecker in East Germany or Todor Zhivkobv in Bulgaria, is the same as system legitimacy. Indeed, one of the few writers on the German Democratic Republic to call the shots right may have been David Childs, who, in his book, *The German Democratic Republic: Moscow's German Ally*, notes that East Germany is especially vulnerable to Western democratic influences.[2] That the protest movement has mushroomed most profoundly in regimes that were politically the most repressive, often moving from hundreds to hundreds of thousands of people in a matter of weeks, gives vivid testimony to the volatility of change behind the now-bent Iron Curtain.

Eastern Europe: A Panoply of Political Problems

The immediate and direct causes of regime instability differ in each nation of communist Europe. What unites them all is the absence of a unifying element, of political legitimacy as such. The Baltic states of Latvia, Estonia, and Lithuania, for example, were independent nations prior to World War Two. After the war, they were simply absorbed into the Soviet postwar empire as part of the booty of victory and the cupidity of Western leadership. They were mourned as "captive states" under Hitler and then given over to Stalin, which has only protracted their captivity.

Recent revelations by an expert working group of Soviet historians have found that the Baltic states became part of the Soviet empire in 1940 as a part and parcel of the Nazi-Soviet Non-Aggression Pact. This confirmed what was widely known and reported elsewhere. But in this instance, this historical reconsideration has led to a historic realignment. Now, everything from linguistic preeminence to a return to a free market is under consideration. Ethnic Russians in the Baltic states are voicing bitter complaints about being discriminated against. This pattern of reconsideration and reform is now underway in every nation, albeit by fits and starts.

In East Germany, the postwar regime was set up as a result of a four-part division of the German nation. In the West, the United States, England, and France held sway; in the East, the Soviet Union dominated. Again, the division was externally and arbitrarily imposed—based on the twin principles that to the victors go war booty and reparation and that a divided Germany would be less of a threat to world peace and stability than would a united Germany. With the direct intervention of Soviet occupying troops after 1953, Berlin and later its Wall became the symbols not only of a divided Germany but of a sealed community, alienated from its own people and not just from the West.

As a consequence, the governing bodies, lacking even a remote popular base, or any sort of differentiation from one another, have had little choice but to derive their power from the Communist party. The government and party have been so closely identified that calls for popular elections and a multiparty system threaten at one fell swoop to undermine all Communist authority—no matter what the popular mandate would reveal. The East German regime, whether under Honecker or Grenz, is faced with the same unpalatable choice: either return to all-out repression or resort to total resignation. Either option betrays the complete bankruptcy of the regime. So it comes to pass that the convulsions in East Germany, starting with the resignation of

Honecker and ending with the collapse of the Berlin Wall, threaten to change the map of all Germany, if not all Europe. But these post-1989 shocks are part of a future chapter of a united Europe and not of this particular moment in time.

Poland, under the tireless leadership of the Solidarity movement, has served as a prototype for developments throughout the region. It never wavered in its belief that parliamentary rather than revolutionary solutions were key. And its very search for legitimacy, under the cautious leadership of Lech Walesa, placed Solidarity in sharp relief to the communist leadership, which accepted Poland as a consequence of the Nazi-Soviet Pact. The Communist party was doomed by its absolute acceptance of the division of Poland to suit the needs of the major players in the postwar epoch. The postwar border adjustments were at the expense of Germany (the nominal loser) and to the advantage of the Soviet Union, which effectively annexed the eastern portion of Poland. But these divisions and redivisions had nothing to do with an internal national consensus. In contrast, Solidarity developed, survived, and thrived because of its consensual base. Its emergence as the governing element resulted from a startling series of developments, brilliantly stage-managed by Lech Walesa. In part, it is also an indirect consequence of the larger incapacity of an externally imposed regime to survive indefinitely, whether in political or military guise.

In Hungary, the effective ruler of the nation was a Communist party that underwent a national communist phase in 1956 only to be decimated by Soviet invasion and occupation. After that, it was evident that the Communist party was a foreign imposition, one extending even to Soviet military advisors helping to administer the Hungarian state apparatus. Thus, the negation of the Communist party itself in 1989 was an understandable consequence of the party's delegitimization. Interestingly, the Hungarian regime has petitioned for membership in the Council of Europe, that West European group founded in 1949 "to uphold the principle of parliamentary democracy."

In Czechoslavakia, we have a similar situation in the natural history of protest but, thus far, without the outcome one notes elsewhere. The Stalinist coup engineered by Klement Gottwald in 1948 destroyed the postwar democratic regime of this fragile democracy. The character assassination of Tomas G. Masaryk followed by his tragic suicide put in place a Communist regime without a shred of legitimacy. It ruled until 1968, when a mass uprising took place, led by Alexander Dubcek, only to be crushed a year later by direct Soviet occupation.

In Czechoslovakia, uneasy relations continue to exist between orthodox and revisionist elements within the Communist party. The government itself has become hostage to party factionalism, leading to a strange condition in which the Soviet authorities warn the Czech hardliners of the risks in their continuing press for power, while protesters face a far more severe challenge than one might have predicted based on the character of the regime or the levels of social and economic development. Regime continuity in Czech politics has been maintained only with the aide of riot police. With a political opposition led by writers like Vaclav Havel and jazz critics like Karel Srp, the potential for full-scale political transformation is curiously more difficult in this nation with a strange democratic past than in places lacking such a past. Legitimacy requires legislators—something not yet developed in Czechoslavakia.

In some nations, such as Yugoslavia, which long ago broke from the Stalinist yoke in organizational terms, the character of opposition to the illegitimate Communist party takes the form of separatist, nationalist movements—with six ethnic segments from Croations to Albanians demanding a share of government or a separate autonomous regional fate. Political leadership rotates not out of a sense of democratic participation but as a consequence of full and mutual mistrust. The relatively benign Communist movement of Yugoslavia, with its workers councils and regional associations, was enough to fend off Soviet blandishments, but could not establish political legitimacy any more than could its Stalinist opponents. Hence, the national and ethnic rivalries in Yugoslavia take on a special role in accelerating national disintegration. As Harold Lydall in his *Yugoslavia in Crisis* properly notes, socialist self-management coupled with ethnic federalism has created a "monstrous amalgam," resulting in an enormous waste of human and material resources.[3]

Even Bulgaria, a nation-state that has tied its fate and fortunes so closely to the Soviet Union that for all intents and purposes it is part of the Soviet government, has begun to witness startling opposition to the conservative regime with the now "normal cycle" of small protests, followed by large protests, followed by bold demands for democratization of the polity and opening up of the economy, and finally ending with the resignation of Todor I. Zhivkob, the longest-running dictator in the Soviet bloc (thirty-five years) and his displacement with a moderate reformist, Petar T. Mladenov. And if Gorbachev's *perestroika, glasnost,* and new thinking has permeated Sofia, with its Independent Discussion Clubs and demands for free elections in a multiparty environment, one can say in all frankness that the last vestiges of the Soviet Empire in Eastern Europe are under mortal siege.

When we turn to the strange case of Rumania we see what Daniel Nelson in his recent book, *Rumanian Politics in the Ceausescu Era,* describes as a textbook case in political immobility, made possible by international isolation from the Eastern and Western blocs alike.[4] But such isolation, while reinforcing the pseudo-Stalinist pivot of Nicolae Ceausescu and his family in the short run, lacks a capacity to resolve domestic conflict and, hence, is but a postponement to any effort to resolve the problem of legitimacy—one that has terrible consequences for the population in the short run but lacking any capacity for legitimization in the long run.

Rumania indicates how a carefully textured policy that cultivates a global image of being the "Switzerland" of the East can yet be coupled with being a domestic variant of a Latinized Stalinism. More exactly, it is a case of dynastic communism that is a special variant of the dictatorship of the proletariat, albeit in this case the dictatorship of the extended family. And whatever weakness such dynastic varieties on the communist theme possess, they offer political tightness, the sense of solidarity that is absent elsewhere in Eastern Europe. Ceausescu's formula of no capitalism and no democracy is likely to resonate well among the threatened Communist party cadres suffering an aftershock of dispossession.

The Bastions of Communism: the Soviet Union and China

We then must turn to the problem of legitimacy in the Soviet Union and the People's Republic of China. For, in these two nations, we witness, however imperfectly, precisely the existence of a legitimate revolutionary upheaval and tradition. And if in both places the destruction of despotic traditional rule also meant the disastrous bypassing of liberal democratic options, one can hardly deny the social basis of revolutionary ferment. It is in these two giant countries, the twin foundations of the communist world in the postwar epoch, that the struggle for mass democracy and free economy takes on the most complex form. Essentially, the very organic nature of communism in these two master nations makes the evolution of reform all the more difficult. For, not only is the overthrow of an imposed administrative cadre involved, but the economic and social structures that came into existence after a huge amount of personal sacrifice and public turmoil are at stake.

In the Soviet Union, every admission of guilt or responsibility comes with great difficulty. Decades of mythology and layers of ideology have to come unglued. Accepting responsibility for the Katyn Forest massacres involves a revision of Soviet history and a reevaluation of the "ethics" of the Soviet armed forces vis à vis the Nazi *Wehrmacht*. The admission of secret pacts for the division of Poland and the Baltic states completely discredits the communist idea of international proletarian solidarity, showing the Soviet Union to be a venal state in the Machiavellian, or, dare one say, czarist mold. The continuing reevaluation of figures like Lenin and Stalin moves in fits and starts—with efforts to describe the death and imprisonment of 245 million Soviet people as "excesses" and "aberrations" within an otherwise perfect system rather than as something endemic to socialist development as such. Political assassinations are linguistically papered over by posthumous "rehabilitations" as a sort of communist-materialist bow in the direction of the province of immortality. Many old Bolsheviks are rehabilitated posthumously, but Leon Trotsky, the presumed dissident leader, remains a non-person.

As a consequence, the movement for reform in the Soviet Union takes place not as unadulterated liberalization of the regime, but as a demand for restoration of nationalist and traditionalist values. Democracy is one element in the Soviet reform movement; ultranationalism and totalitarianism is yet another. Public opinion surveys indicate this two-sided nature of Soviet reform movements: a demand for more democracy and a demand that the state impose more restrictions to insure work and stability. In short, the very legitimacy of the Soviet state and its birth in a revolutionary situation makes the process of reform extremely volatile and taxing. One French author, Jacques Baynac, claims in *The Gorbachev Revolution* that Leninism is itself the ultimate victim of Gorbachev's New Thinking, since appeals for collectives, self-management, and free markets become tactics in the prevention of the downfall of a regime that has little capacity to appeal directly to democratic political slogans.[5]

One finds a similar set of contradictory characteristics in China. Repression in Tiananmen Square was real; twenty-six hundred dead civilians and ten thousand injured people attest to that. The character of the opposition was massive enough to threaten stability but not system legitimacy—certainly as measured by the loyalty of military cadres or urban citizens, for example. On the other hand, reform proceeds top down, with efforts to revive the pre-1989 movement for economic reform again picking up steam by fits and starts. The Chinese leadership itself is divided into pragmatic and hardline elements, as is evident by the change in leadership from Deng Xiaoping to Jiang Zemin. But while a myriad of reforms continue to take place amidst efforts to control their pace and impact, no real challenge to communist rule is possible.

The Cultural Revolution was allowed to run its course in the late 1960s because it simply extended to a new generation the legitimacy of the revolution of the 1940s. This was not the case with events in 1989, which even introduced symbols of Western democracy, such as the Goddess of Democracy, to show to the old regime the displeasure of the largely young opponents. But again, as in France in the late 1960s, the industrial working masses stood with the regime and against the reformers, as painful a reminder as that may be. Even if this mass support for the regime was essentially passive in nature, it was enough to insure the survival of the Deng regime in its time of crisis and in the aftermath of the massacre of students and dissidents.

Huan Guocang, author of *The Chinese View of the World*, puts the matter rightly in noting that "the events of 1989 are likely to make inevitable the rise of Chinese society against the Communist state."[6] His idea that the Chinese people have "a new sense of community, and no longer are they disenfranchised individuals dealing with an all-powerful state" is precisely the subjective core of the weakening of legitimacy of the communist apparatus. Indeed, the events in Tiananmen Square call to mind Marx's famous opening lines on the suppression of the June 1848 Revolution in France:

> The Paris workers are crushed by superior force; they did not surrender. They are beaten, but their opponents are defeated. The momentary triumph of brute force is bought with the destruction of all illusions and imaginings.[7]

However, such a transformation is not likely to display East European characteristics of democratic revival. One has to accept as a given the postponed optimism of Winston Lord in his essay "China and America Beyond the Big Chill" in *Foreign Affairs*, when he says that by "the end of the century, the Chinese may well enjoy a freer press, a more highly developed legal system and a more open political process than would have been the case without the dark phase now being endured."[8] This is so because the facade of legitimacy claimed by the heirs of the Long March has been impaired but not destroyed by the Tiananmen massacre. Internal mechanisms of repression persist because support from the rural elites and military cadres for the regime remain largely intact. And, given the indifferent response to student appeals in the rural areas, it is fair, if painful, to say that the oppositionist elements exaggerated their base of support and paid a heavy price in human suffering and political mobilization in so doing.

I am not suggesting that either the Soviet Union or China are impervious to regime transformation. Clearly nothing could be further from the truth: A great deal of the impulse to the current stage of unrest and protest were made possible, if not overtly stimulated, by the Gorbachev and Deng reforms. But the nature of those national systems must be reckoned quite differently from the small states of Eastern Europe precisely because legitimacy, or the consent of the governed, remains complicated by the quasilegitimacy bestowed by their respective revolutionary origins. Thus, what is not true of Eastern Europe is still true of the Soviet Union and China: that their leadership has a basis, however tenuous, in legitimacy, in this often passive consent of the governed. Indeed, the new parliamentary reforms in the Soviet Union and the political reforms in China, giving more power to regional heads and decentralization of authority, generally indicate an awareness within their leadership cadres of the unique position and opportunity at this juncture for both communist superpowers.

One can expect a serious erosion of Eastern bloc politics, a removal of some of these nations from the political orbit of Soviet life in exchange for a certain amount of Finlandization, i.e., a willingness of these nations to forego any sort of threatening or menacing role in foreign policy and military affairs directed at the Soviet Union. Within Soviet life and Chinese life, Communist party rule will continue unabated and unchallenged—at least until the legitimacy of the system itself can be overcome by largely parliamentary and judiciary networks, by opposition that is recognized and legalized by the broad masses of these nations.

This is a unique moment within the history of twentieth century socialist and communist life; one that Western democracies can ill afford to miss. Every effort should be made to strengthen ties with reform elements in China and the Soviet Union, and, even more, every opportunity seized to present the rulers of each of these master countries with real choices that would not threaten stability. The process of displacing illegitimate with legitimate regimes in Eastern Europe is well underway, however uneven the patterns of reform express themselves. The same process will take far different, more tortuous, complex forms in the great nations of the Soviet Union and China, and will take longer to develop. As a result, the United States would do well to encourage, but not intervene directly, in this exceedingly complicated set of maneuvers.

The Future for the Communist Bloc

This thumbnail sketch of current events in the Eastern bloc is not intended to replace careful study on a nation-by-nation basis. Nor would I wish to deny that each country has internal historical conditions that make their march to democracy tortuous, painful, and uneven. Beyond that, these remarks do not begin to address, much less resolve, questions as to why these forces for basic change took place in 1989 and not last year or next year. It might well be that a certain "J-curve" phenomenon was at work: 1989 being a period of moderate upswing in the economies of Eastern Europe, but insufficient to meet much higher levels of expectations.

One can also speculate that what started out as a national reconsideration in the Soviet Union quickly assumed global dimensions that were unforeseen even by the founding fathers of the New Thinking. Uncapping steam valves may lead to uncontrollable consequences. It is evident that, in direct head-to-head competition, the Soviets fare poorly with respect to the Americans. But it is no less evident that North Koreans fare poorly with respect to South Koreans, East Germans with respect to West Germans; Mainland China with respect to Taiwan. And, in the larger scheme of things, systemic inadequacies of the East have led to a general feeling of relative deprivation throughout the Soviet empire. Even if one can make a case that conditions have improved within an Eastern European context, in comparative terms such changes have been slow in coming, costly in terms of taxation, and even more costly in terms of personal deprivations.

Another factor may be the new technology. The mass media has served to highlight such polarities in the political economy. Advances in everything from satellite television to computer work stations have deprived the communist bloc of its previous insularity. In short, whatever measures one looks at, 1989, like 1789, was neither the worst of times nor the best of times. Rather, its very ordinariness pointed up the stagnancy of the economy, which, along with the illegitimacy of the polity, made the moment of change come together in far-flung parts of the communist empire.

Whatever the specific and immediate factors that produced a combustible situation in so many nations at a single moment in time, the search for structural factors and commonalities is important lest we view the revolutions of 1989 as sporadic, spontaneous, or impervious to any deeper meaning. Beneath the intense rivalries between the Slavic and Romany, the Catholic and Orthodox forms of Christianity, the agrarianism of Hungary and the industrialism of Czechoslavakia, and a myriad of other factors that has made the term "Balkanization" synonymous over the centuries with divisiveness and bald-faced competition, is a common thirst for freedom—even if it signifies the freedom to return to the good days of fratricide. As Walter Laqueur has recently reminded is in his book *The Long Road to Freedom*, it would be half-baked fantasy to assume that out of the rubble of communism will emerge pure, unadulterated, Western-style democracies.[9] The autocratic soil that nourished the current communist regimes is itself sufficient to prevent any easy or ready-made solutions. But whatever does emerge will at least restore a sense of regime authenticity, and hence the revival of political legitimacy in Eastern Europe, the Soviet Union, China, and other blighted portions of civilization.

The recognition by policy analysts and politicians alike of the acute differences in historical antecedents, as measured by the illegitimate versus legitimate origins of each nation, and, more adroitly, degrees of popular consent involved in each of the nations now undergoing upheaval, will be a useful starting point in reviewing the events of 1989. But it bears repeating that historical longevity and political legitimacy are simply bluntly not the same. The monumental effort underway to distinguish legislative enactments from executive dictations is a deep structural recognition of this condition in Eastern Europe. To ignore this truth is to be cast, along with the Bolshevik vanguard, in the widely heralded dust bin of history.

[This chapter is a revised edition of a speech delivered on 25 November 1989 at the "Prodemocracy Movement in China" symposium held at Rutgers University.]

Notes

1   For a fuller discussion of the interrelationship between legitimacy and revolution, see Irving Louis Horowitz, *Foundations of Political Sociology* (New York and London: Harper & Row, Publishers, 1972), pp. 253-325.

2   David Childs, *The German Democratic Republic: Moscow's German Ally*, 2nd ed. (London and Boston: Unwin Hyman,1988).

3   Harold Lydall, *Yugoslavia in Crisis* (New York and London: Oxford University Press, 1989).

4   Daniel Nelson, *Rumanian Politics in the Ceausescu Era* (New York: Gordon & Breach, 1988).

5   Jacques Baynac, *The Gorbachev Revolution* (London: Oxford University Press, 1989). See also, Jeffrey C. Goldfarb, *Beyond Glasnost: The Post-Totalitarian Mind* (Chicago: University of Chicago Press, 1989).

6   In Ezra F. Vogel, One Step Ahead in China: Guangdong Under Reform (Cambridge: Harvard University Press, 1989).

7   Karl Marx, *The Class Struggles in France*, volume 1: *The Karl Marx Library, On Revolution*, edited by Saul K. Padover (New York: McGraw-Hill Book Company, 1971), pp. 154-242.

8   Winston Lord, "China and America Beyond the Big Chill," *Foreign Affairs* 68(4) (Fall 1989): 1-27.

9   Walter Laqueur, *The Long Road to Freedom: Russia and Glasnost* (New York: Scribners/Macmillan Publishers, 1989). See also Zbigniew Brzezinski, *The Grand Failure: The Birth and Death of of Communism in the Twentieth Century* (New York: Scribner/Macmillan, 1989).

Appendices

Report on Checking the Turmoil and Quelling the Counter-Revolutionary Rebellion

Proclamation of the National Day of Mourning

Glossary of Terms

Bibliography

Contributors

Report on Checking the Turmoil and Quelling the Counter-Revolutionary Rebellion
Chen Xitong, mayor of Beijing and state councillor

Chairman, vice-chairman, and committee members, during late spring and early summer, namely, from mid-April to early June 1989, a tiny handful of people exploited the student unrest to launch a planned, organized, and premeditated political turmoil that later developed into a counter-revolutionary rebellion in Beijing, the capital. Their purpose was to overthrow the leadership of the Chinese Communist Party and to subvert the socialist People's Republic of China. The outbreak and development of the turmoil and the counter-revolutionary rebellion had an extensive international background and social basis at home. As Comrade Deng Xiaoping put it, "This storm was bound to happen sooner or later. As determined by the international and domestic climate, it was bound to happen and was independent of man's will."

In this struggle involving the life and death of the party and the state, Comrade Zhao Ziyang committed the serious mistake of supporting the turmoil and splitting the party, and was responsible for the shaping up and development of the turmoil. In face of this very severe situation, the Party Central Committee made correct decisions and took a series of resolute measures, winning the firm support of the whole party as well as people of all nationalities in the country.

Represented by Comrade Deng Xiaoping, the proletarian revolutionaries of the older generation played a very important role in winning the struggle. The Chinese People's Liberation Army, the armed police, and the police made great contributions in checking the turmoil and quelling the counter-revolutionary rebellion. The vast numbers of workers, peasants, and intellectuals firmly opposed the turmoil and the rebellion, rallied closely around the Party Central Committee, and displayed a very high political consciousness and sense of responsibility as masters of the country. Now, entrusted by the State Council, I am making a report to the Standing Committee of the National People's Congress on the turmoil and the counter-revolutionary rebellion, mainly the happening in Beijing, and the work of checking the turmoil and quelling the counter-revolutionary rebellion.

One. The Turmoil Was Premeditated and Prepared for a Long Time

Some political forces in the West have always attempted to make the socialist countries, including China, give up the socialist road, to eventually bring these countries under the rule of international monopoly capital and put them on the course of capitalism. This is their long-term, fundamental strategy. In recent years, they have stepped up the implementation of this strategy by making use of some policy mistakes and temporary economic difficulties in socialist countries. In our country, a tiny handful of people both inside and outside the party stubbornly clung to their position of bourgeois liberalization and went in for political conspiracy. Echoing the strategy of Western countries, they colluded with foreign forces, ganged up at home, and made ideological and organizational preparations for years to stir up turmoil in China, overthrow the leadership by the Communist party, and subvert the socialist People's Republic of China. That is why the entire course of brewing, premeditating, and launching the turmoil, including the use of varied means, such as creating public opinion, distorting facts, and spreading rumors, bore the salient feature of mutual support and coordination between a handful of people at home and abroad.

This report will mainly deal with the situation since the Third Plenary Session of the Thirteenth Central Committee of the Chinese Communist Party. Last September, the Party Central Committee formulated the policy of improving the economic environment, straightening out the economic order, and deepening the reform in an all-round way. This policy and related measures won the broad support of the masses and students. The social order and political situation were basically stable. Good evidence of this was the approval of Comrade Li Peng's government work report by an overwhelming majority (with a mere two votes against and four abstentions) at the National People's Congress in the spring of 1990. Of course, the people and students raised many critical opinions against some mistakes committed by the party and the government in their work, corruption among some government employees, unfair distribution, and other problems. At the same time, they made quite a few demands and proposals for promoting democracy, strengthening the legal system, deepening the reform, and overcoming bureaucracy. These were normal phenomena. The party and government were also taking measures to solve them. At that time, however, there was indeed a tiny group of people in the party and society who ganged up together and engaged in many very improper activities overtly and covertly.

What deserves special attention is that, after Comrade Zhao Ziyang's meeting with a U.S. "ultraliberal economist" on 19 September last year, some Hong Kong newspapers and journals, which were said to have close ties with Zhao Ziyang's "brain trust," gave enormous publicity to this and spread the political message that "Beijing is using Hong Kong mass media to topple Deng and protect Zhao." In his article entitled "Big Patriarch should Retire," published in Hong Kong's *Economic Journal,* Li Yi (alias Qi Xin), editor-in-chief of the reactionary *Nineties* magazine, clamored for "removing the obstacle of super old man's politics" and "giving Zhao Ziyang enough power." Another article in *Nineties* appealed to Zhao to be an "autocrat." Hong Kong's *Emancipation* monthly also carried a lengthy article, saying that some people had "overt or covert" relations with certain persons in Hong Kong media circles, which "are sometimes dim and sometimes bright, just like a will-o'-the-wisp," and that such subtle relations now "have been newly proved by a drive to topple Deng and protect Zhao, launched in the recent month." The article also said that "in terms of the hope of China turning capitalist, they settle on Zhao Ziyang." To coordinate with the drive to "topple Deng and protect Zhao," Beijing's *Economics Weekly* published a dialogue on the current situation between Yan Jiaqi (a research fellow at the Institute of Political Science under the Chinese Academy of Social Sciences), who had close ties with Zhao Ziyang's former secretary Bao Tong, and another person. It attacked "the improvement of the economic environment and the straightening out of economic order," saying that would lead to "stagnation." It also said that a big problem China was facing was "not to follow the old disastrous road of nonprocedural change of power as in the case of Khruschev and Liu Shaoqi." It said that nonprocedural change of power as in the Cultural Revolution will no longer be allowed in China." The essence of the dialogue was to whip up public opinion for covering up Zhao Ziyang's mistakes, keeping his position and power and pushing on bourgeois liberalization even more unbridedly. This dialogue was reprinted in full or in part in Shanghai's *World Economic Herald,* Hong Kong's

Mirror Monthly and other newspapers and magazines at home and abroad.

Collaboration between forces at home and abroad intensified toward the end of last year and early in 1990. Political assemblies, joint petitions, big- and small-character posters and other activities emerged, expressing fully erroneous or even reactionary viewpoints. For instance, a big seminar called "Future China and the World" was sponsored by the Beijing University Future Studies Society on 7 December last year. Jin Guantao, deputy chief editor of the Towards the Future book series and advisor to the society, said in his speech that "attempts at socialism and their failure constitute one of the two major legacies of the twentieth century." Ge Yang, chief editor of the fortnightly *New Observer*, immediately stood up to "provide evidence," in the name of "the eldest" among the participants and a party member of dozens of years' standing, saying, "Jin's negation of socialism is not harsh enough, but a bit too polite." On 28 January 1990, Su Shaozhi (a research fellow at the Institute of Marxism-Leninism-Mao Zedong Thought under the Chinese Academy of Social Sciences), Fang Lizhi, and the like organized a so-called "neoenlightenment saloon" at the Dule bookstore in Beijing, which was attended by more than one hundred people, among them Beijing-based U.S., French, and Italian correspondents as well as Chinese. Fang described this gathering as "smelling of strong gunpowder" and "taking a completely critical attitude toward the authorities." He also said "what we need now is action" and professed to "take to the street after holding three sessions in a row." In early February, Fang Lizhi, Chen Jun (a member of the reactionary organization Chinese Alliance for Democracy), and others sponsored a so-called "winter jasmine get-together of famed personalities" at the Friendship Hotel, where Fang made a speech primarily on the two major issues of "democracy" and "human rights," and Chen drew a parallel between the May Fourth Movement and the "democracy wall at Xidan." Fang expressed the "hope that entrepreneurs, as China's new rising force, will join forces with the advanced intellectuals in the fight for democracy." At a press conference he gave for foreign correspondents on 16 February, Chen Jun handed out Fang Lizhi's letter addressed to Deng Xiaoping, and another letter from Chen himself and thirty-two others to the Standing Committee of the National People's Congress and the Central Committee of the Chinese Communist Party, calling for amnesty and the release of Wei Jingsheng and other so-called "political prisoners" who had gravely violated the criminal law.

On 23 February, the *Taiwan United Daily News* carried an article headlined "Beginning of a Major Movement—a Megashock." It said: "A declaration was issued in New York, and open letters surfaced in Beijing. As the thunder of spring rumbles across the Divine Land (China), waves for democracy are rising."

On 26 February, Zhang Xianyang (a research fellow at the Institute of Marxism-Leninism Mao Zedong Thought under the Chinese Academy of Social Sciences), Bao Zhunxin (an associate research fellow at the Institute of Chinese History under the Chinese Academy of Social Sciences), Ge Yang, and thirty-eight others jointly wrote a letter to the Communist Party Congress Central Committee calling for the release of so-called "political prisoners."

Afterwards, a vast number of big- and small-letter character posters and assemblies came out on the campuses of some universities in Beijing, attacking the Communist party and the socialist system. On 1 March for example, a big-character poster titled "Denunciation of Deng Xiaoping—a letter to the nation" was put up at Qinghua University and Beijing University simultaneously. The poster uttered such nonsense as "the politics of the Communist party consists of empty talk, coercive power, autocratic rule, and arbitrary decision," and openly demanded "dismantling parties and abandoning the Four Cardinal Principles (adherence to the socialist road, to the people's democratic dictatorship, to the leadership by the Communist party and to Marxism-Leninism and Mao Zedong thought)." A small-character poster titled "Deplore the Chinese" turned up in Beijing University on 2 March, demanding to overthrow "totalitarianism" and "autocracy."

On 3 March, there appeared in Qinghua University and other universities and colleges a "letter to the mass of students" signed by the Preparatory Committee of the China Democratic Youth Patriotic Association and urging students to join in the "turbulent current for democracy, freedom and human rights under the leadership of the patriotic democratic fighter, Fang Lizhi." On the campuses of Beijing University and other schools of higher learning on 29 March, there was extensive posting of Fang's article, "China's Disappointment and Hope," written for the Hong Kong *Ming Pao Daily News*. In the article, Fang claimed that socialism had "completely lost its attraction" and there was the need to form political "pressure groups" to carry out "reform for political democracy and economic freedom." But what he termed as "reform" actually is a synonym for total Westernization.

The big-character poster "Call of the Times" that came out in Beijing University on 6 April questioned in a way of complete negation "whether there is any rationale now for socialism to exist" and "whether Marxism-Leninism fits the realities of China after all." On 13 April, the Beijing Institute of Post and Telecommunications and another school received a "message to the nation's college students," signed by the Guangxi University Students' Union, that called on students to "hold high the portrait of Hu Yaobang, the great banner of democracy, freedom, dignity and rule by law, in celebration of the May Fourth Youth Day."

Meanwhile, so-called democratic salons, freedom forums and various kinds of seminars, conferences, and lectures mushroomed in Beijing's institutions of higher learning. The democratic salons presided over by Wang Dan, a Beijing University student, sponsored seventeen lectures in one year, indicative of its frequent activities. They invited Ren Wanding, head of the defunct and illegal Human Rights League, to spread fallacies about the so-called "new authoritarianism and democratic politics." At one point, they held a seminar in front of the Statue of Cervantes, openly crying to "abolish the one-party system, force the Communist party to step down, and topple the present regime." They also invited Li Shuxian, the wife of Fang Lizhi, to be their "advisor." Li fanned the flames by urging them to "legalize the democratic salon," "hold meetings here frequently," and "abolish the Beijing Municipality's ten-article regulations on demonstrations."

All this prepared, in terms of ideology and organization, for the turmoil that ensued. A *Ming Pao Daily News* article commented:

> The contact-building and petition-signing activities for human rights initiated by the elite of Chinese intellectuals exerted enormous influence on students. They had long ago planned a large-scale move on the seventieth anniversary of the May Fourth Movement to express their dissatisfaction with the authorities. The sudden death of Hu Yaobang literally threw a match into a barrel of gunpowder." In short, as a result of the premeditation, organization, and engineering by a small handful of people, a political situation emerged in which the "rising forebodes a coming storm."

Two. Student Unrest Was Exploited by Organizers of the Turmoil from the Very Beginning

Comrade Hu Yaobang's death on 15 April prompted an early outbreak of the long-brewing student unrest and turmoil. The broad masses and students mourned Comrade Hu Yaobang and expressed their profound grief. Universities and colleges provided facilities for the mourning on the part of the students. However, a small number of people took advantage of this to oppose the leadership of the Communist party and the socialist system under the pretext of "mourning." Student unrest was manipulated and exploited by the small handful of people from the very beginning and bore the nature of political turmoil.

The turmoil found expression first in the wanton attack and slander against the party and the government and the open call to overthrow the leadership of the Communist party and subvert the present government, as contained in the large quantity of big- and small-character posters, slogans, leaflets, and elegiac couplets. Some of the posters on the campuses of Beijing University, Qinghua University, and other schools abused the Communist party as "a party of conspirators" and "an organization on the verge of collapse"; some attacked the older generation of revolutionaries as "decaying men administering affairs of the state" and "autocrats with a concentration of power"; some attacked by name the Chinese leaders one by one, saying that "the man who should not die has passed away while those who should die remain alive"; some called for "dissolving the incompetent government and overthrowing autocratic monarchy"; some demanded the "abolishment of the Chinese Communist Party and adoption of the multiparty system" and "dissolving of party branches and removal of political workers in the mass organizations, armed forces, schools, and other units"; some issued a "declaration on private ownership," calling on people to "sound the death knell of public ownership at an early date and greet a new future for the republic"; some went so far as to "invite the Kuomintang back to the mainland and establish two-party politics," etc. Many big- and small-character posters used disgusting language to slander Comrade Deng Xiaoping, clamoring "down with Deng Xiaoping."

This turmoil, from the very beginning, was manifested by a sharp conflict between bourgeois liberalization and the Four Cardinal

Principles. Of the programmatic slogans raised by the organizers of the turmoil at the time—either the "nine demands" first raised through Wang Dan, leader of an illegal student organization, in Tiananmen Square or the "seven demands" and "ten demands" raised later—there were two principle demands: one was to reappraise Comrade Hu Yaobang's merits and demerits; the other was to completely negate the fight against bourgeois liberalization and rehabilitate the so-called "wronged citizens" in the fight. The essence of the two demands was to gain absolute freedom in China to oppose the Four Cardinal Principles and to realize capitalism.

Echoing these demands, some so-called "elitists" in academic circles, that is, the very small number of people stubbornly clinging to their position of bourgeois liberalization, organized a variety of forums during the period and indulged in unbridled propaganda through the press. Most outstanding among the activities was a forum sponsored by the *World Economic Herald* and the *New Observer* in Beijing on 19 April. The forum was chaired by Ge Yang, and its participants included Yan Jiaqi, Su Shaozhi, Chen Ziming (director of the Beijing Institute of Socioeconomic Science), and Liu Ruishao (head of Hong Kong Wen Hui Pao's Beijing office). There were two main topics: one was to "rehabilitate" Hu Yaobang; the other was to "reverse" the verdict on the fight against liberalization. They expressed unequivocal support for the student demonstrations, saying that they saw from there "China's future and hope." Later, when the Shanghai Municipal Party Committee made the correct decision on straightening things out in the *World Economic Herald*, Comrade Zhao Ziyang, who consistently winked at bourgeois liberalization, refrained from backing the decision. Instead, he criticized the Shanghai Municipal Party Committee for "making a mess of it" and "landing itself in a passive position."

This turmoil also found expression in the fact that, instigated and engineered by the small handful of people, many acts were crude violations of the Constitution, laws, and regulations of the People's Republic of China and ran gravely counter to democracy and the legal system. They put up big-character posters en masse on the campuses in disregard of the fact that the provision on "four big freedoms" (speaking out freely, airing views fully, holding great debates, and writing big-character posters) had been abrogated, and they turned a deaf ear to all persuasion; they staged large-scale demonstrations day after day in disregard of the ten-article regulations on demonstrations issued by the Standing Committee of the Beijing Municipal People's Congress; late on the night of 18 and 19 April, they assaulted Xinhuamen, headquarters of the Party Central Committee and the State Council, and shouted "down with the Communist party," something which never occurred even during the Cultural Revolution; they violated the regulations for the management of Tiananmen Square and occupied the Square by force several times, one consequence of which was that the memorial meeting for Comrade Hu Yaobang was almost interrupted on 22 April. Ignoring the relevant regulations of the Beijing Municipality and without registration, they formed an illegal organization, Solidarity Student Union (later changed into Federation of Autonomous Student Unions in Universities and Colleges), and "seized power" from lawful student unions and postgraduate unions formed through democratic election. Disregarding law and school discipline, they took by force school offices and broadcasting stations and did things as they wished, creating anarchy on the campuses.

Another important means that the small number of turmoil organizations and plotters used was to fabricate a spate of rumors to confuse people's minds and agitate the masses. At the beginning of the student unrest, they spread the rumor that "Li Peng scolded Hu Yaobang at a Political Bureau meeting and Hu died of anger." The rumor was meant to spearhead the attack on Comrade Li Peng. In fact, the meeting focused on the question of education. When Comrade Li Tieying, member of the Political Bureau, state councillor and minister in charge of the State Education Commission, was making an explanation of a relevant document, Comrade Hu Yaobang suffered a sudden heart attack. He was given emergency treatment right in the meeting room and was rushed to a hospital when his condition allowed. There was definitely no such thing as Hu flying into a rage.

On the night of 19 April, a foreign language student of Beijing Teachers' University was run down by a trolley bus on her way back to school after attending a party. She died despite treatment. Some people spread the rumor that "a car of the Communist party's armed police knocked down a student and killed her," which stirred up the emotions of some students who did not know the truth.

In the small hours of 20 April, policemen whisked away those students who had blocked and assaulted Xinhuamen, and sent them back to Beijing University by bus. Some people concocted the rumor of an "April 20 bloody incident," alleging that "the police beat people at Xinhuamen, not only students, but also workers, women, and children," and that "More than one thousand scientists and technicians fell in blood." This further agitated some people.

On 22 April, when Li Peng and other leading comrades left the Great Hall of the People at the end of the memorial meeting for Comrade Hu Yaobang, some people perpetrated a fraud with the objective of working out an excuse for attacking Comrade Li Peng. First, they started the rumor that "Premier Li Peng promised to come out at 12:45 and receive students in the Square." Then they let three students kneel on the steps outside the east gate of the Great Hall of the People for handing in a "petition." After a while, they said, "Li Peng went back on his word and refused to receive us. He has deceived the students." This assertion fanned strong indignation among the tens of thousands of students in Tiananmen Square and almost led to a serious incident in which the Great Hall of the People was almost assaulted.

Rumor mongering greatly sharpened students' antagonism toward the government. Using this antagonism, a very small number of people put up the slogan: "The government pays no heed to our peaceful petition. Let's make the matter known across the country and call for a nationwide class boycott." This led to a serious situation in which sixty thousand university students boycotted classes in Beijing and many students in other parts of China followed suit. The student unrest escalated and the turmoil expanded.

This turmoil was marked by another characteristic, that is, it was no longer confined to the institutions of higher learning or the Beijing area; it spread to the whole of society and to all parts of China. After the memorial meeting for Comrade Hu Yaobang, a number of people went to contact middle schools, factories, shops, and villages, made speeches in the streets, handed out leaflets, put up slogans, and raised money, doing everything possible to make the situation worse. The slogan "Oppose the Chinese Communist Party" and the big-character poster "Long live class boycott and exam boycott" appeared in some middle schools. Leaflets saying "Unite with the workers and peasants, down with the despotic rule" were put up in some factories. Organizers and plotters of the turmoil advanced the slogan "Go to the south, the north, the east, and the west" in a bid to establish ties throughout the country. Students from Beijing were seen in universities and colleges in Nanjing, Wuhan, Xian, Changsha, Shanghai, and Harbin, while students from Tianjin, Hefei, Anhui, and Zhejiang took part in demonstrations in Beijing. Criminal activities of beating, smashing, looting, and burning took place in Changsha and Xian.

Political forces outside the Chinese mainland and in foreign countries had a hand in the turmoil from the very beginning. Hu Ping, Chen Jun and Liu Xiaobo, members of the Chinese Alliance for Democracy, which is a reactionary organization groomed by the Kuomintang, wrote "an open letter" from New York to Chinese university students, urging them to "consolidate the organizational links established in the student unrest and strive to carry out activities effectively in the form of a strong mass body." The letter told the students to "effect a breakthrough by thoroughly negating the 1987 campaign against liberalization," "strengthen contacts with the mass media," "increase contacts with various circles in society," and "enlist their support and participation in the movement." Wang Bingzhang and Tang Guangzhong, two leaders of the Chinese Alliance for Democracy, made a hasty flight from New York to Tokyo in an attempt to get to Beijing, and had a direct hand in the turmoil. A number of Chinese intellectuals residing abroad who stand for instituting the Western capitalist system in China invited Fang Lizhi to take the lead, and cabled from Columbia University a "Declaration on promoting democratic politics on the Chinese mainland," asserting that "the people must have the right to choose the ruling party" in a bid to incite people to overthrow the Communist party.

Someone in the United States, using the name of "Hong Yan," sent in by fax "ten pieces of opinion on revising the Constitution," suggesting that deputies to the national and local people's congresses as well as judges in all courts should be elected from among candidates without party affiliation in an attempt to keep the Communist party completely out of state organs of power and judicial organs.

Some members of the formed *China Spring* journal residing in the United States hastily founded a China Democratic party. They sent a "letter addressed to the entire nation" to some universities in Beijing, inciting students to "demand that the conservative bureaucrats step down" and "urge the Chinese Communist Party to end its autocratic rule."

Reactionary political forces in Hong Kong, Taiwan, the United States, and other Western countries were also involved in the turmoil through various channels and by different means. Western news agencies showed unusual zeal. The Voice of America, in particular, aired news on three frequencies beamed to the Chinese mainland for a total of more than ten hours every day, spreading rumors, stirring up trouble, and adding fuel to the turmoil.

Facts listed above show that we were confronted not with student unrest in its normal sense but with a planned, organized, and premeditated political turmoil designed to negate the Communist party leadership and the socialist system. It had clear-cut political ends and deviated from the orbit of democracy and legality, employing base political means to incite large numbers of students and other people who did not know the truth. If we failed to analyze and see the problem in essence, we would have committed grave mistakes and landed ourselves in an extremely passive position in the struggle.

Three. The *People's Daily* 26 April Editorial was Correct in Determining the Nature of the Turmoil

From the death of Comrade Hu Yaobang on 15 April to the conclusion of the memorial service on 22 April, Comrade Zhao Ziyang tolerated and even pretended to ignore the increasingly evident signs of turmoil during the period of mourning, thus facilitating the formation and development of the turmoil. In the face of the increasingly grave situation, many comrades in the central leadership and Beijing municipality felt that the nature of the matter had changed, and repeatedly suggested to Comrade Zhao Ziyang that the central leadership should adopt a clear-cut policy and measures to quickly check the development of the situation. But Zhao kept avoiding any serious analysis and discussion on the nature of the matter. At the end of the memorial meeting for Comrade Hu Yaobang, comrades in the central leadership again suggested to Zhao that a meeting be held before his visit to the Democratic People's Republic of Korea on 23 April. Instead of accepting this suggestion, Zhao went golfing as if nothing had happened. Owing to his attitude, the party and the government lost a chance to quell the turmoil.

On the afternoon of 24 April, the Beijing Municipal party and people's government reported to Comrade Wan Li. At his proposal, members of the Standing Committee of the Politburo met that evening, presided by Comrade Li Peng, to analyze and study seriously the development of the situation. A consensus was reached that all signs at that time showed we were confronted with an antiparty and antisocialist political struggle conducted in a planned and organized way and manipulated and instigated by a small handful of people. The meeting decided that a group for quelling the turmoil be established in the central leadership, requiring at the same time that the Beijing Municipal Party Committee and people's government mobilize the masses fully, win over the majority so as to isolate the minority, and strive to put down the turmoil and stabilize the situation as soon as possible.

The following morning, Comrade Deng Xiaoping made an important speech, expressing his full agreement and support for the decision of the Politburo Standing Committee and making an incisive analysis of the nature of the turmoil. He pointed out sharply that this was not a case of ordinary student unrest but a political turmoil aimed at negating the leadership of the Communist party and the socialist system. Deng's speech greatly enhanced the understanding of the cadres and increased their confidence and courage in quelling the turmoil and stabilizing the overall situation.

The *People's Daily* editorial on 26 April embodied the decision of the Politburo Standing Committee and the spirit of Comrade Deng Xiaoping's speech, and pointed out the nature of the turmoil. At the same time, it made a clear distinction between the tiny handful of people who organized and plotted the turmoil and the vast number of students. The editorial made the overwhelming majority of the cadres feel reassured. It clarified the orientation of their activities, thus enabling them to carry out their work with a clear-cut stand.

After the editorial of the *People's Daily* was published, the Beijing Municipal Party Committee and people's government, under the direct leadership of the Chinese Communist Party's Central Committee and the State Council, convened in quick succession a variety of meetings inside and outside the party to uphold the principle and unify their understanding. They then proceeded to clear up rumors and reassure the public by any means; to render support to the leadership, party and Youth League members and student activists in educational institutions, and to encourage them to work boldly; to persuade those students who took party in the demonstration to change their course of actions; and actively to conduct a variety of dialogues. Whether conducted by the State Council spokesman Yuan Mu and other comrades with the students, or by leaders of relevant central departments with the students and principal leaders of the Beijing Municipal Party Committee and people's government with the students, all achieved good results.

Meanwhile, earnest work was being carried out in the factories, villages, shops, primary and secondary schools, and neighborhoods to stabilize the overall situation and prevent the turmoil from spreading to other sectors of society. Various provinces, municipalities, and autonomous regions did a good job in their respective localities according to the spirit of the editorial to prevent the influence of Beijing's situation from spreading to other parts of the country.

The clear-cut stand of the 26 April editorial forced the organizers and the plotters of the turmoil to make an about-turn in strategy. Before the publication of the editorial, large numbers of posters and slogans had been against the Communist party, socialism, and the Four Cardinal Principles. After the publication of the editorial, the illegal Beijing Federation of Autonomous Student Unions in the Universities and Colleges issued on 26 April the "No. 1 Order of the New Student Federation" to change their strategy, urging students to "march to Tiananmen under the banner of supporting the Communist party" on 27 April. The designated slogans included "Support the Communist Party," "Support Socialism," and "Safeguard the Constitution." The Federation also, at the suggestion of Fang Lizhi, changed its subversive slogans, such as Down with Bureaucratic Government, Down with Corrupt Government, Down with Dictatorial Rule, etc., into slogans such as Oppose Bureaucracy, Oppose Corruption and Oppose Privilege and other slogans that could win support from people of various circles.

The Japanese Jiji News Agency then dispatched from Beijing a news story entitled "Young Officials Form a Prodemocracy Group," describing some figures in the so-called "Zhao Ziyang's brain trust" as "young officials of the Chinese Communist Party's Central Committee and the government," noting that they "made frequent contacts with representatives of the new autonomous student unions in Beijing's universities and colleges, including Beijing University, Qinghua University, People's University, and Beijing Teachers' University, which took part in the demonstrations and offered advice to the students." It also said that during the mass demonstration on 27 April, the students held "placards of Support Socialism and Support the Leadership of the Communist Party at the instruction of the same group."

Student leaders originally planned to stage "a hundred-day demonstration and student strike of indefinite duration." But the students lost such enthusiasm after publication of the editorial.

Compared with the demonstration on 27 April, the number of students taking part on 4 May dropped from over thirty thousand to less than twenty thousand, and the number of onlookers also decreased by a big margin. After the 4 May demonstration, 80 percent of the students returned to class as a result of the work of the party and administrative leaders of various universities and colleges. After the publication of the *People's Daily* 26 April editorial, the situation in other parts of the country also stabilized quickly. It was evident that with some more work, the turmoil, instigated by a small handful of people making use of the student unrest, was likely to calm down. A host of facts showed that the *People's Daily* 26 April editorial was correct and played its role in stabilizing the situation in the capital and the whole country as well.

Four. Comrade Zhao Ziyang's Speech on 4 May was the Turning Point in Escalating the Turmoil

When the turmoil was about to subside, Comrade Zhao Ziyang, as general secretary of the Chinese Communist Party, adopted a capricious attitude of going back on his word. At first, when members of the Politburo's Standing Committee solicited his opinion during his visit to Korea, he cabled back and explicitly expressed "full agreement with the policy decision made by Comrade Deng Xiaoping on handling the current turmoil." After he returned on 30 April, he once again expressed at a meeting of the Politburo's Standing Committee his agreement with Comrade Deng Xiaoping's speech and the determination of the nature of the turmoil as made in the 26 April editorial, and maintained that the handling of the student unrest in the previous period had been appropriate.

A few days later, however, when he met with representatives attending the annual meeting of the Asian Development Bank on the afternoon of 4 May, he expressed a whole set of views diametrically opposed to the decision of the Politburo, to Comrade Deng's speech, and to the spirit of the editorial. First, as the turmoil had already come to the surface, he said, "there will be no big turmoil in China." Second, when a host of facts had proved that the real nature of the turmoil was the negation of the leadership of the Communist party and the socialist system, he still insisted that "they are by no means opposed to our fundamental system. Rather they are asking us to correct mistakes in our work." Third, although facts had shown that a tiny handful of people was making use of the student unrest to instigate turmoil, he merely said that it was "hardly avoidable" for "some people to take advantage of this," thus totally negating the correct judgment of the party's Central Committee that a handful of people were creating turmoil.

This speech of Comrade Zhao Ziyang's was prepared by Bao Tong beforehand. Bao asked the Central Broadcasting Station and Chinese Central Television to broadcast the speech that very afternoon and to repeat it for three days running. He also asked the *People's Daily* to "front-page" the speech the following day and to carry a large number of positive responses from various sectors. Differing views were held up and not even allowed to appear in confidential materials. Comrade Zhao Ziyang's speech, publicized throughout the *People's Daily* and certain newspapers, created serious ideological confusion among the cadres and the masses and inflated the arrogance of the organizers and plotters of the turmoil.

The great difference between Comrade Zhao Ziyang's speech and the policy of the party's Central Committee not only evoked many comments at home but was also seen clearly by the media abroad. A Reuters dispatch said that Zhao's remarks constituted a sharp contrast to the severe condemnation of the students a week earlier and that it was a major revision of the previous week's judgement. An article in *Le Monde* on 6 May stated that it seemed that the party chief (referring to Zhao Ziyang) remarkably turned the development of the situation to his advantage.

After the speech was thrown into the open, leading officials at various levels, the party and Youth League members, and the activists among the masses, particularly those working in the universities and colleges, all became confused. They were at a loss as to what to do, and many voiced their objection. Some said, "There are two voices in the central leadership. Who is right and who is wrong? Whom are we supposed to follow?" Some queried, "We are required to maintain identical views with the central leadership, but with which one?" Others complained, "Zhao Ziyang plays the good guy at the top while we play the villains at the grass roots." Cadres in universities and colleges, and student activists as a whole, felt betrayed and troubled; some even shed tears.

At that time, the Beijing Municipal Party Committee and the people's government were also in a wretched plight. Although they knew opinions differed in the central leadership, they had to say against their will that the central leadership was unanimous and was only stressing different points. They had to ask the central leadership for instructions on many things, but Comrade Zhao Ziyang, as general secretary, was reluctant to call a meeting. Under the strong demand of the Beijing Municipal Party Committee and people's government, a meeting was convened on 8 May. But Zhao refused to hear the briefing of the Beijing authorities. At the meeting, some comrades said that Comrade Zhao Ziyang's speech on 4 May was not in accord with the spirit of the 26 April editorial. Zhao sternly retorted, "I'll be responsible for what was wrong in my speech." At another meeting, when some one said that comrades at the grass-roots level were complaining that they "had been betrayed," Comrade Zhao Ziyang rebuked, "Who betrayed you? People were betrayed only during the Cultural Revolution." In those days, quite a few people, echoing Hong Kong and Taiwan newspapers, repeatedly attacked the comrades in Beijing Municipal Party Committee and people's government who were working at the front lines. Hooligans yelled in the demonstrations: "the Beijing Municipal Party Committee is guilty of making false reports to deceive the central leadership." In face of the worsening situation, certain contemplated measures could not be implemented.

In contrast to the above, organizers and plotters of the turmoil were encouraged by Comrade Zhao Ziyang's speech. Yan Jiaqi, Cao Wiyuan (director of the Research and Development Institute of the Sitong Company) and others said that "things have turned for the better. It is necessary to mobilize the intellectuals to support Zhao Ziyang." Zhang Xianyang said, "Aren't we supposed to make use of the students? Zhao Ziyang is now doing just this."

Egged on by Comrade Zhao Ziyang and manipulated by a few others, leaders of the Autonomous Student Unions of Beijing

University and Beijing Teachers' University declared the resumption of a class boycott that night. Many other universities followed suit and organized pickets to prevent students from going to their classrooms.

After that, a new wave of demonstrations surged ahead. On 9 May, several hundred journalists from more than thirty press units took to the streets and submitted a petition. About ten thousand students from a dozen universities, including Qinghua and People's universities, Beijing Teachers' University, and the University of Political Science and Law, staged a demonstration supporting the journalists, distributing leaflets, and calling for a continued class boycott and a hunger strike.

Henceforth, the situation took an abrupt turn for the worse and the turmoil was pushed to a new height. Influenced by the situation in Beijing, the already calmed down situation in other parts of China became tense again. Shortly after Comrade Zhao Ziyang's speech, a large number of student demonstrators assaulted the office buildings of the Shanxi Provincial Party Committee and the Provincial Government in Taiyuan on 9 and 10 May. They also assaulted the ongoing International Economic and Technological Cooperation Fair, the Import and Export Commodities Fair, and the Folk Arts Festival. The above incidents exerted a very bad influence both at home and abroad.

Five. Hunger Strike Was Used as Coercion to Escalate the Turmoil

Good, kindhearted people asked if the government's lack of understanding, consideration and concession had brought about the students' behavior. The facts are just the opposite.

From the very beginning of the turmoil, the party and government fully acknowledged the students' patriotism and their concern about the country and people. Their demands to promote democracy, promote reform, punish official profiteers, and fight corruption were acknowledged as identical with the aspirations of the party and government, which also expressed the hope to solve the problems through normal democratic and legal procedures.

But such good intentions failed to win active response. The government proposed to increase understanding and reach a consensus through dialogues of various channels, levels, and forums.

The illegal student organizations, however, put forward very demanding conditions for the dialogue. They said that their partners to the dialogues "must be people holding positions at or above membership in the Standing Committee of the Politburo of the Party Central Committee, or vice-chairman of the National People's Congress Standing Committee and vice-premier"; that "a joint communiqué on every dialogue must be published and signed by both parties"; and that the dialogues should be "held in locations designated in turn by representatives of the government and students."

This was nothing like a dialogue, but more like setting the stage for political negotiations with the party and government. Especially after Comrade Zhao Ziyang's speech on 4 May, the very small number of people, regarding the restraint on the part of the party as a sign of weakness, put forward harsher terms, adding increasing heat to the turmoil and escalating it.

Even under such circumstances, the party and the government still took the attitude of utmost tolerance and restraint, with the hope of continuing to maintain the dialogue in order to educate the masses and win over the majority.

At 2:00 A.M. on 13 May, leaders of the Federation of Autonomous Student Unions in Universities and Colleges raised the demand for a dialogue, which was accepted two hours later by the General Office of the Party Central Committee and that of the State Council.

However, the students went back on their own word and cancelled the dialogue at daybreak. On the morning of 13 May, the Bureau for Letters and Visits of the general offices of the Party Central Committee, the State Council, and the National People's Congress Standing Committee again notified them of the decision to hold a dialogue with the students on 15 May.

Despite their agreement, the students began maneuvering for the number of participants in the dialogue. After the government agreed to their first proposed list of twenty people, they then demanded that the number be raised to two hundred.

Without waiting for further discussion, they accused "the government of insincerity in wanting to hold a dialogue." Then, just four hours after they had been informed of the dialogue, the students hastily made public their long-prepared "hunger strike declaration," launching a seven-day fast that involved more than three thousand people and a long occupation of Tiananmen Square. Thirteen May was chosen as the starting date of the hunger strike "to put pressure on them [the government] during Gorbachev's China visit," said Wang Dan, leader of the Federation.

The very small number of people who had organized and plotted the turmoil used the fasting students as "hostages" and their lives as a bet to blackmail the government by vile means, making the turmoil more serious.

During the hunger strike, the party and government maintained an attitude of utmost restraint and did everything they could in various aspects. First of all, staff members of various universities, leading officials at all levels, and even the party and state leaders went to Tiananmen Square to see the fasting students on many occasions and to reason with them.

Second, efforts were made to help the Red Cross and to mobilize more than one hundred ambulances and several hundred medical workers to keep watch at the fasting site day and night. Fifty-two hospitals were asked to have some two thousand beds ready so that students who suffered shock or illness because of the hunger strike could get first-aid and timely treatment.

Third, all sorts of materials were provided to alleviate the suffering of the fasting students and to ensure their safety.

The Beijing Municipal Party Committee and people's government mobilized cadres, workers, and vehicles to provide the fasting students day and night with drinking water, edible salt, and sugar via the Red Cross.

The Municipal Environmental Sanitation Bureau sent sprinklers and offered basins and towels for the fasting students.

Adequate supplies of medicine preventing sunstroke, cold, and diarrhea were provided by pharmaceutical companies and distributed by the Red Cross.

The Provisions Department sent a large amount of soft drinks and bread to be used during the emergency rescue of the students.

A total of six thousand straw hats were provided by commercial units, and one thousand quilts were sent by the Beijing Military Area Command, in response to the city authorities' request to protect the fasting students from heat in the day and cold at night.

To keep the hunger strike site clean, makeshift flush toilets were set up and sanitation workers cleaned the site at midnight. Before the torrential rain on 19 May, seventy-eight coaches from the public transport company and four hundred thick boards from the materials bureau were sent to protect the fasting students from rain and dampness. No fasting student died in the seven-day hunger strike.

But all this failed to get any positive response. The facts told people time and again that the very small number of organizers and plotters of the turmoil were determined to oppose us to the very end and that the problem could not be solved even with tolerance on one thousand occasions and ten thousand concessions. It needs to be pointed out in particular that Comrade Zhao Ziyang did not do what he should have done when the situation quickly deteriorated, but instead stirred up the press to give wrong guidance to the public, making the deteriorated situation more difficult to handle.

In his 6 May meeting with Comrades Hu Qili and Rui Xingwen, both then in charge of propaganda and ideological work in the Central Committee, Comrade Zhao said, "[the press] has opened up a bit and there have been reports about the demonstrations. There is no big risk to opening up a bit by reporting the demonstrations and increasing the openness of news." He even said: "Confronted with the will of the people at home and the progressive trend worldwide, we could only guide our actions according to circumstances."

Here, he even described the adverse current against the Chinese Communist Party and socialism as "the will of the people at home" and "a progressive trend worldwide."

His instructions were passed on to major news media units in the capital the same day and many arrangements were made afterwards.

As a result, the *People's Daily* and many other national newspapers and periodicals adopted an attitude of full acknowledgment and active support of the demonstrations, sit-in, and hunger strike, devoting lengthy coverage with no less exaggeration. Even some Hong Kong newspapers expressed their surprise over this unique phenomenon.

Under such wrong guidance, the number of people who took to the streets to support the students increased day by day. The number of people involved grew from tens of thousands to a hundred thousand and several hundred thousand in addition to the two hundred thousand students who came from other parts of the country to show their support for the fasting students.

For a time, it looked as if refusal to join in the demonstrations was "unpatriotic," and refusal to show support equal to "indifference to the survival of the students."

Under these circumstances, the fasting students were put "on the back of the tiger and found it difficult to get off." Many teachers and parents of the students wrote to or called top governmental agencies, press organizations, and radio and television stations, asking them not to force the fasting students onto the path of death, to save the children, and to stop this form of "killing by public opinion."

But this did not work. The students' hunger strike and the Beijing citizens' demonstrations threw Beijing into chaos and seriously disrupted the Sino-Soviet summit, which was being closely followed worldwide. These events forced some changes in the agenda, and some activities were even cancelled.

Meanwhile, demonstrations in various major cities throughout China and even all provincial capitals registered a drastic increase in the number of people involved, while people also took to the streets in some small and medium-sized cities, producing a large-scale involvement and a serious disturbance never seen since the founding of the People's Republic of China.

In order to show support for the students and add fuel to the flames of turmoil, some of the so-called "elitists," who stubbornly stood for bourgeois liberalization, threw away all disguises and came to the front.

On the evening of 13 May, the big-character poster "We can no longer remain silent," written by Yan Jiaqi, Su Shaozhi, Bao Zunxin, and others, appeared at Beijing University urging intellectuals to take part in the big demonstrations they had sponsored to support the students' hunger strike.

On 14 May, "Our urgent appeal for the current situation" was jointly made by twelve people, including Yan Jiaqi, Bao Zunxin, Li Honglin, Dai Qing, Yu Haocheng, Li Zehou, Su Xiaokang, Wen Yuankai, and Liu Zaifu. They demanded that the turmoil be declared a "patriotic democratic movement" and the illegal student organizations be declared legal, saying that they would also take part in the hunger strike if these demands were not met.

This appeal was published in *Guangming Daily* and broadcast on China Central Television. These people also went to Tiananmen Square many times to make speeches and agitate. They slandered our government as "an incompetent government," saying that through the fasting students "China's bright future can be envisioned."

Then these people formed the illegal Beijing Union of Intellectuals and published the "16 May Declaration," threatening with countercharges that "a promising China might be led into the abyss of real turmoil" if the government did not accept the political demands of the very small number of people.

As the situation became increasingly serious, Comrade Zhao Ziyang used the opportunity of meeting Gorbachev on 16 May to direct deliberately the fire of criticism at Comrade Deng Xiaoping, thus making the situation even worse.

Right at the beginning of the meeting, he said, "Comrade Deng Xiaoping's helmsmanship is still needed for the most important issues. Since the Thirteenth National Party Congress, we have always reported to Comrade Deng Xiaoping and asked for his advice while dealing with the most important issues." He also said that this was "the first" public disclosure of the "decision" by the Communist Party of China.

On the following day, Yan Jiaqi, Bao Zunxin, and others published their most furious and vicious "17 May Declaration." They made accusations that "because the autocrat holds unlimited powers, the government has lost its own sense of responsibility and human feelings"; that "despite the Qing dynasty's demise seventy-six years ago, there is still an emperor in China though not in name, a senile and fatuous autocrat"; and that "General Secretary Zhao Ziyang declared publicly yesterday afternoon that all decisions in China must be approved by this decrepit autocrat." They cried out in rough voices: "Gerontocratic politics must end; the autocrat must resign."

Some newspapers and periodicals in Hong Kong and Taiwan echoed their reactionary clamor. The Hong Kong newspaper *Express* published an article on 18 May titled "Down with Deng and Li but not Zhao." It said, "Zhao Ziyang's speech was full of hints that the foul atmosphere at home now was caused by Deng Xiaoping's helmsmanship ... At present the masses are eager to get rid of Deng and Li, while Zhao's role is almost open upon calling." It also added, "It is good news for Hong Kong if Deng could be successfully ousted and China's reform embarks on the path of legal rule with the realization of democracy."

Against the backdrop of such screams, slogans smearing Comrade Deng Xiaoping and attacking Comrade Li Peng were all around. Some demanded "Deng Xiaoping step down" and "Li Peng step down to satisfy the people." Meanwhile, slogans like "Support Zhao Ziyang,"

"Long live Zhao Ziyang," and "Zhao Ziyang be promoted to chairman of the Central Military Commission" could be seen and heard in the demonstrations and at Tiananmen Square.

Plotters of the turmoil attempted to use the chaos as an opportunity to seize power. They distributed leaflets, proclaiming the founding of the Preparatory Committee to the People's Conference of All Circles in Beijing to replace the Municipal People's Congress. A call was made to establish "a Beijing regional government" to replace the legal Beijing Municipal People's Government. They attacked the State Council, which had been formed in accordance with the law, as "pseudogovernment." They also made rumors saying that the Ministry of Foreign Affairs and a dozen other ministries had already "declared independence" from the State Council, and that about thirty countries in the world had broken diplomatic relations with our country. After the rumor that "Deng Xiaoping has stepped down" was made, some went to demonstrations carrying a coffin, burned Comrade Xiaoping's effigy, and set off firecrackers on Tiananmen Square to celebrate their "victory."

The situation in Beijing became increasingly serious, with anarchism spreading rapidly and many areas sinking into complete chaos and white terror. If our party and government did not take resolute measures under these circumstances, another precious chance would be missed and further irretrievable damage would be done. This would not be permitted by the broad masses of the people.

Six. The Government Had no Alternative but to Take the Correct Measure of Declaring Martial Law in Parts of Beijing

To safeguard social stability in the city of Beijing, to protect the safety of the lives and property of the citizens, and to ensure the normal functioning of party and government departments at the central level and of the Beijing Municipal Government, the State Council had no alternative but to declare martial law in parts of Beijing as empowered by Clause 16 of Article 89 of the Constitution of the People's Republic of China, and this at a time when police forces in Beijing were seriously inadequate to maintain normal production, working, and living conditions. This was a resolute and correct decision.

The decision on taking resolute measures to stop the turmoil was announced at a meeting called by the central authorities and attended by cadres from the party, government, and military institutions in Beijing on 19 May. Comrade Zhao Ziyang, persisting in his erroneous stand against the correct decision of the central authorities, neither agreed to speak at the meeting together with Comrade Li Peng, nor agreed to preside over the meeting. He didn't even agree to attend the meeting. By doing so, he openly revealed his attitude of separating himself from the party before the whole party, the whole country, and the whole world.

Prior to this, members of the Standing Committee of the Politburo of the Party Central Committee had met to discuss the issue of declaring martial law in parts of Beijing on 17 May. On the same day, a few people who had access to top party and state secrets gave that information away due to their counter-revolutionary political stand. A person who worked at the side of Comrade Zhao Ziyang said to the leaders of the illegal student organization: "The troops are about to suppress you. All others have agreed. Zhao Ziyang was the only one who was against it. You must get prepared."

On the evening of 17 May, Bao Tong summoned some people from the Political Structural Reform Research Center of the Party Central Committee for a meeting. After divulging the secret of declaring martial law, he made a "farewell speech" in which he warned the attendants not to reveal the schemes worked out at the meeting, saying that anyone who revealed them would be a "traitor," a "Judas." On 19 May, Gao Shan, deputy bureau director of this Political Structural Reform Research Center, hurried to the Economic Structural Reform Institute to pass on to those who were holding a meeting the so-called instructions from "above." After that, the meeting, presided over by Chen Yizi, the institute's director, drafted a "six-point statement on the current situation" in the name of the Economic Structural Reform Research Institute, the Development Institute of the China Rural Development Research Center under the State Council, the Institute on International Studies of the China International Trust and Investment Corporation, and the Beijing Association of Young Economists. The statement, which was broadcast at Tiananmen Square and distributed widely, demanded "publicizing the inside story of the top leadership's decision making and the divergence of opinions" and "convening a special session of the National People's Congress" and "a special congress of the Chinese Communist Party." It also urged the students on Tiananmen Square to "end their hunger strike as soon as possible," hinting that the government "would adopt an extreme action [military control]."

Soon after that, some people, who identified themselves as employees of the State Commission for Restructuring the Economy, went to Tiananmen Square to deliver a speech in which they said, "with deep grief and extreme anger, we now disclose a piece of absolutely true news: General Secretary Zhao Ziyang has been dismissed from his post." The speakers called on the workers, students, and shopkeepers to carry out nationwide strikes and instigated the masses to take immediate actions to fight a life-and-death struggle. The speech was soon printed in the form of a *People's Daily* Extra that was widely distributed.

On the same evening, leaflets titled "Several Suggestions on the Tactics of the Student Movement" were found at the Beijing railway station and other public places. They said that

at present, hunger strike and dialogues should no longer be our means and demands. We should hold peaceful sit-ins and raise clear-cut new political demands and slogans:

1. Comrade Ziyang mustn't be removed;
2. A special National Congress of the Chinese Communist Party must be convened immediately; and,
3. A special session of the National People's Congress must be held immediately.

They also said that people "shouldn't be terrified by the coming troops" and that "this attitude should be explained time and again to the students before their coming." Some leaders of the Autonomous Students' Union of Beijing Universities and the Beijing Autonomous Workers' Union who had been arrested also confessed that, at about 4:00 P.M. on 19 May, someone holding a piece of paper and identifying himself as a staff worker of a certain organization under the Party Central Committee went to the "Tiananmen Square headquarters" and revealed the news that martial law was about to be declared.

As a result of the close collaboration between a small number of people who had access to top party and state secrets and the organizers and schemers of the turmoil, the organizers made timely adjustments to their tactics. That night, forty-five minutes before the meeting called by the central authorities and attended by cadres from the party, government, and military institutions in Beijing, they changed the hunger strike to a sit-in in a bid to give people the false impression that, since the students had already ended their hunger strike, it was not necessary for the government to declare martial law. By so doing they also gained time to organize people and coerce those who were in the dark to set up roadblocks at major crossroads to stop the advance of the troops and to continue to mislead public opinion and confuse people's minds. While viciously cursing Comrade Deng Xiaoping and other proletarian revolutionaries of the old generation, saying that "we don't need Deng Xiaoping's wisdom and experience," they lavished praises on Comrade Zhao Ziyang by saying that "the country is hopeless without Ziyang as the party leader" and "give us Ziyang." They also plotted to rally forces for greater turmoil, claiming that they were going to mobilize two hundred thousand people to occupy Tiananmen Square and to organize a citywide general strike on 20 May. Dovetailing with Comrade Zhao Ziyang's three-day sick leave that started on 19 May, they spread the word that a "new government" would be established in three days.

Under these extremely urgent circumstances, the Party Central Committee and the State Council decided resolutely to declare martial law in parts of Beijing, starting from 10:00 A.M. on 20 May, to prevent the situation from worsening and to grasp the initiative to stop the turmoil so as to give support to the broad masses who were opposed to the turmoil and longed for stability. However, as the organizers and schemers of the turmoil had learnt of our decision before it was implemented, there were tremendous difficulties and obstacles to the troops' entry into the city.

On the eve of declaring martial law and in the first two days after it was declared, all major crossroads were blocked. More than 220 buses were taken away and used as roadblocks. Transportation came to a standstill. Troops to enforce martial law were not able to arrive at their designated places. The headquarters of the Party Central Committee and the State Council continued to be surrounded. Demagogic speeches could be heard everywhere on the streets. Leaflets spreading rumors could be seen everywhere in the city. Demonstrations, each involving thousands of people, took place in succession and Beijing, our capital city, fell into total disorder and terror. In the following few days, martial law troops managed to enter the city by different ways.

Meanwhile, the armed police and security force continued to perform their duties by overcoming tremendous difficulties. Urban and suburban districts organized workers, residents, and government office workers, as many as one hundred twenty thousand people altogether, to maintain social order. The outer suburban counties also sent out militiamen. The concerted efforts of the troops, police, and civilians helped improve the transportation, production, and living order in the capital and people felt much at ease. But the very small number of people never stopped for a single day their activities to create turmoil and never changed their goal of overthrowing the leadership of the Communist party. Things were developing day by day toward a counter-revolutionary rebellion.

One of the major tactics the organizers and schemers of the turmoil used after martial law was declared was to continue to stay on Tiananmen Square. They wanted to turn the Square into a "center of the student movement and the whole nation." Once the government made a decision, they planned to make a "strong response" at the Square and form an "antigovernment united front." These people had been planning to stir up blood-shedding incidents on the Square, believing that "the government would resort to suppression if the occupation of the Square continues" and "blood can awaken people and split the government."

To ensure that the situation on the Square could be maintained, they used funds provided by reactionary forces both at home and abroad to improve their facilities and install advanced telecommunication devices, spending one hundred thousand *yuan* a day on an average. They even started the illegal purchase of weapons. By using the tents provided by their Hong Kong supporters, they set up "villages of freedom" and launched a "democracy university" on the Square, claiming they would turn the university into the "Huangpu military school of the new era." They erected a so-called goddess statue in front of the Monument to the People's Heroes. The statue was formerly named the Goddess of Democracy, showing that they took American-style democracy and freedom as their spiritual model.

Fearing that the students who took part in sit-ins could not hold on, Liu Xiaobo and other behind-the-scenes schemers went up to the front stage and performed a four-man farce of a forty-eight-to-seventy-two-hour hunger strike so as to pep the students up. They said: "As long as the flags on the Square are still up, we can continue our fight and spread it to the whole country until the government collapses."

Taking advantage of the restraint that the government and the troops still exercised after martial law was declared, the organizers and plotters of the turmoil continued to organize all kinds of illegal activities. Following the establishment of the Autonomous Students' Union of Beijing Universities, the Beijing Autonomous Workers' Union, the Fasting Contingent, the Tiananmen Square Headquarters, and the Union of Capital's Intelligentsia, they set up more illegal organizations, such as the Patriotic Joint Conference of People from All Walks of Life in the Capital for Upholding the Constitution and the Autonomous Union of Beijing Residents. In the name of the Research Institute for Restructuring the Economic System, the Development Institute of the China Rural Development Research Center under the State Council, and the Beijing Association of Young Economists, they openly sent telegrams to some of the troops in an attempt to incite defection. They engaged in such underground activities to topple the government as organizing a special team in charge of molding public opinion and making preparations to launch an underground newspaper.

They organized their sworn followers by taking a secret oath, claiming "under no condition should we betray our conscience, yield to autocracy, and bow to the emperor of China in the 1980s." Wan Runnan, general manager of Stone Company, listed the following six conditions for retreating from Tiananmen Square when he called together some leaders of the Autonomous Students' Union of Beijing Universities in the International Hotel: to withdraw the troops, cancel martial law, remove Li Peng, ask Deng Xiaoping and Yang Shangkun to quit, and let Zhao Ziyang resume his post." During the meeting, they also planned to organize "a great march to claim victory at midnight." Moreover, as they believed that there was almost no hope of solving problems within the party after Zhao Ziyang asked for sick leave, they pinned their hopes on an emergency meeting by the Standing Committee of the National People's Congress.

Yan Jiaqi, Bao Zunxin, and others sent a telegram to the leaders of the National People's Congress Standing Committee, saying that "as the Constitution is being wantonly trampled on by a few people, we suggest that an emergency meeting of the Standing Committee of the People's National Congress be held immediately to solve the current critical problems."

Inspired by a certain member of the National People's Congress (NPC) Standing Committee, the Institute of Social Development of the Stone Company issued a letter soliciting the opinions of the Committee members on "a suggestion to immediately hold an emergency meeting of the NPC Standing Committee." After getting the signatures of part of the Standing Committee, it sent urgent telegrams to other members of the Standing Committee outside Beijing. But in these letters and telegrams, they conspired to say nothing about their true motives in an attempt to deceive those comrades who did not know the truth. They even illegally used their name to force them to cooperate.

After doing all this, Yan Jiaqi and Bao Zunwin published an article in Hong Kong's *Ming Pao Daily News*, titled "Solve China's Present Problems in a Democratic and Legal Way—Also a Letter to Li Peng," that called on "every member of the Standing Committee and every member of the National People's Congress to cast a sacred vote to abolish martial law and dismiss Li Peng as premier."

The organizers and instigators of the turmoil also agitated and organized acts of violence in an unbridled fashion. They linked up with local hoodlums, ruffians, and criminals from other parts of the country, unreformed former convicts, and others who have a hatred of the Communist party and socialism to form the so-called Dare-to-Die Corps, Flying Tigers Team, The Brave-Righteous Army, and other terrorist groups threatening to detain and kidnap party and government leaders. They planned to seize state power by adopting the tactics of "storming the Bastille." They distributed leaflets to stir up counter-revolutionary armed rebellion, advocating "a single spark can start a prairie fire" and calling for establishing "armed forces that might be called the peoples' army," for "uniting with various forces including the Kuomintang in Taiwan" and for "clear-cut stand to oppose the Communist party and its government and not hesitating to sacrifice lives."

They declared they would settle accounts with the party and the government after the event and even prepared a blacklist of cadres to be suppressed. The Hong Kong *Ming Pao Daily News* published a "dialogue" on 2 June between Liu Xiaobo, one of the organizers and planners, and "a mainland democratic leader," in which Liu said: "We must organize an armed force among the people to materialize Zhao Ziyang's comeback."

The activities of the instigators of the turmoil have strong financial backing. In addition to materials worth some hundreds of thousands of dollars from the Stone Company and others, they also got support from hostile forces overseas and other organizations and individuals. Some people from the United States, Britain, and Hong Kong offered them nearly 1 million U.S. dollars and millions of Hong Kong dollars. Part of the money was used for activities to sabotage enforcement of martial law. Anyone who took part in establishing obstacles to stop traffic and black army vehicles could get thirty *yuan* a day. Also, they set high prices to buy off rioters to burn military vehicles and beat soldiers, promising to offer 3,000 *yuan* for burning one vehicle and more money for capturing or killing soldiers.

A high-ranking official from Taiwan launched a campaign to "send love to Tiananmen" and took the lead of donating 100,000 Taiwan dollars. A member of the Central Committee of the Kuomintang in Taiwan suggested that 100 million Taiwan dollars be donated to establish a "fund to support the mainland democratic movement." Some people of the Taiwan arts and cultural circles also launched "a campaign supporting the democratic movement on the mainland." A letter by the Autonomous Students' Union of Beijing Universities to "Taiwan friend in art circles" said that "we heartily thank you and salute you for your material and spiritual support at this crucial moment."

All this shows that the turmoil planned, organized, and premeditated by a few people could not be put down merely by making some concessions on the part of the government or just by issuing an order to impose martial law, contrary to the imagination of some kind-hearted people.

They had made up their minds to unite with all hostile forces overseas and in foreign countries to launch a battle against us to the last. All one-sided goodwill would lead only to their unscrupulous attack against us. The longer the delay the greater the price.

Seven. How Did a Small Minority of People Manage to Stir up the Counter-Revolutionary Rebellion?

The Chinese People's Liberation Army undertakes not only the sacred duty of "strengthening national defence, resisting aggression, and defending the motherland" but also the noble responsibility of "safeguarding the people's peaceful labor, participating in national reconstruction, and working hard to serve the people," all of which is provided for in Article 29 of the Constitution of the People's Republic of China. It was exactly to carry out the tasks entrusted to them by the Constitution that the troops entered the city proper and safeguarded social order.

After the announcement of martial law in some areas of the capital on 20 May, the troops, despite repeated obstructions, were mobilized to march toward the city proper in accordance with a deployment plan, and by different ways to take up appointed positions.

The handful of organizers and plotters of the rebellion were well aware that they would not be able to continue their illegal and counter-revolutionary activities and that their conspiracy would come to nothing if the martial law troops took up positions in the center of Beijing. Therefore, they started to create trouble deliberately and did their best to aggravate the unrest, which eventually developed into a counter-revolutionary rebellion.

On 1 June, the Public Security Bureau detained a few of the ringleaders of the illegal Federation of Autonomous Workers' Unions. The agitators of the rebellion then took advantage of this opportunity to incite some people to surround and attack the offices of the Beijing Municipal Public Security Bureau, the Municipal Party Committee and Government, and the Ministry of Public Security.

On the evening of 1 June, a police jeep on loan to the Chinese Central TV Station was involved in a traffic accident in which three people died. None of the victims was a student. This was deliberately distorted as a provocation by martial law troops. The conspirators attempted to seize the bodies and parade them in coffins, stirring up the people and making the atmosphere extremely tense. After this incitement and uproar, they lit the fire of the counter-revolutionary rebellion.

In the early hours of 3 June, while martial law troops were heading for their positions according to schedule, agitators urged crowds to halt military and other motor vehicles, set up roadblocks, beat soldiers, and loot trucks of materials at Jianguomen, Nanheyan, Xidan, Muxidi, and other road crossings. Some twelve military vehicles were halted by crowds near Caogezhuang. Soldiers marching past the Yangjing Hotel were stopped and searched by rioters, and military vehicles parked in front of the Beijing Telegraph Office had their tires slashed and were surrounded with road dividers.

About dawn, military vehicles on the Yongdingmen Bridge were overturned, others at Muxidi had their tires slashed, and some four hundred soldiers in Chaoyangmen were stoned. In the Liubukou and Hengertiao areas, military vehicles and soldiers were surrounded by unruly crowds.

Around 7:00 A.M., some rioters swarmed over military vehicles that had been halted at Liubukou and snatched machine guns and ammunition. From Jianguomen to Dongdan and in the Tianqiao area, martial law troops were surrounded and beaten. On the Jianguomen flyover, some soldiers were stripped and others severely beaten.

Later in the morning, troops in the Hufangqiao area were beaten by rioters and some were blinded. The mob prevented some injured soldiers from reaching hospitals by deflating ambulance tires, and the victims were dragged from the vehicles. From Hufang Road to Taoranting Park, twenty-one military vehicles were surrounded and halted. Policemen escorting the soldiers were beaten by the rioters.

From noon onward, many of the soldiers trapped by mobs and barricades at the southern end of the Fuyoujie and the northern end of the Zhengyilu, Xuanwumen, Hufangqiao, Muxidi, and Dongsi crossroads were injured and their equipment taken away. At Liubukou, policemen tried several times to recover a military truck loaded with arms and ammunition from an enraged mob but failed. They were then forced to use tear gas to disperse the rioters and recapture the dangerous cargo.

About the same time, mobs began to surround and assault buildings housing state organizations and establishments of vital importance, including the Great Hall the People, the Propaganda Department of the Chinese Communist Party Central Committee, and the Ministry of Radio, Film and Television, as well as the west and south gates of Zhongnanhai, the seat of the Party Central Committee and the State Council. Dozens of policemen and guards there were injured.

As the situation rapidly deteriorated, the instigators of the upheaval became more vicious. At about 5:00 P.M., the ringleaders of the illegal Beijing Federation of Autonomous Students' Unions of Universities and Colleges and of the Federation of Autonomous Workers' Unions distributed knives, iron bars, chains, and sharpened bamboo sticks, inciting the mobs to kill soldiers and members of the security forces. In a broadcast over loudspeakers in Tiananmen Square, the Federation of Autonomous Workers' Unions urged the people "to take up arms and overthrow the government." It also broadcast how to make and use molotov cocktails and how to wreck and burn military vehicles.

A group of rioters organized about one thousand people to push down the wall of a construction site near Xidan and stole tools, reinforcing bars, and bricks, ready for street fighting.

They planned to incite people to take to the streets the next day, a Sunday, to stage a violent rebellion in an attempt to overthrow the government and seize power at one stroke.

At this critical juncture, the Party Central Committee, the State Council, and the Central Military Commission decided to order troops poised on the outskirts of the capital to enforce martial law and quell the counter-revolutionary rebellion.

Eight. How Did the Counter-Revolutionary Rebels Injure and Kill People's Liberation Army Men?

Since the enforcement of martial law in Beijing, the martial law troops heading for Beijing proper tried their best to avoid conflict, exercising great restraint in accordance with instructions of the Party Central Committee. After the 3 June riot happened and before the troops entered the city, the Beijing Municipal government and the headquarters of the martial law enforcement troops issued an emergency announcement at 6:30 P.M. that said, "All citizens must heighten their vigilance, keep off the streets, and not go to Tiananmen Square as of the issuing of this notice. Workers should remain at their posts, and other citizens must stay at home to ensure their security." The announcement was broadcast over and over again on television and radio.

About 10:00 P.M. on 3 June, the various martial law troops carried out their orders and entered the city limits. But at every major intersection they were seriously obstructed. Even so, the troops were quite restrained, while the counter-revolutionary rioters harboring a deep hatred of the People's Liberation Army troops took advantage of the situation and proceeded to beat and kill soldiers, to seize and smash military materials, and to burn military vehicles.

From 10:00 P.M. to 11:00 P.M. on the same day, at Cuiweilu, Gongzhufen, Muxidi, and Xidan, twelve military vehicles were burned. Some people threw bricks at soldiers. And some rioters pushed trolleybuses to the crossroads, set them on fire, and blocked the roads. When some fire engines got there, they were also smashed and burned.

Around 11:00 P.M., three military vehicles were wrecked, one jeep was overturned at Hufangqiao, and military vehicles on Andingmen overpass were surrounded. In Chongwenmen Street, a regiment of soldiers was surrounded, and, on Jianguomen overpass, thirty military vehicles were halted by barricades while another three hundred military vehicles were halted to the west of the Beijing Coal Industrial School.

Trying to persuade the rioters to let them through, PLA men from warrant officers to generals were beaten up or kidnapped.

To avoid conflict, the barricaded military vehicles in Nanyuan Sanyingmen made a detour. When they reached the southern gate of the Temple of Heaven, they were halted again, and many of these vehicles were wrecked and burned. One military vehicle was halted in Zhushikou and a group of people swarmed over it. When a man looking like a cadre came up and tried to persuade them to leave it alone, he was severely beaten and no one knows whether he died or not.

Just after dawn on 4 June, more military vehicles were burned. Several hundred military vehicles on dozens of road crossings in Tiantan Dongche Road, at the northern gate of the Temple of Heaven, the western exit of the subway in Qianmen, Qianmen Donglu, Fuyou Street, Liubukou, Xidan, Fuxingmen, Nanlishilu, Muxidi, Lianhuachi, Chegongzhuang, Donghuamen, Dongzhimen, Dabeiyao, Hujialou, Beidougezhuang, and Jiugongxiang in Daxing County were attacked with Molotov cocktails. Some soldiers were burned to death; others were beaten to death. In some areas, several dozens of military vehicles were burned at the same time.

At the Shuangjing crossroad, more than seventy armored personnel carriers were surrounded and machine guns ripped from twenty of them.

From Jingyuan crossroad to Laoshan crematorium, more than thirty military vehicles were burned at the same time. Some rioters with iron bars and gasoline drums waited on the crossroads to burn passing motor vehicles. Many military vehicles carrying food, bedding, and clothing were hijacked.

Several mobs drove armored personnel carriers along the Fuxingmen overpass area and fired their guns. The Federation of

Autonomous Workers' Unions claimed in their own broadcast that they had taken away a military transceiver and a cipher code book.

The mobs also assaulted civilian installations and public buildings. Shop windows, including those of the Yanshan Department Store in Xicheng District, were broken. Pine trees in front of Tiananmen Gate and the western part of Chairman Mao's Memorial Hall were burned. Some public buses, fire engines, ambulances, and taxis were also wrecked and burned. Some people even drove a public bus loaded with gasoline drums toward the Tiananmen rostrum and attempted to set fire to it. They were stopped by martial law troops on the southern side of the Golden Water Bridges.

The mobs also murdered soldiers in various bestial ways. About dawn on 4 June, some mobs beat up soldiers with bottles and bricks at Dongdan crossroad. In Fuxingmen, a military vehicle was surrounded and twelve soldiers dragged off the vehicle. They were searched and severely beaten. Many of them were badly injured. In Liubukou, four soldiers were surrounded and beaten up, and some were beaten to death. In the Guangqumen area, three soldiers were severely beaten. One was rescued by some bystanders; the other two have not yet been found. In Xixingshen Lane of the Xicheng District, more than twenty armed policemen were beaten up by mobs; some were badly injured, and the others' whereabouts are unknown. In Huguosi, a military vehicle was halted and soldiers on it were beaten up and detained as hostages. Submachine guns were snatched. A truck full of bricks drove from Dongjiao Minxiang to Tiananmen Square, and people on the truck shouted, "if you are really Chinese, attack the soldiers."

After dawn, a police ambulance carrying eight injured soldiers to a hospital was halted by mobs. They beat a soldier to death and shouted that they would do the same to the other seven. In front of a bicycle shop in Qianmen Street, three soldiers were severely beaten by hooligans, who threatened anyone who tried to rescue them. On Changan Avenue, a military vehicle broke down suddenly, and was attacked right away by about two hundred rioters. The driver was killed inside the cab. About thirty meters to the east of Xidan crossroad, another soldier was beaten to death. Then the mob poured gasoline over his body and set fire to it. In Fuchengmen, another soldier's body was hung over the overpass after he had been savagely killed. In Chongwenmen, a soldier was thrown from the overpass and burned alive. Near the Capital Cinema on West Changan Avenue, an officer was beaten to death, disemboweled, and his eyes plucked out. His body was then strung up on a burning bus.

In the several days of the rebellion, more than 1,280 military vehicles, police cars, and public buses were wrecked, burned, or otherwise damaged. Of the vehicles, over one thousand were military vehicles, more than sixty were armored personnel carriers, and about thirty were police cars. More than one hundred twenty public buses were destroyed as well as more than seventy other kinds of motor vehicles. During the same period, arms and ammunition were stolen. More than six thousand martial law soldiers, armed police, and public security officers were injured, and the death toll reached several dozen. They sacrificed their blood and even their precious lives to defend the motherland, the Constitution and the people. The people will remember their contributions.

Such heavy losses are eloquent testimony to the restraint and tolerance shown by the martial law troops. The PLA is an army led by the Chinese Communist Party and serves the people wholeheartedly. They are ruthless to the enemy but kind to the people. They were able to defeat the 8 million Kuomintang troops armed by U.S. imperialism during the war years, able to defeat U.S. imperialism that was armed to the teeth, and able to effectively safeguard the sacred territory, territorial waters, and air space of our country. So why did they suffer such great casualties in quelling the counter-revolutionary rebellion? Why were they beaten and even killed, even while they had weapons in their hands? It was just as Comrade Deng Xiaoping pointed out: "It was because bad people mingled with the good, which made it difficult for us to take the firm measures that were necessary." It also showed that the PLA love the people and are unwilling to injure civilians by accident.

The fact that they met death and sacrificed themselves with generosity and without fear fully embodies the nature of the PLA. Otherwise, how could there be such great number of casualties and losses? Doesn't this reflect that the army defends people at the cost of its own life?

In order to quell the counter-revolutionary rebellion and to avoid more losses, the martial law troops, having suffered heavy casualties and been driven beyond forbearance, were forced to fire in the air to open the way forward after repeated warnings.

During the counterattack, some rioters were killed. Because there were numerous bystanders, some were knocked down by vehicles, some were trampled on or were hit by stray bullets. Some were wounded or killed by ruffians who had seized rifles.

According to the information we have so far gathered, more than three thousand civilians were wounded and over two hundred, including thirty-six college students, died during the riot. Among the nonmilitary casualties were rioters who deserved the punishment, people accidentally injured, and doctors and other people who were carrying out various duties on the spot. The government will do its best to deal with the problems arising from the deaths of the latter two kinds of people.

Due to a rumor spread by the Voice of America and some people who deliberately wished to spread rumors, people talked about a "Tiananmen bloodbath" and "thousands of people massacred." The facts are that, after martial law troops reached Tiananmen Square at 1:30 A.M., the Beijing municipal government and the martial law headquarters issued an emergency notice that stated: "A serious counter-revolutionary rebellion occurred in the capital this evening" and "all citizens and students in Tiananmen Square should leave immediately to ensure that martial law troops will be able to implement their tasks." The notice was broadcast repeatedly for three hours through loudspeakers. The sit-in students gathered around the Monument to the People's Heroes in the southern part of the Square. At around 3:00 A.M., they sent representatives to the troops to express their desire to withdraw from the Square voluntarily and this was welcomed by the troops.

At 4:30 A.M., martial law headquarters broadcast the following notice: "It is time to clear the Square and the martial law headquarters accepts the request of the students to be allowed to withdraw." At the same time, another notice on quickly restoring normal order to the Square was issued by the municipal government and the headquarters and broadcast. After hearing this, several thousand students organized hand-in-hand pickets and started to leave the Square in an orderly manner, carrying their own banners and streamers.

At about 5:00 A.M., the troops vacated a wide corridor in the southeastern part of the Square to ensure the smooth and safe departure of the students. At the same time, a few students who refused to leave were forced to leave by martial law troops. By 5:30 A.M., the clearing operation of the Square had been completed.

During the whole operation, no one, including the students who refused but were forced to leave, died. Tales of "rivers of blood" in Tiananmen Square and the rumor mongers themselves "escaping from underneath piles of corpses" are sheer nonsense. The counter-revolutionary rebellion was put down with Tiananmen Square returning to the hands of the people and all martial law enforcement troops taking up their assigned positions.

During the quelling of the counter-revolutionary rebellion, the People's Liberation Army, the armed police, and the public security police fought valiantly and performed immortal feats. Many people gave first aid to the wounded and rescued besieged soldiers, rendering their cooperation and support to the martial law enforcement troops.

Due to the turmoil and counter-revolutionary rebellion, Beijing has suffered heavy losses in its economy, and losses in other fields cannot be counted with money. Workers, peasants, and intellectuals are working hard to retrieve the losses. Now, order in the capital has fundamentally returned to normal and the situation throughout China is also tending to become calm, which shows that the correct decision made by the Party Central Committee has benefited the Chinese people. Yet, the unrest and the rebellion are not completely over, as a handful of counter-revolutionary rioters refuse to recognize defeat and still indulge in sabotage, even dreaming of staging a comeback.

In order to achieve thorough victory, we should mobilize the people completely, strengthen the people's democratic dictatorship, and spare no effort to ferret out the counter-revolutionary rioters. We should uncover instigators and rebellious conspirators, and punish the organizers and schemers of the unrest and the counter-revolutionary rebellion—that is, those who obstinately stuck to the path of bourgeois liberalization and conspired to instigate rebellion, those who colluded with overseas and other foreign hostile forces, those who provided illegal organizations with top secrets of the party and state, and those who committed the atrocities of beating, smashing, grabbing, and burning during the disturbances. We should made a clear distinction between two different types of contradictions and deal with them accordingly through resolute, hard, and painstaking work. We must educate and unite people as much as possible and focus the crackdown on a handful of principal culprits and diehards who refuse to repent. On this basis, we will retrieve all the losses suffered in the unrest and the counter-revolutionary rebellion as soon as possible. For this we must rely on the people, try to increase production, practice strict economy, and struggle arduously.

Chairman, vice-chairmen, and Standing Committee members, our country's just struggle to quell the unrest and the counter-revolutionary rebellion has won the understanding and support of governments and people in many countries. We extend our wholehearted gratitude for this. However, there are also some countries, mainly the United States and some West European countries, that have distorted the facts, spread slanderous rumors, and even uttered so-called condemnations and imposed sanctions on our country to set off an anti-China wave and wantonly interfer in our country's internal affairs. We deeply regret this. As for the outside pressures, our government and people have never submitted to such things, not this time nor any time. The rumors will be cleared away; the truth and facts will come out.

Our country will unswervingly take economic construction as the central task and persist in the Four Cardinal Principles and in economic reform and opening up to the outside world. Our country will, as always, adhere to our independent foreign policy of peace, continue to develop friendly relations with all countries in the world on the basis of the Five Principles of Peaceful Coexistence, and make our contributions to the safeguarding of world peace and the promotion of world development.

Proclamation of the National Day of Mourning
Wu'er Kaixi of the Beigaolian (Beijing Students' Union)
Yan Jiaqi of the Beizhilian (Beijing Intellectuals Union)
4 July 1989

Today marks the passing of the first month of the 4 June massacre. We appeal to Chinese people all over the world to mourn silently for our martyred compatriots.

On 4 June 1989, Deng Xiaoping, Li Peng, and Yang Shangkun of the reactionary clique committed an act that courted worldwide condemnation. They mercilessly dispatched tanks and armored personnel carriers to launch the world's cruelest massacre against the unarmed and peaceful Chinese students and citizens of Beijing. Subsequently, they carried out a vicious campaign throughout Mainland China to pursue, arrest, and execute all outstanding members of the Chinese student movement and the prodemocracy movement. In fact, their premeditated criminal plan, the so-called "leave no stone unturned" policy, strives to extinguish the spark of the Chinese democracy movement once and for all.

But the democratization process, like the Yellow River, has already overflowed its dikes. It cannot be contained. Even though they are living under a reign of white terror, Chinese students are continuing their patriotic prodemocracy movement under various guises. At the present time there is total silence over the whole of China; this is precisely the time for demonstrators to prepare for another, greater storm in the future.

In order to continue the endeavor begun by our compatriots who martyred themselves with their blood and lives in the Tiananmen incident, in order to urge the Chinese student movement and the prodemocracy movement to greater heights, the Beijing College Students' Autonomous Association (Beigaolian) and the Beijing Intellectuals Autonomous Association (Beizhilian) held a joint meeting from 27 June to 3 July. Wu'er Kaixi, head of the Beigaolian, and Yan Jiaqi, head of the Beizhilian, jointly presided over the meeting. During the conference, they made a preliminary analysis of the Chinese student movement and the prodemocracy movement since April. They also reflected on the history of the Chinese prodemocracy movement since 1979. They held substantive discussions on the present political situation of the Chinese government and took concrete steps toward fulfilling their goals.

The conference resulted in the general agreement that the 4 June massacre should not be considered the conclusion of the 1989 Chinese prodemocracy movement, but instead provide precisely a new awakening and fresh start that the Chinese movement needed.

The 1989 Chinese prodemocracy movement is the brightest page in modern Chinese history. The significance of the movement has already far surpassed that of the May Fourth Movement seventy years ago and the April Fifth Movement thirteen years ago. The nature of this movement is that it is neither a struggle by the common people for survival under tyranny nor a movement brought about solely by an internal power struggle within the Communist party. This movement stands alone as a great struggle by a people who never will compromise their demand for the privilege of self-government. Its basic objectives transcend national and cultural boundaries. The movement belongs to all the people of all civilizations for the attainment of freedom, democracy, rule by law, and human rights. It shall blossom forth on Mainland China and bear fruit. Therefore, this movement that was led by the students of Beijing, and responded to by people of all social classes, is in essence a universal struggle for the dignity and sovereignty of all mankind. For this reason, the Deng-Li-Yang reactionary clique's bloody suppression is not only an unforgivable crime against Chinese students and people, it is a mad challenge to the basic human rights of all of mankind. During this struggle, all nations and peoples of the world who revere freedom, democracy, rule by law, and human rights, naturally and without reservation stand on the side of the Chinese students and the Chinese people.

The prodemocracy movement of 1989 is since 1979 the high point in the development of China's prodemocracy movement. This government, by adopting measures that run counter to world opinion, has fully exposed the true nature of the present system as autocratic and dictatorial. It also raised this central question to the world: Should the "reform" of all communist countries have "political democratization" as its basic responsibility? As early as 1979, the precursors of the Chinese prodemocracy movement raised the shining motto of "The Fifth Modernization." This cry is finding a distant echo among people in the Soviet Union and the Eastern European countries who are demanding political reform, uniting these countries together as they discard Stalinism and gradually march toward the international climate of political democratization. The aspect in which Deng Xiaoping and the small group around him are reactionary is that from the very beginning they have stood on the very opposite end of this worldwide historical trend. They arrested Wei Jingsheng, closed down Democracy Wall, initiated the so-called "cleansing the spiritual pollution" and the "antibourgeois liberalization" campaigns, and even carried out the unconscionable "June Fourth Massacre." Their sole purpose was, as they themselves have claimed, to turn around the "international climate" and to set another model for international communism. In other words, they are stubbornly holding on to the dictatorial, autocratic model of Stalinism; they have promoted even more viciously than before the line of the "antirightist" movement and the "class struggle" of the "cultural revolution." Therefore, this struggle of the Chinese students and Chinese people not only affects whether the matter of China's reform can continue but also whether the overall reform in all Communist countries can vigorously develop into an all-out trend. When one faces the fact of the 4 June massacre, all the communist countries must carry out a painful reflection and examination. All nations and peoples that love peace and democracy have the right to rebuke and restrain antirevolutionary, antidemocratic, and antihumanist forces.

At the same time, the Chinese prodemocracy movement of 1989 became a great symbol of the unprecedented solidarity among the Chinese people all over the world. Chinese people on the mainland, in Hong Kong, Macao, Taiwan, Asia, the United States, Europe, Australia, and the world over have never experienced this kind of emotional bonding and shared unity as today. This has become a truly patriotic movement for Chinese people throughout the world. It demonstrates in a profound manner that only under the banner of freedom, democracy, rule by law, and human rights can the livelihood of this ancient race, the Chinese people, reach its full potential. Issues such as the peaceful reunification of China's two shores, the restoration of Hong Kong and Macao to the fatherland, or even the willingness of overseas sojourners to devote themselves to the country do not matter now. Only when the principles of freedom, democracy, rule by law, and human rights are realized throughout China will these matters become truly significant. If these are rejected, the Chinese people will have no alternative!

The most precious facet of the Chinese prodemocracy movement of 1989 was not only that the significance of freedom, democracy, rule by law, and human rights has been deeply ingrained in the minds of every Chinese, but that, from the beginning until the end, the movement adopted goals that corresponded to its original purpose and tactics. Those goals were rationality, peaceful demonstration, and nonviolence. Even at dusk on 4 June, when they were encircled by troops, the students on the Square still resolutely destroyed all captured guns and bullets. They clearly demonstrated their determination not to use violence to fight violence. Amidst the guns and bullets, the students called out: "The supreme principle of peace is self-sacrifice." This earth-shattering and gut-wrenching motto reflected precisely the ancient Chinese philosophical beliefs that peace will triumph over violence, that civilization will triumph over barbarousness, that reason is certain to prevail over irrationality, and that righteousness will triumph over evil! For those few of us who were lucky to survive the movement, the only comfort we can derive is that the image of those unarmed, self-possessed Chinese youths facing scores of advancing tanks has become a symbol of peaceful resistance to tyranny for all mankind. For the students' movement and the democracy movement, they left an indelible imprint on the memory of the peoples of the world.

The fundamental cause of the evolution of the prodemocracy movement of 1989, which began as an "April shower" by students but developed rapidly into a powerful hurricane by May, was that it focused and expressed the united plea of all the nation's people. This plea was to regulate government profiteering, to eradicate corruption, to institute a free press, and to implement a system of balance of power in government. All of these problems did not arise accidentally or in isolation. They are instead the inevitable result of China's promoting economic reforms without pursuing corresponding political reforms during the past ten years. As long as the press has no freedom, then official profiteering cannot be fully exposed; as long as power and authority cannot be curbed, then corruption is bound to occur. And finally, if officially profiteering is widespread and corruption is rampant, then China's economy cannot truly have the vitality to grow. Therefore, all of contemporary China's problems can be focused on one crucial point: Genuine political reform must be implemented. China's students, citizens, workers, and intellectuals all have raised precisely this demand. In actuality, this demand has received the support of the majority of the membership of the Communist party, the People's Alliance, the People's Revolutionary party, and other organizations. But the Deng-Li-Yang clique has taken its minority opinion and forced it on the heads of the Chinese people. It is using a military dictatorship, the blood-and-iron repressive tactics of barbarians, to derail a China full of high hopes.

However, even though large-scale massacre and massive repression have created a temporary period of white terror, they cannot solve the political and economic crisis. On the contrary, they can only exacerbate this kind of crisis. At the moment, the Deng-Li-Yang clique, other than confronting the original political and economic crisis, must also confront a credibility crisis that it didn't have before. In fact, this clique has lost all vestiges of legitimacy in the eyes of foreigners and the people. Since it has forcibly blocked the road to political democratization, it can only cause an economic reversal. Political corruption will become more widespread and thus lead to further discontent among the people. It can be predicted that, in the not too distant future, a student movement and democratic movement will arise again in China on an even larger scale. A reactionary political authority that depends only on tanks and machine guns for support will inevitably be thoroughly destroyed by this storm.

In order to welcome the coming of this new high tide of student and democratic movements in the future, the conference decided to jointly establish an organization of the Beigaolian and the Beizhilian to unify all democratic forces overseas and to prepare for the establishment of a Committee for the Chinese Student and Prodemocracy Movements. At the same time it was suggested that, at the appropriate time, to follow the methods of overseas supporters of the Beijing students and democracy movement and establish a Chinese Student and Prodemocracy Movement Foundation.

During the joint conference, we made clear that in our efforts to secure the democratization of China we will still maintain our position of "rationality, peaceful demonstration, and nonviolence." We will oppose under all circumstances the use of terrorist tactics. China's modern and recent history has taught us that the principle that "power comes from the barrel of a gun" cannot lead China to a true state of freedom and democracy. This was the resolution of the martyrs who sacrificed themselves on 4 June.

The symbol of the Beijing students' 27 April Peace March was the peaceful methods used by the Chinese people to oppose violence. and to obtain democracy. It constituted the greatest day in the history of modern Chinese history. On 27 May, at a joint meeting of all the various organizations at the capital, a ten-point declaration discussing all aspects of the state of affairs was drafted. Among them was the proposal that 27 April be designated Chinese Freedom and Democracy Day. This proposal was readily approved at this joint meeting.

During the month's time since the 4 June massacre, we who have lived and fought on Tiananmen Square and who have escaped unreasonable arrest by hiding out and fleeing, look at the distant skies of our country and cry uncontrollably. The brave souls of those who heroically met a tragic death have not yet received their final rest. Of those fighters who stood shoulder to shoulder with us, many are perhaps under arrest or their whereabouts unclear, and those countless ones who were on hunger strikes for many days and whose bodies became weak have not received consolation but, on the contrary, have incurred great spiritual and psychological hardship. We hereby, in the name of those above mentioned, and in the name of those whose blood flowed on Tiananmen Square, respectfully make the following appeal to all descendents of the Chinese race and to all peace-loving people of the world:

1. On 12 September 1989, simultaneously in various parts of the world, commemorate the hundredth day after the 4 June massacre with a service to honor the students, teachers, citizens, doctors, and nurses who died in the tragedy.
2. Initiate a campaign to promote Chinese students and Beijing citizens for the 1990 Nobel Peace Prize; respectfully remember the unprecedented act of hundreds of thousands of students who in an orderly manner camped out on Tiananmen Square for several weeks, carried out hunger strikes, and peacefully petitioned the government; and commend the people of Beijing for their bravery in confronting and obstructing the advancing troops empty handed.
3. Make 4 June a Chinese National Day of Mourning.

As of now, the high idealism and fearless spirit of the martyrs have already been made clear to the world! The Chinese prodemocracy movement will continue undaunted; the future of the Chinese nation is bright! We believe firmly that the day is not too distant when the criminals of Tiananmen Square will be publicly tried and the Goddess of Democracy erected again!

Our compatriots who died on 4 June will live forever!

Long live the Great Prodemocracy Movement of 1989!

Long live freedom, democracy, rule of law, and human rights!

Glossary of Terms

Anti-Rightist Campaign: the 1957 reaction to the "Hundred Flowers Campaign" (see below) that was designed to root out individuals who questioned Communist rule. Such individuals were accused of having contacts with the West or being influenced by Western ideas. Hundreds of thousands of people were imprisoned, banished from their jobs, or otherwise persecuted.

Beigaolian: the Autonomous Student Union of Beijing Universities and Colleges formed in late April 1989 to take the place of the official, government monitored student organizations.

Bourgeois Liberalization: the Communists' term for Westernization. The term is frequently used to describe social and political trends that, in the leadership's eyes, go too far. For example, the notion of consulting with the people in the development of policy was acceptable to the leadership, but actually giving the power to select or depose their leaders was considered "Western" and therefore evidence of "bourgeois liberalization" (see Spiritual Pollution).

Cadre: an operative for the Communist party. Cadres are used to spread and implement party policies.

Central Committee: a committee consisting of five members who are considered to be the top policy makers in China. Deng Xiaoping's personal approval, however, is necessary on crucial matters. At the time of the Tiananmen Square demonstrations, the members were General Secretary Zhao Ziyang, Premier Li Peng, State President Yang Shangkun, Chairman of the Standing Committee of the National People's Congress Wan Li, and Politburo Standing Committee member Hu Qili.

Changan Boulevard: a broad avenue that crosses Tiananmen Square in the heart of Beijing from east to west. "Changan" means "eternal peace" in Chinese.

Chinese Communist Party (CCP) : founded in 1921 and the leading party in China since 1949. There are other political parties in China. However, they exist in name only and never challenge the supremacy of the CCP.

Corruption: a term that broadly defines any method by which government officials used their power to enrich themselves or their family and friends. Corruption was partially a result of China's having both a state-controlled economy and a market economy. Officials could withhold or even buy cheap, state-supplied goods and sell them off at a higher price on the market economy. Officials also were known for setting their children up in a government business or arranging to have them educated overseas, which was also considered corruption. These problems became acute in the 1980s because the government was encouraging people to make money and yet had set few guidelines on legal means to do it.

Cultural Revolution: a tumultuous period from 1966 to 1976 during which Mao and his closest advisors, the Gang of Four (see below), persecuted their opponents and intellectuals in general. The targets of the Cultural Revolution were sent to work in the country, tortured, harassed, and sometimes even killed by youth groups called Red Guards. The ostensible purpose of the campaign was to wipe out all traces of contact with Western values and influences; in the process, some traditional ideas, such as Buddhist and Confucian values, were also challenged. The Cultural Revolution traumatized the nation, causing questions to be raised about the nature of communism and reinforcing traditional fears of instability and "turmoil," a key term during the 1989 student movement.

Democracy Wall: a period in 1978 and 1979 in which posters demanding democratic reforms were posted on a wall in the Xidan district of Beijing. The posters, called either big-character posters or small-character posters, were allowed ostensibly as a way to show Deng Xiaoping's openness while at the same time discrediting some of the policies of Mao Zedong. Eventually, Democracy Wall was closed and some of the writers arrested. One of them, Wei Jingsheng, is still in jail.

Face: a person's reputation or credibility. In Chinese culture, losing face is to be avoided at all costs.

Four Cardinal Principles: Deng Xiaoping's "basic prerequisite for achieving modernization." They are: keeping to the socialist road; upholding the dictatorship of the proletariat; upholding the leadership of the Communist party; and upholding Marxism-Leninism and Mao Zedong Thought (see chapters 3 and 8).

Four Modernizations: China's recipe for economic development in the post-Mao era, calling for advances in industry, defense, agriculture, and science and technology. The Four Modernizations were initiated by Mao's original successor, Hua Guofeng, and were subsequently adopted by Deng Xiaoping.

Gang of Four: four Communist party leaders who, in the aftermath of Mao Zedong and the Cultural Revolution, were blamed for excesses of that period. Many experts agree, however, that the Gang of Four served merely as scapegoats for Mao's mistakes after his death. The new regime did not want to denounce its former leader, fearing that criticism would undermine the Communist party and thus their own power. The members of the gang were Jiang Qing (Mao's widow), Wang Hongwen, Zhang Chunqiao, and Yao Wenyuan. See also Cultural Revolution.

Gerontocracy: the system of rule by elders. In China it carries special significance because of the traditional respect for elders.

Gongzilian: the Workers' Autonomous Union formed in late May 1989 in Beijing, after the declaration of martial law, to support the student movement. The support was minimal and no strikes were organized.

Great Hall of the People: one of ten large-scale civic projects undertaken during the 1950s. The Great Hall of the People was the site of formal occasions such as state dinners and funerals. It sits on the western side of Tiananmen Square.

Hundred Flowers Campaign: a short-lived policy in 1956 in which intellectuals were encouraged to voice their complaints, the idea being to "let a hundred flowers bloom, a hundred thoughts contend." Some intellectuals, however, used the period to begin questioning the right of the Communist party to be the sole instrument of government power in the nation, a charge so threatening to Mao that he subsequently suppressed the campaign.

Kuomintang (KMT): the Nationalist party, currently based on Taiwan, that fought a bitter war with the Communists in the 1930s and 1940s for control of the country. The Kuomintang has continued to claim that it is the rightful government of China; consequently, the Communist government frequently blames its problems on Taiwan.

Lin Biao: minister of defense under Mao Zedong. Lin was considered Mao's heir apparent when he was accused of plotting to overthrow him. The party line is that Lin was killed in a plane crash over Mongolia in 1971, although recent reports from that country state that his body was never found there. A more plausible explanation is that Mao began to fear Lin's growing power and ousted him.

Mao Zedong: chairman of the Communist party and paramount Chinese leader from the founding of the People's Republic of China in 1949 until his death in 1976. Mao enjoyed cult-like popularity among a large sector of the Chinese population, virtually giving him dictatorial powers. But the devastation caused by the Cultural Revolution tarnished his reputation, and the party has struggled to redefine his rule in such a way as to stress his contributions while disavowing his flaws.

May Fourth Movement: a student demonstration on 4 May 1919 protesting the Versailles Treaty, which granted portions of Shandong province to Japan. The May Fourth Movement was the first patriotic movement by intellectuals and students in modern China, giving rise to Marxist and Leninist influences in China as well as an era of great literary and artistic creativity.

Muxidi: a district about three miles west of Tiananmen Square on Changan Boulevard. The students marching to and from their universities in northwestern Beijing would turn at Muxidi. In the 3 June attack, soldiers are believed to have trapped demonstrators in Muxidi as they began their assault.

National People's Congress (NPC): officially, the parliament for the People's Republic of China. However, it functions less as a forum for genuine political debate than as a rubber stamp, approving the senior leaders' policies.

Open door policy: Deng's policy of increasing ties between China and other nations, particularly Western countries. Academic, commercial, and political exchanges increased under this policy, whereas Mao Zedong had closed China off to several Western nations.

People's Daily: the official party newspaper of China. Its contents are considered to reflect official government position on every issue it addresses. There is also an overseas edition for students and officials who are abroad.

Politburo: a twenty-member committee that handles the daily affairs and major policies of the Chinese Communist Party.

Reform: another term used to describe China's general effort to modernize its economy in the 1980s. It represented a step away from the planned, centralized economy of previous eras and allowed more autonomy for regional economies, petty capitalistic ventures, and the introduction of free market mechanisms.

Responsibility System: part of the reform program of the 1980s. The responsibility system introduced free-market mechanisms to the agricultural sector, giving farmers more control over which crops to sow, where they could sell it, and what prices they could charge, and allowing them to engage in other sideline capitalist ventures.

Reversal of Verdict: stemming from a traditional Chinese practice, refers to reassessing a person's reputation and standing, usually changing it from bad to good. It can occur both while a person is alive, enabling him to regain his position in society, or after his death, which is often taken to mean that the principles or ideas for which he stood are now acceptable.

Sanjiaodi: the triangular area at the heart of Beijing University where the students often congregated to hear speeches and announcements.

Shanghai Commune: a brief period in 1967 in which self-government by workers, or a "proletarian dictatorship," was to have been established in Shanghai. The workers, heeding the call of the Cultural Revolution, had overthrown the existing party structure in Shanghai in January and attempted to set up a structure modeled after the Paris Commune. However, factionalism fractured the commune, and Mao became interested in other methods of restructuring party power. Mao suggested that the commune transform itself into a "revolutionary committee" in which the army would have a substantial share of power. The demise of the Shanghai Commune amounted to the first of several retreats from the original aims and promises of the Cultural Revolution.

Spiritual Pollution: a term akin to "bourgeois liberalization" (see above) and referring to the influence of Western values on the Chinese people. "Spiritual pollution" can encompass anything from criminal activities to a preference for Western clothes and pop music to liberalized attitudes about sex. A campaign against "spiritual pollution" was carried out from late 1983 to early 1984, with limited success.

Student Movement of 1986-87: In December 1986, students at universities in Hefei demonstrated for democratic reforms. The movement spread to campuses in other cities. The party leadership split in its decision on how to deal with the situation. The movement was suppressed nonviolently and labelled "turmoil." General Secretary Hu Yaobang refused to suppress the students, leading to his dismissal.

Tiananmen Square: the spiritual heart of the People's Republic of China and the site of numerous political rallies during the Mao Zedong era. "Tiananmen" means "Gate of Heavenly Peace."

Waigaolian: short for the Autonomous Student Union of Non-Beijing Universities and Colleges.

Wei Jingsheng: See Democracy Wall.

Xinhuamen: an area just west of Tiananmen Square that is the entrance to Zhongnanhai (see below) and where Communist party headquarters are located. Xinhuamen means "New China Gate."

Yuan: unit of currency in China usually designated as RMB (*renminbi*). Its official exchange rate in 1989 was about 4:1 in with the U.S. dollar, but the black market value was closer to 7:1.

Zhongnanhai: a lake and the surrounding district on the northwestern corner of Tiananmen Square where the Communist party headquarters are located.

Zhou Enlai: prime minister of China and second-in-command to Mao until his death in 1976. Zhou was highly regarded for his tenacity, grace under pressure, and staunch defense of the party. At his funeral services, violent demonstrations broke out on Tiananmen Square.

Bibliography

Books

Ban Gu. *Han Shu* (History of the Han Dynasty). Beijing: Zhonghua shuju edition, 1962.
Buci-Glucksmann, Christine. *Gramsci and the State*. London: Lawrence and Wishart, 1980.
The China White Paper (August 1949). Palo Alto: Stanford University Press, 1967.
Chow Tse-tsung. *The May Fourth Movement, Intellectual Revolution in Modern China*. Cambridge: Harvard University Press, 1960.
Creel, H.G. *Chinese Thought from Confucius to Mao Tse-tung*. Chicago: University of Chicago Press, 1953.
Deng Xiaoping. *Selected Works of Deng Xiaoping, 1975-1982*. Beijing: Foreign Language Press, 1984.
Eisentadt, S.N., ed. *Max Weber on Chrisma and Institution Building*. Chicago and London: The University of Chicago Press, 1968.
Etzioni, Amitai. *A Comparative Analysis of Complex Organizations*. New York: The Free Press, 1961.
_____, ed. *A Sociological Reader in Complex Organizations*, 2nd ed. New York: Holt, Rinhart and Winston, 1969.
Fairbank, John King, ed. *Chinese Thought & Institutions*. Chicago: University of Chicago Press, 1957.
Fan Ye. *Hou Han Shu* (History of the Later Han Dynasty). Beijing: Zhonghua shuju edition, 1965.
Fang Tung-mei. *The Chinese Way of Life: The Philosophy of Comprehensive Harmony*. Hong Kong: The Union Press, 1957.
Fei Xiaotong. *Rural China*. Shanghai: Guanchashe, 1948.
Fukuyama, Francis. "The End of History?" *The National Interests* 16 (Summer 1989).
Fu Locheng. *Fu Mengzhen xiansheng nianpu* (A Chronological Biography of Fu Sinian). Taibei: Biographical Literature Society, 1969.
Fung Yulan. *A History of Chinese Philosophy*. Translated by Derke Bodde. Princeton: Princeton University Press, 1952.
Gurr, Ted Robert. *Why Men Rebel*. Princeton: Princeton University Press, 1970.
Harmin, Carol Lee and Timothy Cheek. *China's Establishment Intellectuals*. Armonk, N.Y. and London: M. E. Sharpe, 1986.

Hoare, Quintin Hoare and Geoffery Nowell Smith, eds. *Selections from the Prison Notebooks of Antonio Gramsci*. New York: International Publishers, 1971.

Hou Wailu, ed. *Zhongguo sixiang tongshi* (A General History of Chinese Thought). Beijing: People's Press Beijing, 1960.

Hsu, Francis L.K. *Americans and Chinese: Passage to Difference*. 3rd ed.. Honolulu: University Press of Hawaii, 1981.

_____."Eros, Affect, and Pao." In *Kinship and Culture* Chicago: Aldine Publishing, 1971.

Hu Hsien Chin. "Emotion, Real & Assumed, in Chinese society." Unpublished manuscript on file with Columbia University Research in Contemporary Culture, 1949, document no. CH 668.

Hu Songping. *Hu Shihzhi xiansheng nianpu changbian chugao* (A Draft Chronological Biography of Hu Shih). Taibei: Lianjing Press, 1984.

Huang Xianfan. *Songdai Taixuesheng Jiuguo Yundong* (Patriotic Student Movements of the Imperial Academy During the Song Dynasty). Shanghai: Commercial Press, 1937.

Lee, Peter Nan-shong. *Industrial Management and Economic Reform in China, 1949-1984*. Hong Kong, London and New York: Oxford University Press, 1987.

Lin, Yu-sheng. *The Crisis of Chinese Consciousness*. Madison: University of Wisconsin Press, 1979.

Lin, Yutang. *My Country and My People*. New York: Reynal and Hitchcock, 1935.

_____. *The Importance of Living*. Hong Kong: Heinemann Educational Books (Asia), 1977.

Madsen, Richard. *Morality and Power in a Chinese Village*. Berkeley: University of California, 1984.

Mao Zedong. *Mao Zedong sixiang wansui* (N.p., 1969)

_____. *Selected Works of Mao Tse-tung*. Beijing: Foreign Language Press, 1967.

Moore, Barrington, Jr. *Injustice: The Social Bases of Obedience and Revolt*. London: Macmillan Press, 1978.

_____. *Social Origins of Dictatorship and Democracy: Lord and Peasants in the Making of the Modern World*. Boston: Beacon Press, 1966.

Munro, Donald J. *The Conception of Man in Contemporary China*. Ann Arbor: The University of Michigan Press, 1977.

Perry, Elizabeth J. and Christine Wong, eds. *The Political Economy of Reform in Post-Mao China*. Cambridge, Mass. and London: the Council on East Asian Studies, 1985.

Su Xiaokang, et al. *Heshang*. Hong Kong: China Books Press, 1988.

Pitcher, George, ed. *Wittgenstein: The Philosophical Investigations, A Collection of Critical Essays*. Garden City, N.Y.: Anchor Books, 1966.

Prize-Winning Stories from China, 1978-1979. Beijing: Foreign Languages Press, 1981.

Pye, Lucian W. *Chinese Commercial Negotiating Style*. Cambridge, Mass.: Oelgeschlager, Gunn & Hain Publishers, 1982.

_____. *The Dynamics of Chinese Politics*. Cambridge, Mass.: Oelgeschlager, Gunn & Hain, Publishers, 1981.

_____. *The Spirit of Chinese Politics: A Psychocultural Study of the Authority Crisis in Political Development*. Cambridge: The MIT Press, 1968.

Sassoon, Anne Showstack. *Gramsci's Politics*. London: Croom Helm, 1980.

Smelser, Neil J. *Theory of Collective Behavior*. New York: Free Press, 1962.

Solomon, Richard H. *Mao's Revolution and the Chinese Political Culture*. Berkeley: University of California Press, 1971.

Toulmin, Stephen. *Cosmopolis, The Hidden Agenda of Modernity*. New York: The Free Press, 1990.

Tsou, Tang. *The Cultural Revolution and Post-Mao Reforms: A Historical Perspective*. Chicago and London: The University of Chicago Press, 1987.

Wang, James C.F. *Contemporary Chinese Politics: An Introduction*. 3rd ed. Singapore: Prentice-Hall International, 1989.

Xin shinian zhengyi zuopin xuan, 1976-1986 (Controversial Works of the Past Ten Years, 1976-1986). Guangxi: Lijiang Press, 1987.

Xiao Gongchuan. *Wenxue jianwanglu* (Memoirs of a Scholar). Taibei: Biographical Literature Society, 1972.

Yi, Mu, and Mark V. Thompson. *Crisis at Tiananmen: Reform and Reality in Modern China*. San Francisco: China Books & Periodicals, 1989.

Zhang Zhiying, et al., eds. *Binfende xiaoshuo shijie*, (The Riotous Profusion in the World of Fiction). Shijia'zhuang: Huashan wenyi press, 1988.

Periodicals

American Journal of Sociology 92 (1987)

Beijing Review 10 April 1989, 22 August.1989

Caizheng(Finance) 12 (1983)

Columbia Journalism Review September/October 1989.

Dangdai zuojia pinglun January 1989

Inside China Mainland 11(1) (January 1989)

Jiushi niandai December 1988

National Review 4 August 1989

PS (or *APSA*) 2 (Spring 1987)

Psychiatry 1949
Renmin ribao (*People's Daily* overseas edition) 19 July 1989
Soviet Studies 25(3) (July 1983)
The China Quarterly 39 (July-September 1969)
Washington Journalism Review September 1989
Zhengmin September 1988

Other periodical sources include articles from several major U.S. newspapers, including the *New York Times*, the *Los Angeles Times*, and the *Washington Post*.

Recent Books on the Tiananmen Incident

[In the year since 4 June 1989, there has been a proliferation of books on the Chinese student movement of 1989 and its bloody aftermath. In January of 1990, the latest bibliographical list showed about thirty titles. When we checked again in May, the list had grown to over sixty items.]

Bajiu Zhongguo minyun jishi (Chronology of the Chinese Democracy Movement). U.S.: n.p., 1989.
Beijing Spring 1989. Armonk, N.Y.: M.E. Sharpe, 1990.
Beijing xueyun (The Student Movement in Beijing). Kowloon: Xingdao chubanshe, 1989.
Beijing xueyun wushi'ri, 1989, 4.15-6.3 (Fifty Days of the Student Movement in Beijing, 15 April-3 June 1989). Taibei: Shibao wenhua chuban jiye youxian gongsi, 1989.
Beijing zuihou caifang (Last News from Beijing). Taibei: Zili baoxi wenhua chubanbu, 1989.
Beizhuangde minyun (The Tragic and Stirring Democracy Movement). 5th printing. Hong Kong: Mingbao chubanshe youxian gongsi, 1989.
_____. In English translation, *June Four*. Fayetteville: University of Arkansas Press, 1989.
_____. In Japanese translation, *Dokyumento tenanmon*. Shohan. Tokyo: Promotions Gianni and Co., 1989.
_____. In Chinese/English edition, *Dedicated to Freedom*. New York: Roxene Corp., 1989.
Children of the Dragon. New York: Collier Books, 1990.
China in Crisis: the Role of the Military. Coulsdon, Surrey, U.K. & Alexandria, Va.: Jane's Defence Data, 1989.
Ching, Julia. *Probing China's Soul: Religion, Politics, and Protest in the People's Republic of China*. New York: Harper & Row, 1990

Cong Wei Jingsheng dao Wu'er Kaixi, 1957-1989 (From Wei Jingsheng to Wu'er Kaixi). Taibei: Haifeng chubanshe, 1989.
Cries for Democracy. Princeton N.J.: Princeton University Press, 1990.
Deron, Francis. *Chine, La Révolution Inachevée.* Paris: Denoel, 1989.
Duke, Michael S. *The Iron House.* Salt Lake City: Peregrine Smith Books, 1989.
Feigon, Lee. *China Rising.* Chicago: I.R. Dee, 1990.
Fengqi Tiananmen (The Wind from Tiananmen). Taipei: Zhonghua minguo chiaowu weiyuanhui huaqiao tongxunshe, 1989.
"Heshang" (The River Elegy). Television program, 1988. Two video cassettes. Broadcast on Chinese television.
Huang Tian. *Zhonghua minzhu xuelu* (The Bloody Road of Chinese Democracy). Hong Kong: Limin chubanshe, 1989.
Kuhan ziyou (Tearful Cries for Freedom). Taipei: Wenxun zazhishe, 1989.
Lanham, Megan Gabriel. *Snatched from the Dragon.* Nashville: T. Nelson, 1990.
Li, Lu. *Moving the Mountain.* 1st U.S. ed. New York: Putnam, 1990.
Liangci Tiananmen shijian (Two Tiananmen Incidents). Hong Kong: Tianhe chubanjigou, 1989.
Lishide chuangshang (The Wound of History). Hong Kong: dongxi wenhua shiye gongsi, 1989.
Liu, Pin-yen. *Tell the World.* New York: Pantheon Books, 1989.
Lord, Bette. *Legacies.* New York: Knopf, 1990.
Massacre in Beijing. New York: Warner Books, 1989.
Munier, Bruno. *Voyage au Printemps de Pekin.* Montreal: Meridien, 1989.
Pang, Pang. In *Tangxuede Beijing cheng* (The City of Beijing Flowing with Blood). Taibei: Fengyun shidai chuban gongsi, 1989.
The Peking Massacre. Taipei: Kwang Hwa Pub. Co., 1989.
Renmin buhui wangji (The People Will not Forget). Hong Kong: Hong Kong jizhe xiehui, 1989.
Salisbury, Harrison Evans. *Tiananmen Diary.* Boston: Little, Brown, 1989.
Shogeki no chugoku chi no nichiyobi (China Shock: Bloody Sunday). Shohan. Tokyo: Gaifusha, 1989.
Sijiao yu huixiang (Cries and Echoes). Kowloon: Kunlin chuban youxian gongsi, 1989.
Simmie, Scott, and Bob Nixon. *Tiananmen Square: An Eyewitness Account of the Chinese People's Passionate Quest for Freedom.* Seattle: University of Washington, 1989; also Vancouver/Toronto: Douglas & McIntyre, 1989.

Sui, Haoping. *Kantian tian* (Looking to Heaven). Taibei: Shinu chubanshe, 1989.

Tenanmon moyu (The Burning at Tiananmen). Tokyo: Yomiuri Shinbunsha, 1989.

Tiananmen 1989 nian (Tiananmen 1989). Rev. ed. Taibei: Lianjin, 1989.

Tiananmen can'an jianzheng (Eyewitness accounts of the Tragedy at Tiananmen). Taipei: n.p., 1989.

Tiananmen fengyun (Disturbance at Tiananmen). Taibei: Lechun wenhua shiye youxian gongsi, 1989.

Turnley, David C. *Beijing Spring*. Hong Kong: Asia 2000, 1989; also New York: Stewart, Tabori and Chang, 1989.

U.S. Congress, House. Committee on Foreign Affairs. Subcommittee on International Operations. *The Role of the United States Embassy and the Voice of America in the Recent China Uprising*. Washington : US GPO, 1989.

Voices from Tiananmen Square. Montreal: Black Rose Books, 1990.

Wang Ling. *Taochu Beijing* (Escape from Beijing). Hong Kong: Guoji chubanshe, 1989.

Wode xin zai Tiananmen (My Heart is at Tiananmen). Enlarged ed. Taibei: Zhengzhung shuju, 1989.

Xuechao, dongluan, baoluan (Student Demonstrations, Turmoil and Violence). Chengdu: Sichuan kexue jishu chubanshe, 1989.

Xue'se de liming (The Blood-Red Dawn). Haverhill, MA: Zhizhuang chuban gongsi, 1989.

Xuewo zhonghua (China Bathed in Blood). Hong Kong: Hong Kong Xinyidai wenhua xiehui, 1986.

Xuewo minzhu'hua (The Bloodied Flower of Democracy). Hong Kong: Baixiang wenhua shiye youxian gongsi, 1989.

Yang Du. *Tiananmen jishi* (Chronology of the Tiananmen Incident). Chuban. Taibei: Shibao wenhua chuban qiyeh youxian gongsi, 1989.

Yeh Zhiqiu. *Baozheng, fengyen, tucheng* (Cruel Government, Beacon Fire, and Massacre City). Hong Kong: Wenyi shuwu, 1989.

Yi, Mu. *Crisis at Tiananmen*. San Francisco: China Books & Periodicals, 1989.

Zhao Chiang. *Xue'rande fengcai* (Bloodstained Elegance). 3rd ed. Hong Kong: Haiyan chubanshe, 1989.

Zhongguo minyun yuanziliao jingxuan (Selected original documents of the Chinese Democracy Movement). Hong Kong: Shiyue pinlunshe, 1989.

Zuojiade nahan (Cry of the Writers). Hong Kong: Fanrong chubanshe youxian gongsi, 1989.

Archives and Collections: The Student Movement

[In establishing the "China Witness 1989" archive at Yale University in June
of 1989, historian Jonathan D. Spence wrote that only by creating this
archive can we pay tribute to those brave individuals who were either
brutally slain or fortunate enough to have survived the protests and
demonstrations. It is in this light that we have listed below some
institutions that have established collections and archives for gathering
information regarding the student movement of 1989 and the events
preceding and following the brutal crackdown. As of May 1990, the
editors know of six institutions having fairly extensive archives that
would facilitate scholars who would like to do further research on the
events of 1989. Undoubtedly, other archives and collections will be
created in time.

Historians have lamented the fact that not enough records were kept of the
May Fourth Movement of 1919 for them to study. With the creation of
these archives on the student movement of 1989, future historians
should have no regrets.]

University of Chicago.
Tiananmen Incident Archive.
Far Eastern Institute of the University of Chicago and The Center for
Psychosocial Studies
111 E. Wacker Dr., Chicago, IL.

> This is the earliest documentary center established for the collection of
> materials related to the Tiananmen incident. It was established on 4
> June after it was verified by telephone that the bloody crackdown had
> actually taken place. The working members of this group, including
> Shao Jing, were holding a conference on Modern Chinese Literature
> when news of the suppression broke on the evening of 3 June. The
> meeting was abruptly adjourned and on the following day the archive
> was established.

Columbia University
C.V. Starr East Asian Library
Columbia University
New York, NY.

> Director Marsha Wagner was in Beijing during the Prodemocracy
> movement and took photographs of many of the wall posters.

Harvard University
Charles L. and Lois Smith Collection on Contemporary China
Harvard University
Cambridge, MA.

> Efforts are concentrated on collecting handbills, petitions, declarations, pamphlets, etc. issued by demonstrators in Beijing and other cities in China, as well as similar materials published by the Chinese government. Eyewitness accounts, personal letters, and audiovisual materials such as videotapes, tape recordings, and photographs are also being solicited. Materials on the overseas reaction, particularly in Hong Kong and Taiwan, to the movement and the subsequent crackdown will also be collected.

New York Public Library
Tiananmen Archive
New York Public Library
Oriental Division
New York, NY.

> This collection is part of the library's continuing effort to chronicle important events in the history of modern China. Several thousand items of historical significance have been acquired by the library to date, including a wide variety of primary source material from democracy groups in China. More than seven hundred items from democratic organizations in China were painstakingly gathered and brought to the United States under conditions of great secrecy by Robin Munro, a research associate with the Asia Watch human rights organization. Among the highlights are a complete set of the widely read *New Herald* daily newspaper from 24 April to 30 May featuring sharp criticism of the country's widespread corruption and rigid political structures.

University of Toronto
China Documentation Center
The University of Toronto
Toronto, Ontario, Canada

> This project, under the direction of Professor Timothy Brook, is designed to establish an objective record of the events in Beijing before and after the government's deployment of troops on 4 June, to monitor the arrest and disappearance of those associated with the democracy

movement (in coordination with Amnesty International), and to assess the continuing impact of the suppression on government functioning. In addition to collecting documentary evidence, the project is conducting debriefings of foreigners who were evacuated from China.

Yale University
China Witness 1989
Manuscripts & Archives Division
Sterling Memorial library
Yale University
New Haven, CT.

Initiated by historian Jonathan D. Spence of Yale University, this collection is directed toward collecting materials in Chinese, English, and other languages, including individual eyewitness accounts, notes, newspaper clippings, recordings, videotapes, photographs, FAX materials, telegrams, recorded telephone messages, etc.

The Chinese University of Hong Kong
Shatin, Hong Kong

The Chinese University of Hong Kong, being the nerve center of East Asia, has an extensive collection of books and documents on the Tiananmen Square incident.

Contributors

IRVING LOUIS HOROWITZ is Hannah Arendt distinguished professor of sociology and political science at Rutgers, The State University of New Jersey. He is also president of Transaction Publishers, located at Rutgers, which is the largest social science publisher in the United States. Among his major writings in this area are *Foundations of Political Sociology*; *Ideology and Utopia in the United States*; *Three Worlds of Development*; and, more recently, *Beyond Empire and Revolution*, all published by Oxford University Press.

PETER N.S. LEE is chairman of the Department of Government and Public Administration at the Chinese University of Hong Kong. He has written extensively on the contemporary Chinese political and social scene. His works include *Industrial Management and Economic Reform in China, 1949-1984* (Oxford University Press, 1987).

MARJORIE H. LI is the Acting East Asian librarian at Rutgers University and series coeditor of Transaction Publisher's Series on East Asian Culture and Politics.

PETER LI teaches Chinese Literature and Civilization at Rutgers University. He has written extensively on Chinese literature and cultural topics. His works include *Classical Chinese Fiction: Its Study and Appreciation*; *Modern Chinese Fiction: Its Study and Appreciation*; *Understanding Asian Americans: A Resource Curriculum Guide*. He is series coeditor of Transaction Publisher's Series on East Asian Culture and Politics.

STEVEN MARK is a journalist who has worked in Los Angeles and Texas. He recently traveled in China.

KING K. TSAO is a doctoral candidate in the Department of Political Science at the University of Chicago. He was at Beijing University (Beida) from September 1987 to June 1989 and did research on economic reforms on the factory level. He is currently assistant lecturer in the Department of Government and Public Administration at the Chinese University of Hong Kong.

CHUNG-FANG YANG received her Ph.D. in social psychology in 1972 and has taught at the Department of Psychology, University of Hong Kong for over six years. Her major research interest is in establishing social psychology for the Chinese people using an indigenous approach. She frequently visits and gives lectures in many universities in the People's Republic of China (PRC). She was actually in the PRC when the 4 June crackdown occurred and she has visited various parts of the mainland since 4 June.

YING-SHIH YU is Michael Henry Strater University Professor of East Asian Studies at Princeton University and a member of the Academia Sinica. A historian of great breadth and depth, he has written extensively on Chinese intellectual and cultural history. His many works include New Tendencies in Modern Culture, Democratic Revolution, and History and Thought.

Index

Printed in the United States
212880BV00001B/1/P